TEACHING STRATEGIES

TEACHING STRATEGIES

A Guide to Better Instruction

Second Edition

Donald C. Orlich
Washington State University

Robert J. Harder
Washington State University

Richard C. Callahan
Shipley Associates

Constance H. Kravas
Washington State University

Donald P. Kauchak
University of Utah

R. A. Pendergrass
Wright State University

Andrew J. Keogh
North Dakota State University

105096

D. C. Heath and Company   Lexington, Massachusetts   Toronto

Photograph Credits

p. 1, Jean-Claude Lejeune/Stock, Boston; p. 31, Frank Siteman/Stock, Boston; p. 53, Arthur Grace/Stock, Boston; p. 77, Robert V. Eckert Jr./The Picture Cube; p. 123, Ellis Herwig/Stock, Boston; p. 161, Elizabeth Crews/Stock, Boston; p. 201, Rick Friedman/The Picture Cube; p. 251, Jean-Claude Lejeune/Stock, Boston; p. 295, Susan Lapides; p. 335, Susan Lapides.

PREFACE

The goal of *Teaching Strategies: A Guide to Better Instruction*, Second Edition, is to provide proven teaching methods, coupled with effective instructional theory, to preservice and inservice teachers. We develop the premise that the teacher is an educational leader and decision-maker who both directly affects the students and influences the presentation of subject matter.

In this text, we offer a broad spectrum of instructional methodologies, techniques, and approaches that are workable in today's classroom. We hope that prospective teachers will find this book valuable as a basis for identifying sound educational practices and as a guide for making systematic, logical, and humane instructional choices. *Teaching Strategies* is intended for education-related courses dealing with instructional methods or techniques, but it may be profitably used as a reference book for a variety of other purposes. For example, we have received numerous reports that inservice teachers have found the book valuable as a "refresher" and guide. This Second Edition attempts throughout to reflect the energy associated with educational reform movements of the 1980s as well as the impact of the microcomputer on the classroom teacher.

Each chapter focuses on a major theme, which is explored in great depth, including the more significant research studies. In Chapter 1, we provide a brief introduction to schooling and broad educational goals. We also introduce our major concepts of instructional decision-making and teacher responsibility. In Chapters 2 through 5, we present the basic "tools" for effective and systematic teaching. The major topics include: specifying instructional objectives, sequencing learning activities, applying the various taxonomies, preparing lesson plans, and conducting micro-teaching. Collectively the first five chapters present the basics for instructional planning and stress the future teacher's comprehension of the fundamentals. We have analyzed and synthesized instructional and educational trends so that the student gains a broad perspective of the field. We want students to develop their own individual framework for instruction, based on the best of well-proven educational practices.

The last five chapters present instruction as a dynamic process operating within a social context (the classroom)—with the realities of interaction between teacher and student our foremost concern. How to make this interaction most productive is our key objective. Chapter 6, on how to pose questions, is perhaps one of the most detailed in any methods textbook. In revising this chapter, we have altered some of our previous techniques, incorporating feedback from users of the first edition. Chapter 7, Decisions About Discussions, provides the background for successful discussion techniques and synthesizes the essential principles from social psychology so that they may be easily applied by classroom teachers. We have revised this chapter to illustrate contemporary problems and useful new techniques. In Chapter 8, the topics of inquiry and simulations illustrate some of the higher-level and interactive techniques for teachers at all levels. Finally Chapter 10 views classroom management from four different perspectives, again stressing an underlying tenet of the book—the teacher as a decision-maker.

In addition, we present several techniques that will help teachers—both new and experienced—stimulate the development of critical thinking skills. These thought-producing techniques include the appropriate use of hierarchy charts, specialized grids to apply the taxonomies, "wait time," question mapping, probing, student-directed discussions, inquiry, simulations, and so forth. We are very deliberate in specifying entry-level skills of students so that the teacher will be successful in using this information in highly interactive and complex instructional environments.

At the beginning of each chapter is a set of intended learner outcomes to help focus the users' study efforts. As the themes develop, we subtly interject "affective" statements for the user—to illustrate how affective and cognitive objectives relate. At appropriate points, *formative evaluations* are introduced to give students immediate feedback on how well they have met the intended objectives. Our formative evaluations also provide the student with models preparing similar instruments for future classroom use.

Overall, the topics introduced reflect a wide range of teaching and instructional strategies, presented as a unified—albeit an eclectic—system. All topics have been used, critiqued, and reviewed several times by our own preservice students and by fellow teachers. All techniques are presented as realistic and practical classroom methods—not simply theoretical ones. Our rather conservative approach to the microcomputer is based on up-to-date research findings—that it frees the teacher for higher-level instruction. Examples of all strategies are provided in a variety of instructional contexts to illustrate abstract concepts. The techniques described herein also work in multicultural settings; several professors who teach in such settings have commended the first edition for its usefulness in this context.

As a whole, the topics are those most often taught in basic methods of instruction courses. These topics appear on state or national lists of generic teacher competencies required by all those entering the profession. We were deliberate in the selection of topics to avoid duplicating those taught in separate education courses at most universities and colleges.

We wrote the book with the sincere desire to improve classroom teaching and to make a genuine contribution to the profession by providing a rationale and applying it. We are indebted to Mollie B. Bailey, Jack Cousins, Elaine McNally Jarchaw, and Geoffrey L. Hughes for their critiques and suggestions of the first manuscript, to Susan Reimer-Sachs for her insightful critique of the first edition, and to Judith Leet for her contributions to the second edition. We would like to express our appreciation to Dr. Dorothy I. Hellene for her contributions to the first edition. We especially acknowledge the efforts of many professors, teachers, and administrators for their suggestions and evaluations. Finally we thank our students for their patience and recommendations as these materials were developed, field-tested, and revised.

Donald C. Orlich

CONTENTS

7 DECISIONS ABOUT DISCUSSIONS   201

8 DECIDING TO USE INQUIRY   251

9   MORE DECISIONS ABOUT INQUIRY AND SIMULATIONS   295

10 DECIDING HOW TO MANAGE A CLASS   335

1

TEACHING AS
DECISION-MAKING

The schools of America are its single largest "industry." Few teachers ever recognize that, as members of this "industry," they must have a broad understanding of teaching. Too few teachers or administrators acknowledge the need to be able to analyze *how* they teach in terms of *what* and *whom* they are teaching. This book views such an approach as an important ideal, and the authors present this chapter as a rationale that gives a theoretical and practical structure to guide action in the classroom. Our intent is to provide a general instructional guide for all teachers.

The general objectives for Chapter 1 are

1. To illustrate one general theory of teaching
2. To discuss decision-making as a teaching theory
3. To identify areas that have an impact on the teacher
4. To provide an abbreviated study of societal goals that form the framework for instruction in the schools
5. To present an overview of curricular and instructional decision areas
6. To list general areas where teachers must make decisions
7. To summarize the concept of "effective schools"
8. To synthesize major studies that could affect American education
9. To provide a list of future-oriented questions for prospective teachers
10. To summarize the remaining chapters of the text
11. To introduce the concept of formative evaluation

THE TEACHER AS DECISION-MAKER

The art and science of effective teaching may be defined from many points of view. There are those who sincerely believe that "good teachers are born, not made." If this were the case, good teachers could simply be identified without the expense of schooling. But as yet, no one has been able to identify those "natural" tendencies that produce good teachers. At the opposite pole, there are those who claim that teaching is nothing more than the simple application of the correct reinforcers so that appropriate learner behaviors are elicited. The only problem with this position is that no one has discovered all of the positive reinforcers to be used each day with millions of children and by hundreds of thousands of teachers.

These two positions can be viewed as two extremes of a broad continuum. Teaching as an "art" relies heavily on intuition as a basis for action, whereas teaching as a "science" depends primarily on a behaviorally oriented model. In the former approach, teaching is conducted by a more

2

subjective, spontaneous method; in the latter, the process of education tends to be perceived as a very simple stimulus-response interaction—a reductionist position—with every skill subdivided into component tasks or procedures. On the one hand, it is very possible that there are natural traits in some people that predispose them to being better teachers; on the other, it is also essential that all teachers master a set of tested teaching skills to be successful. Thus it is difficult to subscribe totally to either perspective because both tend to be closed prescriptive systems. However, both approaches do influence what happens in the classroom.

Teaching as Interaction and Decision-Making

We propose an alternate theory. The act of teaching is always a dynamic interaction of individuals (teachers and teachers, teachers and learners, learners and learners), in which decisions constantly are being made by all concerned. We believe that teaching must be deliberate and planned.

For example, a teacher may decide to give one mass assignment to all students from a single textbook or to give multiple assignments from a variety of sources so that the students can select the ones of their choice. A decision may also be made to use multiple objectives, with accompanying learning materials that have been tailored to fit the instructional needs of various individuals or groups in the class. The teacher may then choose among a wide variety of options concerning how he or she will behave. Will there be a lecture, a short quiz followed by a recitation period, a film, a filmstrip, or an audio tape? Decisions, decisions, decisions!

Phillip W. Jackson (1968) suggests that elementary teachers engage in as many as 1,000 personal interactions each day. His findings are similar to Paul V. Gump's observations (1967) that there are as many as 1,300 teacher acts in a single day of teaching. Most of these interactions involve minor as well as major decisions.

Not all of the decisions are made as the result of systematic and organized planning. Sometimes the choices are made intuitively. The use of intuition in teaching is quite prevalent. Many choices must be made intuitively because the rapid pace of classroom learning demands instant decision-making. In these instances, teachers depend on experience and quick thinking to provide the most appropriate instructional technique. We may assume that the intuition of the experienced teacher is likely to be superior to that of the novice. Intuition is like an opinion in that its usefulness is dependent on the experiential background on which it is based. Yet, in many cases, teachers depend on intuition when systematic and organized planning would be more appropriate. For example, a teacher may believe that a new activity ought to be offered in the school setting, so a particular course of action is taken. Sometimes these "hunches" prove to be right and the results are beneficial to the students. But sometimes they are not effective or are inappropriate for the needs of the learners.

Intuition as a sole guide to instructional behavior represents a very limited view of the teaching process. Like the proposition that "good teachers are born, not made," the use of intuition alone restricts teachers from considering teaching as both science and art. It negates the development of a systematic planning pattern from which rational and consistent decisions can be made. It implies that intuition is the beginning and end of instructional effectiveness, rather than one aspect of the teaching process.

Too often the teacher who relies exclusively on intuition determines objectives and selects procedures that are more reflective of instructor needs than student needs. Thus if a teacher feels like lecturing, a lecture is delivered. If a teacher feels like showing a film, a film it is! Few of us would tolerate this mode of operation in arenas outside the realm of education. Consider for a minute how much confidence you would place in a bus driver who repeatedly changed the bus route because of a belief that such changes were inherently good and relieved both the driver and the riders of boredom.

Of course, we also propose that through meaningful experiences, a teacher may know instinctively how to handle or react to a specific situation. For example, students are almost always "restive" prior to vacation periods. Thus a teacher should not try to introduce a new topic on the Friday before a one-week vacation. Teachers can shift from an intuitive mode of operation to a more critical one simply by being *aware* that they are constantly making decisions that affect the intellectual, attitudinal, and psychomotor skills of learners.

Implicit within the concept of decision-making is the notion of *responsibility*. Teachers cannot pass the buck. If teachers make decisions, they must be willing to take the responsibility for both their implementation and their possible consequences. For example, if teachers deliberately bias a discussion to fit their opinions, religious dogmas, or political tenets, then they are being agents of indoctrination. Some teachers whom we have known refuse to acknowledge that they are, in fact, being doctrinaire and claim that "this is good for the students." Of course, they would *not* consider it "good" if the students were to be swayed toward the opposite doctrine.

We illustrate this potential problem area because, in our opinion, many teachers do not recognize their responsibility for making decisions. There is often a tendency to blame the "administration" or the "school board." To be sure, administrative regulations and school-board policies do govern selected instructional procedures and even content. But most of the classroom instructional decisions are, in fact, made by the teacher. (We will discuss these and other curricular matters later in Chapter 1.) Our plea is that the teacher will take the responsibility for making these decisions, and that most decisions will be made on a logical, systematic basis—and not on impulse.

One way to raise one's level of cognitive consciousness (awareness) is to begin thinking with the "if-then" logic. *If* the teacher desires to encourage the students to learn through inquiry techniques, *then* he or she must provide the students with the initial learning skills with which to inquire and must supply the learning materials in a sequential, systematic fashion so that the students may apply the concepts being learned to real situations.

The if-then logical paradigm provides the teacher with a cognitive "map" similar to that used in generating rules and principles. The teacher starts thinking about causes and effects of actions and statements and about relationships between classroom activities and students. The teacher learns to obtain as much information as possible about both students and subject matter prior to the lesson and then develops a plan for success. This plan of instruction is based on the conclusions developed about the interaction between the subject matter, the student, and the teacher.

Finding the Panacea

If there is one truism in teaching, it is that there is no *one way* to teach anything or anyone. With alarming frequency, educational authorities or critics announce that they have discovered *the* answer to teaching problems. The literature is full of such examples. Read about the advocates for behavioral objectives, team teaching, individually guided instruction, educational television, phonics or other reading techniques, new math, activity-oriented science, and new social studies. Many of these approaches are based on sound analysis and investigation of the teaching-learning act. Typically each approach is related to a specific kind of teaching activity, a specific philosophy of education, or a specific perspective of the structure of the basic discipline for which the program is developed.

Unfortunately many advocates, in their eagerness to "spread the word" about particular approaches or methodologies, myopically attempt to convince other educators that *their* method is, at long last, the right one. Such pronouncements, no matter how well intentioned, tend to be naive. The chances are likely that many teachers will not use *the* method; indeed, teachers who have never heard about *it* will find success simply by using more eclectic methods combined with wisdom, logic, and a sound knowledge of educational psychology.

For example, during the late 1960s and the entire 1970s, standardized test scores for students above grade 3 tended to decline. By 1984, some scores began to stabilize and even to increase somewhat. To improve education (and test scores), nearly four-fifths of the state legislatures passed "accountability" laws. Nobody could really define *accountability,* but the term sounded impressive. In general, the accountability movement became a simple extension of testing and evaluating. The typical grades at which statewide tests were administered tended to be grades 4, 8, and 11. Other state legislatures or state boards of education established "minimum competency levels" for high school graduation as a measure of accountability. Almost no one listened to critics who asked, "Why are standardized test scores acceptable and satisfactory in grades 1, 2, and 3 but not in others?" Few legislators, school-board members, administrators, or teachers asked the question, "Of what use are test scores to a child six or eight months after the testing period?" We must, however, add a warning statement issued nationally by the president of the Educational Testing Service (ETS) in 1983: Gregory R. Anrig, addressing the ETS annual invitational conference, warned that the "quick fix" of using standardized tests to improve education was, in fact, a *test abuse*. An analysis of the history of the 1980s will tell us if anyone heeded Anrig's stern warning (see page 12).

It appears that much of the methodology of educators tends to be based on simplistic thinking. During the 1950s and 1960s, furious conflicts developed about the way to teach reading—by sight, phonic, phonetic, psycholinguistic, or eclectic methods. Experts know that a variety of techniques is important to develop a broad set of reading skills. Exclusive use of any one method will not bring instant reading success to all children, but will strengthen certain skills over others. The literature shows that one program after another is proposed as a cure-all but eventually proves to be not entirely effective when used alone.

Thus we caution you from the beginning: we will never say that we have *the* method. We will present a series of options that are all usable and that will all yield humanely conceived educational results. In other words, we are following our own theory. If teaching is a decision-making activity, then there ought to be divergent means by which to accomplish any instructional objective. That is what this book is about: to learn when to use a technique and what one can expect from using it. The context in which any method is used predicates its success; this is the notion of relevance.

Content and Process as Decisions

As you plan the teaching of a subject, you must remember that not only is the *content* of the lesson important, but of equal importance may be the *processes* that the students need to master the content. The Cunard Steamship Lines once advertised that getting there was half the fun! With teaching, the same logic as that expressed by Cunard is applicable. The students must know how to accomplish what you want. Let us examine a few situations.

If a teacher wants to teach about mathematical ratios (the content) and the applications of this concept, then the students must master various skills and processes. They must be able to understand the meaning of division, comprehend the concept of whole numbers, conceptualize the notion of proportions, and perform a few other basic arithmetic operations. In certain cases, the processes associated with content are at times indistinguishable from the content; that is, both the thought processes and the resultant knowledge, skills, or information *are* the content. In this sense, there is "procedural content" and there is "cognitive content." The "modern math" movement was an attempt to build systematically on mathematical cognitive processes. The only trouble was that some professors of mathematics who wrote books on "modern math" forgot that it takes practice, drill, and application to learn a concept. Instead of providing the necessary procedural exercises, the mathematicians provided concept after concept without supplying concrete learning experiences. In short, the lack of procedural techniques—knowing how to know—tended to be ignored in favor of highly sophisticated math topics that were beyond the comprehension of most young people. Now, a decade or two after the "math revolution," there is a "counter-revolution." Teachers and publishing companies are returning to the teaching of a broader spectrum of math rather than exposing the students to random sets of math concepts. And, in some cases, the content of math textbooks today looks remarkably similar to that in 1950!

When prospective teachers are asked "As you anticipate teaching, what concerns you most?" many, if not most, secondary education majors identify "knowledge of subject matter" as their chief problem. It must be noted that, although there is a tendency for prospective secondary school teachers to be "subject-oriented," elementary school teachers tend to be "child-oriented." Their primary objective is to help the child to grow and mature both mentally and physically—not just to teach mathematics, physics, or English literature. Thus the early school experiences of children are oriented toward helping them to adjust from their home environment to the institutional dimensions of school. However, the elementary school teacher's approach, in which the child comes first and the subject content second, may create some conflict within any school system.

In the junior high schools or middle schools, there is a transition period in which the emphasis shifts from a human-growth orientation to a subject orientation. It is critically important for middle school and junior high school educators to understand that children (young adolescents) in these institutions are just beginning to emerge from Jean Piaget's *concrete operations* stage and are entering the initial *formal operations* stage. To teach this large group effectively, teachers must combine "hands-on" activities and "thinking" activities for all major concepts or lessons. Techniques such as preparing time lines, conducting experiments, preparing charts and graphs, classifying, and sequencing all help the learners. Lecturing and abstract discussions simply do not aid learning for these children. But in nearly all high schools, teachers tend to be very academically inclined. The subject matter is first, last, and always the focus, although not to the exclusion of all personal considerations.

Who decided on these emphases? One could argue that "society" did. However, that would be a bit irresponsible. We argue that the teachers determined these priorities in response to the subtle pressures placed on them by institutions of higher education and perhaps even by society at large. It is commonly agreed that the schools of any society mirror that society. The wishes and beliefs of a society are subtly translated into the values, curricula, and instructions of the schools. Yet there are a large number of secondary school educators who desire to "humanize" the secondary schools and to make them more process oriented. But when newspaper writers, school board members, legislators, and parents begin to pressure high school teachers to improve test scores, to raise academic standards, and to add content, those same teachers become acutely aware of content.

It is hard for all of us in education to realize that processes must be taught with content, and it is even more difficult to understand the motives of any teacher who says, "Well, if they didn't have the knowledge or techniques before they got into my class, that's too bad. . . ." If students do not have the so-called prerequisite skills, then you as a teacher must provide them! If you do not, then your students will suffer failure. If you provide the basics, then your students will be successful. The decision is yours.

GOALS AND SCHOOLS

In elementary and secondary education, goals are continually stated, clarified, changed, and converted into school programs and ultimately into classes. But what are goals? Goals are broadly conceived statements that express, in general, what the schools should try to accomplish. However, goals, in a large sense, can be thought of as fairly constant. The major goals of schools and education in the Western world have changed very, very little in the last 2,500 years. If you challenge this assertion, examine any set of goals for any period of time. They will probably contain the following common elements:

1. The need for healthy people (the ancient Greeks, especially Spartans, overemphasized this goal)
2. The need for political indoctrination (the ancient Egyptians were among the first to stress this need)
3. The need for *acculturation,* the process of conditioning a child to the customs of the culture (this goal is universal, permeating all societies, even those without written languages)
4. The need for values (this is universal and is closely related to the need for acculturation)
5. The need for a vocation (this need is also universal and probably began with the Greeks)
6. The need for leisure time (this was first discussed in 1861 by the British philosopher Herbert Spencer, although it originates with the ancient Romans)

Depending on the society, other major goals also are apparent. These include religious, nationalistic, and economic goals, among others.

National Goals in the United States: The World War Eras

Seven Cardinal Principles

In the United States, one classic and still used statement of goals is the Seven Cardinal Principles of Secondary Education. These principles were discussed widely during the period of World War I. They set the stage for the ever-reformulated goals of our schools. The writers of the Seven Cardinal Principles first observed that secondary education had as its overriding goal "a clear conception of the meaning of democracy. It is the ideal of democracy that the individual and society may find fulfillment in the other. . . ."

Thus the Seven Cardinal Principles of Secondary Education (1918) concerned the following:

1. Health
2. Command of fundamental processes
3. Worthy home membership
4. Vocation
5. Civic education
6. Worthy use of leisure
7. Ethical character

Each of these seven items was extensively discussed in the original text of the Seven Cardinal Principles.

The Postwar Era

We are presenting only a "mini-capsule" history of the goals of schools so that you will have some background information with which to judge the present. If you are interested in a detailed history, then you should refer to one of the many extensive treatments of the subject that are available.

During the 1920s and 1930s, little concern was voiced over elementary and middle or junior high schools—concern, that is, as measured by major national pronouncements or studies.

The period between 1945 and 1970 was marked by the building of new school plants to accommodate the increasing adolescent and young adult population, by experimentation with curriculum, and by general expansion of and sensitivity toward educational goals. In addition, a "great debate" was held about the function of secondary schools during this era. One position stressed that our schools should look more to their European (French or Russian) counterparts. A more radical position urged the elimination of high schools and compulsory education. The middle position was best illustrated by James B. Conant (1959) in his best-selling book, *The American High School Today: A First Report to Interested Citizens.*

In 1959, Conant defended the goal of having a comprehensive high school—one in which, under "one roof," educational objectives would be espoused relating to (1) vocational education; (2) college preparation; and (3) general education. The impact of the "Conant Report" was to fix, seemingly for the remainder of the twentieth century, the concept of a nonelitist high school system in the United States.

To improve our high schools, Conant presented twenty-one recommendations. To list but a few, these included (1) counseling; (2) required programs of study; (3) programs for the academically talented; (4) an academic supplement to the high school diploma; (5) career education; (6) developmental reading programs; and (7) elimination of small high schools. Conant visualized the high schools as being the institution through which the Seven

Cardinal Principles might be attained. What is interesting is that during these times the elementary schools were the foci of thousands of innovations and widespread experimental practices—for example, the "Initial Teaching Alphabet"—but the elementary school generally was not criticized by any major reform faction.

In 1961, yet another critic, John W. Gardner, former Secretary of the Department of Health, Education, and Welfare (HEW), noted in his outstanding book, *Excellence: Can We Be Equal and Excellent Too?*, that schools act as a sorting institution today just as they have since the nineteenth century. Gardner described the dilemma inherent in any school system that attempts to provide egalitarianism, individualism, and social stratification. He pointed out that it was almost impossible to reach a point of equality in educational opportunity. The children of well-educated, professional, middle-class people would, according to Gardner, assuredly grow up and mature in an atmosphere more conducive to intellectual striving than would children of semi-literate, lower-class laborers. Theoretically, Gardner argued, educational opportunities are equal; but in actuality they are not.

One observation of Gardner's was later verified through tests, questionnaires, and inferential statistics in the monumental "Coleman Report" (1966) issued by the U.S. Office of Education under the direction of James S. Coleman. The report concluded that, when all factors are considered, the most important variable affecting a child's scholastic performance is the parents' educational background. The next most significant factor is the educational background and social class of the families of the other children in school. One point that Coleman noted, but which seemed to have been ignored, was that the verbal abilities *of the teacher* had a significant impact on the verbal skills of the students!

The 1970s: Reexamination Amid Criticism

The 1970s can be viewed as a period of reexamination of directions for education. As an institution, the schools had been criticized as being not open or truthful with the populace or with the students. *Irrelevant* had been the keyword of the 1960s; but that concept quickly outlived its usefulness, as *relevance* too often meant shoddy scholarship or irresponsible teaching. While educators in the 1970s stressed the advantages of innovations, the public became alarmed at the declining levels of the achievement tests, especially in the basic skills area. Declining test results led to growing criticism on a nationwide scale and to a call for a return to "basics." Numerous groups of citizens and educators met to reexamine the nature and future direction of education in the United States and released position papers on the subject.

In 1975, the National Association of Secondary School Principals (NASSP) issued another statement about high school concerns entitled, *Secondary Schools in a Changing Society: This We Believe*. The NASSP task force revised their 1944 position statement to reflect contemporary needs. Their endorsements included (1) greater assumption of educational leadership by the schools at the secondary level; (2) increase in opportunities for students to exhibit responsibility; (3) expansion of the curriculum to include community activities; (4) compulsory education to include a community component for those who may benefit more from it than from school classes; (5) redefinition and expansion of guidance services; (6) more student activities to meet more effectively the current needs of youth; and (7) greater community participation in the governance of the school. These statements were not listed as goals but as areas that needed greater attention. The 1975 list provided evidence that schools mirror society—or at least its social problems—and emphasized the need for greater interaction between high schools and their surrounding communities.

In 1978, the U.S. Commissioner of Education, Ernest L. Boyer, stated that our system needed reshaping. He suggested a three-level system built around (1) a basic school (elementary), (2) a middle school for core or general knowledge that focused on our heritage, institutions, and social issues, and (3) a three-year transitional school (high school).

By now you may have inferred that goals tend to be created by individuals, associations, governmental agencies, governing boards, and citizens at large. The last group, citizens, tends to be unique in the establishing of goals for schools. In the United States, all of our public schools, including universities, are controlled primarily by their respective state legislatures. Each legislature then delegates responsibilities to its respective citizens— university boards of regents, state boards of education, and local school boards. All of these groups at some time or another express their ideals for American schools.

There is currently a massive effort to encourage local citizens to participate in the preparation of goal statements for the public schools. There are thousands of lists giving community suggestions. To publish them all would require a book, but to provide you with a quick summary, we have reduced them to eight rather generalized goals:

1. Education should respect the uniqueness of each individual.
2. Education should provide an opportunity for individual self-direction.
3. Education should emphasize that cultural, ethnic, and racial differences contribute positively to our nation's future.
4. Education should instill a desire in each individual to perform well and to take pride in learning.
5. Education should include out-of-school learning experiences.
6. Education should provide a basis for good citizenship.
7. Education should provide the basics for vocational choice.
8. Education should make available the best of our cultural heritage.

What does this very brief orientation about goals have to do with teaching and decision-making? The answer is very simple: while there is a consensus on what ought to be done in the schools, there are also concurrent efforts being made to convert these general principles into school programs—curriculum units, modules, chapters, and tests.

The 1980s: Another Batch of Studies

In the United States, we tend to analyze high school problems or crises by way of committee reports. To illustrate the phenomena of school reports, at least eight major and twenty-one minor national reports were published during 1983 and 1984. We could write at length—even an entire book—on just the eight major reports and their implications. However, we will limit ourselves to mentioning four important reports in a general overview and then will reflect on their collective implications for instruction.

Every good researcher explicitly states the limitation of the study. Unfortunately, most of the reports tend to ignore their major limitations, assumptions, or omissions. Despite their flaws, these reports will cause some changes in the schools. States will tighten up high school graduation standards and add more academic subjects—or perhaps a foreign language. Physics will still be taught in the junior or senior year, without much substantive change. The new batch of studies will not prevent some obscure mathematics professor from installing the concept of *function* at grade 6 where the concept is totally inappropriate. Science will still be ignored by elementary school teachers and their principals.

A Nation at Risk (1983), a study sponsored by the U.S. Department of Education, presents the strongest criticism of the schools. It states, "If an unfriendly foreign power had attempted to impose on America the mediocre instructional performance that exists today, we might well have viewed it as an act of war." Such rhetoric is nonsense. The report, however, has been almost uncritically accepted by school boards, state boards of education, and others who know little of research or our educational history.

A Nation at Risk suggests (1) a tougher set of academic basics for high school graduation; (2) higher standards for universities; (3) a longer school year or school day; (4) merit pay for top teachers; and (5) more citizen participation in the public schools. In actuality, this report calls for a two-track high school: college preparatory and vocational. Used as a blueprint, it offers virtually nothing on instruction, but it will have a conservative impact on the program of studies.

Academic Preparation for College (1983) is the College Board's offering to improve the high schools. This report identifies basic academic competencies for intended study: reading, writing, speaking, listening, reasoning, studying, and mathematics. Several specific objectives are listed for each of the basic competencies. This list offers a useful set of criteria by which to judge selected aspects of any high school curriculum. As with all the studies, the College Board stresses the importance of "computer competency." The basic academic high school subjects are defined as English, the arts, mathematics, science, social studies, and foreign languages.

Obviously, this report focuses on only the college-bound student. Thus it does not represent a realistic view of the American public high school.

A Celebration of Teaching: High Schools in the 1980s (1983) is a national study written by a productive educator and scholar—Theodore R. Sizer. Sizer provided a case study of fifteen public and private high schools. He then listed a series of elements for an "essential school." He strongly advocates (1) incentives for learning; (2) emphasis on encouraging quality; (3) more student responsibility; (4) awarding of high school diplomas only when mastery of defined skills is achieved; and (5) inculcation of ethical values. Several of the elements Sizer advocates could be implemented in any high school. His study might be called the "1983 Conant Report."

A Place Called School (1984) was also written by a scholar—John I. Goodlad. This report is the most comprehensive of the set. Goodlad has examined a series of "feeder" schools—elementary, junior high, and senior high schools. He provides detailed case studies and generalizations about the sample of schools being studied. He then addresses a series of issues that impinge on the school: teacher preparation, instruction, curriculum, leadership, research, and entry ages of students. Fully understanding the complexities of these issues, Goodlad provides no simplistic solutions.

All the studies of the early 1980s focus attention on the public high schools. Perhaps this emphasis is their collective asset. Yet other than Goodlad's extensive study, the elementary and middle or junior high schools are all but ignored. Thus we observe educational history repeating itself by researchers focusing on only the high school and not the entire K–12 system. Over the years few prominent studies have examined the obvious links among our elementary, middle, and high schools. Of course, high schools get more attention than elementary and middle schools and have the extracurricular activities that are reported in the newspapers and other media.

The 1980s will produce changes in the schools but at this point the changes are not clearly in focus.

Interpreting Goals Through Legislation

National Defense Education Act

Although our broad educational goals have changed very little during the last few centuries, major political, social, and economic events have caused changes in the emphasis of goals. For example, during the period between 1957 and 1969, the United States placed heavy emphasis on improvements in math and science curricula as a national goal. The year 1957 marked a major shift in our goals. On October 4, 1957, the Russians successfully launched their "Sputnik." It was a memorable day for one of the authors, for he was teaching junior high school science at the time. All that day, for five different class periods, the students discussed nothing but the fact that "*we are behind!*" These twelve- to fifteen-year-olds truly reflected our national concerns.

The Congress quickly responded with the now famous National Defense Education Act (NDEA), which provided the schools with hundreds of millions of dollars to "catch up" in mathematics, science, foreign languages, and counseling. The National Defense Education Act was signed by President Eisenhower in September 1958. The enabling clause states that the NDEA was designed "to strengthen the national defense and to encourage and assist in the expansion and improvement of educational programs to meet critical national needs . . ." (U.S. Statutes at Large, 1958). The main motive was "to meet critical national needs," not to meet school needs or the needs of children or young adolescents.

Elementary and Secondary Education Act of 1965

In 1965, President Lyndon B. Johnson signed into law the now historic Elementary and Secondary Education Act (ESEA). This act pumped billions of dollars into all segments of education, ranging from preschool to university graduate school. As the original act became amended, it provided *categorical aid* (that is, aid to specific activities in the school) to help remediate problems.

Billions of dollars were made available under ESEA for the improvement of state departments of education, for educational research and development, for devising and testing of innovative practices in the public schools, for installation of educational technology in the schools, and for improvement of teaching skills. In 1981, the ESEA was changed rather drastically with the passage of President Ronald Reagan's legislation, the Education Consolidation and Improvement Act (ECIA). This act tended to reduce the massive federal aid to education and to allow local school districts greater flexibility and discretion in the use of funds. The ECIA signaled the demise of general *categorical* aid to public schools.

Public Law 94-142

The year 1975 witnessed yet another consequential federal act, Public Law 94-142, the Education for All Handicapped Children Act. How important is this law? Dean C. Corrigan wrote in 1978 that "this act is the most important piece of educational legislation in the history of this country."

The basis for this act is the assumption that all handicapped children can benefit from public education. Although the law and its accompanying regulations tend to be technical, *every* teacher in the United States must understand its implications, for there is no teacher, school, or class that may be exempt. There are five concepts that, at this stage in your career, you must understand about PL 94-142.

Basically, this law establishes that all handicapped children between the ages of three and twenty-one are entitled to free public education. *Handicapped* is defined by the law as those who are mentally retarded, hard of hearing, deaf, speech-impaired, visually handicapped, seriously emotionally disturbed, orthopedically impaired, multihandicapped, or those who have other health impairments or have specific learning disabilities and, because of impairments, need special educational services.

It is estimated that approximately 12 percent of the children in age group three to twenty-one are included in this broad definition of *handicapped*. Thus the numbers of persons covered under the law would range in the millions!

The second point that will affect you as a teacher is the need to prepare a written *individual education plan* (IEP) for every handicapped child in your class. This plan must be developed to meet that specific child's needs. The IEP must specify the goals of the educational services, the methods of achieving those goals (objectives), and the exact number and quality of exceptional services to be rendered to the child.

The federal laws require that the IEP be formulated by (a) a parent, (b) a child, (c) a teacher, (d) a professional who has evaluated the child within a "recent" time span, and (e) others as designated by the local education agency. The last category usually includes the school principal or a special education resource person.

The IEP must list all special activities and "regular" class activities in which the child will participate. Dates and duration of services must be stated. Objectives and evaluation procedures must also be given. A minimum of one IEP meeting must be held each year. The law is most specific in requiring that parents receive written notice of the IEP meeting.

If you wonder whether you will have the skills to complete an IEP, this book (Chapters 2 and 5 especially) will provide many of the technical skills that all teachers need to devise any educational objective or plan.

The third stipulation of PL 94-142 requires that a handicapped child's records be kept secure. Actually, as the law is written, a federal investigator could not examine a child's record without first getting parental permission. Thus you must recognize that the parent has unlimited access to all educational records. Furthermore, a parent may amend (in writing) any statement in that child's file. If there is disagreement (for example, between a parent and a teacher) on what is in the file, the parent has a right to an impartial hearing. Finally, the school must keep a record of all persons who have access to the child's record and why.

The fourth element of PL 94-142 requires that when an agency (the school) and the parents fail to agree on an IEP or an evaluation of the child's abilities, then an impartial hearing must be held. The rules for conducting the hearing are very explicit. A hearing can be lengthy and time-consuming for all. For example, if the parents *or* the school district disagrees on the IEP, there is the final recourse of suing in a court of law. Let us, as an example, assume that the parents are dissatisfied with the IEP that has been devised for their child. The parents can sue the school district for redress of their grievances. The judgment of the court will then take precedence over the IEP. However, it is feasible for the case to go all the way to the U.S. Supreme Court for solution.

What happens to the child while the courts are determining the appropriate IEP? The child will remain in the school setting to which he or she was originally assigned. This is done so that the child has the benefit of some formal schooling.

The final component of PL 94-142 prescribes that all handicapped children have the right to be served in the "least restrictive environment." The latter phrase led to a general interpretation of "mainstreaming"—that is, placing handicapped children in "regular" classrooms. A least restrictive environment means that handicapped children must be educated and treated in a manner similar to nonhandicapped peers. So there can be no separation of handicapped children in lunchrooms, recess, games (where appropriate to the child's abilities), classes, or any education service or function if the child is able to participate in these activities.

However, a least restrictive environment may simply mean that the child will always be placed in a special room, not in a regular classroom. It may even mean that the child can be institutionalized in a special school or even in a private school. The deciding factor in placement is whether the child can receive profitable services. For example, a school district can place a deaf child in a regular class with a special interpreter if, in the professional judgment of school personnel, that child can profit educationally from that arrangement.

"Education's 'Three Mile Island': PL 94-142," the title of McCay Vernon's paper (1982), provides another point of view—very different in emphasis from Corrigan's. Vernon argues most persuasively that the ultimate impact of PL 94-142 is that for the first time the federal government is dictating to local schools exactly how handicapped children will be educated. He then raises a set of issues that focus on this general question: should we invest the largest per capita educational investment on those who are least able to return dividends to our society? Obviously, that question will be debated as the impact of this law is felt.

We discuss this law at some length because it illustrates how the goals of respecting the uniqueness of each individual and of providing for individual self-direction are implemented through a federal act. As members of society, we obviously feel it is in the best interest of *all* persons to extend the concept of the "general welfare" to every child who is capable of profiting from public schooling.

State and Local Impact on Goals

Obviously, state laws and local regulations all have an impact on the schools. State legislatures, state boards of education, and local boards of education all have the legal right to require that the schools teach certain subjects, skills, or ideals. Arizona, for example, requires a course on the free enterprise system of economics. Virginia and several other states require a state history course for high school graduation. Nearly every state has a legislated physical education curriculum. As national goals become converted to laws and then to curricula—as reflected in books, tapes, films, teacher guides, and the like—there is also a tendency on the part of the state to establish the content and the processes that will help teach the content.

All this means—and our treatment of local influence is very superficial—that teachers must ultimately make the decisions regarding how to teach and what to teach. Teachers must begin to sift through the goals, establish priorities, and select those goals that they think are important. The most valuable goals will then take precedence in the classroom.

But remember: it is not the goal that is taught. The goal is simply the framework within which content, skills, processes, attitudes, and the like are taught.

We believe that goals are not subdivided like apple pies. Goals become abstractions that inspire action. Goals are almost never attained. Rather, objectives are stated as action elements stemming from goals. Objectives then become the means by which we seek to achieve our goals, a topic that is expanded in Chapter 2.

However, we must provide one caveat. The people of the United States have many nationalities, races, classes, occupations, philosophies, religions, attitudes, outlooks, and values. The diversity of our nation has led to a pluralistic society. Such pluralism also leads to a conflict of goals. Observe that in the typical school system there are social, moral, intellectual, political, and vocational goals. Some teachers tend to stress the goal regarding the improvement of our society. Others try to emphasize the goal to develop critical thinking. Still others attempt to develop individual students so that they may maximize their fullest potential. All of these accepted goals have led to eclecticism as a means of operating—i.e., we tend to mix parts of goals. The problem with eclecticism is that ultimately it leads to conflicts within goals. One cannot teach critical thinking and at the same time stress that "teacher knows best." If a teacher is *unknowingly eclectic,* then that teacher is probably inconsistent in teaching practices. If you are cognitively aware of your eclecticism, you at least should attempt to avoid placing your own students in those situations that promote personal conflicts. In our society there probably always will be confusion and disagreement over some goals. As a teacher you may or may not be able to resolve either the confusion or the disagreement, which is all part of being pluralistic.

CONTEMPORARY REFLECTIONS ON INSTRUCTION

During the 1980s, the many "publics" of public education became concerned that the public schools were declining in quality at an unprecedented rate. The decline, of course, referred to the decline in standardized test scores.

What caused those declines? Many studies were conducted to investigate test score decline by high school students. A plethora of such studies yielded only one useful finding: if students did not attend school regularly or did not take basic academic courses in science, English, and mathematics, they scored poorly. Annegret Harnischfeger and David E. Wiley (1975) prepared one of the more objective studies about the decline of test scores and concluded that no single variable could be identified to account for these declines.

By the late 1970s, several researchers began to identify public high schools whose graduates had test scores higher than the national average or which were showing growth rather than decline. The totality of this trend became labeled the "effective schools movement."

Effective Schools Movement

Roots of the Movement

One of the leading proponents of the effective schools movement was the late Ronald Edmonds—a prominent and well-respected researcher. Edmonds died in 1983 before he could successfully challenge the predominant social sciences theory that familial effects outweighed any school effects on learning. In short, Edmonds began to collect evidence to repudiate the work of James Coleman and his associates (1966) and of Christopher Jencks and others (1972). The Coleman and Jencks studies tended to establish *correlational* data that the higher the family's socioeconomic status, the better the school achievement of its children. Coleman and Jencks did provide an easy-to-use alibi for teachers and administrators, especially those in urban or predominantly minority schools: we cannot expect much from minority or poor students since social background and luck are far more important than the influence of school. Thus the hypothesis of a sociologist and an economist was used by public educators as an excuse for not improving the schools in an active, rigorous manner.

Thomas L. Good's research summary (1982) pointed out that what teachers expect of their students is usually what they get from them. His statement was nothing new, for Robert Rosenthal and Lenore Jacobson (1968) initially had reported this finding as the "Pygmalion effect." However, Good's summary did report that (1) teachers tend to treat low-achieving students with less favorable responses than high-achieving students; (2) teachers demand less from low-achievers; (3) teachers interact in a less friendly manner with low-achievers; (4) low-achievers seldom get the benefit of the doubt in tests, whereas high-achievers do; and (5) when expectations are forced on the school through community pressure, the performance of all students is increased. In one study (Rist, 1970), the teachers of inner-city children tended to expect their students to do poorly. It seems to have been amply demonstrated that if you expect children to perform poorly in school, they will perform poorly (Rosenthal and Jacobson, 1968). On the other hand, if you expect them to do well—they will do well.

You may well ask yourself why teachers and administrators do not rectify such poor instructional expectations. We again conclude that many public school educators have uncritically accepted the *familial effects* theory: teachers cannot be held accountable for some students' failure to learn when they know that the students come from poor home environments. Just as

Ron Edmonds has cautioned all educators, a theory that is not applicable in all cases may be used as an alibi because it is convenient.

Describing Effective Schools

The most important question for teachers to address is how to provide *effective schools*. In the previous sentence, we deliberately put the emphasis on the institutions, the *schools,* and not on individuals, the teachers or principals. For we feel strongly that it takes all the resources of the institution to make learning efficient, excellent, and effective. There are several so-called school effectiveness projects in the United States and Canada, but we will select one project that synthesizes the entire movement—the Alaska Effective Schooling Program.

In 1980, the State Board of Education for the state of Alaska inaugurated a school improvement plan that was subcontracted to the Northwest Regional Educational Laboratory (NWREL). After a review of school effectiveness studies, the NWREL staff identified five major elements that lead to effective school practices. The five elements are

1. leadership
2. school environment
3. curriculum
4. classroom instruction and management
5. assessment and evaluation

Because the focus of this text is on instruction and management, we will discuss only that major element; it must be noted, however, that the principal is the key person for any effective school. With a strong instructional leader who plans, organizes, staffs, coordinates, and directs the school improvement effort, almost any school can be transformed quite rapidly from an ineffective to a very effective place for learning. The total interaction of all the adults and students in the school helps to shape the environment.

Effective Classroom Instruction and Curriculum

There are at least eleven separate elements that collectively improve schooling, as noted by the effective schools movement.

Expectations for Behavior.   It is no surprise that the first criterion relates to expectations for student behavior. In an effective school environment, all staff members expect all students to learn. All adults hold high expectations that are clearly defined for the learners. *Everyone* accepts the idea that school is a place for learning. Every activity relates to learning.

Student Behavior.   A written code of conduct specifies acceptable student behavior, and all faculty and staff members are familiar with the code. The code is written and given to all students, usually in the form of book covers, notebook inserts, or composition holders. Behavioral expectations are uniformly enforced with disciplinary actions quickly following any infractions.

Class Routines and Procedures.   Teachers are taught how to handle administrative matters quickly and efficiently. Everyone keeps class interruptions to a minimum; learning time is considered "sacred." Classes start promptly with few wasteful transitions.

Standards.   Teachers, administrators, and parents agree on reasonable standards for their students and always let them know what is expected.

Grouping.   It has been found that whole-group instruction tends to be most effective for learning basic skills. Small groups are formed to aid students in learning these skills thoroughly. However, all groups are heterogeneous and tend to be temporary. In elementary and middle or junior high schools, the schedules are arranged so that similar subjects are being taught at the same time. Students who lack entry-level skills or need more review may be shifted to a different group. Groups exist solely to help a student learn better.

Stage Setting.   The teachers help the students get ready to learn. The teachers provide objectives, they repeat the learning objectives, and they continually determine what entry-level skills are needed by all students and bring them all up to that level.

Instruction and Direction.   Teachers always give background information and clear directions—oral and written. During the conduct of classroom recitations or activities, teachers make sure that every student is involved in the instruction. One technique is to use "mass" responses for some questions or activities—one of the techniques used with "direct instruction" or "teacher-directed instruction."

Learning Time.   Everyone concentrates on using class time for learning; little time is used for nonlearning activities. Everyone makes an effort to use classroom time for learning. (If each teacher wastes ten minutes per day, this would account for the waste of more than ten days of school time a year—and would also be a hefty waste of taxpayers' money.)

Reteaching.   You may hear a standing joke that there are "six R's": remedial reading, remedial . . . There are no remedial classes in schools where the staff adopts an effective schooling plan. Teachers reteach all priority content until all students learn it. This is usually called *mastery learning.* Content is reviewed continually, especially key concepts. Learning activities are plentiful.

Teacher-Student Interactions.   Do not assume that the classrooms in effective schools are cold and impersonal. To be certain, they are businesslike. The teachers, however, are enthusiastic supporters of their students and pay attention to student interests, problems, and accomplishments—both in and out of the classrooms. Teachers make sure that the students know that they really care.

Student Rewards and Incentives. All student rewards are made in terms of specific student achievements. Exemplary student work and projects that show high standards are proudly displayed for all to see, including shop projects, English papers, art works, mathematics solutions, and social studies outlines. The incentive to continue to strive for excellence is continually reinforced. The most impressive results from this effort have been reported from ghetto schools in which school effectiveness projects have been instituted.

After considering these eleven points, we may conclude, yes, it takes a great effort to change a mediocre school into an effective one. Yes, the teachers go home tired after a day's work because they are teaching all-out all day. Yes, the teachers have great satisfaction each day because they have been able to teach creatively and with enthusiasm—the name of the game for effective schools and effective teachers.

A Few Emerging Instructional Problems for Teachers

The preceding discussion examines some of the major institutional problems. But what of the teacher? Following is a list of questions on trends that will affect the teacher in the future.

1. *The computer.* How will the microcomputer revolution change the role of teacher at all levels?
2. *Textbook selection.* How will textbooks be selected to best augment computer-aided instruction?
3. *The basics.* How will each teacher actually implement the basics in his or her individual classroom?
4. *Controversial issues.* Will the classrooms of America be more or less "open" for discussion of controversial issues?
5. *School prayer.* Will the public schools become a battleground for a new round of public school prayer advocates?
6. *Creationism.* To what extent will creationist forces continue their efforts to impose their religious views on the teaching of empirical science?
7. *Educational psychology.* To what extent will teachers begin to use tested instructional concepts from the field of educational psychology?
8. *The future.* How can the school teacher honestly prepare children for a future when there is little agreement on what the future will be?

AN OVERVIEW OF OUR TEXT

As you read this text, keep in mind that you, as teacher, will make decisions as an individual practitioner or collectively through some type of group consensus. Here, then, is an overview of selected areas that affect the teacher's decisions and *how* instruction takes place—that is, the methods the teacher will ultimately choose to use.

Goals to Be Emphasized

It is all well and good to realize that our society and specific states have generated lists of goals for the schools. Yet it is imperative to understand that it is the individual teacher who selects and identifies those goals that will be emphasized and those that will be minimized or even eliminated. You, as teacher, make the decisions about aims, outcomes, or purposes. Through your social and cultural values, you determine and interpret the specific objectives that will be emphasized in your classes. We submit that you are the one who is responsible for translating general or ideal goals into operationally accomplished objectives.

Deciding on what will be taught is influenced by a whole series of factors that we often tend to discount. These factors include (1) the geographic location of the school; (2) the types of persons who are hired to teach; (3) the social class orientation of the instructor and the instructional materials; (4) the "neutral" or "noncontroversial" positions subscribed to by teachers when instructing or when avoiding controversial issues; (5) the actual instructional materials available to the teacher; and (6) the cultural, intellectual, emotional, and social attributes of the students. All of these factors are considered by you, as teacher, in your decision to teach a particular subject.

Objectives to Be Taught

The cognitive dimension of the schools rests on instructional objectives, which are either specified or implied. The teacher makes decisions on the instructional focus—for example, content, concepts, and generalizations. When these decisions are made, the teacher then states, in writing or orally, what specific lessons or outcomes are desired.

In Chapter 2 we illustrate this process by providing instructional experiences in specifying written learner-oriented objectives. Again we add the cautionary note: You, as the teacher, should decide the specific instructional objectives deliberately by analyzing your students' needs. This task requires a sequencing of the objectives, a subject that is addressed in Chapter 3.

Levels of Instruction

One major decision that is almost totally controlled by every teacher is the level of instruction. How much effort, time, and resources should be spent on what we might call "lower intellectual learnings"? How do you structure "thinking" abilities? We believe that you, as teacher, must make these fundamental decisions in a systematic fashion.

If history is taught predominantly as the memorization of the "fifty great names," then the instructor has chosen to teach history at the lowest possible intellectual level.

Concomitantly, that same history teacher may choose to provide a low-level historical perspective *and* then begin to evaluate the more advanced generalizations or theses of historians.

Chapter 4 is devoted to three models that can help you to decide on the levels of instruction that you will use in selecting experiences.

Deciding How to Plan a Lesson

Chapter 5, "Decisions About Lesson Planning," introduces the concept of lesson planning. Teachers now incorporate several specific activities into the instructional whole. When preparing a lesson plan, they "screen" many elements of the lesson and make decisions that directly affect the classroom environment. They survey resources, both print and nonprint materials. Assessments of possible instructional designs and methods are conducted. Interactions between individuals and groups must be planned. Estimates on student pacing must be considered, and motivational and evaluational techniques must be specified. All of these decisions tend to fall into a "non-interactive" dimension of teaching. The teacher is not yet interacting with the real people of the school—the students. The remaining decisions focus on interaction. The teacher ought to be the one to determine both the content and the processes of instruction, *but* in an enlightened and systematic manner. The teacher should always know why he or she is teaching what is being taught—and should know other alternatives to accomplish the same objective!

Deciding on Appropriate Interactions

After the prerequisite decisions are made, you as teacher must make a decision on how the classroom interaction will take place. The primary verbal interaction is through teacher questioning. But did you know that there are several different styles and techniques of classroom interaction? There are even ways in which you can decide that the students ought to ask the questions. The process of questioning (Chapter 6) can be fun and worthwhile. Bear in mind that all of this should be accomplished after planned, systematic analysis.

Chapter 7 presents one of the more detailed discussions of its kind about the decisions that must be made if meaningful classroom discussions are to take place. A thoroughly tested set of discussion strategies is presented so that you can decide which technique will accomplish the process and cognitive goals. By the way, most teachers really do not conduct discussions—they conduct recitations. But that is their decision.

Many teaching techniques are defined as being "expository." The teacher tells or has the students tell. In Chapters 8 and 9 we introduce a realm of decision-making that will cause your students to "think." Several techniques are presented so that you, as teacher, may decide on the appropriate ones to be used. Also given are some methods that you can use with inquiry teaching—how to teach inductive-oriented lessons, problem-solving exercises, and even deductive inquiry strategies.

In our opinion the activities given in Chapter 9 are so enjoyable that the students will not notice the work involved. The teaching methods given here require that fundamental instructional decisions be made by the teacher, because they demand a different set of teaching behaviors from the teacher.

Simulations are also introduced in Chapter 9. When is a game or simulation considered to be a learning experience? In recent years, more and more simulations are being marketed for school use. You, as teacher, must decide on their appropriateness, the time allocations, the roles, what learning will take place, and, most difficult, how to evaluate student participation in simulations. We know that you will be very surprised at the number of decisions that must be made when using all the interactive techniques described in this text.

Deciding About Classroom Procedures

One fact will stand out more clearly than all others: teaching requires the use of trust, power, and responsibility. It would be simple if all you had to do was to plan for instruction and interact with the students. But real life is tough. The public schools draw students who are quiet, shy, and gentle as well as those that are loud, angry, and unruly. What decisions do you, as teacher, make to structure the organization and management of your class? These are the topics that form the framework for Chapter 10.

Teachers do not leave teaching because of incompetence, but mainly because they cannot "handle" the students in the classes. Many teacher dropouts just did not know what kind of decisions had to be made by whom, when, where, and for whom. We want you to be better prepared.

You should also understand that there are some decisions that are made for you, whether you like them or not. Often, you must use the already selected learning materials, because there are no others available. If you do not find the adopted materials to be to your liking, then you must make the effort to begin the change process. Furthermore, you do not decide on what students you will teach; you simply take them all! The latter is one aspect of teaching in the public schools that is not apparent in the private schools. It also implies that you have no command over the students' home lives or value structures—outside the school context. To be sure, you will affect their values and, in some cases, profoundly change both their standards and outlooks in the future. We submit that the moment one is taught to read, one's values are changed.

But we wish to caution you that schools have their constraints as well as their opportunities for experimentation. Schools are institutions and, as such, like it or not, the institutional dimensions usually take precedence over personal ones. If you decide to humanize the institution, then you must decide to commit yourself to a long-term change effort. For example, report cards, attendance reports, athletic teams, and administrative channels are all part of the institutional structure of the school. You can change these in any desired direction, but it requires a great knowledge about the politics of change.

By now you should begin to appreciate that one just does not "stand up front and teach." What to teach, what the students should learn, how to teach, how to manage the environment, and what and how to evaluate all require professional decisions. This is where you begin.

INTRODUCING FORMATIVE EVALUATION

Prior to moving to the next chapter, you will be asked to complete a short evaluation. A basic objective of any evaluation system is to determine the extent to which the intended learner objectives are being achieved and the impact that the instruction or assignments are having on the learners. To accomplish this evaluation objective, two well-known evaluation methodologies are used by educators: formative and summative. The first, formative evaluation was originally proposed by Michael Scriven (1967).

Formative Evaluation

Formative evaluation is designed to provide feedback in a rather immediate sense. Formative instruments are designed specifically to monitor selected aspects of any assignment or to determine where learning problems are emerging. By using formative evaluation, problems may be quickly identified and corrected. For example, if some methodology is being used that causes the students to do poorly, quick remediation may take place through formative evaluation. Often the teacher gives assignments but does not check the students' work until the conclusion of the unit, which is usually too late. By continually checking the "small steps," the teacher may identify instructional problems. This means that the teacher observes many different facets of a course while it is being conducted.

Only a few selected items need to be checked in any one formative evaluation. These items would all be based on the stated or intended learning objectives. One does not need a lengthy set of test items. The important point is that the feedback is collected while there is adequate time to make adjustments for the student.

The rationale for formative evaluation is to provide data to the student and teacher so that they may make corrections—immediately, if not sooner! When both students and teacher realize that instructional activities are being monitored constantly, they tend to become more responsible and more productive. The instructional climate and total program environment become positive and supportive. This is precisely the kind of learning climate that the teacher always ought to foster when teaching. Conversely, classes have "gone on the rocks" because the teacher was not evaluating student activities over short periods of time, but waited until the very end of the course or unit to accomplish a one-shot final evaluation.

Using formative evaluation is much more subtle than simply specifying performance objectives. Formative evaluation requires that the teacher carefully observe a selected set of *experiences* for all participants. For example, in most courses, some form of activity is used to build a cluster of skills for future use. A teacher subscribing to formative evaluation monitors the skills and, when a student performs inadequately, a new set of experiences that relate to the instructional objectives are provided. To correct any noted learning deficiency, it is important not to wait until the "final exam." Thus periodic correctives are an integral part of the formative evaluation plan.

One simple method by which to record formative data is to tabulate the absolute numbers or percentages of both individual and group activities. The teacher can compare group data on a graph so that the directions of the students could be displayed for instant visual analysis.

The essential characteristic of formative evaluation is that "hard data" are being collected for decision-making. But, more importantly, corrections are built into the scheme, so that feedback is used when it is needed most— not stored for future judgment.

Summative Evaluation

Evaluation that is conducted as the final or concluding task is called summative evaluation. We should note that summative evaluation may be the final formative evaluation of a course or unit. Summative evaluations may take several forms, as long as they are consistent with the prescribed objectives of the unit, course, or module. Again, summative data can be tabulated as absolute responses, and then a percentage is calculated for each item. Comparisons between students also can be made from summative data (but not from the formative measures). The final grade is, of course, determined by the summative evaluations. Note the use of the plural: good teachers do not have one summative evaluation. They place evaluations at logical points in the course, such as at the ends of units, chapters, modules, or learning activity packages. The summative sets can then be arranged in a profile to illustrate the sum of evaluation activities. Formative data thus provide feedback, whereas summative scores lead to "grades" or to "judgments" about the quality of the performances.

Of course, it may be argued that formative and summative techniques will cause the teacher to change directions for several students. We agree and submit that if these techniques are properly used, the objectives of the entire class may even be altered.

Success is the underlying goal of this technique. If a course needs to be modified because of unrealistic expectations (objectives), then why not alter it?

Perhaps the most convincing advantage of the formative and summative model is that there are no "surprises" at the end of the prescribed work block. With early feedback evaluations built into the system, all elements should stress student success.

The Authors' Technique

At the end of each chapter, or in some cases integrated within it, will be a set of formative evaluation questions. If you score perfectly on the set, you have adequately studied the chapter. If, however, you miss several items, we suggest that you restudy at least that section. Or you may even ask your instructor for another, more detailed book that relates to the topic.

Now let us move on to the formative evaluation—and then to Chapter 2.

FORMATIVE EVALUATION
Decision-Making

How well did you achieve the basic objectives that we presented? To aid you, we have developed a short formative evaluation (test) by which you may check how well you did. If you miss any questions, review the appropriate section in Chapter 1.

1. Goals, according to the text,
   (a) Remain rather constant over time.
   (b) Change drastically over time.
   (c) Are different; goals change very slowly while objectives are very transient or ephemeral.
   (d) Are quite unimportant.
2. In American education
   (a) Pluralism leads to agreement on goals.
   (b) Pluralism leads to conflict over goals.
   (c) There are no conflicting goals.
   (d) There are no goals.
3. It appears that American teachers are oriented toward the values of the
   (a) Lower class.
   (b) Middle class.
   (c) Upper class.
   (d) Aristocratic class.
4. One of the more commonly accepted functions of our schools is that of
   (a) Deterring cultural change.
   (b) Transmitting the ideals and values held by social groups and aiding the realization of those ideals.
   (c) Changing social patterns to coincide with economic progress.
   (d) Maintaining all the *cultural patterns* of our ancestors.
5. From what you know about theories of learning and their effects on the curriculum, to which type of curriculum pattern might the following quote from the philosopher George Santayana best belong? "He who cannot learn from the past is doomed to repeat it."
   (a) Activity.
   (b) Child-centered.
   (c) Progressive.
   (d) Subject-centered.

6. According to the curriculum analysis, it was implied that there is a tendency for the public school curriculum to be
   (a) Oriented toward a critical review of our institutions.
   (b) Quite conservative in nature.
   (c) Influenced by the political party in power.
   (d) More liberally oriented owing to the liberal views of most teachers.
7. What do all of these have in common—the IEP, least restrictive environment, and yearly conference?
   (a) All are a part of the NDEA act.
   (b) They are parts of PL 94-142.
   (c) They are goals of education.
   (d) They are a part of ESEA.
8. According to the text, the teaching of handicapped children
   (a) Is unimportant.
   (b) Is now required by federal law.
   (c) Is now a local option to be determined by local school boards.
   (d) Is now a state function.
9. Objectives and goals are
   (a) Identical.
   (b) Universal.
   (c) Quite different.
   (d) Unessential for schools.
10. Decision-making is being
    (a) Intuitive.
    (b) Responsible.
    (c) Child-centered.
    (d) None of these.
11. Which agency or group has plenary control over education?
    (a) University professors.
    (b) Federal Congress.
    (c) Local superintendents.
    (d) State legislatures.
12. List four or five areas in which process and content seem to be indistinguishable.
13. Select one or two of the studies conducted in the early 1980s. Analyze the implied or stated assumptions; also list the conflicting points of view.
14. Why is it essential that teachers understand decision-making?
15. In what way will you influence *how* you teach?
16. Prepare a checklist of the eleven main points about effective schools. Compare that list with your personal schooling experience.
17. What impact will "high tech" (computers) have on the way we teach?

RESPONSES
Decision-Making

1. (a). Goals tend to remain somewhat static over time.
2. (b). Pluralism does lead to conflict over goals.
3. (b). American teachers strongly reflect the middle class.
4. (b). Transmitting culture is the best selection from this set.
5. (d). This is George Santayana's classic quote and must be considered subject-centered.

6. (b). The schools are not the great changers of society. This is consistent with No. 4 above.
7. (b). These were all discussed in the section on PL 94-142.
8. (b). This is required by federal law PL 94-142.
9. (c). They are essential, but quite different. Goals are broad, while objectives are very specific.
10. (b). We imply throughout the text that decision-making is one act of being professionally responsible.
11. (d). We may have only touched on this in passing, but the state legislature of each state has control over education.
12.–17. These questions require some activity from you. We suggest that you work with a peer or a small group of three or four and discuss these questions.

REFERENCES

Academic Preparation for College: What Students Need to Know and Be Able to Do. New York: The College Board, 1983.

"Alaska Effective Schooling Program." Portland, Ore.: Northwest Regional Educational Laboratory, 1981.

Bloom, Benjamin S., J. Thomas Hastings, and George F. Madaus. *Handbook on Formative and Summative Evaluation of Student Learning.* New York: McGraw-Hill, 1971.

Boyer, Ernest L. Interviewed in: *Your Public Schools.* August 28, 1978, p. 1.

Coleman, James S., et al. *Equality of Educational Opportunity.* Washington, D.C.: U.S. Government Printing Office, 1966.

Commission of the Reorganization of Secondary Education, National Education Association. *Cardinal Principles of Secondary Education.* Washington, D.C.: U.S. Government Printing Office, 1918.

Conant, James B. *The American High School Today: A First Report to Interested Citizens.* New York: McGraw-Hill, 1959.

Corrigan, Dean C. "Public Law 94-142: A Matter of Human Rights, A Call for Change in Schools and Colleges of Education." In *Teacher Education: Renegotiating Roles for Mainstreaming,* Judith K. Grosenick and Maynard C. Reynold, eds. Reston, Va.: Council for Exceptional Children, 1978.

Edmonds, Ronald. "Effective Schools for the Urban Poor." *Educational Leadership* 37:1979, 15–27.

Eisner, Elliot W., and Elizabeth Vallance. *Conflicting Conceptions of Curriculum.* Berkeley, Calif.: McCutchan, 1974.

Gardner, John W. *Excellence: Can We Be Equal and Excellent Too?* New York: Harper and Row, 1961.

Good, Thomas L. "How Teachers' Expectations Affect Results." *American Education* 18(10):1982, 25–32.

Goodlad, John I. *A Place Called School.* New York: McGraw-Hill, 1984.

Gump, Paul V. "The Classroom Behavior Setting: It's Nature and Relaxation to Student Behavior." Lawrence: University of Kansas, Department of Psychology, 1967, pp. 51–56, 80. EDRS/ERIC ED 015 515.

Harnischfeger, Annegret, and David E. Wiley. *Achievement Test Score Decline: Do We Need To Worry?* Chicago ML-Group for Policy Studies in Education, Central Midwestern Regional Educational Laboratory, 1975.

Jackson, Phillip W. *Life in Classrooms.* New York: Holt, Rinehart & Winston, 1968, p. 11.

Jencks, Christopher, et al. *Inequality: A Reassessment of the Effect of Family and Schooling in America.* New York: Basic Books, 1972.

A Nation at Risk. Washington, D.C.: National Commission on Excellence in Education, U.S. Department of Education, 1983.

National Association of Secondary School Principals. *Secondary Schools in a Chang-*

ing Society: This We Believe. Reston, Va.: National Association of Secondary School Principals, 1975.

Rist, Ray C. "Student Social Class and Teacher Expectations: The Self-fulfilling Prophecy in Ghetto Education." *Harvard Educational Review* 40:1970, 411–451.

Rosenthal, Robert, and Lenore Jacobson. *Pygmalion in the Classroom.* New York: Holt, Rinehart & Winston, 1968.

Scriven, Michael. *The Methodology of Evaluation.* AERA Monograph Series on Curriculum Evaluation, 1967, No. 1, pp. 39–83.

Sizer, Theodore R. *A Celebration of Teaching: High Schools in the 1980s.* Reston, Va.: The National Association of Secondary School Principals and the Commission on the Educational Issues of the National Association of Independent Schools, 1983.

"Standardized Exams Aren't a 'Quick Fix' for Education." *Lewiston Morning Tribune,* Oct. 30, 1983, p. 4. From the Associated Press Wire Service reporting Gregory R. Anrig's comments.

U.S. Statutes at Large. 85th Cong., 2d sess., 1958, p. 1580.

Vernon, McCay. "Education's 'Three Mile Island': PL 94-142." *Peabody Journal of Education* 59:1982, 24–29.

2

DECIDING ON OBJECTIVES

The first step in systematic decision-making is the planning phase. In this chapter, two major concepts are presented to begin that phase: (1) the specifying of student objectives; and (2) the preparing of standards of student performance. This chapter is designed so that you will be able to

1. Realize that there are three levels of objectives generally used in the teaching-learning process
2. Identify four domains under which objectives are classified
3. Identify and write performance objectives in various styles
4. Prepare performance objectives
5. Describe why performance objectives are necessary for selected instructional strategies
6. Defend or criticize the use of performance objectives

PLANNING FOR SUCCESSFUL INSTRUCTION

One hallmark of schooling as an organized activity is the process called planning. If you as a teacher wish to instruct in a systematic manner, then a substantial proportion of your time and activity will be concentrated on planning—deciding what and how you want your students to learn. It appears that teachers who are most successful exhibit three common traits: (1) they are well organized in their planning; (2) they communicate effectively with their students; and (3) they have high expectations of their students.

We may generalize that, although learning can take place anywhere and spontaneously, the more systematic the teacher, the greater the probability for success. Instructional planning or lesson planning implies the establishment of priorities. The setting of priorities mandates a continuous set of teacher decisions. The objectives that you specify establish learning priorities for the students. We do not wish to imply that the learners may not specify their objectives. But, to be realistic, the teacher, through lectures, discussions, learning modules, assignments, textbooks, and other educational experiences, is responsible for establishing the priorities.

By means of written lesson plans, the priorities about time, learning materials, objectives, and type of instruction are all made known in advance so that success may be maximized for two important groups—the teachers and the students. Chapter 5 is devoted to lesson planning, so we mention that subject only briefly here.

Performance or Behavioral Objectives

The types of objectives that currently are being advocated by many educators are different from those that were in vogue as late as 1968. There is one large group of educators that stresses that objectives ought not emphasize what the teacher will be doing—for example, teach about photosynthesis—but rather should identify the performance or behavior that is to be expected of the students as a result of instructional experiences. For example, if the instructional topic happens to be the introduction to photosynthesis, then one performance objective may be for the student to "illustrate the general reaction of the photosynthetic process, using the components of O_2, H_2O, CO_2, glucose, sunlight, and chlorophyll in the correct sequence of events"; or "illustrate the major steps of the Krebs Cycle, using the textbook as a source."

Because the emphasis is on student outcomes, these objectives are called *performance* or *behavioral objectives*. Instructional, learner, and specific objectives are also used as synonyms, but these terms should not confuse you. The main point is that you should demonstrate the ability to distinguish between objectives that emphasize student behavior and those that state what the teacher is supposed to do.

Another distinction is made between performance and process objectives. *Performance objectives* generally refer to student mastery of the *content* to be taught. Content is the cognitive material (facts, concepts, skills, and generalizations) that makes up the body of information that we want students to learn. *Process objectives* focus on the *mental skills* (observations, evaluations, or inferences) that allow students to interpret the content they master. Performance and process objectives are not exclusive outcomes but are complementary. Whenever you prepare a performance objective that emphasizes content to be learned by the student, some mental skills are always involved in the student's learning. When the student needs to learn mental skills to make use of the content, that is, when learning skills are the principal purpose of instruction, you should prepare process objectives that aid the student's ability to assimilate that content.

One important use of behavioral objectives is that they give the teacher some clear and precise guidelines to achieving specific student outcomes—for example, the expected student performances or behaviors for which the teacher is responsible in class. That is, the objectives prescribe exactly which behaviors the students must manifest as a result of the instruction. Likewise, performance objectives are given to students prior to instruction to inform them specifically of what they will learn to do. This eliminates much of the guesswork related to teaching ("What should I teach today?") or to the student's learning ("What should I study for the test?").

Note that there is an implicit assumption that, because the student is told in advance what is expected, the student will be self-motivated to do the tasks. This is not always the case, just as it is not always the case if general statements are made to students about what is expected of them. A more detailed critique of the uses and abuses of performance objectives is presented on page 44.

Performance objectives are widely used and, as a prospective teacher, you need to understand and develop the technical skills that are necessary to prescribe and state these types of objectives. If you ever become involved in any "individualized" program, it is mandatory that you skillfully write and analyze performance objectives because nearly all individualized programs using "mastery" learning techniques refer to performance objectives. Furthermore, by law, some states require that they be specific, as do some school districts by policy.

A particular demand on teachers to make use of performance objectives has come from the Education for All Handicapped Children Act of 1975 (Public Law 94-142), which requires that all handicapped children be taught in the regular classroom to the greatest possible extent. As part of "mainstreaming" handicapped children into the classroom, an Individualized Educational Plan (IEP) must be prepared for each special student. Each IEP must identify the specific learning outcomes expected of the student.

Beginning the Process

The identifying and writing of performance objectives take much planning. Often one begins by identifying objectives at a very broad level, then works toward specifics. Developing performance objectives is, therefore, a deductive process. The direction of movement is from a general frame of reference to more specific ones. Most simply, there are three levels of specificity. These levels may be classified as (1) general—very broad objectives; (2) intermediate; and (3) specific behavioral or performance. This chapter deals only with these specific behavioral, performance objectives. General goals were discussed briefly in Chapter 1.

Intermediate-range objectives, while useful as guidelines, are still too general for direct implementation in instruction; thus the classroom teacher states even more specific objectives so that explicit direction is given to learning. These specific objectives usually are called behavioral objectives, because learning is defined as an observable change in the behavior of students. That is, learning is assumed to have occurred when the student demonstrates some behavior that could not be shown prior to the learning experience. Therefore, at the instructional level, objectives are statements about the *behavior of the student*. Rather than describing what the teacher will do, *specific performance objectives describe what the learner will do*.

Deciding which objectives are valid and relevant in any course or program is a very important and difficult part of curriculum planning. To help in this important decision, educators have been urged to examine three principal sources of objectives by Ralph W. Tyler, the founder of behavioral objectives. Tyler (1949) stated that the sources for objectives ought to be (1) the learner;

(2) studies of contemporary life outside the school; and (3) the subject matter itself—the respective disciplines.

If you were to follow the rationale of some proponents of performance objectives to its ultimate conclusion, you would find yourself creating an individual set of objectives for every student. Although this may be an interesting and worthy "goal," we view it as being fiscally and procedurally not feasible. It is doubtful that any society with limited resources would decide to pay for total individualization of instruction. Fortunately, such individualized instruction is not required to provide effective, appropriate, and meaningful learning opportunities for all students.

We have discussed previously some of the past attempts to identify a consensus on the kinds of goals that could be of value to American schools. The common factor in these statements was that the student should be able and willing to demonstrate some acceptable behaviors as a consequence of the educational experiences. These statements have been of use to teachers, curriculum planners, and test-makers in that they have contributed some agreement regarding the specification of student behaviors. The state of Washington has established, for the Common Schools, both long-range goals and intermediate-range objectives.

Rationale for Performance Objectives

Whereas many teachers are able to recognize educational goals and to translate them into effective conditions for learning, others have not carried their thinking beyond the stage of selecting the content to be presented. The danger is that the teacher will not recognize effective ways of reaching the necessary objectives if, in fact, the objectives are not individually formulated. Also, unless students know what the objectives are, they are likely to resort to memorization and mechanical completion of exercises rather than to attempt more relevant learning activities. When the teacher tells the student what is expected, a model is provided around which learning activities can be individually organized. When this is done, the teacher and student have established a "perceived purpose" for all that is to follow. Unless objectives are specifically stated, it is impossible to determine the student's achievements at any given moment. Therefore, statements that define what is expected of the learner must be available. These are the basic assumptions associated with the performance objective movement.

Currently, more than four-fifths of the state legislatures or state education agencies are considering or have already mandated plans that "make the schools accountable." In general, making schools accountable means that teachers will be evaluated in terms of how their students perform. The only way that teachers can "prove" that their students have learned is by providing measurable evidence that their students are different at the completion of a sequence of instruction than they were before instruction. The only way teachers can provide measurable evidence is by stating in advance of instruction the performance they expect of their students—performance objectives. Therefore, in the many states where accountability programs are a part of the teacher's daily life, performance objectives have become a primary part of planning and implementing of instruction.

It is assumed that teachers involved in preparing and using behavioral objectives have a mastery of their academic disciplines. This, however, is not applicable to the majority of preservice individuals (prospective teachers) who have just begun intensive study of their respective disciplines. Therefore, because the preparation of behavioral objectives demands a critical analysis of the subject matter to be learned, a variety of aids— such as textbooks, curriculum guides, and print and nonprint materials— may be useful to preservice teachers.

Taxonomies of Behaviors

In 1948, after an informal meeting of evaluation specialists, a decision was made to formulate a theoretical framework to facilitate more precise communication about the learning process. It was agreed that such a framework would best be devised through a system of classification of the goals of the educational processes. It was the assumption of the group that educational objectives, stated in behavioral form, are reflected in the behavior of individuals. That is, behavior can be observed and described, and these descriptive statements can be classified.

The plan for classification involved a complete taxonomy in four major parts—the cognitive, the affective, the psychomotor, and the perceptual domains.

The Cognitive Domain includes those objectives that deal with the recall or recognition of knowledge and the development of intellectual abilities and skills. This is the domain in which most of the work in curriculum development has taken place and in which the clearest definitions of objectives phrased as descriptions of student behavior occur.

The Affective Domain is the area that concerns attitudes, beliefs, and the entire spectrum of values and value systems. This is an exciting area that curriculum-makers are now exploring.

The Psychomotor Domain attempts to classify the coordination aspects that are associated with movement and to integrate the cognitive and affective consequences with bodily performances.

The Perceptual Domain, less developed than the others, provides a hierarchical structure for sensory perceptions organized on the principle of integration. This taxonomy may be useful to teachers in preparing objectives, plans, and instructional materials that take into account individual differences based on differences in perceptual orientation (Moore, 1967).

These taxonomies or domains were designed as classification systems for student behaviors that represent the intended outcomes of the education process. By combining the principles of any taxonomy with the careful preparation of performance objectives, the teacher can focus instruction on outcomes that vary from the simple to the complex. Using any taxonomy, the teacher can prescribe objectives to build simple, entry-level skills for students or to develop complex, high-level skills that meet the individual student's needs. This analytic "tool" is most useful when the teacher is attempting to develop a specific IEP or when he or she is building entry-level skills for educationally disadvantaged children. Thus, by the tool of the taxonomy, the same types of learning behavior may be observed in all subject areas taught at all different levels of education. Chapter 4 is devoted entirely to the topic of learning the taxonomies and to further clarification and amplification of this educational tool.

ELEMENTS OF PERFORMANCE OBJECTIVES

Although performance objectives are written in a wide variety of styles, three elements generally can be included in the specification of a performance objective.

1. The statement of an observable behavior or performance on the part of the learner.
2. An elaboration of the conditions under which learner behavior or performance is to occur.
3. The prescription of a minimally acceptable performance on the part of the learner.

You will observe the first element in almost all performance objectives—that is, the specification of the *intended* behavior or performance. According to purists of the skill, *only* when all three elements are stated is an objective written appropriately. As learners of the skill, you should always state the three elements for practice. This repetition will then give you insights (nonbehavioral term) into how you will feel (affective term) about their use in your teaching or how to evaluate (cognitive term) curricula that use such objectives. Again, it will be your decision (affective behavior) as to what style *you* choose. It was *our* decision (arbitrary and cognitive behavior) to illustrate a three-element type.

Element One: Performance Statement

The first element of a behavioral objective is the specification of a word, generally a verb, that indicates how the learner is performing, what the learner is doing, or what the learner is producing. Verbs such as *match, name, compute, list, assemble, write, circle,* and *classify* result in observable learner behaviors that will help you to evaluate the achievement of behavioral objectives.

For example, if you state that the student must name the capitals of ten states listed, the student's behavior is manifested when this performance takes place; everyone will know that the student has attained the stated student objective.

The specifications of the performance, of course, come from the general goals and intermediate objectives. If you teach social studies, one goal always will be to provide instruction about our form of government and the Constitution. An intermediate objective surely will be to study the Bill of Rights. Specific performance objectives may be as follows. The learner will

1. Write verbatim or paraphrase the first ten amendments to the U.S. Constitution.
2. Distinguish between statements from the Bill of Rights and those that are not.
3. Conduct a survey to determine how many students in the high school can identify the Fifth Amendment.
4. Select one of the amendments and prepare a 200-word essay on its meaning to the learner.
5. Observe a court trial to determine whether the Fifth Amendment is really upheld.
6. Assemble the titles of magazine articles written about the Bill of Rights.

All of these objectives are written with a prescribed student performance in mind. Table 2–1 contains a handy list of action verbs that will help you in constructing the first element of performance objectives.

Careful examination of the table will show you that it contains mainly *transitive verbs,* the "action verbs." They suggest that the actions are done *to direct objects,* which must also be specified. This is critical, since the intended action is meaningless unless the verb and its direct object are specified. The performance objective thus tells what will be done in observable and measurable terms.

Words such as *know, understand, analyze, evaluate, appreciate, comprehend,* and *realize* are not action verbs. While such terms are important in the processes of learning and behaving, they are not observable actions and thus cannot be used when writing performance or behavioral objectives. We suggest that terms such as these be used in specifying goals or intermediate objectives. Remember that you make the decisions about the kind of performance you think is most appropriate or relevant.

Thus, the first and most important element of any performance objective is the selecting of the action verb and its direct object. In certain cases, this is the main performance objective. However, according to Robert F. Mager (1962), an exponent of the performance objective movement, there must be two additional elements to make a performance objective truly communicative: the conditions under which the performance is to take place and the evaluative statement.

Element Two: Elaboration of the Conditions

The second element in the prescribing of a behavioral objective is the statement of the *conditions* under which the learner is to perform the behavior. The conditional element prescribes the circumstances under which the

TABLE 2–1   Some Action Verbs That Describe Observable Cognitive Behavior

A	E	L	R
add	enumerate	label	rank
alphabetize	extrapolate	list	rate
alter		locate	recall
amend	**F**		reproduce
apply a rule	factor	**M**	
arrange	figure	manipulate	**S**
assign values	fill in	mark off	select
	find	match	set down
B	fix	measure	specify
bisect	fold	memorize	state
	formulate	mix	state a rule
C		multiply	substitute
calculate	**G**		subtract
capitalize	gather	**N**	
chart	graph	name	**T**
circle	group		tabulate
classify		**O**	transcribe
combine	**H**	order	translate
complete	hit	outline	
compute	hold		**U**
construct		**P**	underline
correct	**I**	perform	undertake
count	identify	place	
	inscribe	point out	**V**
D	insert	predict	verbalize
define	integrate	print	
delineate	interpolate	punctuate	**W**
describe	itemize	put in order	write
diagram			
discriminate among	**J**	**Q**	**X**
dissect	join	qualify	x-ray
distinguish between		quote	
divide	**K**		**Y**
draw	keep		yell
duplicate	knit		
			Z
			zip

learner must perform. If location is important to accomplishing the objective, then this must be stated in the conditional element of the objective. Generally, conditional elements refer to

1. What materials may be used to do the tasks
2. How the performance may be accomplished—for example, from memory, from the textbook, or from a handout
3. Time elements (although time may also be used in evaluation)
4. Location of the performance (in the classroom, in a gymnasium, or in the library)

Observe this example: "With the aid of the Periodic Chart, the student will list the atomic weights of the first ten elements . . . ." Note that the conditional statement is "with the aid of the Periodic Chart." This tells a student that there is no need to memorize the atomic weights; the student should simply identify them from the Periodic Chart. We often refer to the conditional component of a performance objective as a "statement of givens": "Given this" or "given that," the learner will accomplish something.

Perhaps the conditional element of a performance objective is the "fair play" part of the instruction. How many times have you walked into a class only to find that when the teacher said to "study" a lesson, the actual or implied meaning, at least according to the teacher, was to "memorize" the lesson? The imprecision of such conditions is confusing, if not demoralizing, to students and can often lead to discipline problems for the teacher. We recommend that this element of instruction always be given explicitly to students whether you use performance objectives or not.

The following is a list of a few conditional statements that could be included in the appropriate performance objectives.

1. "From memory . . ."
2. "Using a map of . . ."
3. "On a handout, which describes . . ."
4. "Given six different material samples without labels . . ."
5. "From the notes taken while viewing technicolor 35 mm slides . . ."
6. "Using all 20 problems on page 128 in the textbook . . ."
7. "Within a 10-minute time span and from memory . . ."
8. "When given the names of the Provinces of Canada . . ."
9. "Using the Income Tax Form 1040A . . ."
10. "With a compass, ruler, and protractor . . ."
11. "Using an electric typewriter . . ."
12. "Using the chemicals and glassware provided in the tray . . ."
13. "Using the film 'The Joel E. Ferris Story' . . ."
14. "Given the paper, thermofax machine, and all other materials . . ."
15. "With the use of a microcomputer . . ."

These are some general examples of the conditions under which a student can achieve a desired performance objective. In most cases, the condition will be singular and simple—for example, from memory; however, the condition may be multiple in nature. The conditional statement is set by the teacher and given to the learners in advance. We recommend that the condition be written as the first component of the performance objective, although its placement is not a major issue over which to argue. We simply view it as having significant impact on instructional planning and teacher behavior and so should not be omitted.

In addition, conditions must be realistic. Even though feasible, "reciting the Declaration of Independence from memory in five minutes" would be a very irrelevant condition. One must always ask, "What is my main priority for the objective?" If memorizing is the priority, then that condition will effect the attainment of the objective. If identifying the key elements of the Declaration of Independence is the priority, then a condition less rigorous than memorization would be more compatible with the objective.

We highlight this point, not to be facetious, but to warn you of possible pitfalls. In our collective experiences, we have witnessed performance objectives with outrageous conditions. Conditions must not act as an unreasonable impediment to the student in completing an objective in an effective manner.

Element Three: The Criterion Measure

Perhaps the third element is the most difficult decision of all to make in a three-part performance objective—the definition of an acceptable standard of performance. This standard is usually called the "criterion measure," "level of performance," "minimum criterion," or the "minimum acceptable performance." Whatever the term used to define this element, it must be kept in mind that the designated level is the *minimum or lowest level of acceptable performance*. Traditionally, this level is indicated by a grade of C, the average level. With this truly unique element in instruction, a student knows in advance exactly what the standards are by which the work will be judged.

Examine the following criterion measures, remembering that the condition and the performance verb are missing from the statements.

1. ". . . 70 percent of a given list of problems."
2. ". . . within 2mm. . . ."
3. ". . . 9 out of 10 of the elements. . . ."
4. ". . . within five minutes, with no more than two errors of any kind."
5. ". . . the project will be compared to the two models completed by the instructor."
6. ". . . without any grammatical or spelling errors."
7. ". . . containing one dependent and one independent clause."
8. ". . . meeting all the criteria that are elaborated in detail on page 214 in the textbook."
9. ". . . in 10.0 seconds or less."
10. ". . . 8 out of 10 consecutive trials."

Each of these criterion elements illustrates a well-defined standard toward which the student will strive. These standards are always devised so that the students have a high probability of achieving them and thus will be encouraged to continue to achieve the established criterion. We also caution that many teachers expect far too much from their students and set standards that are too high or impossible to reach. You must know at what level your students are working so that you may establish "reasonable" minimum standards—an accomplishment that is both an art and a science!

Frequently an instructor will require 100 percent of the class to attain 100 percent of the objective—that is, complete mastery. Such criterion measures are called 100/100 criterion measures because 100 percent of the class must obtain a 100 percent score. There are many times when an instructor will require mastery, such as when building skills, applying knowledge, constructing something, using equipment, stressing safety procedures, and doing other key tasks. In these cases, mastery or the top level is the minimum acceptable level. Again, you, the professional, must make that decision. When completing prerequisite or entry-level tasks, the mastery criterion is most appropriate, since later skills are contingent on performing the initial ones.

Criterion Grading

A word of caution must be expressed about criterion levels. Far too frequently, a percent number or a time is prescribed by the teacher as establishing the evaluation element of the performance objective. If time is a critical factor in the real world—as in life-saving, in brake-reaction situations, and in manipulating machinery—then a timed criterion is appropriate. But to set the time of early or initial experiences identical to that of practitioners in the field is inappropriate on the teacher's part. Skills can be built or improved by using variable criterion measures just as with any systematic method aimed at improving skills. Thus, a criterion measure of 30 seconds for a skill in the first experience may be reduced systematically as the learners improve. Typing teachers have observed this principle in action many times. As time progresses in the course, the students are allowed fewer mistakes per selected time period. In short, the standards for an A or top grade or even a C or average grade are shifted to higher levels of achievement as the course progresses.

Some educators have criticized performance objectives for seeming to force them into giving A grades for minimum student performance. This need not be the case. As a teacher, you may write performance objectives with clear criterion measures and make the meeting of those objectives worth any letter grade you choose. You may establish the standard that the meeting of criterion measures in your objectives will earn your students a C grade. Not meeting the criterion measures in your objectives will earn students a grade of less than C, and achieving a grade higher than C will require performance beyond those prescribed in your objectives.

Several other alternatives concerning performance objectives and grades are available to the teacher. You may choose to write several performance objectives for a sequence of instruction. Each objective can be progressively more difficult, with each worth a higher letter grade. Thus, performance objective 1 is worth a grade of D, while objective 2 is worth a grade of C, and so on.

Another alternative, a variation on the one above, is to prepare performance objectives that have several progressively more demanding criterion measures. In this instance, each criterion measure represents a higher letter grade when the learner improves enough to achieve it.

Rather than pressuring the teacher into giving a high grade for mediocre performance, careful use of performance objectives gives the teacher the ability to prescribe precisely the value and meaning of letter grades in terms of overt learner performance.

We have a wide continuum of assessment techniques by which to judge student performances. Following is a list of techniques that may be easily applied in the classroom:

1. Observation of the student's performance
2. Prepared product
3. Practical application tests
4. Laboratory quizzes
5. Proportion of successful trials
6. Timed tasks
7. Checklists with specific criteria
8. Scales to rate activities or products
9. Objective tests
10. Essay tests
11. Teacher anecdotal records
12. Student self-reports

Perhaps the establishment of reasonable levels of excellence is the most difficult task in writing a three-element performance objective. It certainly is the part that requires teacher decisions that reflect discretion and fairness.

Models of Completed Performance Objectives

The following is a series of performance objectives that contain the three elements described in this chapter. As you read each objective, identify each element; then compare your analyses with those in the model set that follows.

1. From those alternatives discussed and listed in this class, the student, from memory, must list three of the apparent causes of the American War Between the States.
2. Using the textbook and the supplemental readings listed in the bibliography, the student will compare the events leading to Richard M. Nixon's resignation from the presidency with Lyndon B. Johnson's refusal to run for reelection in 1968. The criteria for evaluation will be the six major points prepared by the instructor and distributed to the class.
3. Using the six descriptions of elements for a good short story, the student will identify in writing the six elements in the short story by O. Henry, with complete accuracy.
4. Given a compass and a straightedge, the student will construct a pentagon, within 5 degrees of accuracy, on any of the inside or outside angles.
5. After completing the chapter on environmental issues, the student will list at least six problems that could become issues in our city.

6. Following the pattern for a "hot mitt," construct a mitt from the materials in the class bin so that a steam iron set at 400°F may be held for 6 seconds without burning the mitt and without making your hand feel uncomfortably hot. The project must be completed in two class periods.

The model set of responses that follows is coded to reveal each element. Conditions are identified between the parentheses (   ). Each learner performance is stated between the square brackets [   ]. The criterion measure is underscored.

1. (From those alternatives discussed and listed in this class, the student, from memory), [must list] three of the apparent causes of the American War Between the States.
2. (Using the textbook and the supplemental readings listed in the bibliography), [the student will compare the events leading to Richard M. Nixon's resignation from the presidency with Lyndon B. Johnson's refusal to run for reelection in 1968.] The criteria for evaluation will be the six major points prepared by the instructor and distributed to the class.
3. (Using the six descriptions of elements for a good short story), [the student will identify in writing the six elements in the short story by O. Henry,] with complete accuracy.
4. (Given a compass and a straightedge), [the student will construct a pentagon,] within 5 degrees of accuracy, on any of the inside or outside angles.
5. (After completing the chapter on environmental issues), [the student will list] at least six problems that could become issues in our city.
6. (Following the pattern for a "hot mitt,") [construct a mitt from the materials in the class bin] so that a steam iron set at 400°F may be held for 6 seconds without burning the mitt and without making your hand feel uncomfortably hot. The project must be completed in two class periods.

ARE PERFORMANCE OBJECTIVES NECESSARY?

The establishing of behavioral objectives is not an educational panacea that will resolve all learning problems. It must be emphasized that there are limited purposes for writing performance or behavioral objectives. *Behavioral objectives are only a means to an end, not an end per se.* The purpose of the objective is to communicate the exact intent of the lesson, the behavioral objective being one component of the lesson plan. *The teacher can construct technically correct objectives but can fail completely in the classroom because of a lack of teaching skills and interpersonal competencies or strategies.*

When developing lessons that use behavioral objectives, the teacher must accept the following assumptions:

1. Learning is defined as a change in the learner's observable behavior.

2. Behavioral changes are observable in some form and may be measured by *appropriate* measuring devices over a specified period of time.
3. Observed learner outcome is *primary* to the teaching strategies, the content, or the media used.
4. The majority of all children at all ages can master appropriate subjects at some acceptable level if they are given enough time *and* adequate, appropriate learning experiences.

Problems in Writing Appropriate Objectives

We have noticed at least four major problems that teachers encounter when writing behavioral objectives. Each of these four problems is discussed in the following sections.

Confusing Instruction with the Conditional Statement

One of the common traps into which teachers fall is that of writing a behavioral objective that is nothing more than the condition under which the instruction is to take place. For example, written objectives that state, "after viewing a film" or "after classroom instruction," are statements referring to teaching behaviors that take place prior to student performance. They are not performance conditions as we have defined the term. Thus we have found that teachers confuse their instructional behavior with their students' learning behavior. Condition statements refer to the circumstances of the student at the moment of performance. More appropriately written conditions may specify "from memory" or "using classroom notes taken while viewing a movie" when the student is to recall a concept or a set of concepts.

Incomplete Criterion Statement

In developing the criterion statement for an objective, it is very easy to make a statement such as "define eight out of ten terms," which specifies only the quantity of the performance but not the quality. In such a case, the instructor must first have a set of criteria by which to judge the quality of each definition before determining whether the student has given the *minimum* number of eight definitions.

Unspecified Level of Performance in Criterion Statement

For a long time our society has accepted a graded level of performance: 90 percent = A, 80 percent = B, 70 percent = C, and so on. Using the behavioral objective approach to teaching requires a different system of grading because the criterion level is related to the performance. A teacher must ask two questions: (1) "At what level must my students perform in order to be successful in subsequent instructional tasks?" and (2) "What level is considered successful in the world in which the student lives?" In a beginning reading class, the teacher strives for a 95–100 percent mastery of vocabulary and sounds, whereas in a beginning archery course, the instructor considers an acceptable level to be 50 percent of the arrows hitting the target. At best, the teacher establishes a hypothetically acceptable level of performance and keeps collecting data to substantiate, modify, or reject that level. Remember that in nearly all cases standards are subjective, if not arbitrary!

Another problem related to the establishment of minimal levels of performance is the tendency to convert all levels to percentage scores. Asking the student for 80 percent of a definition or for 100 percent of an essay is a misuse of a criterion measure and is inappropriate. A more reasonable approach would be to define clearly the elements necessary for an acceptable essay. Once the attributes or elements are stated, it may be reasonable to request that a certain percentage of these attributes or elements be included. For example, the criterion that "each written sentence must have a subject and predicate" provides a valid standard by which to judge the essay.

Still another problem is the overuse of time statements within the criterion measure. By placing time in the statement, the instructor is suggesting that time is at least as important as quality, and even more important, if the quality criterion is omitted from the objective. Putting a time limit on exercises that require written or constructed products usually defeats the intended outcome, such as *quality* writing or *quality* construction. The decision to include time must be deliberate and not just a habit developed by a clock-watching teacher.

Avoiding Irrelevant Objectives

We assume that at this point you have asked yourself, "Couldn't all this performance-objective writing lead to compilations of millions of trite, useless, and seldom-used lesson plans?" Advocates of performance objectives sometimes fail to caution that you can fall easily into the trap of working out mechanically a series of performance objectives that are totally and irrevocably irrelevant.

If you make the decision to use this instructional technique (or if someone with higher authority makes the decision for you), then you must be careful not to generate trite, redundant lists. We have seen teachers who hand their students pages of performance objectives and simply tell them that they are on their own. Furthermore, we have witnessed the publication of hundreds of thousands of objectives that are on exchange so that teachers can borrow from each other. We have also heard discussions in which teachers find themselves trying to prescribe every single learner activity with such specificity that the objectives, not the learner's achievement of them, become all important.

In short, we are cautioning that overuse of performance objectives is just as absurd as not using any at all. Your decision to use them must always be predicated on the potential benefit to the learner.

Reasons for Using Behavioral Objectives: Summary

Behavioral objectives clarify the intent of the lesson for the teacher. With clearly stated outcomes in mind, the teacher is better able to design appropriate learning experiences for the class—and for each child, if the program is individualized.

Behavioral objectives also clarify the intent of the lesson for the learner. The student is able to use time more efficiently, since he or she knows what is to be performed. If the approach is employed in a self-instructional program, the student may have the alternative of individually selecting learning experiences.

Behavioral objectives make it easier to measure student achievement. Since the criteria are stated in the objective, both student and teacher know what is expected of the student, and the student gets immediate feedback about the performance. It is simpler—but unfair—to assign students an A, B, C, or F arbitrarily without specifying what is being measured. You may recall those extremely biased essay tests in which no learner objectives or grading criteria were specified.

A teacher may still assign A's, B's, and F's, but only with a *prior* explanation of the criteria by which such grading standards will be applied. Also, by specifying behavioral objectives, a contract grading system may be developed, or a different *qualitative* component may be prescribed, for each different level of performance for each grade.

Behavioral objectives make it easier to measure effectiveness of instruction. The teacher's job is to aid student learning. Because the level of performance is stated, it is easy to determine if the selected materials, visual aids, and teaching strategies have been helpful to the student in achieving the stated objectives. As a result, effectiveness of instruction is based on student achievement of the instructional objectives.

Behavioral objectives should help develop a more effective communication system among teachers, students, administrators, and parents. A well-stated behavioral objective gives them all a common frame of reference for discussion. Because instruction is the primary purpose of education, precisely written instructional objectives are essential to any meaningful interaction.

Reginald F. Melton (1978) reviewed the research concerning the effect of behavioral objectives on student learning. He noted that the findings of reported research are very conflicting. However, there do seem to be several generalizations that are supported by some research evidence.

1. Behavioral objectives do act as guides to student learning and as advance organizers. (This is discussed in Chapter 3.)
2. Performance objectives tend to depress incidental learning.
3. Providing students with behavioral objectives after a learning sequence tends to improve incidental learning.
4. Distributing performance objectives throughout the textual material

may improve learning—that is, distributing the objectives over an assignment may be more effective than giving all the objectives at once.

If you teach in a school that uses "direct instruction," "teacher-directed instruction," or "mastery learning," then you must master the process of writing three-part performance objectives. If you teach in a school that has adopted Madeline Hunter's "Instructional Theory into Practice" (ITIP) model (1979, also called "Science of Teaching"), then you will also use performance objectives. Finally, many state accountability laws require their use.

Performance Objectives and Microcomputers

One of the greatest technological revolutions ever, the microcomputer, is now being integrated into the classroom. As computer software must be carefully planned, it is essential that the students be given lists of both performance and process objectives to help them know what is required of them as they work at the microcomputers. As an instructional tool, the microcomputer can also be programmed to process individual and class learning outcomes. This processing capacity saves valuable teacher record-keeping time.

Microcomputers also provide a means by which drill and practice—as well as individualized instruction—may be made part of the classroom routine. Performance objectives must be built into such programs so that students understand what degree of accuracy is required in an individualized system.

Microcomputers easily allow for student self-pacing. Self-pacing requires each user to know expected outcomes and standards. If you use student performance contracts with the microcomputer, then outcomes and standards of achievement are critical. Finally, interactive computer programs allow the student to achieve both performance and process objectives with a speed and efficiency that no other system can attain. We perceive the microcomputer as one powerful means by which careful and systematic learning may be incorporated into your instructional decision-making process.

A Final Caution

Specifying learning activities in behavioral form is just *one* element in the totality of teaching acts. A teacher who uses appropriately designed behavioral objectives may develop into a better instructor. A disorganized, haphazard, or slovenly teacher with or without behavioral objectives will still be disorganized, haphazard, or slovenly. But more important, the *quality* of the objectives is of prime concern. A teacher with well-conceived and relevant objectives will help students demonstrate more relevant learning behaviors.

FORMATIVE EVALUATION

Congratulations. You have just completed the text of Chapter 2. Below are two components of a formative evaluation with which to check your knowledge and understanding of the concepts presented in this chapter. Section 1 contains three lists with four items each. The appropriate responses for each list follow. If you score 4 for each list, continue to Section 2 of the formative evaluation. If you score 3 or less, restudy the text on that section so that you may bring yourself up to mastery for each list.

Section 1

A. Read each item below. Place an X next to each item that states an identifiable behavior or an observable performance.

_____ 1. The learner will understand that multiplication requires a place value numbering system.
_____ 2. The student will appreciate the writings of Mark Twain.
_____ 3. The learner must know microcomputer programs.
_____ 4. The learner will describe the function of baking powder in the making of bread.

RESPONSES

1. Item 1 should not have an X, as the verb *understand* does not offer an observable behavior.
2. Item 2 should not have an X, as the verb *appreciate* does not offer an observable behavior.
3. Item 3 should not have an X. *Know* is internal to the learner and there is no observable behavior.
4. Item 4 should have an X. The verb *describe* offers an observable behavior.

Next Task

If you got 3 or fewer correct, restudy the text on observable behavior or reexamine the performance words. If you got 4 correct, do the formative evaluation on conditions, which follows.

B. Read each of the following items. Place an X next to each item that states a condition under which the learner's behavior is to occur.

_____ 1. Given ten different leaf samples, the student will correctly identify all the plants from which they come.
_____ 2. Identify all the nouns and adjectives.
_____ 3. The student will name the artists and medium used when presented with reproductions of their work.
_____ 4. The student will orally identify the provinces of Canada when shown an outline map of the country.

RESPONSES

Items 1, 3, and 4 should be marked with an X. The following are the conditions for these items:

Item 1: Given ten different leaf samples
Item 3: When presented with reproductions of their work
Item 4: When shown an outline map of the country

All of these phrases *tell the condition* under which behavior is to occur, what will be provided to the student, or where something is to be done. Item 2 does not present any condition at all.

Next Task

If you got 3 or fewer correct, restudy the text on "Element Two: Elaboration of the Conditions." If you got 4 correct, do the formative evaluation on criterion measures, which follows.

C. Read each of the following items. Place an *X* next to each statement that establishes a minimum level of acceptable learner performance.

_____ 1. The student will reduce 70 percent of a given list of fractions to their lowest terms.

_____ 2. Given a printed copy of a 100-line program, the student will enter the program so that it runs without error.

_____ 3. The student will assemble the DNA model within 15 minutes.

_____ 4. The student must create a program using Basic or Pascal.

RESPONSES

Items 1, 2, and 3 should have an *X*. The criterion measures are as follows:

Item 1: 70 percent; to their lowest terms
Item 2: Runs without error
Item 3: Within 15 minutes

Item 4: does not provide any information on minimal standards

Next Task

Now proceed to Section 2 of the formative evaluation, in which you are given six objectives to evaluate.

Section 2

Examine each of the following six objectives and mark an *X* as appropriate for all correct responses.

1. *To list the criteria for evaluating "user friendly" computer software.* This objective is worded in terms of the learner performing or producing something. Yes_____ No_____

2. *Use a straightedge and compass to construct a geometric form.* This statement is worded in terms of the learner performing or producing something. Yes_____ No_____

3. *To identify a parallelogram, given five different geometric shapes.* This objective describes the conditions under which the learner's behavior is to occur. Yes_____ No_____

4. *Using a copy of "The Student Users Library Handbook," the student will prepare a three-page report on the United States' relations with Central America that contains six references to articles in the periodical literature, none of which are more than three years old.* This statement contains the minimum acceptable criteria. Yes_____ No_____

5. *Given three articles, the textbook, and class lectures, the student will understand*

the relationship between the "prime rate," changes in the money supply, and consumer interest rates.

_____ (a) This statement contains all the elements of behavioral objective.

_____ (b) This statement does not contain a minimum acceptable criterion.

_____ (c) This statement does not contain a verb that identifies observable learner behavior.

6. *Given a theorem to prove by coordinate geometry, the student will apply the coordinates that make the least complex algebraic calculation.*

_____ (a) This statement does not contain the conditions under which learner behavior is to occur.

_____ (b) This statement does not contain minimum acceptable criterion.

_____ (c) This statement contains all the elements of a behavioral objective.

Check your answers in the key that follows. If you got all 6 items correct, you are certified as being able to identify and analyze performance objectives. Of course, we don't know if you can write one! If you got 5 or fewer correct, restudy the entire chapter.

ANSWER KEY: SECTION 2

Responses	Review Reference in Text
1. Yes	Element 1, Performance
2. Yes	Same
3. Yes	"given five different geometric shapes"
4. Yes	". . . six references . . . old."
5. C	"will understand" is not an observable behavior
6. C	

REFERENCES

Aten, Rosemary. "Formative and Summative Evaluation in the Instructional Process." *Journal of Physical Education and Recreation* 51:1980, 68–69.

Bloom, Benjamin S., et al. *Handbook on Formative and Summative Evaluation.* New York: McGraw-Hill, 1971.

Bloom, Benjamin S., et al. *Taxonomy of Educational Objectives: Handbook I, The Cognitive Domain.* New York: David McKay, 1956.

Bosco, James. "Behavioral Objectives: Caveat Emptor." *Peabody Journal of Education* 42:1980, 106–109.

Broekhoff, Marna. "Behavioral Objectives and the English Profession." *English Journal* 12:1980, 55–59.

Carroll, John B. "A Model for School Learning." *Teachers' College Record* 64:1963, 723–733.

Eggen, Paul D., Donald Kauchak, and Robert S. Harder. *Strategies for Teachers: Information Processing Models in the Classroom.* Englewood Cliffs, N.J.: Prentice-Hall, 1979.

Hunter, Madeline. "Teaching Is Decision Making." *Educational Leadership* 37:1979, 62–64, 67.

Kimpston, Richard D., and Harlan S. Hansen. "Accountability—Doing What We Say." *Educational Leadership* 39:1982, 274.

Krathwohl, David R., Benjamin S. Bloom, and Bertram B. Masia. *Taxonomy of Educational Objectives: Handbook II, The Affective Domain.* New York: David McKay, 1964.

Mager, Robert F. *Preparing Instructional Objectives.* Belmont, Calif.: Fearon, 1962.

Mager, Robert F. *Preparing Instructional Objectives.* 2nd ed. Belmont, Calif: Fearon, 1975.

Melton, Reginald F. "Resolutions of Conflicting Claims Concerning the Effect of Behavioral Objectives on Student Learning." *Review of Educational Research* 48:1978, 291–302.

Moore, Maxine Ruth. "A Proposed Taxonomy of the Perceptual Domain and Some Suggested Applications." Princeton, N.J.: Educational Testing Service, 1967.

Roberts, Wesley K. "Preparing Instructional Objectives: Usefulness Revisited." *Educational Technology* 22:1982, 15–19.

Scott, Roger O., and William Brock. "File Three: Tests, Texts, Curriculum Alignment: Improving Instruction in Essential Skills." From *What's Noteworthy on School Improvement and Technology with a Special Section on Rural Education.* St. Louis, Mo.: Mid-Continent Regional Educational Laboratory, 1983.

Shannon, John R. "Performance Objectives: Powerful, Yet Limited." *Journal of Business Education* 55:1980, 350–352.

Tyler, Ralph W. *Basic Principles of Curriculum and Instruction.* Chicago: University of Chicago Press, 1949.

Tymitz-Wolf, Barbara. "Guidelines for Assessing IEP Goals and Objectives." *Teaching Exceptional Children* 14:1978, 198–201.

3

DECISIONS ABOUT
SEQUENCING INSTRUCTION

In Chapter 1 we discuss teaching as a decision-making process. Some of your decisions as teacher are made before you teach the lesson (*planning*), some are made during the lesson (*instructing*), and some are made after the lesson has been taught (*evaluating*).

One of the basic components of planning is the writing of educational objectives, a skill amply illustrated in Chapter 2. In this chapter we will present two other components of planning: (1) the sequencing of instruction; and (2) the use of hierarchies to illustrate relationships among bodies of knowledge. After completing this chapter, you should be able to

1. Provide several reasons for using sequencing in the planning process
2. Explain how hierarchies will provide teacher assistance in the planning process
3. Provide some examples of hierarchical or task analysis
4. Provide an overview of "Instructional Theory into Practice" (ITIP), also called "Science of Teaching"
5. Develop hierarchies for your teaching area

SEQUENCING

By sequencing instructional tasks, one assumes that the student can better master any organized body of knowledge or discipline when the content is carefully interrelated. One also assumes the learning of skills or knowledge in a systematic manner helps the student to develop those skills that ultimately aid with information-processing, that is, thinking. Finally, one assumes that the closer that sequenced instruction approaches a "programmed format," the greater the probability for student success.

If we are willing to accept these key assumptions about schooling, then sequencing has two basic purposes. One is to isolate knowledge (a fact, concept, generalization, or principle) so that the student can understand the unique characteristics of the selected information or to isolate a thinking process so that the student can master the process under varying conditions. The second purpose is to relate the knowledge or process being taught to the larger organized body of knowledge. The first function—isolating what is being taught—helps *make learning more manageable,* and the second function—relating the information—*makes learning more meaningful.*

For example, if you want to teach the concept of *metaphor,* you teach the characteristics of metaphor using illustrations of metaphors. This process provides students with a manageable amount of information and with the focus for their study. You proceed to a second figure of speech—*simile*—and use the same process. After the students have mastered both concepts, you then can illustrate how both concepts are figures of speech—that is, they have common characteristics. This process illustrates the relationship of the lesson content to a larger body of knowledge.

This example also shows the relationship between sequencing and hierarchies of knowledge. *A hierarchy is content-related* in that it usually portrays the relationships among items of information, whereas *a sequence is process-related* in that it establishes a schedule for learning the various parts of the related content. In a subject area such as mathematics, in which there is an accepted hierarchy of knowledge, the sequence and hierarchy are very similar because the relationships of the content almost dictate a sequence of learning activities. In a subject such as English literature, in which it is difficult to establish a hierarchy of information, the sequencing of learning is usually established by either the interest or the experience of the teacher. If a learning hierarchy exists, it influences the instructional sequence. If a learning hierarchy does not exist, the sequences of instructional learning establish a loosely knit hierarchy for the student.

At this point, we must once again emphasize how important it is for the teacher to specify objectives to be learned. In Chapter 2, we recommend the three-part performance objectives made popular by Robert F. Mager (1962). From our observation in many classrooms, we sense that the great majority of teachers do not specify their objectives explicitly. Most teachers tend to specify objectives somewhat like a shopping list: they know that they are trying to build a body of knowledge or skills, but the objectives do not have any definite pattern. In short, the objectives are not sequenced. To be an effective teacher, the student learning objectives must be sequenced to illustrate the relationship between the various components of the curriculum. More important, prerequisite conditions or entry level competencies can be identified and taught at an early stage.

A LEARNING HIERARCHY MODEL

Suppose you were teaching your class a lesson and you assumed that the students would be able to answer successfully nearly all of the questions asked on an examination covering the materials of the lesson. From all indications, the students were enjoying the lesson and no big problems emerged. Then, to your dismay, the class performed poorly on the examination. Could the test have been poorly constructed? An incident similar to this one happened to one of America's foremost learning theorists, Robert M. Gagné (1962), several years ago. The lesson was in elementary school mathematics, but the content could have been high school chemistry, college calculus or, for that matter, social studies, English, physical education, or *any* other field of study. What is important is that Gagné was not satisfied with the results and wanted to determine why.

Gagné began to study the sequence in which the learning activities (teaching) were planned. He soon concluded that some instructional elements should have preceded others and that some concepts that he had not taught the students should have been introduced prior to attempting the particular learning objective. This initial study led Gagné to rearrange some of the learning sequences and to try the lesson again. As a result, there was a dramatic change in student success as measured by test results. The concomitant learning experiences were arranged in a chartlike format, so that the top of the chart contained the end of the instructional sequence, usually called the *terminal objective*. Those objectives below the terminal objective are called *intermediate* or *entry-level objectives*. The terminal objective is what the students finally should achieve after a series of planned instructional encounters. Note in Figure 3–1 that the terminal objective is to "solve solubility product problems," and it is labeled with a roman numeral. In Gagné's model, roman numerals are sequenced by levels, with roman numeral I being most difficult and the larger roman numerals being those leading to the terminal objective—that is, the prerequisite behaviors. Figure 3–1 outlines a hierarchy chart that James R. Okey and Robert M. Gagné (1970) devised for a chemistry class. Typically the lowest level objective is to acquire *prerequisite* or *entry-level skills*. Unless a student has already mastered these basic skills, he or she will probably *not* be able to reach the learning objective in any levels above them.

Task Analysis

To study the effects of a hierarchical structure on learning, Gagné employed a methodology that has long proved valuable in the sphere of business and industry. That method is known as "task analysis." Careful sequencing of tasks has been and continues to be a critical element of efficient production in the industrial and technological sectors and even in education. You can imagine how chaotic and costly your education would be if there were no grade levels or if there were no method of identifying the difficulty level of your university courses. If you think that your program of studies seems disorganized, think of the problems you would have if each piece of information you learned were taught in isolation and not as a part of a course and if the courses had no titles or identifying numbers. Your education would be longer and more expensive.

Industry has not been alone in recognizing the value of carefully analyzing tasks and of identifying the sequential relationships of component activities. In education, the importance of sequencing *subject matter content* for instructional purposes has been acknowledged for a considerable length of time. Ralph W. Tyler (1949) viewed sequencing as one of the three major criteria that must be met in organizing a curriculum; continuity and integration were the other two.

Through the impetus of Gagné's investigations of learning sequences, however, emphasis shifted from the sequencing of content per se to the

FIGURE 3–1   Learning Hierarchy for a Science Topic

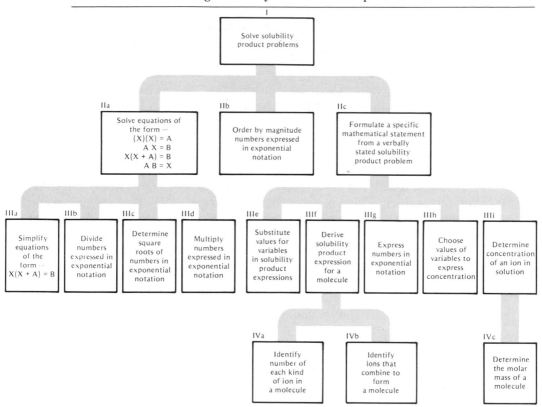

Source: From James R. Okey and Robert M. Gagné, "Revision of a Science Topic Using Evidence of Performance on Subordinate Skills," *Journal of Research in Science Teaching,* vol. 7, no. 4 (1970), p. 323. Reprinted by permission of the National Association for Research in Science Teaching and John Wiley & Sons, Inc.

analyzing and ordering of content *as it relates to the learning process.* The Gagné (1970) model asserts that before the learner can acquire a complex cognitive skill, such as problem-solving, he or she must first advance through a series of *enabling learning conditions.* Rather than relying on arm-chair theorizing to determine the nature and order of these enabling skills, Gagné empirically investigated and tested prerequisite performances that were needed prior to the learning of a particular higher-order skill. He used numerous refined psychological methodologies and techniques to construct these learning hierarchies. He amply demonstrated that skilled teachers should no longer rely exclusively on the organization of subject matter to determine sequence. How a teacher does a task analysis is fully developed on pages 63–65.

It seems noteworthy that "logical" is frequently the term used to describe the type of order imposed on content, and this logical sequence more often reflects the instructor's, rather than the students', thinking processes. In addition to being sensitive to patterns of organization in subject matters, educators are encouraged by learning theorists such as Gagné to focus on the sequential relationships of the subskills (thinking processes and behaviors) that must be acquired *prior* to learning higher-ordered behaviors and skills (Gagné, 1961, 1970). The content to be learned, in other words, is subdivided into descending levels of *cognitive products and processes*—from the most abstract to the most concrete.

If you use the hierarchy of content illustrated in Figure 3–2 to plan a lesson, you must take into consideration the relationship of levels 1 and 2 to levels 3 and 4. Principles and generalizations are formed from facts through observational and inferential processes. For example, each time two magnets are manipulated so that like poles repel and unlike poles attract, there is a single event; the action is observable; and the single event itself does not predict values. This single event is a fact. A series of such events (facts) provide data that can be used to develop a principle about magnets, one of many principles that we teach students in our public schools. The teacher has the option of either presenting the principle first and then substantiating it with the facts or organizing and presenting the facts and then allowing the students to develop the principle. These two options constitute another important teaching decision. Both options demand that the teacher plan for sequencing of lesson activities.

FIGURE 3–2   Hierarchy of Knowledge and Processes of Thinking

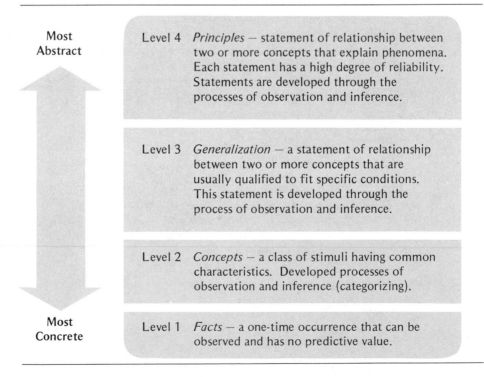

Most Abstract	Level 4 *Principles* — statement of relationship between two or more concepts that explain phenomena. Each statement has a high degree of reliability. Statements are developed through the processes of observation and inference.
	Level 3 *Generalization* — a statement of relationship between two or more concepts that are usually qualified to fit specific conditions. This statement is developed through the process of observation and inference.
	Level 2 *Concepts* — a class of stimuli having common characteristics. Developed processes of observation and inference (categorizing).
Most Concrete	Level 1 *Facts* — a one-time occurrence that can be observed and has no predictive value.

Concept Analysis

In teaching concepts, the teacher must use both sequencing and task analysis. In sequencing, there are two options: (1) the teacher may start the lesson by describing the concept, followed by an analysis of characteristics (facts) and a series of illustrations or examples (facts) so that the students have a thorough knowledge of concept; or (2) the teacher may provide examples (facts) of the concept and allow the student to discover the concept. In either instance, a procedure called *concept analysis* is helpful. For example, if you were teaching the concept "proper noun," it would be helpful to develop an outline of the content to illustrate the characteristics of the content (show its uniqueness) and its relationship (make it meaningful) to the larger body of content covered by the course. An example of this kind of outline is shown in Figure 3–3.

The concept analysis procedure provides the teacher with a sequence-planning technique. To teach the concept "proper noun," the teacher must first teach the characteristics of both "noun" and "proper" as they relate to the concept "proper noun." This is followed by an analysis of characteristics, in which the teacher provides examples that illustrate the characteristics of the proper noun—the *names* of *persons, places,* or *things.*

In the second phase of the procedure, the teacher determines whether the lesson should be taught inductively or deductively. Should the student be given the concept and then provided with examples of its characteristics or should the student be given examples from which to induce the concept? Whether the lesson is taught inductively or deductively, a thorough analysis of concept characteristics and examples is necessary. The concept analysis hierarchy is an excellent procedure to use to accomplish this task. The characteristics of inductive and deductive teaching are presented in Chapters 8 and 9.

To apply the four levels of knowledge in a learning hierarchy (see Figure

FIGURE 3–3   Concept Analysis

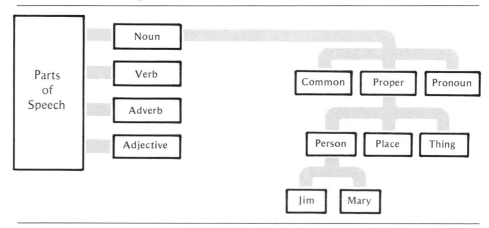

3–2), instruction at levels 3 (generalization) and 4 (principles) must be preceded by instruction at levels 1 and 2. Thus, levels 1 and 2 are prerequisites to levels 3 and 4. You may recall the many teachers you have had who bypassed one or more levels when developing a lesson, thus leaving many of your classmates—if not yourself—totally "in the dark."

Principles of Sequencing

You can arrange almost any set of learning concepts, generalizations, or principles into the Gagné system. Gagné suggested that all instruction *can* (and indeed *should*) follow the systematic identification of content and process illustrated in the preceding hierarchical analyses.

There are several principles that apply to all kinds of sequencing. The first principle is that you always *begin with a simple step*. This does not mean that you "talk down" to your students. Rather, it means that you structure the teaching elements so that easily identified characteristics can be understood by the learners. At this step, you should provide numerous examples. The use of analogies often helps.

The second principle is to *proceed to the concrete*. This means that you may have to use materials, simulations, models, or artifacts that illustrate the lesson, objective, or concept being taught.

The third principle suggests that, from the concrete, you may plan to *structure a lesson or learning sequence so that it becomes more complex*. Additional variables may be introduced, new sets of criteria may be generated, and relationships may be established between the content of the lesson and other content. It is at this level as well as the next level that you should try to get students to apply the information presented by using the two principles previously described.

Finally, you may introduce abstractions. You may require the students to generalize, predict, or explain the information generated, using principles 1, 2, and 3.

Do not be fooled into thinking that on Monday your lesson should be "simple," on Tuesday it should be "concrete," on Wednesday you should address "complex" issues, on Thursday you should deal with "abstract" issues, and on Friday you should test. The four principles may take years to apply when developing sequenced concepts—for example, grammar and creative writing, mathematical analysis, fine arts, or social studies. What we wish to stress is that understanding the interrelationships of these four principles helps students learn. If you realize this, then you will be cognitively aware of the sequential nature of thinking skills and will incorporate appropriate learning experiences to complement the levels. Figure 3–4 is a concrete model of this instructional technique.

Let us examine a concrete example. In the first grade, teachers introduce the concept of graphing, a skill that even college freshmen often do not attain. The overall goal is to provide a series of experiences through which the concept of graphing will emerge. Although the concept of graphing is

FIGURE 3–4   A Hierarchy for Student Success

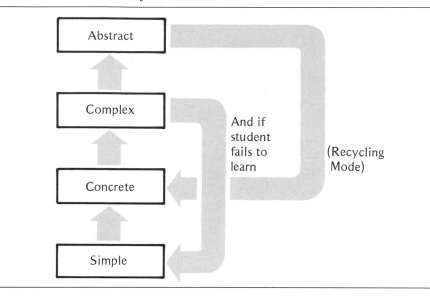

introduced in the first grade, the sequence that includes all types and levels of difficulty of graphs may take as long as ten years. The time duration could be reduced but probably not appreciably.

Systematic graphing experiences require all teachers in the school to communicate with each other over a long period of time concerning what has transpired in their classrooms. In some schools, this process would be articulated by means of a curriculum guide.

The lesson begins in a first grade science class. The children plant bean seeds and begin a study of plant growth. The teacher raises the question of measuring the growth on certain days, say, on every Friday afternoon. All plants are watered as uniformly as possible. As the seeds germinate, the teacher gives each child a strip of paper. The paper is placed by the seedling and the strip is torn to equal the length or height of the plant on the prescribed day. This technique is called a scale of 1:1 or, mathematically speaking, one-to-one correspondence.

The teacher then has each child glue the strip to a large piece of paper, with a label made for the strip and bearing that date. This process continues until the teacher and children grow tired of it. Of course, the teacher asks the children to observe other changes, which they discuss. Finally everyone has a concrete histogram—a simple graph. There will be some variation but, by and large, the results will be somewhat uniform. Then comes a discussion about making histograms, and the concept of a one-to-one scale is introduced. The graphs are saved for the next year. Ultimately, similar histograms are constructed using the concept of scale. The class members can develop a histogram using their own heights, weights, or some other quantifiable, but varying, personal characteristic.

The next year the teacher continues to use the histograms and makes them more complex. Finally, the teacher can show that if a dot is placed at the top of the line and if scales are made in opposite directions (labeling the axes), all the information will be available in a form that is easier to use. This will take us through the second, maybe the third, grade. (We caution that some learning tasks take a long time to develop.)

Ultimately the teacher provides other data, such as daily maximum temperatures, then maxima and minima simultaneously. Thus the graphing concepts become more complex and begin to approach the abstract. Yet these activities reflect an experience that the class shares in common. The culmination of the set of experiences would be to have the children obtain data of their choosing and make their own graphs. The initial instructional episode may take three or four years.

Obviously not all concepts take that amount of time. In a high school, it often takes three to four days to complete a segment (module) of work. Often the modules are sequenced to progress to more complex aspects of instruction. Each module should illustrate the use of the principles described previously.

Our main point is that you, as teacher, control the learning environment. If you desire to make learning more systematic, then here is one technique that has been tested. You have to *decide* how you will apply hierarchies in your teaching so that students learn better—that is the fun of live instruction!

Using Teaching Hierarchies

The value of using a *learning hierarchy approach* to sequencing learning activities is that the prospective teacher as well as the experienced teacher can quickly learn the technique. You can arrange any number of learning components or tasks into a "map" to be accomplished. In this manner your students will have a better chance at success. Often students get "hung up" on learning concepts or principles because the teacher made too large an intellectual leap. By developing hierarchies, the teacher is able to identify learning deficiencies before lessons are assigned.

You will notice that even though the learning hierarchy described in this section is similar to the concept analysis process, its function is different in that it is designed to show relationships between large bodies of information. These relationships may involve any of the four kinds of information illustrated in Figure 3–2.

As a teacher of science, one of the authors once observed that teachers often have difficulty teaching the concept of density. Then, by observing student errors, he inferred that if the tasks associated with the learning concept were identified and structured, some of the problems would be reduced. Table 3–1 lists the various tasks or elements that were prerequisites to mastering the concept of density. On examining the table carefully, are you surprised at the number of operations, skills, and prerequisite skills that are needed? Several teachers were, and so were we.

TABLE 3–1 Task Analysis for the Concept of Density

Concept: Density

Tasks associated with concept

1. Weighing in metric system units
2. Using linear measurement in metric system
3. Understanding two-dimensional measurements: compute areas for rectangle and circle
4. Computing volumes
   (a) Rectangular
   (b) Cylindrical
   (c) Irregularly shaped objects
       (1) Those that float in water
       (2) Those that sink in water
5. Defining and using a "Unit Standard"
   (a) Linear
   (b) Volumetric
6. Using mathematics skills
   (a) Division
   (b) Multiplication
   (c) Ability to solve sample linear equations (a = b/c)
7. Knowing that the mass of water in grams approximates the volume of water in cubic centimeters (cc)
8. Deriving that density is mass per unit of volume

After all the major tasks were listed, as in Table 3–1, they were then sequenced, using Gagné's approach. Figure 3–5 illustrates a simplified task analysis and hierarchy chart for the concept of density.

What becomes apparent is that it is useless to even try to teach this concept before the seventh grade. The children simply do not have the necessary intellectual background until that time—and may not until one year later. Nonetheless, we still find teachers and professors who wonder why their students cannot learn certain concepts or principles. Therefore in many cases you the teacher must revise even the order of the text pages to be read by the students. In short, you may have to sketch "rough" hierarchy charts for every chapter, unit, or module that you assign, so that the benefits to the learner will be maximized. Preparing a rough chart may take just a few minutes as you analyze a unit of work.

When you observe student learning deficits, you can construct your own hierarchy chart to determine if key elements of the instruction are missing. No doubt other charting modifications can be devised, using these techniques. Try your hand at creating such a chart, say, for a concept in English grammar, biology, mathematics, or social studies. We believe that if more teachers were cognitively aware of this technique, then teaching would be improved immeasurably and both teachers and students would be happier in school—and more successful!

FIGURE 3–5   Simplified Task Analysis and Hierarchy Chart for Concept of Density

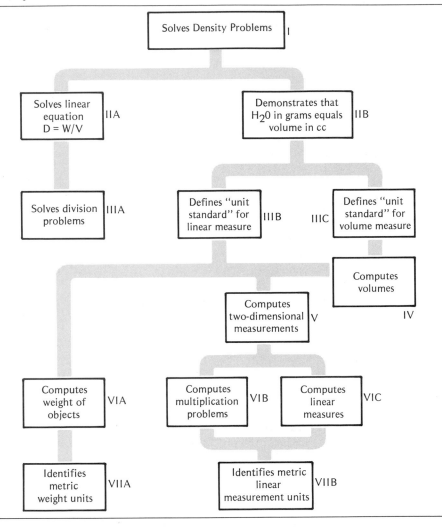

A Rationale for the Hierarchy Model

You may, at this point, think it a bit strange that a teaching methods text is so concerned with task analysis and learning hierarchies. Our rationale is based on the assumption that the processes used in constructing a hierarchy chart are essential for the achievement of clearly specified performance objectives. The Gagné model predicts that if you carefully structure a method by which the identified objectives are taught, then you will be more successful as a teacher. In practice, the hierarchical arranging or sequencing of objectives becomes a handy assessment tool. For example, if children continually fail to learn some generalization or concept, then we must assume that they do not have the prerequisite or enabling experiences by which to be successful. Let us elaborate on this point with a case study.

One of the authors was observing a teacher in the fifth grade trying to teach *an introductory lesson* on graphing. The teacher plunged into the lesson by drawing x and y axes, establishing and naming the scales, plugging in data, and then asking if the children understood. From the vantage point of an observer, it was evident that no one did. The students' facial expressions were uneasy and puzzled—raised eyebrows, frowns, and the like. But the observable evidence of a "disaster area" came with the very first practice problem. Absolutely *no one* in the class got the axes correctly labeled and *no one* had the scales correct. Then the period ended.

The teacher was approached by the author, and a discussion took place about prerequisite learnings, previous graphing experiences, and the like. Since it was recess, there was time to restructure the lesson, identify some critical elements, and arrange them into a hastily devised hierarchy chart.

Then the next class for mathematics came in. The teacher and the class now interacted much more closely. Each element was presented by the teacher according to the hierarchy chart, after which the students did an exercise. Finally the concept of histogram led to the bar graph and the line graph. The class period ended on a positive note.

The hierarchy per se is not enough to help increase student success. The teacher must be *aware* that the students are having learning problems. The awareness may come from nonverbal class cues or from test results that do not meet the teacher's expectations.

To be sure, the construction of learning hierarchies may involve some trial-and-error approaches or may include an intuitive sequencing of objectives. But if you are research-oriented, you may even collect data and empirically test your own hierarchies as did Gagné and his associates when Science—A Process Approach (SAPA) was being developed and field tested.

How Does a Teacher Do a Task Analysis?

The major purpose of task analysis is to discover the relationships of subskills and to use this information to plan for effective instruction. Although it is unrealistic to assume that you as a classroom teacher will have the time or methodological expertise to identify and validate enabling skills empirically with the precision afforded by Gagné's investigations, you can effectively and efficiently use task analysis in your own teaching. The following procedures (tasks) need to be accomplished to analyze learning tasks successfully.

1. *Select an instructional objective that is at the appropriate level of difficulty.* To make this initial determination of what is to be learned, the teacher obviously must know the structure of the content area (such as physics, health, education, mathematics, or social studies). It is essential

that the teacher know what the learner has *already* achieved in the content area.

This first step, which entails the specification of the learning objective, may seem very obvious. (After all, it would be difficult, if not impossible, to analyze an unspecified, ill-defined objective, or to spend laborious hours analyzing the subskills of tasks that are inappropriate for the particular learner.) The importance of this stage of planning is often overlooked. For example, teachers sometimes make such statements as, "When students are in the ninth grade, they should read Chaucer," or "Seventh graders should study world geography." Such curriculum decisions are based on the incremental nature of content but they neglect to identify where *learners* are located in the curriculum plan. For example, it makes little sense to teach students problems of percentage if they do not first understand decimals—regardless of *grade* level considerations.

Therefore, in selecting appropriate learning objectives, you will need to identify the general area where student knowledge ends. This is the point at which to formulate new learning objectives and to analyze the subskills that lead to the attainment of these new objectives. We will refer later to the importance of using *diagnostic vigilance* when you help learners to achieve an objective through a classroom lesson. The technique of diagnostic vigilance allows the teacher to check on whether or not the original objective is, in fact, at the right level of difficulty.

2. *Identify the independent and dependent sequences of enabling skills that lead to the attainment of the desired objective.* For any given set of subskills, there are two basic types of sequences: independent and dependent. (Sometimes the component behaviors may be *both*.) In an independent sequence, the ordering of a particular set of enabling skills is not incremental. For example, in learning to tie a pair of shoes, it does not matter whether one starts with the right or the left foot. These activities are independent of each other. Similarly, in constructing a house, it does not make any appreciable difference if one starts by laying the foundation for the garage or for the main part of the house.

In the dependent sequence, on the other hand, the accomplishment of one subtask (that is, subskill or behavior) is essential before attainment of the next subtask in the series. In putting on shoes and socks, therefore, the ordering of the tasks does make a difference. The socks need to be on before proceeding to the next behavior: putting on the shoes. In the same way, the construction company would be remiss in attempting to shingle the roof prior to raising the walls of the structure.

3. *Arrange the independent and dependent sequences as they relate to each other and perform the task yourself to identify possible steps that were omitted. Use this sequence to construct a lesson that will systematically facilitate the learning of the terminal objective.* Once you have analyzed the objective and discovered its component parts (independent and dependent sequences), these parts (or enabling skills) will provide an entry point of learning for all students. The enabling skills themselves become objectives as you use them to help students reach the terminal objective.

It is doubtful that you will be able to identify all of the prerequisite enabling skills consistently prior to the implementation of the lesson. As you teach, your judgment will allow you to adjust, to add other subskills to the list, and to emphasize certain subskills with particular students. Keep notes about such skills in the daily lesson-plan book that is used by most teachers. These notes will be a handy reference for your next class, as you monitor and adjust your teaching activities.

Applying Task Analysis

As stated at the beginning of the chapter, the two basic reasons for conducting a task analysis are (1) to subdivide the component parts of the learning activity to make learning manageable for students, and (2) to provide coherent relationships among the various components of the learning activity, thereby making learning more meaningful. The process of *task analysis* uses a standard set of questions or an outline to divide the lesson or course objectives into curricular or institutional components. An example of the task-analysis process is one of the components of Instructional Theory into Practice (ITIP) developed by Madeline Hunter (1975). The ITIP program has four main elements.

1. Teaching to an objective
2. Teaching at an appropriate level of difficulty for the learners
3. Monitoring and adjusting instruction
4. Increasing motivation, learning, retention, and transfer

In this approach, the task-analysis process is an important component of the instructional planning process. Although Hunter does not specify precise task-analysis steps, she has given a framework from which educators have developed task-analysis models. One such sequence was developed by our colleagues Sabra Martin and Karen Swoope at Washington State University. The six steps involved in this process are

1. To start with a course goal or set of instructional objectives
2. To define the learning and its crucial attributes
3. To list every step needed to master the learning; use the diagnostic question stem of "Can the learner . . . ?"
4. To examine each step and keep only the *essential* steps
5. To identify dependent and independent sequences
6. To sequence steps in order of difficulty
   a. Simple to complex
   b. Concrete to abstract, i.e., project or activity to words
   c. Pictures to words
   d. Saying to writing
   e. Paragraph to whole story

The subcomponents of step 6 provide a conceptual framework for the sequencing of the learning steps similar to a program described earlier on page 59. Using a conceptual framework reinforces the two basic components of sequencing: isolating information so it can be managed by students and relating material so it becomes meaningful to students. A conceptual framework also allows students to become successful when the learning activity begins with simple or concrete tasks that are easily understood; then the instructional sequence can be developed with additional tasks—of greater complexity or abstraction.

Furthermore, as microcomputers become a part of the instructional technologies of the schools, it behooves all teachers to know how each computer-aided task is sequenced so that meaningful learning will take place in a most systematic manner.

A Sequence of General Tasks

As you plan for the sequencing of specific tasks for the students, you must first plan the sequence in which you will conduct the class. For example, there are some set tasks that *you* must accomplish every time you attempt to reach your objective of preparing and implementing a lesson. You must (1) identify the instructional objectives; (2) plan the appropriate educational activities or experiences; (3) obtain the materials; (4) read the materials yourself; (5) plan the strategies that will be employed in the teaching act; (6) evaluate the students; and (7) critique the lesson—that is, decide how you would improve it.

The sequence of events and the decisions that you make in planning the lesson will be the easy part of teaching. The "moment of truth" arrives when the lesson is taught. Suddenly you will observe that there are students who do poorly despite your best efforts to plan systematically. It is at this point in the teaching process that teacher differences occur. Some teachers simply continue with the lesson plan and complete the unit of study. This technique, of course, is the worst—from the learner's perspective. Others will use another technique, that of a *diagnostic-prescriptive model*.

A Diagnostic-Prescriptive Model

The diagnosis of teaching-learning effectiveness is very complex. However, if some students do not experience success the first time they are exposed to a topic, it behooves the teacher to prepare some type of educational diagnosis similar to that of a medical doctor. The diagnosis is then followed by a prescription. This process may be viewed as a cycle with a minimum of at least four elements: (1) observation; (2) diagnosis; (3) prescription; and (4) evaluation. Figure 3–6 shows this cyclic process.

As you examine Figure 3–6, you will note that we urge that the evaluation phase of teaching be used for decision-making. This may seem to be a novel method of using tests, as most teachers use their tests only for grading. We want you to use tests as one method of making learning more efficient. That is, use your tests to help the students to master the materials in the lesson. This also means that evaluation is used in considering future

FIGURE 3–6   Simplified Diagnostic Model

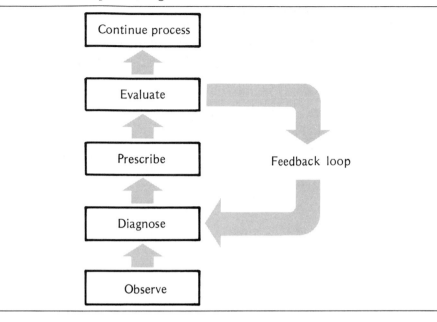

educational material, in substituting lessons, or in identifying other class members who can help as tutors. Let us expand the concept of a diagnostic-prescriptive decision-making tool.

Observation.   The observation phase begins either before an assignment is made or while some specific tasks are being completed by the learners. What does the teacher observe? There are at least three types of clues: activity, verbal, and nonverbal student clues. Most learning takes place through the building or transmitting of concepts or skills. This generalization will hold true for most disciplines and at most grade levels of instruction. As a teacher, you will observe the three types of clues in every class. Do students tend to master selected concepts? Do students prefer to do certain tasks? Do students look amazed when selected tasks are assigned? Do students tend to discuss or evaluate verbally the type of work assigned? The communication network is already established in the classroom. Your job is to monitor it continually.

On a more individual basis, you may observe that only one or two students have trouble with selected, or perhaps most, assignments. The general tendency is to ignore these learners and to allow them to "drift." We suggest that you structure your class period so that if you do identify students who need specific aid, you can establish the mechanism by which they may obtain it. In some cases, you the teacher will do the aiding; in other cases, peers, tutors, programmed instruction, or other assignments will be put into action. But action cannot take place without first observing. In our experience we have known teachers who were simply not aware that students were expressing clues indicating that they needed help in completing the lesson.

Other activity clues relate to incomplete assignments, inaccurate work, plagiarized work, or work that shows that the student has not completed the assignment in the manner in which the teacher expected. In some cases, the observations will be made during oral recitations or discussions. You may sense that a student does not respond to the work or to an oral question in exactly the appropriate manner, that the logic used in responding is a bit faulty, or that a student seems to be making the same type of error repeatedly. Also, when grading papers, you may note that the same kind of mistake prevails throughout a set of examples, or, at worst, throughout the entire assignment. It is at this point that you should begin to implement the elements of the diagnostic-prescriptive model.

Diagnosis. The diagnostic phase of the model begins when you, as teacher, realize that a student or a group of students seems to need additional work in specific skills, processes, or content. At this point, you have made an initial diagnosis, which focuses on small or discrete units of learning (for example, the subskills of the task analysis). Each unit of study is related to the student's learning need. In other words, the teacher who uses this system will never be heard to say to a student, "You've got to try harder." Nobody likes to or tries to fail. Yet teachers mistakenly assign more drill or other such tasks to the student who has been unsuccessful. Such decisions only lead to futility. If a student does not meet the expected standard of performance on the first lesson or set of problems, then it is logical to conclude that more of the same will yield the same result—student failure.

It is the purpose of the diagnostic phase of instruction to determine which prerequisite lessons a student needs in order for success to follow. Also, as the teacher plans the prescription that follows the diagnosis, it is very important that he or she make decisions that allow the student to do the work, rather than have the teacher or tutor do it. Such a strategy helps the student to work more independently and to gain greater self-confidence and self-esteem. The teacher maintains the student's self-confidence by adjusting the difficulty level or by substituting different learning materials.

Diagnosis is an analytic task for the teacher. It is an inductive process in which, after observing specific errors in the student's work or other clues indicating that the student needs help, you begin to frame a general plan that attempts to remedy the problem. You may even think of yourself as the world's greatest detective, with your goal being the eradication of unachieved objectives!

The diagnostic phase of the model is concerned with pinpointing exact problems—for example, the student cannot conjugate a set of verbs; the student does not know the primary colors; or the student cannot compute ratios. Each of these diagnoses identifies a specific learning deficit or behavior.

It is during the diagnostic phase that we suggest that you personally communicate your desire to help the student master the lesson at a higher level. You can test your diagnoses with a few carefully chosen problems or tasks. If the learner exhibits the same learning deficit, then you probably made an incorrect diagnosis and should try again. Now play the part of the kindly medical doctor who writes the necessary prescription after the disorder is identified.

Prescription.   In this model, your prescription is an explicit set of instructional objectives for the student who has *not* achieved at a standard that *you* feel is adequate. The prescription usually contains the following elements:

1. Identification of the prerequisite skills, if any, that the student needs to be able to accomplish the desired objectives.
2. Selection of necessary materials, equipment, and activities that will be made available to the student.
3. Selection of the instructional strategies that are appropriate to the learning episode.

The prescription may be written or stated orally. As you begin this teaching technique, it may be better to write the prescription. This way the learner may check off those objectives that are completed, and you can quickly conduct an evaluation to determine whether the student learned the assignment. Most of the time, you would construct a hierarchy chart that would sequence the prescribed tasks for the learner. The chart need not be elaborate—the simpler the better. The main point is that you should analyze the instruction in a very logical and efficient manner.

Evaluation.   The final phase of the model, evaluation, may be conducted separately, or it may be combined as an active part of the prescription. After the students complete the prescribed activities, they are evaluated immediately. If the errors that were made previously have been corrected, then you have improved their learning. If the prescription was not successful, then—as was illustrated in Figure 3–6—you begin the entire cycle again.

The evaluation may be conducted by several means. You may simply inspect the newly completed work and observe whether or not the work meets your criteria. Or you may conduct an oral evaluation by asking a few key questions of the student. How you conduct the evaluation is unimportant. Striving to improve instruction and learning is important! The evaluation is needed to provide feedback to you, the teacher, for instructional decision-making. Our chief concern is that you know that there is a way of systematically making decisions that will aid those who are not successful on the initial instructional assignment.

Conducting Tutorial Sessions.   The process of task analysis may frighten you into thinking that you must write all kinds of prescriptive learning activities every day for many students. That is the exception, not the rule.

Generally you will find that, after you have made the observations and diagnosis, the prescription element may be very informal and may only be needed for a small number of pupils. As one alternative, you may sit and chat with a student or perhaps a small group of students and may decide to use an oral approach to help each student correct his or her work. In such cases you may employ a set of questions that are diagnostic—at least from the student's point of view. These may be "How did you arrive at this response?" "Are there any words that you do not understand?" "Tell me in your own words what . . . means." "Why . . . ?" "How . . . ?" "What . . . ?"

You must conduct all sessions in a supportive mode. The teacher *must not* be angry, disrespectful, or intolerant toward the students. We mention this because many teachers do exhibit such behaviors, just when they think that they are being helpful to students; in fact, they are perceived by the students as being critical or spiteful, if not vengeful.

CONCLUSION

Every discipline has different types of learning problems. Mathematics is very different from social studies or English. Thus, the general rules presented here must be adapted for specific situations. Perhaps the one generalization that we can validly make is that, more often than not, the teacher assumes that the students have the prerequisite knowledge when, in fact, they do not.

The following quote from one of America's foremost psychologists, Sidney L. Pressey (1959), summarizes our position on the topic.*

> One of the most pernicious problems in teaching is the teacher's desire to "cover ground." Many teachers feel that they do not have time to discover and remedy their pupil's lack of information and skill because they would never be able to "cover" the material called for in the course; so they plunge ahead from a starting point that many of their students have never reached, and they proceed to teach the unknown by the incomprehensible. The result is that the student cannot learn effectively and ends the course about where he started.

A Postscript

In most cases, you will be teaching from a textbook or some type of printed material. Only through a detailed analysis of the content will you be able to determine the sequencing of learning activities, concepts, facts, or skills. The textbook sets the pace for most teachers and learners; however, you

---

*From Sidney Pressey, F. P. Robinson, and J. E. Horrocks, *Psychology in Education* (New York: Harper & Row, 1959), p. 201. Quoted with written permission of the publisher.

may have to supplement the text with short presentations or demonstrations that provide the students with the necessary prerequisite skills or background. Once you have mastered the idea of sequencing major blocks of information, you will be able to implement Gagné's technique in a short period of time.

As was mentioned in Chapter 1, with the advent of PL 94-142 some mainstreaming of special-education children will take place. Every classroom teacher, from kindergarten to grade 12, must be able to provide the most meaningful and effective educational environment for these students. You will be responsible, as a member of the school's instructional team, for helping to prepare an Individual Educational Plan (IEP). The techniques described in this chapter will be the ones that you will probably use most frequently.

In addition, and of greater importance, these same techniques are easily used in teaching children from lower socioeconomic classes who need positive experiences. The diagnostic-prescriptive model discussed here will be of critical importance in this context. It has been verified that many, if not most, of these children have not had the appropriate prerequisite learning experiences to be successful. By spending a little more time with these students and by using the complete set of techniques described in Chapter 2, within a few months you will be able to effect substantial improvement in students who have shown gross educational deficits.

Indeed, Gagné has given us a technique with which even the most difficult and challenging instructional concepts may be made more teachable—and, most important—more learnable.

FORMATIVE EVALUATION
Sequencing and Hierarchies

1. Can you recall the two basic purposes of sequencing?

   (a) _____

   _____

   (b) _____

   _____

2. Describe three ways in which hierarchies provide assistance in the planning process.

   (a) _____

(b) _____

(c) _____

3. Arrange the following task analysis characteristics in an appropriate sequence and explain the reason for each item in the sequence.
   (a) Arrange the independent and dependent sequences.
   (b) Identify the independent and dependent sequences of enabling skills.
   (c) Select an instructional objective.
4. Explain how a hierarchy is helpful in each of the following components of the diagnostic model.
   (a) Observation.
   (b) Diagnosis.
   (c) Prescription.
   (d) Evaluation.
5. Develop a hierarchy on the branches of the federal government that has four levels.

RESPONSES
Sequencing and Hierarchies

1. (a). Isolates the properties and unique characteristics of the desired learning.
   (b). Relates the desired learning to the larger organized unit of learning so that the acquisition of skill or knowledge becomes meaningful.
2. (a). Provides a map for sequencing learning activities.
   (b). Provides a conceptual framework for diagnosing student progress.
   (c). The relational aspect of a hierarchy provides information that can be helpful in selecting the appropriate thinking mode (deductive or inductive) and in choosing the most efficient teaching materials and techniques.
3. (c). *Select an instructional objective.* You must be able to specify first what the student should be able to do at the end of the learning sequence.
   (b). *Identify the independent and dependent sequences.* You must identify the activities necessary to achieve the desired learning and must determine whether the nature of these activities necessitates a specific sequence.
   (a). *Arrange the independent and dependent sequences.* You must arrange the activities so that, if dependent, the sequence is followed and, if independent, the activities are done at the appropriate time.
4. (a). *Observation.* This allows the teacher to look for problems with specifics—that is, the unique characteristics or properties of each component in the hierarchy—or to pinpoint difficulty in relationships between components in the chart.
   (b). *Diagnosis.* This careful observation allows for a detailed probing of the problem situation. A student may not understand a concept characteristic and, therefore, not the concept. Hierarchy provides a map of the possible difficulties.
   (c). *Prescription.* Once a problem is pinpointed, the teacher can select material or procedures to resolve the difficulty. Pinpointing the difficulty helps identify the many solutions available.
   (d). *Evaluation.* This makes the development of measurement items easier. It takes the guesswork out of evaluation.
5. Compare your chart to the one that follows. It should be similar but may differ in the details of the subcategories.

FIGURE 3–7   A Hierarchy on Branches of the Federal Government

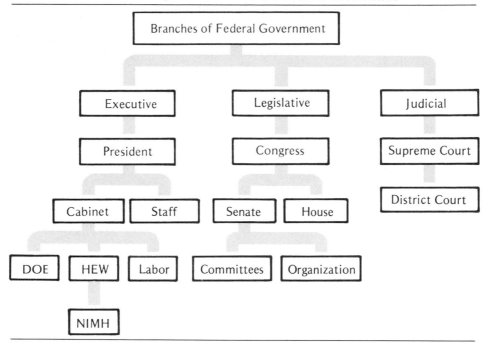

REFERENCES

American Association for the Advancement of Science. *Science: A Process Approach.* New York: Xerox Education Division, 1970.

Gagné, Robert M., and Leslie J. Briggs. *Principles of Instructional Design.* New York: Holt, Rinehart & Winston, 1974.

Gagné, Robert M., and N. E. Paradise. "Abilities and Learning Sets in Knowledge Acquisition." *Psychological Monographs* 76:No. 14, Whole No. 518, 1961, p. 23.

Gagné, Robert M., et al. "Factors on Acquiring Knowledge of a Mathematical Task." *Psychological Monographs* 76:No. 7, Whole No. 526, 1962, p. 20.

Hicks, Clarence E. "Sound Before Sight: Strategies for Teaching Music Reading." *Music Educators Journal* 66:1980, 53–55.

Hunter, Madeline. "Washington State Superintendent of Public Instruction," sponsored workshop (Yakima), 1975.

Livermore, Arthur H. "The Process Approach of the AAAS Commission on Science Education." *Journal of Research in Science Teaching* 2:1964, 271–282.

Okey, James R., and Robert M. Gagné. "Revision of a Science Topic Using Evidence of Performances on Subordinate Skills." *Journal of Research in Science Teaching* 7:1970, 321–325.

Pressey, Sidney L., Francis P. Robinson, and John E. Horrocks. *Psychology in Education.* New York: Harper & Row, 1959, p. 201.

Rink, Judith E. "The Teacher Wants Us to Learn." *JOPER* 52:1982, 17–18.

Tyler, Ralph W. *Basic Principles of Curriculum and Instruction.* Chicago: University of Chicago Press, 1949, p. 85.

4

DECIDING ON LEVELS OF INSTRUCTION: INTRODUCING THE TAXONOMIES

In the previous chapter we discussed the concept of learning hierarchies and
tried to show how these could be used to sequence instruction and to facilitate learning. The present chapter builds on these ideas by describing three
hierarchical classification systems that can be used to sequence instruction
in the areas of cognitive, affective, and psychomotor learning.

Educational objectives can be divided into three main areas on the basis of
their primary focus. Cognitive objectives deal primarily with the development of intellectual skills and abilities. The majority of educational activities is involved with the attainment of cognitive objectives. For the most
part, society as a whole, as well as parents, students, and teachers, views the
cognitive growth and development of students as being the primary function
of the schools. Because of this emphasis, the principal focus of this chapter
will be on developing your understanding of the *cognitive domain*.

The second major area of emphasis in our schools today is in the development of students' attitudes and values. We call this part of the school curriculum the *affective domain*, and later in the chapter we discuss a system
that educators use to describe and sequence instruction in this area.

The third major focus of learning in the schools today is the *psychomotor
domain*, which involves the development of muscular skills and abilities.
We also include the *perceptual domain* as a special application of the
psychomotor domain. The area of the curriculum that places the greatest
emphasis on the psychomotor domain is physical education, but we hope to
show, toward the latter part of this chapter, how all areas of the curriculum
are either directly or indirectly concerned with psychomotor skills.

Central to our discussion of each of these three areas is the concept of a
taxonomy. A *taxonomy* is a hierarchical classification system that can be
used to describe and sequence learning activities. Before describing each of
the three major areas of learning (the cognitive, affective, and psychomotor
domains), we will discuss the idea of taxonomies and their value to prospective teachers.

On completion of this chapter, you will be able to

1. Describe what a taxonomy is and how it can be used in teaching
2. Describe in your own words the differences between the three domains
3. Classify objectives in the three domains as cognitive, affective, or
   psychomotor
4. List the six major levels of the cognitive taxonomy
5. Classify objectives at appropriate levels of the cognitive taxonomy
6. Apply the levels of cognitive taxonomy when constructing classroom
   questions or test items

7. Identify the major elements of the affective taxonomy
8. Identify the major elements of the three psychomotor taxonomies
9. Construct a rationale for the use of the three taxonomies in your major area of interest
10. Construct an outline for a unit plan using the Kaplan Grid Model

TAXONOMIES: AN INTRODUCTION

The concept that underlies all taxonomies as decision-making tools is simply this: not all teacher behaviors are the same. Some are different from others and, accordingly, elicit different responses from the student. That is, if the teacher acts differently, the student will respond in different ways. From this we may infer that the student thus is learning different behaviors. Taxonomies are classification tools that teachers use to describe these different learning outcomes.

Teachers perform various actions in the course of a school day. These actions may include the formulation of performance objectives, of questions to be asked, or of tests to be administered. Within these clusters of teacher behaviors (performance objectives, questions, or tests), teacher actions can vary widely. For instance, teachers can generate very different tests on basically the same topic or content. These different objectives, questions, or tests reflect differences in the teachers' goals. It is clear there is a great difference in emphasis between the questions, "When did Columbus discover America?" and "For what reasons did Columbus set out for America?" One way of examining and comparing the differences in teacher emphasis is to analyze these teacher behaviors in terms of a taxonomy. A *taxonomy* is a classification system that educators use to observe, compare, and evaluate performance objectives, questions, written materials, and evaluation methodologies (tests).

A taxonomy is basically a classification system, a way of grouping selected objects together, such as plants, animals, performance objectives, or questions. But a taxonomy is more than just a classification system. What differentiates a taxonomy from a classification system is that a taxonomy is *hierarchical;* that is, a taxonomy is a classification system with a hierarchy of *classes* or grouping by level or rank. Not all the classes are at the same level. The method by which the classes are arranged in a hierarchy depends on the organizing principle and the type of taxonomy.

In the taxonomy of the animal kingdom, the phyla are arranged according to evolutionary complexity. Thus the phylum Chordata (animals with backbones) is higher than Porifera (sponges), which is higher than Protozoa (one-celled animals). In most educational taxonomies, the organizing principle is that of complexity. The higher levels in taxonomies involve more complex student behaviors than the lower levels. In addition, the higher levels in taxonomies build on the lower levels. If a student can perform at a third level, then we also assume that the student can perform at the two lower levels. This idea is discussed further later in the text.

How Can Taxonomies Be Used?

Teaching can be envisioned as a triad of acts, as illustrated in Figure 4–1. In this model, the formulated objectives should determine the teaching procedures and the evaluation procedures, but with all elements affecting each other. A taxonomy can be used in each of these processes: in formulating objectives at an appropriate level; in developing classroom questions and learning exercises; and in constructing evaluation instruments that are congruent with the objectives and strategies previously employed. In other words, taxonomies can be used to decide what to teach, how to teach, and how to evaluate the effectiveness of our teaching.

Why Use a Taxonomy?

For any educational tool to be useful, it must be regarded as appropriate and effective. Teachers using taxonomies have found them to be useful because they serve the following purposes. (You may want to add your suggestions to this list.)

FIGURE 4–1   A Model of Teaching

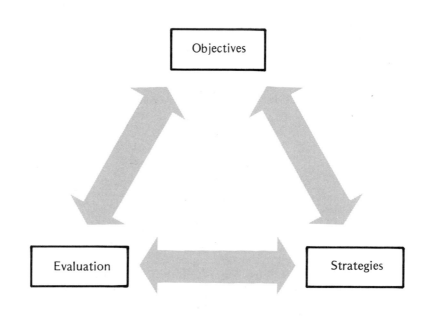

1. Provide a Range of Objectives

A taxonomy provides a list of possible ranges of objectives available in any subject. A close examination of the categories may prevent the teacher from overemphasizing one level, such as the knowledge level, in his or her teaching. In this respect, a taxonomy not only adds variety to the teacher's repertoire but also gives greater breadth to his or her objectives.

2. Sequence Objectives

An analysis of learning tasks will indicate to the teacher the learning experiences necessary for the student to obtain the intended outcomes. A taxonomy provides one means of sequencing learning, from simple to complex outcomes. Other means are discussed in Chapter 3.

3. Reinforce Learning

Because each lower category of the taxonomy is subsumed by the next higher category, reinforcement of previous learning occurs if learning experiences are sequenced in terms of a taxonomy.

4. Provide a Cognitive Structure

Research has shown that students learn and retain information better if it is organized into some type of cognitive structure rather than presented as isolated items. Taxonomies can provide cognitive structure to students by showing them how facts can be used in the application, analysis, synthesis, and evaluation of other ideas.

5. Provide a Learning Model

By experiencing a series of learning activities sequenced in terms of a taxonomy, students are able to perceive that learning can be sequenced according to the relationships of the categories to each other, thus obtaining a model of learning that they too can use when they leave the classroom.

These first purposes of taxonomies can be illustrated by Figure 4–2, which shows the relationship of the sequencing of instruction to the complexity of the levels.

In this figure note that the broader categories are the first to occur in terms of time. In sequencing objectives, teachers typically begin a unit by laying a foundation of lower-level knowledge. Since the taxonomy is hierarchical, each higher objective builds on a sequence of lower ones. In addition, as students progress through each level of the taxonomy they experience a learning sequence that builds on successive levels. Further, it takes greater instructional intensity to achieve higher-level learning goals and objectives.

FIGURE 4–2   Time, Complexity, and Taxonomies

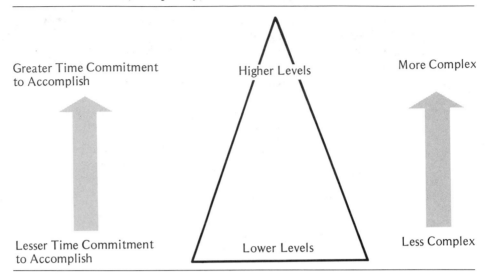

6. Ensure Instructional Congruency

Once an objective (or question) is written and classified at a particular level, it helps the teacher in selecting more appropriate teaching strategies and evaluation techniques that coincide with the level of the objective. If an objective is written at the application level, learning experiences for students must be provided at the application level. In addition, the student should be tested or evaluated at that level. If the goal of a particular Physical Education course is to teach a person how to swim certain strokes, then the teaching activities should be geared toward this goal and the evaluation should match. In this situation, a paper-and-pencil test would be incongruent with the learned behavior. The teacher can prevent such mismatches by analyzing his or her objectives, learning activities, and evaluation procedures, making sure they are compatible.

7. Design Appropriate Test Items

Teachers who understand the principle of fairness will be quick to use the taxonomy as a self-evaluation device to check the appropriateness of test items. There is evidence to show that most teachers at most levels of instruction teach at rather low levels. Yet tests are often constructed to measure higher levels of thinking. This is not fair to the students. The teacher can match learning objectives and teaching activities with the test items to determine whether or not the test approximates the level described in the objective and at which the lesson was taught. This is an application of the concept of congruency.

FIGURE 4–3 Kaplan Grid

Content	Level of Objective	Teaching Activity	Learning Experience	Student Product

8. Provide a Model for Lesson and Unit Planning

Translating ideas into effective lessons and units can be a difficult teaching task. The Kaplan (1979) grid, Figure 4–3, helps teachers coordinate the content they are teaching with the appropriate level of the taxonomy, the learning experience, and the product of the student's effort. This grid is illustrated and discussed in more detail at the end of the chapter.

9. Diagnose Learning Problems

Should a student not achieve the intended outcome at the level specified by the teacher, the teacher can examine systematically at which level the student is encountering the learning difficulty and thereby prescribe cognitive experiences to help the student overcome the specific learning deficit. (Recall the prescriptive-diagnostic model in Chapter 3.) This use of taxonomies may become increasingly important in view of the growing acceptance and retention in our schools of students with diverse cultural backgrounds, as well as the mainstreaming of special education students into the regular classroom.

10. Individualize Instruction

Related to the idea of sequencing instruction is the use of taxonomies as tools for individualizing instruction. Several recent developments in education make this an especially persuasive argument for using taxonomies. One such development is the growing realization on the part of educators that there is a great deal of heterogeneity in most classrooms. Students not only enter classrooms with different experiential and knowledge backgrounds, but they also learn at different rates and in different optimal situations. This problem of heterogeneity is further complicated by the mainstreaming of some special education students into the regular classroom. By identifying and sequencing a number of learning objectives and activities in terms of a taxonomy, the teacher allows the students with differing capabilities to start at different points in a taxonomy and to proceed through the sequenced activities at different rates.

11. Assist in Instructional Decision-making

By using a systematic method of analysis, teachers can decide where the learning will lead and how much time to devote to establishing meaningful prerequisite skills. The taxonomy thus acts as an instructional guide for the teacher.

We are now ready to begin an analysis of the taxonomy of the cognitive domain.

BLOOM'S TAXONOMY: A CLASSIFICATION SYSTEM FOR THE COGNITIVE DOMAIN

As mentioned previously, educators have divided the types of learning that take place in the schools into three areas: affective, psychomotor, and cognitive domains. The affective domain deals with attitudes, interests, and values. The psychomotor domain deals with manipulative or motor-skill activities (for example, printing, typing, or jumping rope). The cognitive domain, the area with which we are primarily interested, concerns knowledge and the development of intellectual abilities and skills. Most of the time, teachers at both the elementary and secondary levels are concerned with the cognitive domain. The most widely used classification system for analyzing objectives in the cognitive domain is Bloom's Taxonomy. Benjamin S. Bloom, in 1956, co-edited a book entitled *Taxonomy of Educational Objectives: Cognitive Domain.* Thus we commonly refer to this classification system as Bloom's Taxonomy. Bloom's Taxonomy classifies cognitive behaviors into six categories ranging from fairly simple to more complex behaviors. These categories are briefly described in Table 4–1.

Like other taxonomies, Bloom's Taxonomy is hierarchical, with learnings at higher levels being dependent on the attainment of prerequisite knowledge and skills at lower levels. These features of the taxonomy will be discussed and illustrated in the text that follows. We begin our discussion of the taxonomy with a description of the first level—knowledge.

Knowledge

Knowledge is the category that emphasizes remembering—either by recall or recognition. An example of a recall operation is a fill-in-the-blank exercise, and an example of a recognition operation is a multiple-choice exercise requiring the recognition of information previously encountered. Both of these processes involve the retrieving of information or facts that are stored in the mind. For the most part, the information retrieved is basically in the same form as it was stored. For example, if an elementary social studies

TABLE 4–1   Six Major Levels of Bloom's Taxonomy

Level	Characteristic Student Behaviors
Knowledge	Remembering; memorizing; recognizing, recalling
Comprehension	Interpreting; translating from one medium to another; describing in one's own words
Application	Problem-solving; applying information to produce some result
Analysis	Subdividing something to show how it is put together; finding the underlying structure of a communication; identifying motives
Synthesis	Creating a unique, original product that may be in verbal form or may be a physical object
Evaluation	Making value decisions about issues; resolving controversies or differences of opinion

Source: From *Taxonomy of Educational Objectives: The Classification of Educational Goals. Handbook I: The Cognitive Domain*, edited by Benjamin S. Bloom et al. Copyright © 1956 by Longman, Inc. Reprinted with permission of Longman.

teacher teaches the students on one day that Washington, D.C., is the capital of the United States, then an appropriate Knowledge-level question to ask on the next day would be "What is the capital of the United States?" In answering this question, the student would be attempting to remember the knowledge in basically the same form as it was learned. Other situations involving Knowledge-level activities include memorizing a poem, remembering the steps to follow in making a dress, learning the lyrics to a song, and answering true-false and matching questions on a test.

Knowledge-level objectives have as their primary focus the storage and retrieval of information. In answering a Knowledge-level question, the student must find the appropriate signals in the problem that will most effectively recall the relevant knowledge stored. In the Knowledge category, the student is not expected to transform or manipulate knowledge but merely to remember it in the same form as it was presented.

Knowledge-level activities may consist of

1. Recalling specific *facts or bits of information* (for example, Who was the first President of the United States?)
2. Recalling *terminology* or *definitions* (for example, What is a noun?)
3. Recalling *conventions* or *rules of usage* (for example, What goes at the end of an interrogatory sentence?)

Teachers generally recognize that the Knowledge category forms the basis for the other categories. In fact, teachers overuse this category. Studies have indicated that the majority of teachers (and textbooks) formulate most of their questions (both in class and on tests) at the Knowledge level.

Consequently the thought processes of the students (and the teachers) are kept at very low levels. Perhaps this is why so many young people find school to be boring and unchallenging.

This is not to say that the Knowledge category serves no purpose. Because of the hierarchical design of the taxonomy, Knowledge serves as the foundation for the other categories. It provides the subject matter on which the higher categories are based. Consequently, Knowledge-level questions can be very useful at the beginning of a lesson or unit by providing necessary background information.

Although the Knowledge level forms the factual foundation for the rest of the categories, there are certain problems with its overuse in the classroom. Some of these problems are as follows:

1. The recall of information is basically a passive operation and does not actively involve the learner. Because of this, students are often poorly motivated when the major part of the curriculum consists of the memorization of facts.
2. Because each Knowledge question usually has one right answer, such questions do not lend themselves to classroom sessions in which the students work together in solving or discussing a problem. Consequently, the students' interpersonal and problem-solving skills are not adequately developed.
3. Related to this second problem is the lack of development of communication skills in students. Because, typically, Knowledge-level questions each have one right answer, classroom dialogue tends to occur between teacher and student rather than between student and student.

Recent work with computers has proven their value in teaching Knowledge-level content (Chambers and Sprecher, 1980). Research with computer-assisted instruction has shown that drill and practice exercises on computers can effectively supplement regular classroom instruction, thus freeing the teacher to instruct students at higher cognitive levels. Unfortunately, computers appear less able at the present time to instruct at these higher levels. Here we see an excellent opportunity for educators to use technology to free the teacher's time and energy for the more important tasks of teaching. In addition, Barak Rosenshine (1983) provides evidence from effective-schooling studies that drill and practice on the lower-level skills do help students learn higher-order skills more effectively.

A general rule of thumb to use in judging whether certain Knowledge-level objectives should be included in the curriculum is to ask the question: "Will this knowledge be useful to the student at a later time in one of the higher categories?" If the answer is no, the teacher should reevaluate the reason for focusing on isolated bits of information and possibly redesign the lesson.

Comprehension

The *Comprehension* category emphasizes the transforming of information into more understandable forms. Like all categories above the Knowledge level, the Comprehension category is used to emphasize ways of handling information that has already been stored. Comprehension activities require students to demonstrate an understanding of the material through some type of manipulation or alteration of the material before answering a question. The distinction between manipulation and recall is important. Knowledge-level questions require recognition or recall by the student ("Where have I heard or seen that before?"). Comprehension-level questions require the student to assemble various ideas and modify them in some way before giving an answer. The comprehension or understanding may be evidenced by oral, written, pictorial, or concrete presentations.

The basic idea behind the Comprehension category is to get students to understand the material and not just to memorize it. This active attempt to understand material thus makes this category one step higher than Knowledge. (An example of the difference between the two would be the difference between second graders reciting the Pledge of Allegiance and understanding what the words mean.) However, unlike some of the higher categories, the Comprehension level does not ask students to extend information but merely to integrate it into their own frame of reference.

A Comprehension-level question requires a greater degree of active participation by the student. In responding to a Comprehension-level question, the student must somehow process or manipulate the response so as to make it more than simple recall. This distinction is important from a learning-theory point of view. That is, material that students rephrase into their own words, or that they organize to "make sense" personally, will probably be learned more quickly and retained longer.

Types of Comprehension Questions

To give an idea of the range of questions that fall into the Comprehension category, this category is divided into four groups: interpretation, translation, examples, and definition. Examples from each of these categories will be provided so that you can become familiar with the variety of questions available to you. Emphasis here should be given to acquainting yourself with possible question formats rather than to memorizing subcategories of subcategories.

1. *Interpretation.* This concept involves the student's ability to identify and comprehend the major ideas in a communication and to understand the relationship between these ideas. For example, asking a student to relate one point in an essay to another requires the process of interpretation. Interpretation involves giving meaning to a response by showing its relationship to other facts. This relationship may be shown by comparing or

contrasting or by demonstrating similarity. "How" and "why" questions often call for some type of interpretation. In answering these questions, the student relates major points and, by so doing, shows an understanding of them. Some interpretation questions may include the following:

(a) *How* do professional and collegiate basketball rules differ?
(b) *What* are some *similarities* between French and German sentence structure?
(c) *Compare* sociology and psychology with respect to their early histories.
(d) *What differences* exist between the high school curricula of today and those of the 1920s?

Note that the italicized key words may be used in a variety of disciplines.

2. *Translation.*   Translation involves the changing of ideas in one form of communication into a parallel form, with the meaning retained. Reading a graph or describing the main point of a pictorial cartoon are both examples of translation. Another type of translation exercise is summarization. When using summarization, the student takes a larger passage and translates it into a shorter, more personal, form. Some translation exercises may include

(a) Describe in your own words the first paragraph of the Declaration of Independence.
(b) Record the results of your laboratory findings in tabular form and summarize your findings.
(c) Reconstruct the main story plot of *Moby-Dick.*

These types of exercises primarily require the student to translate or change the material into a different form.

3. *Examples.*   One of the best ways a person can show his or her comprehension of an idea is to give an example of it. Some exercises requiring examples may include

(a) Give an example of a quadratic equation.
(b) Bring to class tomorrow a poem that uses iambic pentameter.
(c) Name two countries that are constitutional monarchies.

In asking students to provide examples of an abstraction, the teacher should require that these examples be new or previously undiscussed. Otherwise the student would be operating at the Knowledge level, remembering examples from previous classes.

4. *Definition.*   A definition requires the student to construct in his or her own words a description or idea of a term or concept. This involves more than just repeating verbatim a textbook or dictionary definition. Emphasis should be given to having the student formulate the definition with words that are familiar and meaningful to him or her. Some definition exercises may include

(a) Define, in your own words, the Knowledge category.
(b) Give a definition of your particular discipline (for example, home eco-

nomics, mathematics, or physics) that a 15-year-old student can understand.

(c) Explain in your own words the meaning of the term *pornographic*.

Note that, in these examples, the emphasis is on allowing the student to do more than just open the dictionary and copy meaningless words or synonyms.

Application

The *Application* category, as the name implies, involves applying or using information to arrive at a solution to a problem. In operating at the Application level, the student typically is given a problem that is new to him or her and must apply the appropriate principle (method of solving the problem) without having to be prompted regarding how to resolve the problem. Also, the student must know how to *use* the proper method once it has been chosen. When the teacher evaluates an Application problem, he or she should check both the solution and the process. Both of these are important subcomponents in the Application-level problem, because how a student solves a problem may be more important than the answer obtained. To be sure that a question reaches the Application level, a teacher must make the problem *unique* or *novel*. If the problem has been *gone over* the day *before* in class, the *task* for the *student* would involve mere *recall*, thus making it a Knowledge-level activity.

Operations at the Application level can be visualized as a two-step process, as shown in Figure 4–4. In the first step of the process, the student encounters a problem that he or she has not seen before and recognizes it as a subset or type of problem solved before. Note that we have used the words *subset* and *type* rather than *same* with the problem encountered before. The novelty or originality of the problem is an essential characteristic of an Application-level problem.

During the second step of solving an Application-level problem, the student selects an appropriate solution and applies it to the data at hand. This

FIGURE 4–4 Application Problems as Two-Step Processes

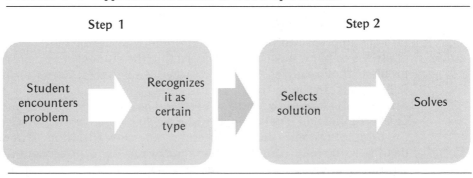

solution can consist of an algorithm, a formula, an equation, a recipe, or a standardized set of procedures for handling a specific type of problem.

Viewing Application problems as a two-step process allows teachers to analyze their students' responses and to diagnose problems on the basis of the error patterns. If students are having difficulty in recognizing certain equations, then they need to be given a wide variety of these types of problems to recognize and prescribe the correct solutions. However, if students are able to perform this function but are unable to plug the values in the problem into the correct formula or equation, then they need to be given practice in the computational aspects of the problem. Here we can see another use of the taxonomy in individualizing instruction for diverse student needs.

A problem at the Comprehension level requires the student to know an abstraction well enough that he or she can correctly demonstrate its use when specifically asked to do so. Application, however, requires a step beyond this. If the student is given a problem new to him or her, the student will apply the appropriate abstraction without having to be prompted as to which abstraction is correct or without having to be shown how to use it in that situation. Thus, a demonstration of comprehension shows that the student *can* use the abstraction when its use is specified, whereas a demonstration of application shows that the student *will* use it correctly given an appropriate situation in which no mode of solution is specified.

Examples of Application

Perhaps a few examples will help differentiate the Application category from other categories. Typically an Application problem has one solution. But there may be other correct ways to solve the problem. This usually involves the use of some formula or principle that has been learned previously.

Observe an example involving mathematics. The formula $a^2 + b^2 = c^2$ describes the relationship between the sides of a right triangle. At the Knowledge level, the student may be asked for the formula concerning the relationship of the sides of a right triangle. The student may reply, "The square of the hypotenuse . . ." At the Comprehension level, the student may be asked to put the formula into his or her own words or, given a triangle with some sides delineated, may be asked to plug the appropriate numbers into the appropriate places. To determine whether or not the student can apply his or her knowledge of the formula, the student may be given a word problem that requires the computation of distances across an imaginary field or lake. In computing these distances, the student would need to recognize that the formula $a^2 + b^2 = c^2$ should be used. To evaluate performance at the Application level optimally, the teacher should wait a few weeks after the original presentation of the content and then introduce a new problem dealing with right triangles. This would ensure that the student can demonstrate the knowledge in a unique and novel situation and not just use the formula on the math test because it is the only topic that has been studied for the previous three weeks.

An example involving home and family living may differentiate between understanding the processes of frying and sautéing and knowing when and why to use each process. The student may know the definition of both sauté and fry (Knowledge level) but, when given foods that have been cooked differently, may not be able to identify which foods have been sautéed and which fried (Comprehension level). An Application-level operation may involve a situation in which the student is given a selected food to cook and told what the food should taste like when cooked. The student should not only choose the correct method, but also correctly apply it to produce the desired product.

An example involving physical education further illustrates the relationship between the three levels. At the Knowledge level, a basketball coach can give a definition of a certain defensive alignment or formation. At the Comprehension level, the coach can explain how the defense strategy works or can identify an example of it in use. At the Application level, the coach can recognize, in a game situation, where the strategy would be appropriate and can successfully implement it.

In all of these examples, note that the student must know *when* and *how* to use a particular method of solving a problem. Now take the formative evaluation on the three previously described levels.

FORMATIVE EVALUATION
Knowledge, Comprehension, Application

Instructions: Place a K next to each Knowledge question or objective.
Place a C next to each Comprehension question or objective.
Place an AP next to each Application question or objective.

1. _____ Approximately what proportion of the population of the United States works in a service industry?
(a) 10 percent (b) 20 percent (c) 35 percent (d) 50 percent (e) 60 percent

2.

HARVARD (51)	B	F	P
Sanders	2	1–2	5
Lewis	9	2–4	20
Mustoe	1	3–10	5
Brown	3	0–6	6
Dover	7	1–2	15
	22	7–24	51

MICHIGAN (84)	B	F	P
Wilmore	10	7–11	27
Johnson	6	3–5	15
Brady	7	2–3	16
Fife	7	0–1	14
Grahiec	5	2–4	12
	35	14–24	84

_____ According to the statistics, which team was more accurate at the free-throw line?

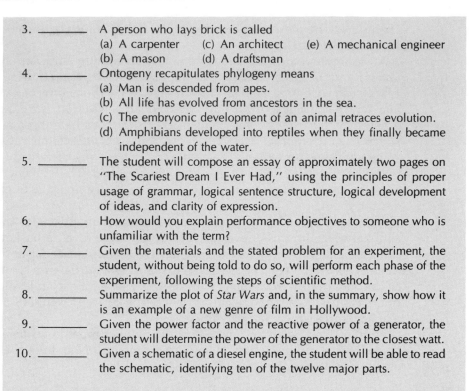

3. _____ A person who lays brick is called
   (a) A carpenter   (c) An architect   (e) A mechanical engineer
   (b) A mason   (d) A draftsman

4. _____ Ontogeny recapitulates phylogeny means
   (a) Man is descended from apes.
   (b) All life has evolved from ancestors in the sea.
   (c) The embryonic development of an animal retraces evolution.
   (d) Amphibians developed into reptiles when they finally became independent of the water.

5. _____ The student will compose an essay of approximately two pages on "The Scariest Dream I Ever Had," using the principles of proper usage of grammar, logical sentence structure, logical development of ideas, and clarity of expression.

6. _____ How would you explain performance objectives to someone who is unfamiliar with the term?

7. _____ Given the materials and the stated problem for an experiment, the student, without being told to do so, will perform each phase of the experiment, following the steps of scientific method.

8. _____ Summarize the plot of *Star Wars* and, in the summary, show how it is an example of a new genre of film in Hollywood.

9. _____ Given the power factor and the reactive power of a generator, the student will determine the power of the generator to the closest watt.

10. _____ Given a schematic of a diesel engine, the student will be able to read the schematic, identifying ten of the twelve major parts.

RESPONSES
Application

1. K. This question requires the student to recall a statistic.
2. C. The behavior required here is a type of table-reading. The student must understand what the different columns mean to answer the question.
3. K. This question requires knowledge of terms.
4. C. This question would be translation, but could be a Knowledge question if the student had seen this particular phrase before.
5. AP. Note how the criteria for evaluation were made quite specific. This component of higher-level objectives is often ignored.
6. C. The key phrase here is "How would *you* . . . ?"
7. AP. Again note how criteria can be applied to Application-level objectives.
8. C. The student is being asked for a summary.
9. AP. In this situation, the student must recognize the problem type, select an appropriate solution, and determine the answer—a sequence that is typical of Application-level objectives.
10. C. This objective requires students to read a schematic and translate it into words.

Analysis

Application involved the bringing together of separate components to arrive at a solution. *Analysis* involves the converse of this process in that complex items—such as speeches, written communications, organizations, or machines—are taken apart and the underlying organization behind them is explained. The emphasis in Analysis-level operations is on explicating how the various parts of a complex process or object are arranged and work together to achieve a certain effect. Another common kind of Analysis question offers an example of reasoning and asks the student to judge whether it is logical. Yet another type of Analysis question asks the student to discover the personal motives behind a communication.

Analysis can be related to Comprehension and Evaluation categories in Table 4–1. Comprehension involves finding similarities and differences and making comparisons. Basically the task at that level is to show relationships that can be discovered by understanding the communication itself. Analysis, however, goes beyond just understanding a communication and involves being able to look beneath the surface and discovering how different parts interact. In this sense, Analysis builds on Comprehension, but goes beyond it. Analysis involves working backwards, taking a situation or event and explaining how all the parts fit together to give a total effect; Comprehension, on the other hand, primarily involves describing what that effect is.

Types of Analysis Questions

As in the Comprehension category, we can subdivide the Analysis category into groups. This is done not to confuse the issue, but to offer you the opportunity to see the Analysis category in various forms.

1. *Identification of Issues.* In this type of Analysis operation, students take a broad communication and subdivide it into its constituent parts. This may be like discovering the "skeleton" of a communication, as the issues involved are sometimes not explicitly stated in the communication. In this sense, the student is asked to go beyond the information in the message and to show the relationship between assumptions and key points, stated or otherwise. Examples of this type of Analysis objective may include

(a) After reading the campaign speeches of presidential candidates, the student should point out the major differences between the candidates.
(b) Given the Bill of Rights, the student will be able to explain its main points in terms of the injustices suffered under British rule.

2. *Implications.* This type of Analysis question requires that students point out relationships between two propositions. The relationships may be expressed by inference, association, or necessary consequences and may not be stated directly. Examples may include

(a) What does the slogan "America: Love It or Leave It" imply about the people to whom it is addressed?
(b) What would be the educational implications of a voucher system that would allow all parents to purchase an education for their children at a school of their choice?

Note that in both the identification of issues and implications subcategories, the main task is to acquire some meaning beyond the denotation level. This is what distinguishes Analysis from Comprehension; the connotation of the message is of great significance.

3. *Motives.* Questions or objectives that ask students to identify reasons for behavior are examples of the motive subcategory. The student must again be able to use connotative meanings and discover two bases of behavior—one overt, the other covert. A caution is in order here. These tasks can lead to speculation on the part of students. The teacher should require that evidence be provided to support the probable motive given. Examples of such questions are

(a) What were some of the motives behind Nixon's historic visit to China?
(b) Why do many organizations keep lobbyists in Washington, D.C.?

4. *Persuasive Techniques.* In this subcategory of the Analysis level, students learn to discover how advertisements or other types of communication are designed to sway opinion. This kind of exercise asks students to find out the "inner workings" of a communication. Examples of such questions are:

(a) Why is the Marlboro man an effective product representative?
(b) How do mouthwash commercials prey on people's sense of insecurity?

The Analysis category has many uses besides those just illustrated. Examples of Analysis objectives from the various disciplines may include

1. *Physical education.* After viewing a game film, the student should then point out the major turning points in the game and explain why or how they contributed to the final outcome of the game.
2. The student should view a videotape of a golf swing and point out those actions that result in a hook or a slice.
3. *Home economics.* Given some dish (or meal) that did not turn out right, the student should pinpoint the error and correct it.
4. *Literature.* Given a poem or other piece of literature, the student should try to explain how the different elements interweave to achieve an effect.
5. *Art.* Given a painting, the student should show how form, color, and texture all blend together to give a certain impression.

All of these examples involve the analysis of a complex phenomenon so that its constituent parts are discovered.

Now complete the next formative evaluation.

FORMATIVE EVALUATION
Analysis

Instructions: Place a K next to each knowledge question or objective.
Place a C next to each comprehension question or objective.
Place an AP next to each application question or objective.
Place an AN next to each analysis question or objective.

1. _____ What logical fallacies do you see in the student demands for more power on college campuses?
2. _____ What are the different parts of the human eye?
3. _____ Why have labor unions and the Democratic party been closely connected in the history of our country?
4. _____ What does the word *taxonomy* mean?
5. _____ What would you say are the authors' motives in writing such books as *Death at an Early Age, 36 Children,* or *Way It's Spozed to Be*?
6. _____ Formulate a definition for the term *urban crisis*.
7. _____ What implications does the advance in medicine, namely, organ transplantation, have for the legal profession?
8. _____ Given a set of data, the student will compute the arithmetic mean to the nearest whole number.
9. _____ Given a description of an experiment that has been conducted, the student will describe how the six steps of scientific method worked together to make a valid experiment.
10. _____ Given $5, the student will plan a dinner for four that will have at least one of each of the basic food types (protein, carbohydrates, etc.) and that will not have more than 1,000 calories per meal.
11. _____ The student will define in his or her own words the function of each of the four components of a computer.
12. _____ The student will write a ten-page paper comparing the idea of "woman" as viewed by two Victorian authors to that by one contemporary author.
13. _____ Given a new problem, the student will design an experiment to solve the problem, using all six steps of scientific method.
14. _____ Given a glazed pot, the student will describe in two pages how the following were achieved: the glaze, form, and texture.
15. _____ With aids, the student will design an electrical distribution system for a city of 100,000 people.

RESPONSES
Analysis

1. AN. "Logical fallacies" should have been the clue here.
2. K. The student is asked to recall information.
3. AN. The student is asked to search below the surface and discover implications and motives.
4. K. It is a hierarchical classification system.
5. AN. The student is being asked to supply motives.
6. C. The student is being asked to formulate his or her own definition.
7. AN. The student is being asked for implications.
8. AP. This classification assumes that the formula for finding the mean is not given to the student.
9. AN. In this problem, students are asked to describe the interrelationship of the component parts of an experiment.
10. AP. The student is asked to use principles of nutrition to solve an everyday homemaking problem.
11. C. "In his or her own words" is the key characteristic here.
12. AN. The student is being asked to show how different novel components (plot, characterization) interact to depict women.
13. AP. The student is applying a solution to a specific problem.

14. AN. Given the final product, the student must work backwards to determine how different procedures affected the finished pot.
15. AP. In this Application exercise, the student is using electrical laws and principles to solve a practical problem.

Synthesis

Synthesis entails the creative meshing of elements so as to *form* a new and unique entity. Because of this emphasis on creativity, the Synthesis category may be the most distinctive and one of the easiest to recognize. Synthesis is the process of combining parts in such a way as to constitute a pattern or structure that did not exist before. A research paper can belong to either the Application or Synthesis category, depending on the level of originality. If the paper is comprehensive and thorough but does not add anything to the topic that is not already known, we consider the writer to be operating at the Application level. However, if the writer puts ideas together in new or unique patterns or creates new idea configurations, then we consider this to be a Synthesis-level activity.

This category probably stimulates the most creative behavior. In fact, by definition, the Synthesis category requires the creation of something unique, a product of the individual and his or her unique experiences. Consequently, the whole of the creation is more than just the sum of its parts; the parts are held together in a unique combination—the whole. This is not to say that every Synthesis operation must be a work of art. A second grader writing a poem can be working at the Synthesis level. What is important in this case is that the second grader is translating a unique experience into poetic expression.

Because the emphasis is on creativity, operations at the Synthesis level are usually difficult to grade objectively. Thus the teacher must use more subjective judgment in evaluating Synthesis operations than in evaluating operations at other levels. The teacher must also be cautious about stifling creativity. Maximum leeway should be allowed for creative expression if creativity is to be encouraged.

Benjamin S. Bloom (1956) differentiates the various subcategories of Synthesis according to product. In one subcategory, the product or performance is a unique type of communication. A poem, essay, or speech is an example of this subcategory. Here the author is trying to communicate certain ideas and experiences to others and does this through the medium of language. Typically, he or she is trying to perform one of the following functions: to inform, to describe, to persuade, to impress, or to entertain. In doing this, the author is attempting to achieve a given effect on an audience. The particular medium of expression used, together with its forms and conventions, is selected to convey certain ideas and experiences optimally. The product or outcome of the Synthesis operation can be considered unique in at least two respects. First, the author has considerable flexibility in communicating the idea and uses this flexibility to create a product unlike any others. Secondly, the product is evaluated partially according to its

TABLE 4–2 Synthesis Operations Involving the Development of a Plan

Proposed Set of Operations	Process (i.e., carrying out the set of operations)	Expected Outcome
Plan for an experiment	Carrying out the experiment	Experimental findings; probability statement
A teaching unit	Teaching	Changes in behavior
Specifications for a new house	Building the house	The house

Source: From *Taxonomy of Educational Objectives: The Classification of Educational Goals: Handbook I: Cognitive Domain,* edited by Benjamin S. Bloom et al. Copyright © 1956 by Longman Inc. Reprinted with permission of Longman.

uniqueness; thus, students are encouraged to add their own personal contributions to the product.

The second subcategory of the Synthesis level involves the developing of a plan or proposed set of operations to be performed. Bloom illustrates this subcategory in Table 4–2. Note that all of these operations result in the creation of a tangible product. This tangible product and the quality of creativity are the two distinguishing characteristics of the Synthesis level. Often, because of resource limitations in our schools, the final product cannot be constructed. Consequently, we often judge the quality of the Synthesis operation on the basis of the plans themselves. This subcategory differs from the previous one in that the product is more tangible and, therefore, sometimes easier to evaluate. Teachers generally feel more comfortable evaluating a project or project plan than an "original" art form.

The third subcategory involves the creation of a set of abstract relations as a product of Synthesis. This set of relations typically is derived from working with observed phenomena or data and forming patterns that did not exist before. These may include the formulation of hypotheses, which are guesses about potentially fruitful directions for research. Also included in this subcategory is the formulation of principles. The Peter Principle is such an example. The Peter Principle states that in an organization people advance or are promoted until they unknowingly (at least before the principle was formulated) reach their level of incompetence. Another example is the Premack Principle (also discussed in Chapter 10), which states that, in psychology, more frequently occurring behaviors can serve as reinforcers for less frequently occurring behaviors. In addition, the taxonomy that we are presently discussing can surely be considered a creative set of abstract relations.

Some examples of Synthesis operations in various disciplines follow.

1. *Home economics.* Creating a new dish or designing a new clothing pattern.
2. *Social studies.* Developing a new constitution for school or designing a survey to measure people's attitudes on a topic.

3. *Language arts*. Writing a play or a short story.
4. *Music*. Putting words to a melody or composing a tune in a certain rhythmic time.
5. *Science*. Designing an experiment or building a new machine (such as an egg hatchery, using everyday materials).

Now proceed to the formative evaluation on the Synthesis category.

FORMATIVE EVALUATION: APPLYING THE SKILLS
Comprehension, Application, Analysis, Synthesis

Based on the information in Figure 4–5, try to construct higher-level questions or objectives of your own: one Comprehension, one Application, one Analysis, and one Synthesis. You may wish to consult the text to refresh your memory and to reexamine the examples given.

Comprehension

_____

_____

Application

_____

_____

Analysis

_____

_____

Synthesis

_____

_____

Some possible questions and objectives follow. Try to write some of your own before consulting them.

RESPONSES
Comprehension, Application, Analysis, Synthesis

Comprehension
1. Which of these powers has increased its expenditures the most in the past ten years?
2. Which of these powers shows the most fluctuations in its military spending?

FIGURE 4–5 Worldwide Military Expenditures in Current Dollars: 1974–1979

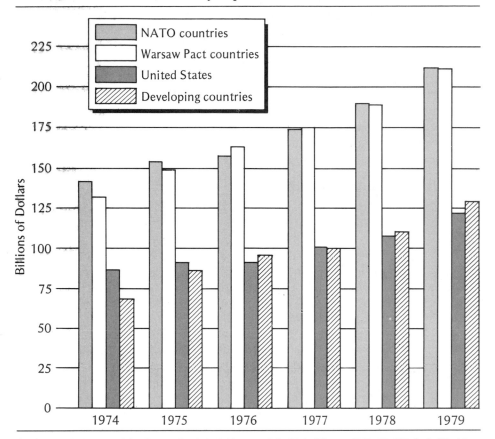

Source: U.S. Bureau of the Census, *Statistical Abstract of the United States: 1982–83,* 103rd ed. (Washington, D.C.: U.S. Government Printing Office, 1982), p. 355, Figure 583.

Application
1. What effect would border conflicts in the following areas have on military expenditures?
   (a) The Middle East
   (b) Eastern Europe
   (c) Southeast Asia
2. What effects would a worldwide recession have on military expenditures?

Analysis
1. Why did the military expenditures for the United States increase so dramatically in 1968? In answering the question, relate your response to the political and economic conditions in both the United States and abroad.
2. What do the increases in military spending over the last ten years tell us about defense priorities for the different groups of countries?

Synthesis
1. Devise a treaty to reduce military spending by 10 percent over the next five years for all the countries listed in Figure 4–5.
2. Given a map of the world and current national military expenditures, develop a United Nations proposal for reducing current military spending.

Evaluation

The *Evaluation* category involves making decisions on controversial topics and substantiating these decisions with sound reasons. Creativity is to Synthesis as judgment is to Evaluation. Evaluation questions ask the students to state what they think and what their opinions and judgments are and to give the criteria on which these thoughts, opinions, and judgments are based. Evaluation involves the use of standards for appraising the extent to which particulars are accurate, effective, economical, or satisfying. To qualify for this category, the student must (1) set up appropriate standards or values; and (2) determine how closely the idea or object meets these standards or values.

The Evaluation category projects the Analysis category into another dimension. In addition to analysis, an Evaluation question also requires that some type of value judgment be made. The criteria for judgment must be clearly identified and the quality of the Evaluation response should be graded according to how well the student has met the criteria. Because Evaluation is the highest category in the taxonomy, it demands the incorporation of all the other levels in responding to a situation or event. The Evaluation category requires the student to make reasonable judgments, to have rational opinions or personal reactions to a stimulus, and to defend them in a logical and coherent fashion.

Although the Evaluation process is subjective to the extent that the student chooses the criteria, emphasis should still be placed on rational, well developed, rather than emotional, responses. This prepares the student for numerous situations in later life in which this type of response will be needed.

An Evaluation response should consist of two parts:

1. The student should establish criteria on which to base judgment.
2. Using the prescribed criteria, the student should make his or her judgment accordingly.

For example, when asking the student "Would Lee Iacocca make a good President?" we are first asking him or her to decide which qualities are necessary for a good President. Then the student should compare these presidential qualities with those possessed by Lee Iacocca. It is obvious that there will be some difference of opinion about the qualities necessary for a good President. This is where the subjective or even creative component of Evaluation can be observed. The student must be analytical in matching these criteria with the subject being evaluated.

Criteria are formed usually from one of three sources:

1. Cultural or social values
2. Religious or historical absolutes
3. Individual justifications

Examples of each follow:

1. "Is it proper for a woman to ask a man for a date?" This question could be answered in several ways, depending on which social or cultural values the person believes are important.
2. "Should abortion be legalized?" To some people this is a religious question, to others it is a personal moral decision, and to still others, it is a medical decision.
3. "Should the Equal Rights Amendment be passed?" Different people would probably arrive at different answers based on different value systems.

The teacher should expect several different responses to the same Evaluation experience because students have varying value orientations. For this reason, the teacher can use Evaluation questions to help students learn to live with and accept the different views of others, thus preparing students for life in a pluralistic society.

The teacher often poses an Evaluation question by asking the student to take a stand on some issue. Questions such as "What do you think is best/worst or more/most important?" serve to elicit Evaluation responses.

FORMATIVE EVALUATION: APPLYING THE SKILLS
Evaluation

Instructions: Write two Evaluation questions for the following passage.

THE ENERGY CRISIS

As each new increase occurs in the price of crude oil, energy experts debate what measures should be taken to remedy possible shortages of oil products and continually rising prices. The United States is affected more by these rises in prices because its technologically oriented economy is heavily dependent upon energy from other countries. With only six percent of the world's population, the United States is using a third of the world's energy. As often happens when the government is asked to take action, the question is not whether it should take action, but what that action should be and which segments of the economy will be affected.

A major energy question involves the kinds of energy sources in which the United States should be investing in the following years. More conservative energy experts claim that the United States, for the next fifty years, will still be heavily dependent on oil and, consequently, should be investing its energy research money in ways to find more oil and to use it more efficiently. More radical critics advocate loosening our grip on oil dependence and exploring alternate sources of energy such as nuclear and solar energy. The latter position is more speculative, but advocates of this position claim that the time is right for bold experimentation.

Even on the topic of oil, experts disagree on how to save the oil that we do have. One controversial method of oil conservation that is being discussed is the limiting of car use either directly or indirectly. Direct means include enforced car pooling and

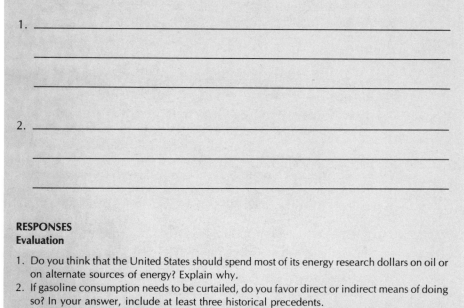

limiting the number of driving days for each vehicle. Indirect means include closing gas stations on weekends and gas rationing. Public debate on these issues has centered on their feasibility and their fairness. For example, opponents of gas rationing contend that extensive bureaucratic controls needed to enforce the gas rationing laws would cost more than they would save. Critics of indirect means of saving gas claim that these methods have not worked in the past and have the potential of being unfair to states with tourist economies.

The energy problem has also spilled over into another area of government control—the air. In an era of plentiful fuels, the environmentalists' demands for clean air seem reasonable and feasible. However, with cleaner fuels becoming increasingly expensive, more and more manufacturing and utility companies are turning to cheaper, dirtier sources of fuel such as coal. Environmentalists contend that now is the time to test the United States population's commitment to a cleaner, more healthy environment and they are advocating the maintenance of present Environmental Protection Agency clean air standards. Opponents say that these standards are unrealistic and should not be enforced in times of energy shortage.

Evaluation Questions

1. _____

_____

_____

2. _____

_____

_____

RESPONSES
Evaluation

1. Do you think that the United States should spend most of its energy research dollars on oil or on alternate sources of energy? Explain why.
2. If gasoline consumption needs to be curtailed, do you favor direct or indirect means of doing so? In your answer, include at least three historical precedents.
3. Should the United States relax its clean air standards during an energy shortage or maintain them as they are? In answering this question, discuss the economic and political implications of one particular position.

BLOOM'S TAXONOMY: A TOOL FOR PLANNING

In the introduction to this chapter, we briefly described how the taxonomy can be used to plan lessons and units. Now that you are familiar with the levels of the taxonomy, we want to return to this topic, describe the uses of

FIGURE 4–6   General Format for Kaplan Grid (Social Studies Unit on Immigrants)

Content, Concepts	Knowledge, Comprehension . . .
Places of origin	
Hardships en- countered	
Contributions of immigrants	

These concepts form the content emphasis for the unit.

the taxonomy in more detail, and illustrate these ideas with some concrete examples. In our discussion of the planning process, we will use a matrix planning model developed by Sandra Kaplan (1979).*

In the first stage of this model, the teacher lists all the major concepts or ideas to be taught. For example, a social studies unit on immigrants might have the topics listed, as in Figure 4–6.

The next step is to take these content areas and translate them into objectives at the various levels, as in Figure 4–7.

Figure 4–8 illustrates how the teacher expands the concepts of cognitive objectives into a working plan that is used both by the teacher and the class. This model, adapted from Sandra Kaplan, shows the relative ease with which detailed planning can be accomplished to provide a broad spectrum of learner experiences.

This approach to planning takes time, but the time spent prior to instruction will pay off in the classroom itself. The teacher will have a clear idea of where each lesson is going, how it relates to other lessons, and the various kinds of learning students will encounter. Further, Kaplan's matrix can help a teacher individualize selected aspects of the curriculum by prescribing a set number of evaluation points to each objective.

*Used with the permission of Sandra Kaplan.

FIGURE 4–7   An Initial Expansion of Performances

Content, Concepts	Knowledge	Comprehension	Application	Analysis	Synthesis	Evaluation
Places of origin	Students will know the dates and the countries of origin of the major immigrant groups to the U.S.	Students will construct a graph showing the national origin of various immigrant groups to the U.S.	Students will predict from where future immigrant groups to the U.S. will come	Students will explain the motives of different immigrant groups in coming to the U.S.	Students will design an immigration policy that is fair to future various immigrant groups	Students will decide whether the current U.S. immigration policy is fair to various immigrant groups and tell why
Hardships encountered						
Contributions of immigrants						

FIGURE 4–8   Teacher-Student Work Plan

Content	Level of Objective	Teaching Activity	Learning Experiences	Student Product
Places of origin	K	Lecture/Recitation Reading assignment Worksheet	Note taking Reading	Worksheet completed
Places of origin	C	Demonstration of how to construct graphs	Note taking Constructing a graph	Graph
Places of origin	AP	Small-group presentations	Each group makes a prediction and presents to class	Presentation by small groups to whole class
Places of origin	AN	Presentation of assignment Discussion of resources Description of final product Break class into groups	Each group focuses on one immigrant group and is responsible for explaining their motives for coming, using references, film strips, and other resources	Report to class

BLOOM'S TAXONOMY: A CRITICAL ANALYSIS

Bloom's Taxonomy has been used as an educational tool to analyze instructional practices since 1956, and an evaluation of his taxonomy with respect to classroom use and other related research seems appropriate. Such an evaluation would point out not only the validations and uses of the taxonomy but also its limitations.

On the positive side, the taxonomy has gained widespread acceptance in the teaching profession and has proved to be a usable tool for curriculum development and instructional and evaluative planning. On the negative side, studies have raised critical questions about the structure and organization of the taxonomy, which have not been answered with either rebuttals or modifications. In addition, educational philosophers such as Edward Furst (1981) have questioned whether the taxonomy is comprehensive and accurately reflects important educational goals.

The great majority of reported research studies on the taxonomy involves articles advocating or illustrating the application of the taxonomy in the classroom. The significance of such positive research and such encouraging articles is that they indicate a generally high level of awareness and acceptance of the taxonomy by teachers. Because it was formulated by educators as an "educational-logical-psychological classification system," the taxonomy has demonstrated great adaptability to many current educational practices.

Responses to Bloom's Taxonomy

Gerald D. Baughman and Albert Mayrhofer (1965) used the taxonomy in a workshop for personnel responsible for curriculum design, construction, and evaluation. They found that instruction in the use of the taxonomy for constructing objectives both extended the range and increased the variety of objectives written by workshop personnel. Most of the change was evidenced by a decrease in the Knowledge category, with concomitant increases in the other categories.

A number of other writers have described how the taxonomy could be used as a curriculum construction guide. John Feldhusen et al. (1974) used an adapted form of the taxonomy to help curriculum designers focus on the higher levels of learning. Donald Bailey and Judith Leonard (1977) demonstrated how the taxonomy could be used to design curriculum for gifted preschoolers.

The taxonomy also has been used as a framework with which to construct test questions. Thomas McDaniel (1979) described uses of the taxonomy in constructing test questions at the college level, and Drew Wolfe and Henry Heikkinen (1979) applied the taxonomy to college chemistry tests. The taxonomy has also been used to construct test banks that were then made available to teachers as potential sources for test questions. Finally, Gerald

Nelson (1978) showed how to use the taxonomy to translate goals at different levels into tangible test items.

Analyses have been done on learning materials. O. L. Davis, Jr. and Francis P. Hunkins (1966) both used the taxonomy to investigate the types of questions used in fifth grade social studies textbooks. They found that the great majority of textbook questions (85 percent or higher) were at the Knowledge level. An updated version of this study by David Trachtenberg (1974), which analyzed more than 60,000 study and test questions, showed high school social studies texts to have a similar overemphasis on the lower levels of the taxonomy. On a more optimistic note, Gilbert Billings (1971) found that although more traditional science texts demonstrated a lack of higher-level questions, such was not the case with the more modern elementary science curricula.

All of these studies demonstrate one potential of the taxonomy as an evaluative instrument—the avoidance of an overemphasis on Knowledge-level objectives, questions, and test items.

Validation of Bloom's Taxonomy

Perhaps some of the most significant research on the taxonomy has focused on its structure. The reason why such research is important is related to assumptions about the construction of the taxonomy. These assumptions have been identified by Russell P. Kropp and Howard W. Stoker (1966):

1. Cognitive processes can be differentiated from others (for example, affective, psychomotor).
2. The categories are hierarchically arranged on the basis of complexity of the processing.
3. The hierarchical categories are cumulative and inclusive of all cognitive behaviors.
4. The mental processes designated in the taxonomy are learned behaviors and are not innate.

The importance of the validity of these assumptions is evidenced in a wide range of taxonomic uses. If cognitive processes cannot be differentiated from others, then the cognitive taxonomy would be an ineffective tool for planning learning activities. If the taxonomy does not include all categories of cognitive processes, then test constructors and curriculum planners may inadvertently omit from training and evaluation procedures important cognitive abilities. If taxonomic categories are not hierarchical and inclusive, the learning experiences planned by educators are likely to be poorly sequenced. If the classes are sequential, then the possibility of diagnostic assessment of student progress as part of a more comprehensive goal becomes plausible (Richard B. Smith, 1968). If the classes of the taxonomy are distinct, learned entities, then each category of performance requires a different set of conditions for learning—with implications for the method of instruction used to elicit the desired behaviors.

Perhaps the most important of these assumptions relates to the categories of the taxonomy being distinct, learned entities. Formulators of the taxonomy have hypothesized that learned behaviors are not all the same, but differ among the six categories as presented in the taxonomy. If the taxonomy is valid, then research workers will need to consider the effects of instructional methods on the different dependent variables represented by the categories of the taxonomy. Similarly, classroom teachers will be concerned with providing instruction that adequately covers each of the categories.

Attempts at validating these assumptions and investigating the structure of the taxonomy have used statistical techniques that focus on products rather than processes. The inherent weakness of such an approach can be seen when one considers that the basis of the taxonomy is the principle of stimulus processing. Stimulus processing occurs when the stimulus inputs of the human organism undergo certain kinds of transformations (thinking processes) into outputs of human performances. These different kinds of transformations of stimuli into human action form a group of events that collectively may be called varieties of stimulus processing, varieties of behavior, or classes of the taxonomy. Formulators of the taxonomy are hypothesizing that different types of thought processes (transformations) are occurring in a student's head when asked "Who discovered America in 1492?" than when asked "How would history have been changed if Columbus had sailed for his mother country of Italy rather than for Spain?" The answers (products) given by students are different for each of the questions and reflect varying cognitive processes. Obviously, this is inferential evidence because we really do not know what is going on in the brain.

Recent research on the brain also indicates some interesting notions about the localization of cognitive and affective functions in the brain (Johnson, 1982). It appears that for most people the *left* half or hemisphere of the brain is involved with logical, sequential, and analytical functions whereas the *right* hemisphere is responsible for intuitive, divergent, and creative behaviors (the more affectively oriented behaviors). Researchers in this area caution against curricula that focus on only one hemisphere to the exclusion of the development of the other. Continued research in the area of cognitive-affective interactions could do much to answer questions not only in the area of learning disabilities but also in the broader area of motivation.

THE AFFECTIVE DOMAIN

Whereas the cognitive domain concerns those intellectually related goals of the schools, there is another domain that involves the development of students' feelings, attitudes, values, and emotions—the affective domain. Lorin and Jo Anderson (1982) describe affective measurement techniques in the classroom and point out that some affective goals, such as honesty and truthfulness, are ends in themselves whereas other goals, such as positive attitudes toward mathematics or science instruction, may be viewed as means toward an end. Most parents, as well as most professionals in the field, tend to view as the most important job of the schools the development of students' thinking skills rather than their attitudes. Our discussion of the affective domain will not be as detailed as that of the cognitive domain because of the cognitive focus of most schools.

The developers of the affective domain (Krathwohl et al., 1964) wanted to establish reference points in this vital area so that instructional objectives could be developed within a systematic framework. Five major areas or categories are described in this domain:

1. Receiving (attending)
2. Responding
3. Valuing
4. Organization
5. Characterization by a Value or Value Complex

These five categories are then subdivided, as are the categories in the cognitive domain. Like those in the cognitive domain, the categories in the affective domain are hierarchically arranged along a continuum, in this case one of internalization rather than complexity. Internalization refers to the extent to which an idea has been integrated into a person's belief structure. If taken through each category of the taxonomy, the learner would begin by being willing to receive a particular attitudinal or value position and would conclude by incorporating or internalizing this position into his or her life style. Following is a very brief outline of the entire affective domain. Refer to the original text (Krathwohl et al., 1964) for further study and details.

Receiving (Attending)

The overall focus of the affective taxonomy is on the development of attitudes and values. The first step in this process and the initial classification in the affective domain relate to the willingness of learners to be open to stimuli and messages in the environment. At this level, students are willing to receive stimuli or to acknowledge that some phenomenon is taking place. To receive an affective message, one must demonstrate *Awareness,* which is the first subdivision of Receiving. Awareness implies that one is conscious that some stimulus is occurring. Awareness is almost equivalent to the cognitive behavior of observing, which we presented previously as being one of the major scientific processes.

Being aware is only the entry step. This is followed by the subcategory of *Willingness to Receive.* One may be aware that some phenomenon has transpired, but does that same individual willingly attend to the stimuli? The attitude of simply being willing to listen to others is a demonstration of Willingess to Receive.

The final subdivision of Receiving is *Controlled or Selected Attention.* Receiving is also contingent on one's ability to focus attention further on a selected set of stimuli. You demonstrated selected attention when you decided to focus on this page rather than on the newspaper, which may be on the same desk on which this text is placed. Students are operating at this level when they make a conscious effort to attend to a classroom presentation rather than to daydream or to look out the window.

Some examples of this level of the taxonomy include the following teacher objectives:

1. Students will listen to and not harbor ill feelings toward other students who disagree with their point of view.
2. Students will develop an openness toward other cultures, so that when other cultures are encountered in and out of the classroom, students will be willing to learn about them.

Responding

The second major element in the affective domain is called *Responding.* Although one may be willing to receive, this is not enough for internalization, which needs an action component. Thus, responding behaviors involve engaging in activities that relate to receiving.

Acquiescence in Responding is the first subdivision of Responding. Acquiescence in Responding is demonstrated when one complies with regulations or conventions. *Willingness to Respond,* the second subdivision, is related to Acquiescence in Responding. The latter suggests that one complies, without knowing the reasons. The former indicates that one complies and knows the reasons why.

The third subdivision in the major category of Responding is *Satisfaction in Response.* This subcategory implies that after one makes a decision within the Responding realm, one is emotionally satisfied. For example, one may have a difficult work assignment that ought to be done. After it is completed, one feels good about having done it.

The following are some objectives that teachers have written for this level of the taxonomy:

1. Students will develop an appreciation for poetry, so that during a free reading period they will select a book of poetry as one of their choices.
2. Students will develop an appreciation of good oral hygiene habits, so that they will voluntarily brush their teeth at least twice a day.
3. Lower elementary students will learn to understand and appreciate the value of sharing, so that in a free play situation, the student will share toys with other children at least once.

Valuing

The third major category in the affective domain is called *Valuing.* Valuing means that one internalizes the concept of "worth." What differentiates this category from the others is that Valuing is exhibited by the individual as a motivated, deliberate behavior and not simply as a willingness to acquiesce.

There are three subdivisions in the Valuing category: (1) *Acceptance of a Value*; (2) *Preference for a Value*; and (3) *Commitment*. These three subdivisions are defined by their titles. Acceptance of a Value means that an individual believes that a certain value is preferable to others, but that this belief is flexible. If one accepts a value and is willing to be identified with it, one demonstrates a Preference for a Value. If one becomes involved and acts in accordance with the value, then one displays behaviors that are classified as Commitment. An important element of behavior is characterized by this level: behavior is motivated not by the desire to comply but by the individual's commitment to the underlying value guiding the behavior.

The following three objectives are examples of this level:

1. Social studies students will learn to value the democratic process, so that in a school election they will not only vote but will also urge others to do the same.
2. Science students will develop a commitment to the need for clean air and water and will demonstrate that commitment by becoming active in organizations set up for this purpose and by encouraging others to do so.
3. Shop students will learn to understand and appreciate the need for safe shop practices and will show this by policing their own and other work areas for unsafe practices.

Organization

As a learner's experiences broaden, there comes a point at which values begin to be ordered or classified. When such behaviors occur, then that individual is operating according to the fourth major category of the affective domain—*Organization*.

Within Organization there are two subcategories. The first is *Conceptualization of a Value,* which is demonstrated when one determines how values relate to each other in an abstract framework. We interpret Conceptualization of a Value as being very similar to the final category of the cognitive taxonomy, Evaluation, in that the individual takes a value position and can defend it if necessary.

The second subcategory of Organization is *Organization of a Value System*. It is at this level that one orders one's commitments. In a broad sense, Organization of a Value System is similar to stating one's "philosophy of life."

Some objectives at this level are as follows:

1. Students will learn the importance of good study habits and will demonstrate this by organizing their free time, both in school and out, so as to complete their assignments.
2. Elementary art students will develop an appreciation for the importance of clean work areas so that, without being prompted, the students will

put away their materials, clean up their area, and be ready for dismissal by the time the bell rings.
3. High school students will accept responsibility for establishing career choices by seeking and organizing information pertinent to their own life situation at a career fair.

Characterization by a Value or Value Complex

The highest category of the affective domain is the demonstration of behaviors that show that an individual acts in a manner consistent with those internalized values in which he or she believes. In the terms of the affective domain, this category is known as *Characterization by a Value or Value Complex*.

Generalized Set is the first of two subdivisions within this category. Generalized Set refers to one's commitment to certain attitudes, beliefs, or values, as reflected in one's consistent behavior. By knowing one's Generalized Set, one's behavior may be predicted for specific situations, which either conflict or converge with those values.

The highest level of the affective domain is described in the final subdivision, *Characterization*. This term implies that one's values so influence one's thinking that one is completely controlled by them. In other words, at this stage in the taxonomy, one's words and actions are entirely consistent with one's value orientation.

Sample objectives for this level of the taxonomy follow:

1. Students will learn to value honesty and will show this by monitoring their own behavior on tests and assignments and by discouraging others from cheating.
2. Students will value the importance of free speech in a society and will demonstrate this by protecting the rights of others—including those they disagree with—to express their views and opinions.
3. Students will learn to value human rights and will demonstrate this by treating other members of the school community in a way in which they would want to be treated.

A Very Brief Analysis

Although we recognize that we have not adequately discussed the affective domain, we will attempt, nevertheless, to analyze this domain as it relates to instruction. We feel that this domain is a complex one, and it is sometimes hard to differentiate objectives at the various levels (a criticism that we realize could also be leveled at the taxonomy of the cognitive domain). The affective domain also poses difficult evaluation problems because of the need for noncoercive and unobtrusive measures. On the positive side, however, the affective taxonomy provides a conceptual framework within which to view the entire instructional process. In other words, an understanding of the major ideas in the affective taxonomy provides teachers with tools with which to improve their educational endeavors.

We also believe that the variations between subdivisions are too artificial and hard to differentiate. Again, if this taxonomy is used as a conceptual framework rather than as a planning tool for instruction, this problem is not too important.

Finally, the time that is needed in the schools to provide all the necessary experiences for both the cognitive and affective dimensions of learning is overwhelming. This problem is becoming increasingly important as teachers and schools are being held more accountable for students' cognitive performance.

Yet we can counter with the question, "What are schools for?" The kinds of attitudes we develop as children and the values we espouse as adults are certainly influenced by the schools. Our attitudes toward learning are school-related; our approaches to personal interaction are shaped largely in school; and our belief in ourselves is school-connected. All of these affective behaviors are more important than learning and promptly forgetting the difference between transitive and intransitive verbs.

Abby L. Hughes and Karen Frommer (1982) devised a system by which to state, identify, and monitor affective objectives. They developed a checklist called "Rating the Affective Domain" (RAD). The seventy-item RAD checklist uses a five-point rating scale. Their system has four major behavioral skill areas: (1) individual tasks, (2) social interaction, (3) relationship to teacher, and (4) emotional responses. By using their RAD system, affective objectives selected for each student may be monitored on a yearly basis.

Perhaps the very best of our teachers subtly interweave both the cognitive and affective consequences into their instruction. Bear in mind that there is a high probability that the teachers whom you liked best just happened to teach the most effectively and to teach the subjects that you liked most. Perhaps this was no accident. Good teachers have been incorporating affective goals into their curricula for years. It is our hope that knowledge of the ideas in the affective taxonomy will help make these teachers more effective and encourage others to be sensitive to the attitudes and values they are developing in students.

We close this section with an observation by Robert F. Mager (1968), the individual singly responsible for popularizing behavioral objectives, who wrote: "If I do little else, I want to send my students away with at least as much interest in the subjects I teach as they had when they arrived." This perceptive statement is the essence of incorporating the affective domain into your *value complex* of instruction.

FORMATIVE EVALUATION
Affective Domain

1. Cognitive domain is to complexity as affective domain is to _____?

2. Cognitive domain is to the head as affective domain is to the _____? (What metaphorical place in the body would form the locus for the affective domain?)
3. True/False. Cognitive and affective behaviors are distinct and separate entities.
4. True/False. Getting someone to listen to an idea is the first step to getting her or him to act on that idea.
5. Is there more of a cognitive emphasis at the lower or higher levels of the affective domain? Explain your answer.
6. Categorize the following statements as cognitive or affective by inserting C or A as appropriate:
   (a) _____ Given a list of ten words, the student will identify all of the five that are nouns.
   (b) _____ The student will follow classroom rules as prescribed by the teacher.
   (c) _____ The student will recite the Bill of Rights.
   (d) _____ In an unsupervised classroom setting, the student will use objectives to plan for instruction at least three times per week.
   (e) _____ During a discussion, the student will listen at least twice to others, demonstrating this by using others' ideas in his or her comments.

RESPONSES
Affective Domain

1. Internalization. The affective domain is hierarchically organized on the basis of internalization. Objectives at the higher levels of this taxonomy require a greater degree of internalization that those at lower levels.
2. The heart. We commonly describe feelings as being from the "heart."
3. False. Though these taxonomies have been presented as separate systems for the purpose of clarity, there are a number of interrelations between the two areas.
4. True. The taxonomy of the affective domain is organized in such a way that a person must first be willing to receive an idea before any other type of internalization can occur.
5. There is more of a cognitive emphasis in the higher levels of the affective domain than at the lower levels because, at the higher levels, an individual must logically organize feelings into a coherent system.
6. (a) Cognitive (Comprehension level)
   (b) Affective
   (c) Cognitive (Knowledge level)
   (d) Affective (the clue here is the phrase, "in an unsupervised classroom setting")
   (e) Affective

THE PSYCHOMOTOR DOMAINS

One of the newer domains to join the taxonomies is that of the *psychomotor domain,* which articulates movement instruction in a systematic manner. There are several classification systems developed in this area in contrast to the previous two domains, which had fewer systems.

The psychomotor domain, which is characterized by the development of muscular skills and coordination, can be thought of as a series of inputs and outputs. The inputs involve perception of information from the outside environment, and the outputs are the actual motions or movements the students perform. Both inputs and outputs are necessary in complex motor activities because movements must be coordinated in terms of the outer environment. Think of a gymnast on a balance beam or a basketball player in a game: both must take in information from the environment (input) and synchronize their movements to this information (output).

Moore's Taxonomy

A logical starting point for our discussion of the psychomotor domain is the *perceptual taxonomy* developed by Maxine Moore (1967, 1970, 1972). Hers was the first developed and places most emphasis on the initial stages of psychomotor development, the perceptual aspect of information.

As shown in Figure 4–9, the lowest levels of Moore's taxonomy deal with discrimination of sensation, starting with simple discriminations and progressing to more complex. At level 4, *perception of meaning,* students not only can perceive complex relationships in a movement but can copy or reproduce those movements. A swimmer, for example, faithfully replicates a dive and a musician plays a concerto as it has been played previously by other musicians. In the final level, *perceptive performance,* students are expected to improvise original variations of the movements replicated in level 4. In keeping with this taxonomy's focus on perception, the emphasis at this level is on the extraction of subtle information from the stimulus and not on the motor skill involved in the behavior. Here we can see a parallel with the emphasis on creativity in the last two levels of Bloom's taxonomy.

Harrow's Taxonomy

Anita Harrow's taxonomy, which was published in 1972, incorporates perceptual elements but places more emphasis on output or performance variables. As shown in Figure 4–10, the two lowest levels deal with basic fundamental movements, the first level dealing with involuntary or knee-jerk

FIGURE 4–9   Moore's Taxonomy of the Perceptual Domain

Level	Example of Behavior
1. Sensation	Ability to discriminate rough detail
2. Figure perception	Resolution of part/whole relationship
3. Symbol perception	Ability to perceive the overall picture and complex relationships within a stimulus
4. Perception of meaning	Ability to reproduce a complex movement
5. Perceptive performance	Ability to reproduce, interpret, and adapt a complex phenomenon

FIGURE 4–10 Harrow's Taxonomy of the Psychomotor Domain

Level	Example
1. Reflex movement	Knee-jerk and other reflex movements innate at birth
2. Basic fundamental movements	Visual tracking of an object, crawling, walking, grasping an object
3. Perceptual abilities	Body awareness, figure-ground differentiation, auditory awareness, memory
4. Physical abilities	Muscular endurance, agility, strength
5. Skilled movement	Simple behaviors such as sawing wood and complex behaviors such as playing tennis
6. Nondiscursive communication	Moving interpretatively and using the body creatively to express ideas or emotions

type motions and the second dealing with learned behaviors. Both of these levels are important because they form the building blocks for later, more complex behavior.

The third level, *perceptual abilities,* is involved with stimulus interpretation and is very similar in focus to Moore's *symbol perception.* Physical abilities, which are at Harrow's level 4, include components such as endurance, strength, flexibility, and agility—considered part of the foundation for higher levels. In the last two levels, *skilled movement* and *nondiscursive communication,* heavy emphasis is placed on performance, or output. At the *skilled movement* level, emphasis is on performance of a skill in a complex environment, such as in a game or in a performance with other musicians. The highest level, *nondiscursive communication,* stresses expressive and creative movement. Here again we can see parallels with the Cognitive Taxonomy.

Jewett and Mullan Psychomotor Domain

The final taxonomy to be discussed is not only the most recent but also the most comprehensive. Its major concepts, endorsed by the American Alliance for Health, Physical Education and Recreation (AAHPER), were synthesized by Ann E. Jewett and Marie R. Mullan (1977). Combining elements of the two previous taxonomies, the Jewett and Mullan psychomotor domain begins with generic movement and concludes with creative movement. As you read through the levels, note the similarities with the taxonomies discussed earlier. Observe also how many of these processes can be applied to vocational, music, and art education.

A. *Generic Movement:* Those movement operations or processes that facilitate the development of characteristic and effective motor patterns. They are typically exploratory operations in which the learner receives or "takes in" data as he or she moves.

1. *Perceiving:* Awareness of total body relationships and of self in motion. These awarenesses may be evidenced by body positions or motoric acts; they may be sensory in that the mover feels the equilibrium of body weight and the movement of limbs; or they may be evidenced cognitively through identification, recognition, or differentiation.

2. *Patterning:* Arrangement and use of body parts in successive and harmonious ways to achieve a movement pattern or skill. This process is dependent on recall and performance of a movement previously demonstrated or experienced.

B. *Ordinative Movement:* The processes of organizing, refining, and performing skillful movement. The processes involved are directed toward the organization of perceptual-motor abilities with a view to solving particular movement tasks or requirements.

1. *Adapting:* Modification of a patterned movement to meet externally imposed task demands. This would include modification of a particular movement to perform it under different conditions.

2. *Refining:* Acquisition of smooth, efficient control in performing a movement pattern or skill by mastery of spatial and temporal relations. This process deals with the achievement of precision in motor performance and habituation of performance under more complex conditions.

C. *Creative Movement:* Those motor performances that include the processes of inventing or creating movement that will serve the personal (individual) purposes of the learner. The processes employed are directed toward discovery, integration, abstraction, idealization, emotional objectification and composition.

1. *Varying:* Invention or construction of personally unique options in motor performance. These options are limited to different ways of performing specific movement; they are of an immediate situational nature and lack any predetermined movement behavior that has been externally imposed on the mover.

2. *Improvising:* Extemporaneous originations or initiation of personally novel movement or combination of movement. The processes involved may be stimulated by a situation externally structured, although conscious planning on the part of the performer is not usually required.

3. *Composing:* Combination of learned movements in personally unique motor designs or the invention of movement patterns new to the performer. The performer creates a motor response in terms of a personal interpretation of the movement situation.*

The *purpose concepts* describe the functions of movement in achieving human goals and thus define the scope of the physical education curriculum. The *processes* by which one learns to move must also be an integral part of curricular planning. The purpose-process conceptual framework promotes

---

*Ann E. Jewett and Marie R. Mullan, *Curriculum Design: Purposes and Processes in Physical Education Teaching-Learning* (Washington, D.C.: American Alliance for Health, Physical Education and Recreation, 1977), pp. 9–10. Reprinted by permission of AAHPER, Washington, D.C.

an action-oriented system focusing on the individual learning to move. Movement processes represent one large category of human behavior. Process learnings are, therefore, essential curricular outcomes. Sequence in physical education can best be facilitated by organizing curricular content in terms of a hierarchy of movement-learning process outcomes. This classification scheme conceptualizes a hierarchy of movement-learning processes and offers a taxonomy for the selection and statement of educational objectives in the motor domain, which is applicable to any curricular area dealing with this domain.

Summary

The functions of the psychomotor domain relate to human movement, and the classification outlines just given analyze instructional objectives through a hierarchy of tasks. Also, learning objectives can be applied in those areas of instruction that make use of the domain. Those areas include mathematics (spatial analysis), home and family living, fine arts, vocational-technical education, science, business, and occupations. Think of how you could use this taxonomy in your own discipline.

FORMATIVE EVALUATION
Psychomotor Domain

1. True/False. The psychomotor domain is only for physical education majors.
2. In which of the following areas would the psychomotor domain *not* be used?
   (a) Music
   (b) Art
   (c) Home economics
   (d) All of the above involve psychomotor learning
3. Categorize the following as cognitive (C), affective (A), or psychomotor (PS).
   _____ (a) In an unsupervised setting, third grade students will obey traffic rules on foot, on bicycle, or on another conveyance at intersections and elsewhere.
   _____ (b) Given a caliper graduated to millimeters, the student will measure objects to within one millimeter of a standard set by the instructor.
   _____ (c) The student will type at least 35 words per minute with a maximum of one error.
   _____ (d) The PE student will abide by the decisions of the officials.
   _____ (e) The student will construct a proof to prove the commutative property of real numbers.
4. Which psychomotor taxonomy is most concerned with the input aspects of movement?
5. Where is creativity provided for in each of the taxonomies?

RESPONSES
Psychomotor Domain

1. False. Psychomotor components exist in virtually all subject matter areas.
2. (d). There are psychomotor components in all of these areas. For example, music students use psychomotor skills in learning how to play an instrument; art and home economics students also use psychomotor skills in manipulative aspects of their subjects.
3. (a) (A) Affective (the key here is the phrase, "in an unsupervised setting").
   (b) (PS) Psychomotor
   (c) (PS) Psychomotor
   (d) (A) Affective
   (e) (C) Cognitive
4. Moore's taxonomy of the *perceptual domain* places the most emphasis on incoming stimuli.
5. All three of the taxonomies place creative behavior at the highest level. In Moore's taxonomy, the final level, *perceptive performance*, stresses interpreting and adapting a complex phenomenon, such as a musical piece. Harrow's taxonomy stresses creativity in the sixth level, *nondiscursive communication*, and Jewett and Mullan's taxonomy does this at the third level, *creative movement*.

CONCLUSIONS

In this chapter we have presented three discrete taxonomies that emphasize cognitive, affective, and psychomotor domains in the schools. We describe these taxonomies as analytical tools that teachers can use purposefully to help them understand more clearly what their objectives are and to help them make their teaching more effective. These taxonomies are treated as separate entities, but interconnections among the three domains are numerous: very seldom do we think without feeling, and action on the part of the learner is a major component of all learning.

Most of the chapter has been consciously devoted to the cognitive domain because we believe that the major thrust of our schools is in the development of cognitive skills and abilities. We describe the taxonomy of the cognitive domain as a hierarchical classification system in which students first know about a topic and then become increasingly familiar with the topic through a series of progressively complex mental operations. These operations, or levels of the taxonomy, require the learner to understand the topic, then to use it in the solution of problems, in the analysis of ideas, in the creation of new ideas, and in the evaluation of other ideas. Each of these steps is sequential, with subsequent steps building on previous ones. Because of this, the taxonomy has been demonstrated to be a valuable tool for sequencing instruction and determining the base of difficulty.

The second area of the curriculum discussed is the affective domain, which deals with feelings, emotions, attitudes, and values. Like the cognitive domain, the affective domain also contains a series of sequential levels in which objectives or student behavior can be categorized. The organizing principle for this domain, however, is one of internalization, or the degree to which feelings and attitudes are integrated into the individual's personality and life style. At the lowest level of this taxonomy, the individual is merely open to messages from other people. Then the person willingly responds to those messages, values them, integrates them into his or her own value structure, and finally leads life according to these ideas. Like that of the cognitive domain, the taxonomy of the affective domain can be used to analyze educational objectives and to order these objectives in a learning sequence.

The final taxonomies that we discuss concern the psychomotor domain. We describe this area of the curriculum as being broader in scope than just physical education skills and including coordinated manipulative movements in a number of disciplines. Like the other two, the psychomotor domain is organized along a sequential continuum—in this case, organizational complexity—with lower behaviors involving simpler movements and higher behaviors requiring more complex and integrated movements.

Although our presentation is admittedly limited, you have at least been introduced to the three interrelated taxonomies; in the case of the cognitive domain, it is hoped that you have acquired more than a superficial understanding of the topic. While not perfect, each taxonomy can contribute to your understanding of what you teach, the possible components that can be included, and the more creative means by which to structure both learning activities and evaluative tasks. We urge you to use these three taxonomies as you analyze the work that you receive in higher education. Finally, ask yourself this question: "How could my classes be made better through the application of the principles and concepts presented in the taxonomies?" If you can become more systematic, analytical, and evaluative, then we have attained one of our goals.

It would be incorrect to conclude that all three taxonomies have been validated. We really do not know if there is such a construct as a Taxonomy of Life's Great Moments. What is important to teachers is that there are systematic methods by which to plan and to structure the activities that are most often associated with schooling. Knowledge of the existence of these taxonomies allows for thoughtful and systematic curriculum construction, which we believe would do much to improve instruction.

We readily conclude that far too many educators give only a cursory glance at the three taxonomies. Many teachers are unaware of their value, and others simply are uninterested in understanding the relationships that may exist in any cognitive area of study.

We feel strongly that if taxonomies were applied to their optimal use, there would be far more cognitive success in the schools of the world; students would be more serious about their studies and would enjoy them more; and physical education would be supported for its own sake rather than considered merely an adjunct of athletics.

As we state in Chapter 1, our aim is to provide you with a better understanding of the decisions that are made by great teachers. By understanding the potentials of the taxonomies, you will be adding one more tool to your "bag of professional skills."

REFERENCES

Anderson, Lorin, and Jo Anderson. "Affective Assessment is Necessary and Possible," *Educational Leadership* 39:1982, 524–525.

Ausubel, David P. *The Psychology of Meaningful Verbal Learning*. New York: Grune and Stratton, 1963.

Bailey, Donald, and Judith Leonard. "A Model for Adapting Bloom's Taxonomy to a Preschool Curriculum for the Gifted," *Gifted Child Quarterly* 21:1977, 97–103.

Baughman, Gerald D., and Albert Mayrhofer. "Leadership Training Project: A Final Report," *Journal of Secondary Education* 40:1965, 369–372.

Billings, Gilbert. "Cognitive Levels of Elementary Science Texts," *School Science and Mathematics* 71:1971, 824–830.

Black, Thomas. "An Analysis of Levels of Thinking in Nigerian Science Teachers' Examinations," *Journal of Research in Science Teaching* 17:1980, 301–306.

Bloom, Benjamin S., Max D. Engelhart, Edward J. Furst, Walker H. Hill, and David R. Krathwohl. *Taxonomy of Educational Objectives. The Classification of Educational Goals. Handbook I: Cognitive Domain*. New York: David McKay, 1956.

Blumberg, Phyllis, Majorie Alshuler, and Victor Rezmovic. "Should Taxonomic Levels be Considered in Developing Examinations?" *Educational and Psychological Measurement* 42:1982, 1–7.

Brophy, Jere. "Teacher Behavior and its Effects," *Journal of Educational Psychology* 71:1979, 733–750.

Chambers, Jack, and Jerry Sprecher. "Computer Assisted Instruction: Current Trends and Critical Issues," *Communications of the ACM* 23:1980, 332–342.

Craig, Grace. *Child Development*. Englewood Cliffs, N.J.: Prentice-Hall, 1979.

Davis, O. L., Jr., and Francis P. Hunkins. "Textbook Questions: What Thinking Processes Do They Foster?" *Peabody Journal of Education* 43:1966, 285–292.

Epstein, Herman. "Growth Spurts During Brain Development: Implications for Educational Policy and Practices." In *Education and the Brain*, J. Chall, ed. Chicago: University of Chicago Press, 1979, pp. 343–370.

Epstein, Herman, and Conrad Toepfer. "A Neuroscience Basis for Reorganizing Middle Grades Education," *Educational Leadership* 35:1978, 656–660.

Feldhusen, John, Russel Ames, and Katheryn Linden. "Designing Instruction to Achieve Higher Level Goals and Objectives," *Educational Technology* 14:1974, 21–23.

Furst, Edward. "Bloom's Taxonomy of Educational Objectives for the Cognitive Domain: Philosophical and Educational Issues," *Review of Educational Research* 51:1981, 441–443.

Guilford, Joy P. *The Nature of Human Intelligence*. New York: McGraw-Hill, 1967.

Harrow, Anita J. *A Taxonomy of the Psychomotor Domain: A Guide for Developing Behavior Objectives*. New York: David McKay, 1972.

Hill, P. W., and B. McGraw. "Testing the Simplex Assumption Underlying Bloom's Taxonomy," *American Educational Research Journal* 18:1981, 93–101.

Hughes, Abby L., and Karen Frommer. "A System for Monitoring Affective Objectives," *Educational Leadership* 39:1982, 521–523.

Jewett, Ann E., and Marie R. Mullan. "Movement Process Categories in Physical Education in Teaching-Learning." In *Curriculum Design: Purposes and Processes in Physical Education Teaching-Learning*. Washington, D.C.: American Alliance for Health, Physical Education and Recreation, 1977.

Johnson, Virginia. "Myelin and Malucation: A Fresh Look at Piaget," *Science Teacher* 49:1982, 41–44.

Kaplan, Sandra. *National Leadership Training*. Ventura, Calif.: Institute for Gifted and Talented, 1979.

Krathwohl, David R., Benjamin S. Bloom, and Bertram B. Masia. *Taxonomy of Educa-*

tional Objectives. The Classification of Educational Goals. Handbook II: Affective Domain. New York: David McKay, 1964.

Kropp, Russell P., Howard W. Stoker, and W. Louis Bashaw. "The Validation of the Taxonomy of Educational Objectives," *Journal of Experimental Education* 34: 1966, 69–76.

Kunen, Seth, Ronald Cohen, and Robert Solman. "A Levels of Processing Analysis of Bloom's Taxonomy," *Journal of Educational Psychology* 73:1981, 202–211.

Lindquist, Alexa. "Applying Bloom's Taxonomy in Writing-Reading Guides for Literature," *Journal of Reading* 25:1982, 768–774.

McDaniel, Thomas. "Designing Essay Questions for Different Levels of Learning," *Improving College and University Teaching* 27:1979, 120–123.

Mager, Robert F. *Developing Attitude Toward Learning*. Palo Alto, Calif.: Fearon, 1968.

Mills, Stephen, Carol Rice, David Berliner, and Eleane Rosseau. "The Correspondence Between Teacher Questions and Student Answers in Classroom Discourse," *Journal of Experimental Education* 48:1980, 194–204.

Moore, Maxine R. "A Proposed Taxonomy of the Perceptual Domain and Some Suggested Applications" (Test Development report 67-3). Princeton, N.J.: Educational Testing Service, 1967.

Moore, Maxine R. "The Perceptual Motor Domain and a Proposed Taxonomy of Perception." *A.V. Communication Review* 18:1970, 379–413.

Moore, Maxine R. "Consideration of the Perceptual Process in the Evaluation of Musical Performance," *Journal of Research in Music Education* 20:1972, 273–279.

Nelson, Gerald. "A Proposed Taxonomy of Student Assessment Techniques in the Cognitive Domain," *Educational Technology* 18:1978, 24–26.

Padilla, Michael, James Okey, and Gerald Dillshaw. "The Relationship Between Science Process Skills and Formal Thinking Abilities," *Journal of Research in Science Teaching* 20:1983, 239–246.

Rosenshine, Barak. "Teaching Functions in Instructional Programs," *The Elementary School Journal* 83:1983, 335–351.

Seddon, G. Malcolm. "The Properties of Bloom's Taxonomy of Educational Objectives for the Cognitive Domain," *Review of Educational Research* 48:1978, 303–323.

Shimmerlik, Susan M. "Organization Theory and Memory for Prose: A Review of the Literature," *Review of Educational Research* 48:1978, 103–120.

Smith, Richard B. "An Empirical Examination of the Assumptions Underlying the Taxonomy of Educational Objectives: Cognitive Domain," *Journal of Educational Measurement* 5:1968, 125–128.

Trachtenberg, David. "Student Tasks in Text Materials: What Cognitive Skills Do They Tap?" *Peabody Journal of Education* 52:1974, 54–57.

Webb, Jeannie. "Taxonomy of Cognitive Behavior: A System for the Analysis of Intellectual Processes," *Journal of Research and Development in Education* 4:1970, 73–83.

Wolfe, Drew, and Henry Heikkinen. "An Analysis of the Construct Validity of a Test of Higher Cognitive Learning in Introductory Chemistry," *Journal of Research in Science Teaching* 16:1979, 25–31.

5

DECISIONS ABOUT LESSON PLANNING

Time—we only have so much of it. The master teacher cannot create a single extra second in the day—any more than can his or her less effective counterparts. But the master teacher certainly controls the way time is used. Master teachers systematically and carefully plan for productive use of instructional time.

One of the primary roles that you will perform as a teacher is that of designer and implementor of instruction. Teachers at every level prepare plans that aid in the organization and delivery of their daily lessons. These plans vary widely in their style and degree of specificity. Some instructors prefer to construct elaborately detailed and impeccably typed outlines; others rely on the briefest of notes handwritten on scratchpads or on the backs of discarded envelopes. Regardless of the format, all teachers need to make wise decisions about the strategies and methods they will employ to help students move systematically toward learner goals.

Teachers need more than a vague, or even a precise, notion of educational goals and objectives to be able to sequence these objectives or to be proficient in the skills and knowledge of a particular discipline. The effective teacher also needs to develop a plan to provide *direction* toward the attainment of the selected objectives. Numerous studies on the characteristics of competent teachers show that being well organized correlates highly with instructor effectiveness.

To aid you in making decisions about the organization of your lessons, the topic of planning is introduced now for your consideration. The principal goal of this chapter is to enable you to be effective and systematic in planning by becoming aware of the decision areas and techniques of lesson preparation. The specific objectives of this chapter are

1. To identify the major elements of lesson planning, including pre-lesson, lesson implementation, and post-lesson activities
2. To provide formats for designing lesson plans
3. To introduce the concept of micro-teaching as a means of applying lesson-planning concepts
4. To consider the many ways that the microcomputer can be used as a tool for lesson preparation and lesson delivery

LESSON-PLANNING PROCEDURES

First we would like to introduce you to the concept of lesson planning and to present a format that has been used by many successful practitioners. We will discuss a general model of lesson planning in much the same way an architect might present the basic design and functions for a new building. When architects first enter their profession, they tend to follow closely the recommendations provided by authorities. But, once they experience success in the process, they make personal adaptations to suit their talents.

Similarly, as a classroom teacher, you will probably begin by imitating a favorite teacher; later you will expand the acquired "basics" for lesson preparation and delivery after study and experience. Classroom innovations usually come once you are in the classroom with your own set of learners, have developed your own instructional resources, and have experimented with various strategies. Although fundamental lesson-planning elements tend to remain stable, their basic formula is always modified to suit the individual teacher's lesson preparations or style of presentation.

A general planning cycle is graphically illustrated in Figure 5–1. The

FIGURE 5–1   The Lesson-Planning Cycle

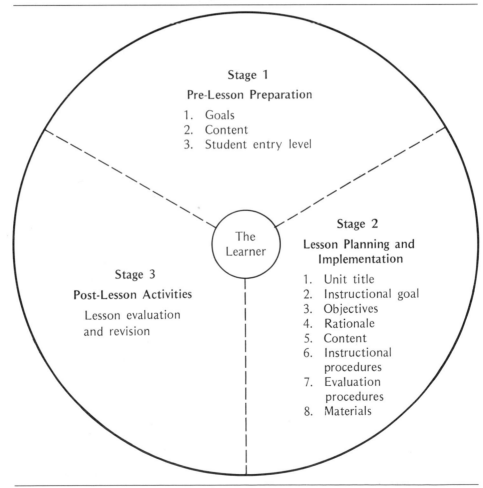

model contains three primary stages, each with several interrelated steps. These stages refer to the major pre-lesson, lesson, and post-lesson activities in which you will engage as you design, implement, and evaluate your daily plan.

Note that the main object of lesson planning is that all activities and processes provide an educative environment for the learner. As noted in Chapter 1, as teachers we often forget about the learner and become more interested in our respective disciplines. Thus, if lesson planning is to be a useful task, it must always focus on the *interaction* between what is to be learned and the learner.

As shown in Figure 5–1, lesson planning involves much more than making arbitrary decisions about "what I'm going to teach today." Many activities precede the process of designing and implementing a lesson plan. Similarly, the job of systematic lesson planning is not complete until after the instructor has assessed both the learner's attainment of the anticipated outcomes and the effectiveness of the lesson in leading learners to these outcomes.

Before we begin our discussion of each element of lesson planning, it is important to add one more caveat. Although we can distinguish logically between various lesson-planning stages and components, in reality these different activities are *not linear*. Even teachers who develop highly structured and detailed plans rarely adhere to them in lock-step fashion. Indeed, such rigidity would probably hinder, rather than help, the teaching-learning process. The lesson-planning elements described in this chapter should be thought of as *guiding principles* to be applied as aids, but not blueprints, to systematic instruction. Precise preparation must allow for flexible delivery. During the actual classroom interaction, the instructor needs to make adaptations and to add artistry to each day's plan. For these reasons, Figure 5–1 depicts the process of lesson planning as being cyclical.

PRE-LESSON PREPARATION

Before you can construct a lesson plan, there are at least three major considerations that must be taken into account. These include (1) information about the major *goals* that are to be pursued through the programs of the school; (2) the *content* to be included in your course; and (3) the *entry level* of your students. Although in actuality these considerations are interdependent, we separate them for the purpose of illustration.

Goals

Within the pages of *Alice's Adventures in Wonderland* by Lewis Carroll, there is a memorable exchange in which Alice, not knowing which road to take, asks the Cheshire Cat for directions. Their subsequent conversation goes like this.

"Would you tell me, please, which way I ought to go from here?"
"That depends a good deal on where you want to get to," said the Cat.
"I don't much care where—" said Alice.
"Then it doesn't matter which way you go."

In contrast to Alice's situation, decisions about destinations and about how to reach them are critical to educators as they plan their courses and lessons. For the teacher or school administrator, the starting point of curriculum planning is usually the identification of broad educational goals.

A *goal* describes the major, culminating outcome that results from the educational process. It is more abstract, more visionary, than an objective. As discussed in Chapter 1, a goal is something toward which to work—a guiding star, so to speak. It gives us that affective quality of commitment.

Whereas goal statements are effective in suggesting certain types of content and actions for the school to include in the curriculum, they are too general for organizing the daily activities of teachers and students. General goals must be translated into progressively specific outcomes as you plan for daily lessons.

The sources of educational goals are many. As a new teacher, you may find some, perhaps all, of the following resources helpful.

State, District, and School Goals

Most states, districts, and schools have developed written statements of general educational goals—outcomes that are to be sought for *all* learners. The *process* of developing goal statements is often as critical as the *content* of the goals. To ensure that the selected goals are accepted widely, they must be formulated by representatives of the many different groups who have a vested interest in them—teachers, administrators, students, parents, and other citizens of the community.

Whether formulated by a national curriculum commission, a state board of education, or a group of local citizens and teachers, goals are usually long-range and inclusive in scope. Note, for example, the comprehensive nature of the following goal statement written in 1983 in the form of a recommendation developed by the Committee on Educational Policies Structure and Management of the State of Washington (1983).

> It is recommended that the core curriculum ensure that *all* high school students pursue a common core curriculum designed to assure graduation with effective communication (written and oral) and thinking and reasoning skills; study in the arts (appreciation or performance); knowledge of American civilization and government; comprehension in at least one language other than English; computation skills and the ability to use computers; understanding of geography, economics, and history; job acquisition and retention skills; and the capability to assume future roles as parents, consumers and home managers. Students with special educational needs should share in this core to the extent of their abilities.

Curriculum Guides and Courses of Study

District and school-level goals often are converted into more concrete goals at the program and course level—social studies, physical education, language arts—and presented in documents known as curriculum guides. As the term *guide* implies, these manuals provide the framework within which you, as a teacher, can organize your course outlines, units, and lessons.

Guides spell out in greater detail than goals the types of competencies students are expected to attain in a course of study. They may or may not include specific student objectives and learning activities.

The content of curriculum guides usually is developed by a group of local teachers after careful consideration of the various subject-matter elements and their relation to the abilities and needs of the children who will receive the instruction. Most districts have guides available for each of the main components of the school's curriculum. The guides that have been developed for the subject you teach will be helpful to you as a new teacher in identifying the major content and learning experiences to which students have been exposed in previous years. They will also suggest topics that are recommended for learners at your particular grade level.

Needs-Assessment Information

Increasingly, school districts are developing new programs and revising current ones based on needs-assessment information. The purposes of such data collections are twofold: (1) to identify the goals of the district; and (2) to determine how well these goals are being met. A discrepancy between what is viewed as ideal (a goal) and what is seen as the present status (the actual condition) is defined as a *need* that should be addressed through curricular or instructional changes.

Clearly, the identification of goals is a critical part of all curriculum planning. One of your tasks as a teacher will be to select from various sources those goals that will provide focus for your course-planning endeavors. Because of the ages and abilities of your particular students, you will want to design lessons that, in an incremental way, assist the students in approaching the selected goals.

At this point, you may begin to realize that there is definitely more to planning a lesson than just assigning the odd-numbered problems for the next day and the even-numbered ones for the day after. This is why teaching is such a demanding profession. Once the goal question is resolved, you must determine what it is that will be taught.

Course Content

Decisions about course content—that is, what subject matter to include and how much material to cover in a course, a unit, or a lesson—are, initially, among the most difficult facing the beginning teacher. They demand that the teacher have a strong command of the discipline and the ability to analyze it carefully to isolate those concepts, principles, rules, and facts that are most significant.

A lesson plan will help a teacher articulate clearly stated ideas, activities, and assignments. M. L. Land (1980) reported that *clarity* was a critical element for effective instruction. He observed that teacher vagueness and lack of clarity had a negative effect on student achievement. Thus for many of you, the lesson plan will become a guide to improving the clarity of verbal or written communication in the classroom.

Several sources of information may be helpful in making these significant choices about content. Two of these sources are experts in the field and local curriculum developers.

Expert Opinion

For each content area taught in our schools, subject-matter specialists have suggested key questions that should be raised and critical concepts that should be learned. Publishers frequently rely on the opinions of content experts to develop textbooks, which in turn establish a "tradition of content" that is typically included in a particular field of study. Although the exclusive use of textbooks for selecting subject matter has certain limitations, it is presently one of the more influential determiners of content.

Curriculum Study Teams

Many schools have content-based curriculum study teams composed of teachers who work together to develop general outlines and materials for one or several areas of study. In a more informal way, your colleagues—particularly those who majored in a particular content area at the college level—may prove to be invaluable resources as you begin the process of developing your courses.

Student Entry Level

At the same time that you are selecting major course goals and choosing content in relation to these goals, another pre-lesson planning task must be accomplished: the identification of student entry levels. This activity requires that you find out what students already know about the content, determine whether there is a need for instruction in the particular area, and assess whether students are at a state of readiness to receive the instruction. It is not an overstatement to say that at *every* step of the planning process, it is imperative to consider our audience, the students. What they already have learned, the degree to which they have retained the learning, their motivations, their abilities, their social and cultural backgrounds, and their academic achievements are all crucial data. Such information takes on special significance as teachers prepare to mainstream handicapped chil-

FIGURE 5–2   Major Components of the Instructional Process Cycle

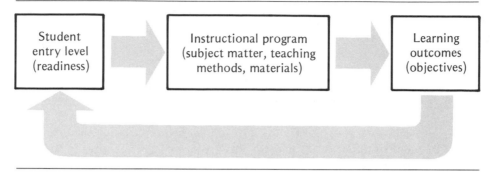

dren into their classrooms. Often the teacher who is aware of special student disabilities can adapt the physical environment and the instructional strategies employed for daily lessons in ways to accommodate unique learner needs.

The function of the student entry level as a prerequisite for planning is demonstrated in Figure 5–2, which shows the major components of the instructional process cycle. Note the direct relationship between the entry level and the subsequent learning experiences provided and the learning outcomes attained. It should also be recognized that this process, like that of lesson planning, is a never-ending cyclical one.

How do you, as a newly hired teacher in a school district, obtain all this information about the students, especially when you may not meet them until the day after school begins in the fall? One technique is to set up a series of conferences with the principal, school counselor, and vice-principal (if the school has one). Inquire about the general kinds of problems that the students have had in your particular grade level or specialization. Ask to examine any class composites on either school-district-sponsored or nationally administered achievement tests.

One critical fact to know is the students' reading achievement levels. If your potential students are two or three years below their grade level in reading, you will have to secure materials that can be comprehended by them. You may even have to prepare taped cassettes so that students with special reading problems can listen to and follow the written assignments.

In short, when you are assigned five or six different classes or preparations per day, you will not have much time to determine student entry levels. (At the start, you may even rely on intuition until you can make more accurate observations.) Perhaps one final method is to ask your colleagues for appropriate advice.

In a very general way, the identification of the student entry level is done by assigning groups of students to specific instructional units and courses and then monitoring their progress closely as they complete the material in a particular sequence. Also, some schools have perfected techniques by which to individualize instruction. On a more specific level, it is much more difficult to determine the entering level of students. The entry level is influenced by numerous interacting factors. However, knowing the entry level of all students is vital if the teacher is to help each pupil learn the material. In determining the entry level, the teacher asks the question, "For which concepts and generalizations do my students have the requisite knowledge, skills, and attitudes?"

In summary, the preliminary preparation stage plays a vital role in teacher decision-making. The choice of a particular lesson, the content selected, and the methodologies used are determined by the knowledge of broader *goals,* by the *subject matter,* and by the entry level of the *learners.* The lesson, in essence, represents the daily implementation of the teacher's interpretation of these important interacting elements.

LESSON PLANNING AND IMPLEMENTATION

Although there is no one best way to develop and present a lesson plan, the format presented here should help you meet the requirements for nearly all instructional activities. You may follow the format or amend it to suit your individual needs as you become proficient in lesson planning. A sketch of the recommended format is provided in Figure 5–3. An explanation of the various components of the format and an example of a completed plan are also provided in the following sections.

Lesson-Planning Elements

Section 1. Unit

As we discussed in the preceding text, daily lesson plans do not spring out of thin air. Rather, they relate to, and originate from, the broader goals and culminating experiences that are planned for the students. These major synthesizing goals are achieved by learners as a result of completing various *units* of study. Thus, the purpose of the first section of the lesson plan is to identify, in a sentence or two, the larger unit of instruction of which the particular lesson will be a part and in the context of which the lesson will be taught.

Section 2. Instructional Goal or Unit Objective

An instructional goal is an outcome that students should achieve on completion of the total unit of instruction. For example:

1. The goal of this unit is to present a variety of musical rhythmic features.
2. The goal of this unit is to classify needleleaf cuttings of selective trees.

An *instructional goal* provides focus and direction to the lesson. The *behavioral* or *performance objectives* that you write represent the more specific

FIGURE 5–3   A Model Lesson Plan Format

Teacher _____

Course Title _____

1. Unit _____

2. Instructional goal _____

3. Performance objectives _____

4. Rationale _____

5. Content	6. Instructional procedures
	(a) Focusing event (b) Teaching procedures (c) Formative check (d) Student participation (e) Closure

7. Evaluation procedures: _____

8. Materials and aids: _____

subskills or behaviors required to demonstrate attainment of the broader instructional goal. Whereas behavioral objectives specify measurable student outcomes, *an instructional goal usually is general and is stated in nonbehavioral terms.* Thus, although it is inappropriate to use verbs such as *know, value,* and *understand* in stating performance objectives, these words are not only acceptable *but preferable* at the instructional goal level of planning where they provide overall guidance and organization to the instructional process. (See also Chapter 2, page 39.)

It is possible that the instructional goal or unit objective will *not* be reached at the end of a single lesson. It represents an organizing element from which to develop as few as one, or as many as a dozen or more, specific performance objectives. Thus, attainment of the instructional goal may take from a few minutes to several days—even weeks—depending on the complexity of the topic and the type of learner change that is sought.

Section 3. Performance Objectives

Once you have selected your instructional goal, the next step is to identify the subordinate skills that your students must learn in order to achieve the goal. This process results in the identification of concepts, rules, and information that each student will need, along with the sequence of behavioral objectives that must be attained before mastering the overall goal.

Each lesson that you prepare should include one or more performance objectives, each consisting of one element of knowledge or skill that forms part of the broader instructional goal or unit objective. Performance objectives describe specifically what the student will be able to *do* as a consequence of the lesson. (Chapter 2 discusses performance objectives in detail.)

Beginning teachers frequently ask, "How many objectives should be included in a single plan?" Because there are so many variables in the instructional process—different outcomes, learners, teachers, and conditions—it is impossible to respond to this question by specifying any set number. In general, the average secondary student can grasp only four or five major ideas (and often only one) within a 45- to 50-minute period. On the average, therefore, the daily lesson plan for secondary classes should contain no more than four to five performance objectives. Lessons prepared for younger students should be even shorter, ranging from 5 to 20 minutes, and should focus on the attainment of perhaps a single performance objective.

Whereas it is permissible to use terms such as *to know, to value,* and *to understand* in writing instructional goals, performance objectives need to contain *active verbs* that explain the form that the understanding, knowing, and thinking will take. This characteristic of performance objectives enables them to be particularly effective aids to you in deciding exactly what will be taught, how it should be presented, what instructional strategy is appropriate, and what evaluation procedures should be used. In addition, it provides a vehicle for communicating precisely with others about the expected outcomes.

To assist students in achieving maximum performance, objectives need to be specific, to present a challenge, and to be "close at hand." Objectives that are perceived by the students as somewhat difficult do result in higher task achievement than those that are viewed as too easy, provided that the challenge is within reach and objectives that are close at hand can be attained within a reasonable time period. Dale H. Schunk and John P. Gaa (1981) observed that motivation is appreciably strengthened when the student perceives that the objective is within reach rather than distant. Finally, the inclusion of explicit performance objectives in a lesson plan should never inhibit you from capitalizing on these unexpected, serendipitous learning opportunities during lesson implementation.

During the instructional implementation stage itself, you will need to monitor student understanding and progress continuously, so that you do not forge ahead to the next objective before the student has mastered related subordinate skills. Such diagnostic activities serve the added purpose of preventing unnecessary duplication of instruction, which should be avoided because it fosters student boredom (unless, of course, the repetition is being used intentionally and sparingly to reinforce earlier learning).

Not all objectives need to be organized and presented in hierarchical fashion. In addition to *dependent* sequences, some learning outcomes can be arranged in *independent* patterns. To use the analogy of the construction of a building, although it is imperative to lay the floor of a house before raising its walls, it is not necessary to wait until the entire house has been completed before constructing the garage. In fact, it makes little difference whether the garage is built before, during, or after the construction of the main house, so long as the overall blueprint is kept in mind. Similarly, departures from the objectives are acceptable, so long as the instructional goals and course outlines are considered.

Many teachers find it useful to mark off items on the outline as soon as they have been attained by students. If used carefully, this technique saves a great deal of misunderstanding and confusion. It may be helpful to think of this outline as a list of subordinate principles of the central idea (the instructional goal).

Section 4. Rationale

A statement of rationale or purpose provides a brief justification of why you feel your students should learn what you are teaching. In preparing this section of your lesson plan, it is helpful to imagine a visitor to your classroom asking, "Why are you teaching this at this time?" The rationale would be your response.

One of the best reasons for including a rationale in your formal planning activities is that it will help to clarify the intent of the lesson for *you*, the teacher. The rationale will prompt you to think about both content and goals, separating the most significant aspects of subject matter from the ephemeral, and the most important learner objectives from the trivial. In turn, you will be more likely to communicate this sense of purpose to your students. When instructors know not only *what* they are trying to accomplish, but also *why* they are attempting to accomplish it, they are more likely to teach with enthusiasm and purpose, to stay on task, and to avoid tangents that confuse their learners.

Section 5. Content

The content section of the lesson plan provides an outline or a description of *what* is to be taught. At the minimum, it should include a "key word" checklist of the material to be presented, arranged in the order that you intend to teach it.

An important question that you will want to address at this juncture of the planning process is, "What is the most appropriate sequence to use in presenting the subject-matter content to my students?" Fortunately, you will have conducted a task analysis to determine the subskills and knowledge that your students must learn prior to reaching a particular unit objective or instructional goal. You will be able to answer this question without too much additional effort. The hierarchical analysis will tell you what entry behaviors are required before students can progress toward the intended outcomes. The analysis will also tell you which lower-level skills must precede higher-level ones and the order in which these subskills should be learned.

Section 6. Instructional Procedures

Whereas in the content section of the lesson plan the teacher lists *what* is to be taught, in the instructional procedures column the teacher states *how* it will be taught. Based on information provided in the five previous sections of the plan, the teacher identifies the strategies that will be most effective in leading students toward the attainment of each of the performance objectives.

Although for any one objective there are probably numerous procedures that teachers could employ, current research and knowledge about learning suggest that five major components should be included in a lesson to maximize student opportunity for learning. The five major elements of an effective instructional procedure on which we will elaborate are:

1. Focusing event
2. Teaching procedures
3. Formative check
4. Student participation
5. Closure

Focusing Event

A memorable lesson usually starts with a memorable beginning. All teachers have just a bit of Shakespeare in their blood. Every one of us has a touch of the dramatic, a flair for the unusual, a mad dream to "put on one they won't forget." It is with these theatrical notions that the stage for learning experiences is set. If the teacher fails to capture the interests and imaginations of the students, the remainder of the lesson is wasted. Irrespective of how significant the subject matter may seem to the instructor or of how capable the students are, if their interests are not stimulated early during the instructional sequence, they will not be motivated to develop an understanding of the content.

The main purposes of the focusing event are to provide *lesson orientation* and *learner motivation*. When presented effectively and creatively, the focusing event makes subsequent learning more efficient because students are prepared to engage actively in the lesson. A motivated learner acquires new knowledge and skills more readily than one who is not motivated. A student's desire to learn can be a mighty force in the instructional process. We need to capitalize on this powerful learning variable as we commence each day's activities.

A focusing event can take many forms: a clever story common to the students' experience, a humorous anecdote, an analogy that relates to the main concept of the lesson, a puzzling experiment or confusing situation, and even a "touch of magic" that encourages students to ask questions. It is important to remember, however, that the focusing event is not an end in itself. It should be used as a building block to influence positively the way your students approach the lesson. If a joke is chosen for the focusing event, it should be used because it relates clearly to the content of the lesson and should not be introduced at the start of the class period simply to relax or to entertain the students. Although a joke can serve effectively as a rapport builder (and rapport is certainly a very important element of teacher-learner interaction), when used as a focusing event, it should serve the additional function of readying the students for the lesson ahead.

To illustrate the use of the focusing event as a lesson "booster," two examples of the ways that a teacher may open a class period are provided.

Imagine you are a student in a sixth grade class and your teacher enters and says:

> "Let me read you a story from today's sports page. 'Reggie Jackson went to bat eight times in yesterday's double-header. He was walked twice, struck out once, flied out in deep center field once, doubled twice, tripled once, and hit a ninth inning grand slam home run in the second game.'"
>
> At this point, a little boy in the back of the room raises his hand and says, "All right!"
>
> The teacher responds, "All right!" Then the teacher states, "Class, we are going to work on fractions today. But first let's figure out what kind of fractions we can find from Reggie Jackson's games for yesterday."

In the preceding example, the mood or climate was established quickly by a focusing event that was relevant to the purpose of the lesson—learning about fractions. Let us look at one more example.* This time you are a student in a tenth-grade class and your teacher begins the lesson by saying:

> "This week we have been studying Southwest history and I have been thinking that there is one area that it would be fun to know a great deal more about. I would like to find out the origin of the names of the towns in our own state of Texas. For example, how many of you know where the name Austin came from?
>
> "Can you tell me why they named Austin Austin? . . . John.
>
> "Can you add anything? . . . Sue.
>
> "It's intriguing to know why towns were given their names, and today we are going to learn a great deal more about the names of towns. At the end of class today, each of you will demonstrate the ability to do research on the names of towns by sharing the origin of the names of two towns with the rest of the class and telling us where you found this information."

The way you present the focusing event is equally as important as its content. To stimulate student interest and motivation, the teacher must present it with a great deal of "gusto." Being enthusiastic does not require

---

*This example was provided by Dr. David Lundsgaard of Highline Public Schools and is reprinted with his written permission.

that you lead your students in a rousing cheer at the start of each period or that you perform a humorous monologue in the tradition of a stand-up comic. It does require, however, that you *believe* in what you are teaching and, even more important, that you *think positively about your learners* as individuals capable of significant growth in all dimensions—cognitive, affective, and psychomotor.

To conclude your focusing event, you may want to *verbalize* the performance objective(s) that you have specified in your lesson plan. Many teachers find that this technique provides a smooth transition to the next stage of the instructional sequence—the presentation of the day's lesson. The teacher, in other words, may use the focusing event to "grab the learner's attention" and then conclude it with a brief announcement of what the student is expected to be able to do at the end of the instructional activities.

It is crucial that, in stating the performance objectives, you translate what you have written on your plan into a form that is both understandable and interesting to your students. Indeed, the language used to specify a performance objective on paper is seldom identical to the language needed to express the objective orally in class. The way we communicate the objectives must correlate with the level of sophistication of our audience. For example, notice the difference between the way the following performance objective is written for a third grade lesson plan (developed for the *teacher's* use) and the way the teacher actually presents it to the third grade students:

> *Lesson plan objective:* Given ten problems, the student will demonstrate the ability to add two-digit numbers and will get nine out of ten correct.

> *Oral statement of objective:* Today we're going to learn to add two-digit numbers. Last week we worked on adding one-digit numbers. Adding two-digit numbers is a lot like what we did then.

Teaching Procedures

At this point in the instructional procedures section, the stage has been set for the lesson. Now it is time for the presentation of content—the "input" that will be provided to foster student learning. But *how* will you give students the intended information? This decision requires you to choose from a wide variety of teaching methods and possible learning experiences those that are most appropriate for the particular lesson.

Because there are so many variables that characterize any given classroom situation, decisions regarding teaching procedures are very complex. Figure 5–4 identifies some of the important components of such decision-making and their apparent interactions with the learning environment that must be considered.

As noted, there are at least four elements associated with the selection of a teaching procedure. Every teacher has a unique set of personal strengths, abilities, previous learnings, and experiences to rely on when selecting teaching methods. The strategies we choose should be ones that bring stu-

FIGURE 5–4   Variables Affecting the Choice of Instructional Procedures

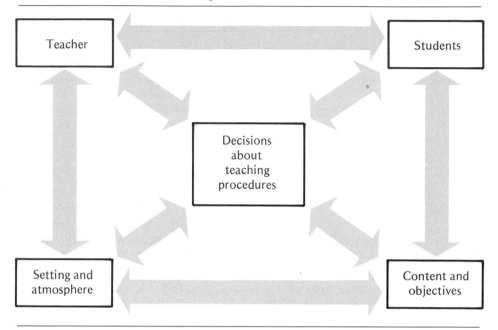

dent success. This does not mean that the teacher should hesitate to try new methods and techniques. Even though your own preferences influence your methodology choices, you should continually seek opportunities to develop your teaching skills in additional directions. With practice, you will feel confident about your ability to use an extensive selection of teaching methods. We are very familiar with the traditional teacher excuse: "That teaching method doesn't match my personality." Such an often-heard statement simply means that the teacher has decided to quit learning. The emphasis of modern curricula is on highly interactive instructional methodologies, not static principles.

The methodology used to impart content also must match the students' experiences. Just as every teacher brings unique skills and preferences to the learning situation, so too every learner enters the classroom with a special combination of likes, dislikes, interests, values, abilities, and needs. It is doubtful that any two students will respond identically to you or to the lesson. Thus it is essential to give careful consideration to these student variables when making decisions about teaching methods. If a student interacts comfortably with peers in a small-group setting but stutters uncontrollably when asked to stand up in front of the entire class, the sensitive instructor will select teaching methods and learning experiences that help the student attain the intended outcomes without experiencing personal frustration or embarrassment.

As we have discussed previously, all lesson planning activities have purposes. The purposes—the desired ends of the learning experiences—involve the goals, the related performance objectives, and the subject matter of the lesson. Obviously, decisions about appropriate methodology must correspond to these other planning elements. If the desired learning is in the affective domain, different methods will be needed than if a psychomotor skill is being sought. Although small-group discussions may be appropriate in helping students clarify their personal values and be tolerant of the feelings and attitudes of others, discussions are not very effective in teaching students a new gymnastics event.

Still another factor that influences the choice of teaching procedures is that of the physical environment, including such related elements as time, place, and context of the learning situation. To use a rather extreme example, a ninth grade biology teacher in Jacksonville, Florida, where abundant marine life can be observed and numerous natural museums visited, will want to plan different types of field trips than a ninth grade biology teacher in Terre Haute, Indiana. Because instructional procedures are often dependent on *where* the learning is to take place, the teacher always needs to ask the question, "Is this environment the best one for the method planned?"

Formative Check

One of the most vital elements of *any* lesson is the formative check, an activity that allows the teacher to assess student understanding up to the point of the check and to make adjustments to the lesson in accordance with this information.

Actually, it is slightly erroneous to imply that the teacher should check for student understanding *after* the content of the lesson has been presented. In reality, formative checking is a continuous process that needs to be done throughout the instructional process from the moment you first introduce a topic for the day (for example, the focusing event) to the time you bring the lesson to closure.

Just as the skillful weather forecaster constantly monitors the movement of fronts, so too the effective teacher conscientiously monitors student understanding and progress by means of the formative check. The resulting data permit the teacher to adjust the lesson to compensate for any confusion, gaps, or advances in learning that were not anticipated during the planning phase.

Formative checks vary widely in their specificity and level of formality. Sometimes it is most appropriate to conduct the formative check on a one-to-one basis, and at other times it is best done in small-group settings; some lessons require written tests, and others call for verbal question-and-answer periods. Curriculum designers, especially developers of programmed instructional materials, frequently rely extensively on formative quiz items to direct the learning sequence. The student, in such cases, cannot progress to the next learning activity until the preceding step has been successfully completed; this is usually demonstrated by answering correctly a true-or-false, multiple-choice, or fill-in-the-blanks test item.

Other formative checks are markedly less structured. For example, on some days you may want to initiate a class session by finding out in an informal way the degree to which students remember the content and outcomes of the previous lesson. You may, for instance, begin by saying: "Please summarize what we learned about the incident at Harpers Ferry yesterday. . . . John?"

The use of formative checks helps ensure that students are not pushed to new topics and objectives before achieving success in the subskills that make attainment of the later task possible. Whatever their format, formative checks help the teacher avoid situations in which learning problems are not identified until the *end* of an entire unit or sequence. Sadly, situations in which students feel "hopelessly lost" and hence consider themselves learning "failures" occur too frequently in education. Many of these problems can be prevented if we conduct frequent and relevant formative checks and then *use* this information to make appropriate changes in our teaching procedures. Sometimes a formative check will alert us to the need for remediation or for enrichment, and sometimes the information will suggest that more student practice is required to foster internalization of the concepts being studied. We realize that formative checks may be difficult to practice in some situations, but these will be the exceptions, not the rule.

Student Participation

Another powerful element in the teaching process is that of student practice accompanied by feedback of success. The purposes of such practice are many. First, a practice session can serve as a *formative check of student understanding*. Second, the *degree that learning is retained* is highly related to the degree to which the student was given an opportunity to practice that learning. Third, student *learning can be enhanced* greatly with practical activities that relate directly to the objectives of the lesson. The activities give relevance and practicality to what may otherwise seem (to the students) to be a series of meaningless words. Finally, student practice, when followed by feedback of progress, can be very informative and *intrinsically rewarding for the student*. It allows the learner to see that "I'm able to *do* this!"

Student practice has to be carefully planned. Requiring students to "fill out a worksheet" or to "do a homework assignment" does not guarantee that the activity will be meaningful or constructive. Practice, unfortunately, is one of the elements of instruction that frequently is abused, particularly in those situations in which the teacher employs it simply as a method of "killing time" by keeping students occupied with "busy work." Even worse, some teachers use student practice as a tool for punishment—for example, they may threaten: "If you don't quiet down, I'm going to assign you extra homework tonight."

In contrast to these forms of abuse and misuse, student practice should be thought of as an integral component of the lesson, and students need to know that you view it as an important, rather than peripheral, part of the learning process. One of the best ways to communicate this belief is by giving students feedback, or knowledge of results, regarding their practice activities. In other words, you conduct a formative check on the practice and report the results to the students so they realize that what they do during the practice is of high priority.

One additional note should be made about student practice. Prior to being asked to perform a particular task or to demonstrate their understanding of a concept via a practice activity, students need to know precisely what it is that the teacher expects them to do. This requires that the teacher *describe the assignment clearly* and *model the correct procedures* as a means of providing students with a good example to follow. For example, after a teacher has *explained* "how to multiply fractions," it is imperative to *demonstrate* "how to multiply fractions" by using the chalkboard, the microcomputer, overhead projector, or bundles of sticks. The old adage "a picture is worth a thousand words" has never been more apt. Once the modeling has been completed and the teacher has conducted a short formative check to assess student understanding, *then* the learners are ready to practice the assigned task.

Closure

Public speakers are often advised that when they deliver their talks they should adhere to the following formula:

1. Tell them (the audience) what you're going to tell them.
2. Tell them.
3. Tell them what you've told them.

This advice has some merit for teachers as well. The focusing event, including the statement of the objective(s), serves as a way of telling students what you are going to help them to learn. The content and methodology components of the lesson serve as a means of helping them to attain the intended outcomes. Lesson *closure* serves to synthesize and summarize all the elements of the lesson at the end.

An effective closing puts the "icing on the cake." As the finale of the learning experience, it not only provides a vehicle for *summarizing* the day's lesson but, more significantly, allows the teacher to *single out those aspects that are of greatest importance*. Closure solidifies the whole lesson by reinforcing what has just been learned, while simultaneously telling students that "now we're ready to move on. You've got it!"

The techniques that you use in bringing a lesson to closure often are as critical as the content of the closure itself. Whenever possible, we recommend that you design closing sequences that actively engage your learners. Ask *them* to identify the main points of the lesson—for example, "What have we been trying to learn today?" Request *them* to suggest meaningful relationships between what the class has learned previously and what it has learned today.

Sometimes, of course, you may not want to bring a lesson to closure, such as when you wish to challenge students to pursue a special research project. On the other hand, some lessons may require the inclusion of three or more separate closures. Lesson closure, like all other aspects of the teaching process, needs to be adapted skillfully to the particular learning situation. Although at the outset it may seem comforting to follow "the perfect prescription for lesson excellence," we will never be able to identify such an all-encompassing system. With teaching, nothing is cast in cement—nor would we want it to be.

Section 7. Evaluation Procedures

Student evaluation, as we are defining it here, entails post-instruction assessment of student performance. It is that stage in the instructional sequence at which the teacher determines to what degree the learner has attained the anticipated outcomes of the lesson. These measurement activities frequently are referred to as student *summative evaluation*.

At the end of the lesson, a clear picture of how well students have mastered the stated objectives should emerge. If the teacher finds a discrepancy between what was intended and what has been achieved, then decisions must be made regarding where additional instruction is needed.

The evaluation procedures should describe in detail the testing technique to be followed in evaluating student summative behavior. These procedures must relate directly to the behavioral objectives stipulated at the beginning of the lesson, including the conditions, content, and criteria that are to be employed to assess student mastery.

A word of caution is in order about evaluation procedures. *Be sure you measure the behavior you have taught students to perform.* Congruence among stated objectives, instruction, and evaluation procedures is very important. It is much fairer to expect students to behave in ways that closely duplicate how they have been taught to behave. Some teachers are notorious for writing clear statements of desired terminal performance, but testing students on other, sometimes even unrelated, behaviors. When this happens, instead of channeling their energies to learn the most important material and skills, students are left in a state of confusion and generalized anxiety about course requirements and testing procedures.

The "condition" element of the performance objective is commonly misconstrued by teachers in planning for evaluation. The *examination* situation needs to parallel closely the *practice situations* in which the learning has taken place. For example, if a student is expected to learn how to swing a golf club, the appropriate testing situation will involve the actual swinging of a club, rather than exclusive reliance on a paper-and-pencil test!

Not all lessons require that the students demonstrate attainment of the behavioral objective—that is, by their performance on the test—on the exact day that instruction is provided. It is hard to imagine a classroom situation in which the teacher would not collect *formative* evaluation data on a daily basis. But *summative* evaluation may be postponed to a more appropriate time, such as when the teacher wants to combine several objectives to show their cumulative relationship before testing student terminal behavior.

Irrespective of when you implement the evaluation procedures, it is advisable to include the recommended procedures within each day's plan. This strategy will help to remind you of the one-to-one correspondence that should exist between the lesson intentions and the measurement of the intended outcomes.

One final point should be mentioned before discussing materials and aids. Although the examples given in this chapter tend to be consistent with a behavioral objective–based curriculum, we recognize that some, if not all, of the important learning may take weeks, months, or even years. Thus, all learning is not neatly divided into daily lesson plans. As you know from the presentation on taxonomies, the higher cognitive levels and most affective levels take a long time to assimilate.

Section 8. Materials and Aids

The materials and aids section of your plan should provide a checklist of everything you expect to use to teach the lesson. The list should include audiovisual equipment, handouts, books, microcomputer and software, and lab facilities—in short, anything that the student does not have that you must supply.

The Medium Is the Massage (McLuhan and Fiore, 1967) is certainly relevant to our discussion. Indeed, the *way* that ideas and skills are presented may have more impact on the learning process than their content.

Although much could be mentioned about the importance of selecting materials and aids that will foster learning, we do not go into detail on this point here. Suffice it to say that it is essential for the teacher not only to identify the types of audiovisual and print media that will enhance the learning environment, but also to *prepare for the use of the selected aids.* You will want to take all of the preliminary steps necessary to ensure that the materials are ordered in ample time and that the equipment required is available for your use (and in good operating condition) prior to the initiation of the lesson.

A Rationale for Post-Lesson Evaluation

Evaluation occurs on a number of levels in the development and implementation of instructional plans. We already have discussed some of these evaluative activities—namely, the formative and summative assessment of student achievement.

Evaluation occurs on another level—that of the lesson itself. At the conclusion of every class session, it is useful for teachers to ask themselves a series of questions about the effectiveness of the plan—for example, Were the objectives realistic and appropriate? Did the instructional methods work? For which learners and to what degree? What components of the lesson succeeded? What aspects could be improved? The answers to these and other inquiries help the teacher to identify difficulties experienced by learners and to relate these problems to specific elements of the lesson.

A lesson plan should be an *emerging document*. Thus the initial creation of a plan is only the *first* stage of its development. After initial use, the *actual* classroom conditions that account for learner entry level, teaching procedures, and learner outcomes need to be compared to the *planned* situation. The resulting data allow for refinement and recycling to make the lesson plan more effective as an instructional tool. In summary, the teacher *continually evaluates* the lesson each time it is implemented and always attempts to improve the techniques and approaches employed.

No plan is a magical elixir that will guarantee intended learning. It can only be as effective as the instructor using it. The critical activity for you as a planner is to identify the type of format that will be most helpful to you in facilitating the learning process. The format you choose should be easy for you to use—a tool to lend direction to the lesson, but not a manuscript from which to read verbatim statements.

OTHER LESSON FORMATS

To complement the lesson-planning format introduced earlier in this chapter, Figures 5–5 through 5–8 illustrate some of the many other options that are available. Some of these styles will be more applicable to your teaching situation than others.

In selecting a format, the teacher needs to consider (1) the subject or content that is taught; (2) the types of instructional methods the teacher is able to use; and (3) the interests and learning styles of the students. Also, you may use several different forms of lesson plans in any one unit or module of instruction.

As you examine the following lesson plan formats, you will quickly observe that each contains a set of common elements: topic, goal or rationale, objectives, and procedures. Furthermore, you will note that each format is logically structured and developed, qualities that are highly critical, as you usually will be introducing or expanding concepts as you teach. It is imperative that a lesson build systematically and logically, so that the learners likewise build systematic and logical study skills.

FIGURE 5–5   Weekly Lesson Plan Format 2

Identify goals _____

Specify objectives _____

Taxonomic levels _____

Sequence objectives (process) _____

    Independent _____

    Dependent _____

Select materials (content) _____

    Textbooks assignments _____

    Laboratory or computer activity _____

    Supplemental materials _____

Prepare hierarchy (content) _____

    Arrange logically _____

    Rearrange for learning _____
      Pre-entry skills
      Entry skills
      New skills
      Apply new skills
      Relate skills
      Review

Formative test _____

Review as needed _____

Report _____

The format in Figure 5–5 encourages the instructor to plan for the inclusion of an array of objectives in a sequential order. Further, this format allows a teacher to build a larger unit of material to be planned, studied, and completed.

FIGURE 5–6   Lesson Plan Format 3

INQUIRY/PROBLEM SOLVING

Subject _____

Teacher _____

Goal _____

Topic for this lesson _____

Objectives _____

_____

_____

Procedures or Steps

1. Problem identification _____

_____

_____

2. Data collection _____

_____

3. Formulation of hypothesis or assumption(s) _____

_____

4. Analysis of data or materials _____

_____

5. Testing hypotheses or assumptions _____

_____

6. Conclusion or judgment _____

_____

This format is easily adapted to any inquiry-oriented lesson.

FIGURE 5–7   Lesson Plan Format 4: Outline of Key Questions
or Key Statements

Unit topic _____

Instructional goal _____

Objectives _____

_____

_____

Procedures for recitation or discussion _____

_____

_____

Key questions

1. _____

2. _____

3. _____

4. _____

   Summary _____

   _____

Key statements

1. _____

2. _____

3. _____

4. _____

   Summary _____

   _____

Conclusion _____

_____

This lesson plan format may be particularly suitable when questioning and/or teacher-led discussion will be the primary learner activities. Further, the addition of "Key statements" reflects the research evidence provided by J. T. Dillon ("Cognitive Correspondence Between Question/Statement and Response," *American Educational Research Journal* 19:1982, 540–551; and "Do Your Questions Promote or Prevent Thinking?" *Learning* 11:1982, 56–57, 59). Dillon suggests that teachers' statements rather than questions will promote more higher-level student responses. (See Chapter 6 for the discussion.)

FIGURE 5–8   Lesson Plan Format 5

Goal _____	
Objectives _____	
Cognitive Levels _____	
Materials _____	

Set (initiating or motivating experience)	Questions
Purpose	Activities
Instructional model	Formative check
Closure	Guided practice
	Independent practice

Advocates of Madeline Hunter's ITIP often illustrate this lesson plan as useful.

THE KAPLAN MATRIX

One of the special challenges facing the teacher is the need to develop lessons that adapt to the specific skills and abilities of students. Nowhere is the challenge more pronounced than in situations involving the gifted student or the student with specific learning disabilities. To assist educators in this critical area, Sandra Kaplan (1979) has created a matrix that *extends* the basic curriculum, thus allowing the instructor to plan appropriate activities for the student's individual level of learning.

The format in Table 5–1 is a sample of the Kaplan matrix. The content (unit objectives) is listed down the left side. The differentiated processes are identified across the top. In each box, the teacher develops an activity or assignment *and* specifies the outcome that aligns the thinking process and objective or content. Through this extended format, the teacher develops a wide array of alternatives to the regular curriculum that can be matched to each student's readiness level.

The Kaplan matrix looks complex but it is not. The behavioral objectives describe student activities that must be performed. We suggest preparing a Kaplan matrix for any activity-oriented topic or laboratory.

MICRO-TEACHING

We now turn our attention to the topic of micro-teaching, a technique that affords both beginning and advanced teachers excellent opportunities to *plan* and *practice* a wide array of new instructional strategies. Our goal is not only to introduce you to micro-teaching, but also to provide instructions to guide you in applying this very widespread teacher-education method. By the end of this part of the chapter, you will be able to plan and present a micro-teaching lesson for school-age children or for peers in your education classes. In subsequent chapters, as numerous teaching methods are described, you will be encouraged to develop and implement additional micro-teaching lessons so as to experience and experiment with various instructional techniques or methods.

What Is Micro-Teaching?

Micro-teaching is a scaled-down sample of teaching. It is essentially an opportunity for pre-service teachers and experienced professionals to develop and/or improve specific teaching skills with a small group of students (4–6) by means of brief (4–15 minutes) single-concept lessons. These lessons are recorded on videotape for reviewing, refining, and analyzing very specific teaching processes. Micro-teaching is a technique that allows the teacher to place small aspects of teaching under the microscope.

More specifically, micro-teaching is an empirically tested procedure that allows one to

1. Practice a new technique, strategy, or procedure in a supportive environment
2. Prepare and deliver a lesson with a reduced amount of anxiety
3. Test new ways to approach a topic or lesson
4. Develop very specific delivery techniques such as introducing a topic, giving an assignment, or explaining an evaluation procedure
5. Be evaluated both by *others* and by *oneself*
6. Gain immediate feedback of one's performance by viewing the video playback

TABLE 5–1   The Kaplan Matrix for Extending the Curriculum

Content or concepts	Behavioral or Performance Objectives and Related Student Activities					
	Knowledge	Compre-hension	Application	Analysis	Synthesis	Evaluation
Volcanoes	List facts about Mount Saint Helens devastation	Compare Mount Saint Helens to the volcanoes of Hawaii	How could we use the piles of volcanic ash?	What do the people near Mount Saint Helens feel?	Make a volcano model for our class	Are all things about Mount Saint Helens bad? Why?
Minerals and Gems	List the important gems found in the Northeast	Contrast the hardness of the minerals found in the Northeast	Field test the hardness of ten minerals	What would happen if the government imposed tougher mining regulations?	Grow crystals of various shapes and colors	What do you think of people who hoard gems? Why?
Space Travel	Name all the people who have gone to the moon	Compare the Russian space program to the U.S. program	If you were an astronaut, what would you study about space?	What do you think would happen if we found life elsewhere?	Make a rocket and fly it	What are some of the negative things about being an astronaut? Why?
Weather and Climate	Name the different types of clouds	Contrast the climates of the Southwest and the Southeast	Chart the amount of rainfall for the next week	What effect did El Chiconal have on the world's weather?	Create a wind generator	Which climate best suits your lifestyle? Why?

Adapted with the permission of Sandra Kaplan.

7. Risk little but gain much in valuable experience
8. Subdivide complex teaching interactions into related elements
9. Manage one's own behavior in a systematic manner

The micro-teaching approach to developing teacher competencies is not without its drawbacks, and two questions have been raised about its effectiveness. (1) How does one apply the effects to real classes? and (2) Does it matter significantly that college peers are not really authentic students? But micro-teaching has considerable merit in its own right because, outside of the actual classroom setting, micro-teaching provides the closest simulation of teaching yet devised. As a future educator you will want to strive for excellent, not merely satisfactory, performance, so we encourage you to practice your skills—with the constant goal of self-improvement. The Far West Educational Laboratory report shows that micro-teaching is a powerful way to change teaching behaviors (Borg and associates, 1970). Janice Bertram Vaughn (1983) provided evidence that it did not matter whether college peers or students from the appropriate grade level made up the "micro-class." The results are equally positive and beneficial.

Micro-teaching has the basic objective of subdividing multifaceted teaching acts into simpler components, so that the task of learning new instructional skills will be more manageable. When prospective or in-service teachers engage in a micro-teaching lesson, they focus on a specific aspect of teaching until a satisfactory minimum competency of that skill has been developed. If a specific skill is not mastered, then a reteach session is scheduled to perfect it. The teacher proceeds to new skills only after success has been achieved with each preceding one.

Before developing any micro-teaching lesson plans, however, several considerations need to be mentioned. First, *not every topic, concept, or process automatically lends itself to every teaching method.* Each concept needs to be analyzed carefully to determine whether or not it is appropriate for the assigned skill or for the specified time allotted to conduct the micro-class.

Second, *in situations where it is not possible to obtain school-age students for the teaching sessions, a modified form of micro-teaching may be used.* For example, students enrolled in your education classes may be recruited to play the role of the school students. Also, because of a limited amount of class time, your reteach sessions may need to be kept to a minimum.

Cognitive *skills* (in the form of single-concept lessons) as well as *processes* may be perfected through micro-teaching. The notion of single-concept lessons will be addressed later in this chapter. But first we need to define what we mean by *processes* of instruction.

Instructional processes concern how you do a specific teaching act. Some illustrations of processes that you may want to learn through the micro-teaching technique include

1. Introducing a new topic or concept
2. Giving an assignment to a class
3. Specifying how the students will be evaluated in the course

4. Asking questions
5. Conducting recitation sessions
6. Tutoring an individual or small group
7. Leading a discussion
8. Practicing inquiry and problem-solving skills
9. Providing summaries of student statements
10. Closing a discussion or a class period

The list is far from complete. You may think of many others. What is comforting to the learner (or prospective teacher) is that micro-teaching allows one to practice a skill in "safety." It is a simulated form of teaching. The reality is there, but not *all* of the realism of a classroom. With the micro-teaching approach, you can isolate one tiny segment of the totality of teaching and practice it until the process is mastered. Few teachers have the opportunity to practice and master a skill before using it in a classroom.

Preparing for Micro-Teaching

Micro-teaching is not just "getting up front and teaching." The technique requires that you first prescribe carefully selected behaviors that you want to practice. As in "regular" daily lessons, the objective(s) must be carefully specified. Furthermore, a set of criteria must be established by which to judge how effectively you were able to accomplish the desired skills, processes, or behaviors. The whole idea of micro-teaching is to *help you improve* your teaching techniques through practice, feedback, and evaluation.

Usually, micro-teaching sessions are only five to ten minutes in length. To conduct your lesson, you will need a portable videotape recorder, one TV camera, and one microphone for a videotape recorder (VTR) setup. This requires that you plan for at least one or two technicians to help you operate the needed equipment. These may be students or your peers in class. If a VTR setup is not available, use a cassette audiotape recorder, which will be nearly as effective.

At this point, you should be able to combine all of the competencies learned in the preparation of a micro-teaching lesson plan based on content from your major discipline. Here is an instructional objective for you to use in designing and demonstrating your lesson.

> Within the prescribed time limitation and focusing on a prescribed process or teaching technique, teach a preselected concept to either a peer group of approximately five students or to five "real" students. The members of your mini-class must achieve the performance objective as it is stated in the lesson plan or you must accomplish the teaching process that you have specified in the plan.

To accomplish this objective, the following tasks should be performed for each micro-teaching session. You should

1. Prepare a lesson plan, using the suggested format. We recommend an abbreviated version of the lesson-plan format described in the early part of this chapter.

2. Make two copies of your lesson plan, one for your group leader and one for your own use while micro-teaching.
3. Teach the lesson to the student group within the time limitation stipulated for the particular micro-teaching session.
4. Evaluate student achievement or your correct use of the process you tested by using a stated performance objective and a specific evaluation device.
5. Play the role of a micro-session student when not teaching, operate the recording equipment, or evaluate other micro-teaching performances.
6. Critique in writing, by using an evaluation instrument, the teaching of the other students in the group. Each group should provide an immediate oral critique following each micro-lesson.
7. Critique your own lesson after viewing and listening to the recording of the teaching. You may want to use a critique checklist or other evaluation criteria to aid you in your self-evaluation (see Figure 5–10).
8. Reteach the lesson, time permitting, to master the new technique.

Deciding on Micro-Lesson Content and Lesson-Plan Format

One of the most critical decisions you will need to make in preparing for your lesson is how to *narrow your topic*. The purpose of micro-teaching is not to demonstrate everything there is to know about effective instruction; rather, it is to focus directly on one aspect of the teaching process at a time. To accomplish this, you will need to select a *single subconcept* from the discipline of your choice and to develop a lesson aimed at helping your micro-session students learn this concept in the short span of five to ten minutes.

Initially, making decisions about the content to be covered in a single-concept lesson is often difficult for the beginning teacher. It demands that you have a strong command of your discipline and the ability to analyze it carefully and to isolate those concepts, principles, rules, and facts that are *most significant*. The work of experts in the various disciplines can greatly assist you with this task. Of course, textbooks, curriculum guides, course outlines, and models or collections of sequenced performance objectives also may be useful tools to employ in this context.

Once you have selected a single concept as the basis for your micro-lesson, the next step is to develop a *limited number* (perhaps only one) of performance objectives. That is, you need to determine what behavior the micro-student is to manifest in relation to the concept and to what extent he or she is expected to recall, recognize, or apply the concept.

To aid you in the development of your single-concept lesson for micro-teaching, we suggest that you follow the organizational format for lesson planning described previously in this chapter. Instead of using the format in toto, however, you will need to make careful "editing" decisions so that the resulting plan will be manageable within the limits of the micro-setting. For example, you may not have enough time to allow for extensive "student

FIGURE 5–9   Micro-Teaching Planning Checklist

Activities	Check When Completed
1. Student entry level known	_____
2. Unit title, instructional goal/unit objective and performance objective(s) properly written	_____
3. Focus is on a *single* concept	_____
4. Rationale clearly stated	_____
5. Content determined	_____
6. Instructional procedures specified	_____
7. Micro-session evaluation or critique form developed	_____
8. Audio-visual materials and special instructional items prepared	_____
9. Two copies (original for instructor; copy for self) of lesson plan completed	_____
10. Lesson delivered and peer evaluations given	_____
11. Tape replayed	_____
12. Self-critique conducted	_____
13. Decision made about whether to reteach	_____

practice." Although the planning procedures recommended previously will be generally applicable, they may need to be abbreviated to fit your particular objective(s) and circumstances. The ultimate criterion of your plan's effectiveness is: *Does it work for you during the actual implementation of the lesson?*

Micro-Teaching Planning Checklist

Since micro-teaching entails much preparation (just as does systematic teaching), the checklist in Figure 5–9 is provided to assist you in this important planning process.

Micro-Teaching Feedback

Once you have completed your lesson and have received immediate verbal and written feedback from your micro-students, you will be ready for what may be the most significant aspect of the technique—your own self-evaluation. The replay of your micro-teaching sessions is potentially of great value in helping you to identify strengths and weaknesses in your use of particular teaching approaches and strategies. The playback (learner feedback) is aimed toward helping you become the best possible teacher. The replay of your micro-teaching gives you an approximation of how you appear, sound, and interact with your students.

In the interest of effectiveness and efficiency, you should view the video recording as soon as possible after the actual micro-teaching session, preferably immediately, but certainly no later than 24 hours after you have taught your lesson.

While observing the replay of your micro-session, it is helpful to use an evaluation form that reflects appropriate criteria by which to judge the effectiveness of your teaching skills. The micro-teaching evaluation form in Figure 5–10 may help you design similar evaluative instruments to assess your own lessons.

PLANNING WITH MICROCOMPUTERS

It is fitting to close Chapter 5 with a short discussion of that apparent wizard of modern technology, the microcomputer, for it is emerging as a powerful aid to lesson preparation and instruction. Without question, microcomputers already have had a significant impact on the classroom, and it is mandatory to discuss their potential.

Technology never has been and never will be the panacea for our educational needs; the microcomputer will not replace the teacher as the basic instructional planner or provider. But insightful educators find that the computer can improve lesson planning and the management of instruction and thereby enhance the teaching and learning process. We will review how the microcomputer can be used (1) as an instructional tool, (2) with teacher- or student-made software, and (3) as an aid for cataloguing lesson plans and software.

The Microcomputer as an Instructional Tool

Computer-assisted instruction (CAI) enables a lesson to be delivered through a computer program without constant teacher interaction. Harper Gaushell (1982) noted that CAI takes one or more of the following forms:

1. *Tutorial programs* present the student with material, followed by a set of questions concerning that information. It is assumed that the pupil has not had prior knowledge of the subject matter. Tutorial programs may be used either in conjunction with or independent of the classroom teacher.
2. *Drill and practice* help ensure that the learner attains complete understanding of concepts that have been taught.
3. *Simulations* provide for the study of events beyond the normal capability of our senses, such as events that occur too quickly or too slowly for us to perceive. For example, the internal operation of an automobile engine,

FIGURE 5–10   A Sample Micro-Teaching Evaluation Form

Name of Micro-Teacher _____

Class Hour _____

Tape No. _____

SCALE

(Needs improvement)	1	2	3	4	5	(Very effective)

I. Lesson Plan
Unit and instructional goal _____

Objective _____

Rationale _____

Focus on single key concept _____

Distinction between content
   and procedures _____

Sequencing of lesson _____

Evaluation procedures specified _____

II. Management and Delivery
Focusing event _____

Teacher-student eye contact _____

Pacing of lesson _____

Monitoring and adjusting _____

Teacher verbal behaviors _____

Teacher nonverbal behaviors _____

Lesson closure _____

Use of materials _____

III. Evaluation (knowing that the
objective was reached)
Evaluation plan followed
   as specified _____

Students performed tasks
   or met stated objective _____

Teacher and students know whether
   objectives were reached _____

General comments _____

_____

_____

which normally operates at very high speeds, may be studied through a simulation of its operation.

Higher-level thinking skills are also promoted through technological advances such as *display devices* in which the computer is used to organize raw data and present information in the form of graphs and charts. *Calculations* can be made that offer relief from the drudgery associated with repetitive mathematical exercises (which sometimes preclude the learning of more important conceptual objectives). *Information retrieval* is made accessible from large library data bases, which provide vast amounts of material not otherwise available to the student. *Word and music processing,* which promote writing and musical composition, are easily programmed.

Teachers of the handicapped have discovered another major advantage of the microcomputer as an instructional tool: computer technology can enable students with speaking, writing, or visual disabilities to communicate at levels that would have been impossible only a few years ago.

Teacher- and Student-Made Software

As school personnel prepare to purchase computer hardware, they must ask the corollary question: "How will we acquire the necessary software?" Adequate planning for computer technology demands that educators conduct a careful needs assessment and plan for the provision of software *prior* to allocating resources for the acquisition of hardware.

Although it may be argued that local production of programs is often inefficient (a similar product already may have been developed elsewhere), locally developed programs do create interested and enthusiastic teachers and students. Another advantage of teacher-made software is that a product developed by a classroom teacher is more likely to relate directly to instructional objectives, course content, and student reading and language skill levels. External products, however sophisticated, may miss the mark in each of these important areas causing frustration and feelings of failure.

When students are involved in computer course development, they too learn quickly that it is not really difficult to program. More significant, they are given an ideal opportunity to exercise effective interpersonal abilities (they need to communicate closely with the teacher about the lesson's objectives and intended audience) and to practice organizational skills. We think of this phase as a new "art form" for students.

Cataloguing Computer Software for Future Use

Just as the organized teacher carefully maintains files of each previous year's curriculum goals, lesson plans, and examinations, the teacher who collects or produces programs needs to catalogue them. Such systematic efforts help ensure their later accessibility and enable good programs to be distributed to other educational settings. The computer itself, of course, provides an excellent vehicle for this cataloguing process.

In conclusion, we urge you to consider seriously the significance of the microcomputer as a powerful force to assist you as a planner of instruction. Our "real world" already is computerized. As a tool for lesson planning and instruction, the computer can be one of our greatest assets. It contributes yet another medium to the teacher's already diverse repertoire of planning and teaching methods—and decision-making skills.

CONCLUSION

Our major intent in this chapter has been to illustrate several guiding principles that can assist you in organizing initial lesson plans. We have by no means described all of the available options. Furthermore, each instructor or school district may have its own required format. If that is the case, you will at least have had some experiences that should allow you to adapt easily. We also recognize that your instructor may not use micro-teaching in the conduct of the course.

Let us now address a very important technique that will probably involve the largest proportion of your decision-making time—the art of questioning, which is the subject of Chapter 6. But first, complete the formative evaluation that follows.

FORMATIVE EVALUATION
Lesson Planning

1. What are the three components of pre-lesson preparation that should precede the process of designing and using a lesson plan?
2. Match the following elements of lesson planning with their definitions by inserting the correct letter in the spaces provided.

_____ Unit	(a) An outline of how the lesson will be taught.
_____ Instructional goal	(b) A description of what the students will be able to do as a consequence of the lesson.
_____ Performance objective	(c) Name of the larger element of instruction of which the particular lesson is a part.
_____ Rationale	(d) Checklist of everything (for example, handouts) the teacher will need to supply to students during the lesson.
_____ Content	
_____ Instructional procedures	(e) An outcome students are to achieve on completion of the total unit of instruction.
_____ Evaluation procedures	(f) Post-instruction assessment of student performance.

_____ Materials

(g) A brief justification of why students should learn what is being taught.

(h) An outline or description of what is to be taught.

3. Identify three sources of educational goal statements that you may find useful in the planning process.

4. Which of the following are goal statements (match with a *G*) and which are objectives (match with an *O*)?

_____ (a) Citizenship training will be learned in this unit.

_____ (b) Each student will list the names of the state's governor and attorney general.

_____ (c) The proper safety habits will be taught in this chemistry class.

_____ (d) Please determine the mass of each of the five samples to the nearest gram.

_____ (e) We will learn Picasso's secrets to success in this art class.

_____ (f) Beside each color on the wheel, you will print in the space the complementary color.

5. What are the two main purposes of the focusing event?

6. An activity that allows teachers to assess student understanding and to make adjustments to the lesson is called a

_____ _____

7. How do formative and summative evaluations differ?

8. List at least four different examples that you might develop as focusing events in teaching the concept of "micro-teaching."

9. Which of the following is not necessarily true of teacher- or student-made computer programs?

(a) Invention is stimulated

(b) Time is saved

(c) It relates to specific objectives and student skill levels

(d) Teachers are likely to reuse and adapt them

(e) Enhances the developer's computer literacy

10. True/False. The Kaplan Matrix for extending the curriculum is based on Bloom's Taxonomy.

RESPONSES
Lesson Planning

1. Goals; content; student entry level.

2. _(c)_ Unit   _(h)_ Content
   _(e)_ Instructional goal   _(a)_ Instructional procedures
   _(b)_ Performance objective   _(f)_ Evaluation procedures
   _(g)_ Rationale   _(d)_ Materials

3. State, district, and school goals; curriculum guides; needs assessments.

4. _G_ (a)   _O_ (d)
   _O_ (b)   _G_ (e)
   _G_ (c)   _O_ (f)

5. Lesson orientation; learner motivation.

6. Formative check.

7. Formative checking is a continuous process that needs to be done throughout the instructional process. The resulting data permit teachers to readjust the lesson to compensate for

any confusion, gaps, or advances in learning that were not anticipated during the planning phase. Summative evaluation entails post-instruction assessment of student performance. It is that stage in the instructional sequence at which the teacher determines to what degree the learner has attained the anticipated outcomes of the lesson.

8. The response to item 8 should be discussed with one or two of your peers and your instructor.

9. ___(b)___

10. True

REFERENCES

Bloom, Benjamin S. *Human Characteristics and School Learning.* New York: McGraw-Hill, 1976.

Borg, Walter R., Majorie L. Kelley, Phillip Langer, and Meredith Gall. *The Mini-Course: A Microteaching Approach to Teacher's Education.* Beverly Hills, Calif.: Macmillan Educational Services, Inc., 1970.

Gaushell, Harper. "Microcomputers in Education," April 1982. Educational Resources Information Center/Education Document Reproduction Service, ED 225 540.

Hunter, Madeline. "Diagnostic Teaching." *The Elementary School Journal* 80:(September) 1979, 41–46. (a)

Hunter, Madeline. "Teaching is Decision-Making." *Educational Leadership* 37:(October) 1979, 62–64, 67. (b)

Kaplan, Sandra N. *Inservice Training Manual: Activities for Developing Curriculum for the Gifted/Talented.* Ventura County Schools, Calif.: 1979.

Land, M. L. "Teacher Clarity and Cognitive Level of Questions: Effects on Learning." *Journal of Experimental Education* 49:1980, 48–51.

McLuhan, Marshall, and Quentin Fiore. *The Medium Is the Massage.* New York: Bantam Books, 1967.

"The Paramount Duty: The Interim Report of the Temporary Committee on Educational Policies, Structure and Management." Olympia, Wash.: State of Washington, Superintendent of Public Instruction, November 1983.

Schunk, Dale H., and John P. Gaa. "Goal-Setting Influence on Learning and Self-Evaluation." *Journal of Classroom Interaction* 16:(Summer) 1981, 38–44.

Vaughn, Janice Bertram. "A Comparison of Peer Teaching and Child Teaching in the Preservice Teacher Acquisition of Enthusiasm, Praise, Probing and Questioning Behaviors" (Ph.D. diss., University of Cincinnati, 1983). *Dissertation Abstracts International* 44:(August) 1983, 377–A.

6

DECIDING HOW TO ASK QUESTIONS

Next to lecturing, the single most common teaching method employed in the schools of America and, for that matter, in the world may well be the asking of questions. As an art, it may have started with Socrates and remains the most often used of all teaching strategies. Therefore, to become a highly competent educator, it is very important that you master the development and application of questioning.

After studying this chapter, you will be able to

1. State the general conclusions from a given review of literature on classroom questions
2. Distinguish between convergent, divergent, or evaluative questioning operations
3. Distinguish between sequential hierarchies and nonsequential hierarchies, which relate to the classification of questions
4. Use the following techniques:
   (a) Prompting
   (b) Handling incorrect responses
   (c) Promoting multiple responses
   (d) Framing review questions
   (e) Encouraging nonvolunteers
   (f) Encouraging students to ask questions
   (g) Using "wait time"
5. List techniques that interfere with student responses
6. List areas relating to questioning where there is some empirical disagreement

In addition, you should demonstrate the following affective behaviors:

1. Be considerate and courteous to students during a recitation period
2. Be open-minded as students respond
3. Appreciate the feelings of students who may be too shy or too reticent to participate in class recitation
4. Be positive in outlook, not sarcastic or cynical

REVIEW OF SELECTED STUDIES

Having gained familiarity with performance objectives, task analysis, lesson planning, and the taxonomies, you may be wondering how to implement

The authors wish to thank Carol Mandt Doughty for her efforts in preparing the prototype materials originally used for this chapter.

these concepts to aid in your teaching decisions. One of the most effective and underestimated teaching *strategies* used to implement the previously discussed elements is classroom questioning. There is little doubt that questioning plays a critical role in teaching. If teachers are to "teach logically," then they must be knowledgeable in the process of framing questions so that student thought processes can be guided in the most skillful and meaningful manner. This implies that teachers must design questions that will help students attain the specific goals (that is, performance objectives) of a particular lesson. Although textbook and examination questions contribute to the learning process, most questions that occur in the classroom are verbal and teacher-formulated. As Meredith D. Gall (1970) pointed out, questions are critical elements with which teachers stimulate student thinking. By studying question patterns, one may even determine the types of verbal interactions that take place in the classroom.

The Status of Classroom Questioning

The purpose of this chapter is to indicate the functions of questions, their use as a teaching strategy, and the effects they have on learning. Our brief review of classroom questioning will provide you with an indication of the apparent effects that questioning techniques have on learning processes.

Although questioning is an important instructional strategy, it appears that teachers may have mistakenly equated quantity of questions with quality. One of the earliest studies of questions in the classroom was done in 1912 by Romiett Stevens. She estimated that 80 percent of school time was used for question-and-answer recitation. Half a century later, a sample of high school teachers was found to have asked an average of 395 questions a day, with most of them being memory questions (Clegg, 1971). Meredith D. Gall (1970) cited several studies in which large numbers of questions were used by elementary teachers—ranging from 64 to 180 questions in one class period to an average of 348 questions during the school day!

In Gall's excellent research paper (1970), he cited eight studies that spanned a period from 1912 to 1967, which all showed that questioning practices changed little over this time. In 1982, Delva Daines reported that her data on elementary and secondary social studies teachers revealed that literal types of questions were posed most often by the teachers at a rate of 1.5 per minute. No question about it: teachers do practice the art of questioning.

Several reasons have been proposed for why teachers use so many fact (low-level) questions. One rationale supported by many teachers is that students need facts for high-order thinking. This is a cogent point, but there are additional ways to teach facts, such as programmed instruction.

Another apparent reason why teachers overuse fact questions is the lack of systematic teacher training in the use of questioning strategies. The Far West Laboratory for Educational Research and Development developed a self-contained, in-service mini-course to improve teachers' questioning skills. The Laboratory program uses 16-mm films to explain the concepts and also includes modeling, self-feedback, and micro-teaching. The program was used with forty-eight elementary teachers in the Far West Laboratory field tests, and the results showed an increase in redirection questions (those requiring multiple student responses) from 26.7 percent to 40.9 percent; in thought-provoking questions, from 37.3 percent to 52.0 percent; and in probing (that is, prompting) questions, from 8.5 percent to 13.9 percent. There was also a concomitant decrease in the repetition of students' answers from 30.7 percent to 4.4 percent. The repetition of the teacher's own questions decreased from 13.7 percent to 4.7 percent, and the answering of the teacher's own questions by the teacher decreased from 4.6 percent to 0.7 percent (Borg et al., 1970).

We must note here that it is the micro-teaching component of the Far West Laboratory's mini-course that allows the teacher to practice and perfect questioning skills. Studies by Donald C. Orlich et al. (1972, 1973) revealed that when teachers were trained in questioning, the frequency of higher-level questions used in the classroom increased significantly.

Still another reason why there have been so many low-level questions is that, until recently, teachers have lacked an easy-to-use system to organize and classify questions. They have also lacked a means of evaluating the effects that different questioning techniques have on the learning process. This is where Bloom's and other taxonomies can be of use. A majority of the researchers use Bloom's Taxonomy to evaluate the potential for critical thinking in the classroom. Rodney P. Riegle (1976) wrote that the use of a taxonomy per se will not improve the quality of questions but does make the teacher more aware of the process. He implied that students also should understand the various levels of questions. In this chapter we present a total of seven different taxonomies or hierarchies by which to categorize questions.

Questions and Cognitive Effects

Before attempting to demonstrate the ways a teacher may use a classification system such as Bloom's to improve questioning, let us examine a few of the hundreds of published studies to determine how varying the levels of questioning affects student thinking.

Francis P. Hunkins (1969) undertook this task in a study with 260 sixth-graders in eleven social studies classes. From this study, Hunkins concluded that the use of high-level questions helped students not only evaluate better but also improve in understanding lower-level facts.

If teachers emphasize low-level questions whereas high-level questions are needed to stimulate thinking and evaluation, then we may have discovered one of the basic reasons why students find school boring. However, all the blame for low-level questions does not rest with the teacher. O. L. Davis, Jr., and Francis P. Hunkins (1966) investigated textbook questions and the thinking processes they apparently foster. They randomly chose a third of the chapters from three recently published fifth-grade social studies textbooks. They used the *Taxonomy of Educational Objectives, Handbook I: Cognitive Domain* by Bloom (1956) to categorize the questions. All three books consistently emphasized Knowledge questions and uniformly avoided higher-order questions. A summary of their data indicated that the averages for all three were as follows: Knowledge—87 percent; Comprehension—9 percent; and Application—4 percent. Of the 732 questions that were analyzed, Davis and Hunkins found that none required analysis, one required synthesis, and two required evaluation!

However, analyses published by J. T. Dillon revealed wide discrepancies between the teachers' cognitive level of questions and the students' responses. Dillon (1982a) observed that there was a 50 percent chance that a student would respond with a lower-level response when asked a higher-level question, and *vice versa*. Dillon (1982b) further wrote that teachers may have become doctrinaire in their almost exclusive use of teacher questioning at the expense of greater student participation. He very accurately observed that teacher-question student-recitation periods seldom lead to meaningful classroom discussion. (We very much concur with Dillon; see Chapter 7, "Decisions About Discussions.")

Dillon (1981a) also cautioned teacher educators that if teachers dominate classroom verbal interactions, then class members ultimately become dependent on the teacher and illustrate passive behaviors. Indeed, the latter traits would hardly foster ingenuity, creativity, or thinking—traits we all consider desirable.

Dillon (1981b) offers an alternative to the use of teacher questions. He provides some persuasive evidence that teachers should stimulate student responses and thinking by using *declarative statements* rather than questions. Dillon writes that by using declarative statements rather than questions, teachers elicit longer and more complex student responses. Obviously the entire field of classroom questioning has become unsettled—although in the late 1970s it seemed as though there was "no question" about questioning!

Using Student Questions

There is another source of questions that is often overlooked—the students. Walter R. Borg and his associates (1970) stated that classes should be oriented toward student communication, giving students a chance to express opinions and ideas; but evidence shows that teachers do most of the talking and questioning.

In 1975, Catherine Cornbleth presented some relevant studies and evidence to support teacher encouragement of student questioning behavior. In general, she found that: (1) students can be encouraged to ask productive or higher-level questions; (2) the more questions a student asks per period the more probable the questions will be higher level; (3) praise will encourage and stimulate more productive thinking processes with children of lower socioeconomic status; and (4) students become more involved in the classes when they are encouraged to ask questions.

In yet another study, Meredith D. Gall and associates (1978) reported that their experiments on questioning, recitation, and learning seemed to support the idea that recitation teaching was more effective in promoting student learning than a nonrecitation instructional experience lasting the same period of time. They also noted that students learned equally well when the teacher gave the answer to a question a student did not know or when information was provided by their peers. This study provides evidence that fact questions were not harmful to the learning of higher cognitive skills.

Gall's studies draw two conclusions: (1) well-designed questions and strategies may be more important than the level of questions; and (2) when you work with very small groups, there is a tendency for greater efficiency in learning. The latter is discussed in Chapter 7.

Although the evidence is somewhat inconclusive, there does appear to be a direct relationship between the level of questions asked by the teacher and the level of student responses. Furthermore, it appears that if a teacher decides to raise his or her expectations for the class and *systematically* raises the level of his or her questioning, then the students accordingly raise the level of their responses. Of course, this implies a carefully planned questioning sequence that would probably span several weeks of instruction. The major caution is not to jump haphazardly into high-level questions without making the necessary teacher-student attitude adjustments. This means that teachers must plan for the utilization of appropriate questions just as they plan for the next week's reading assignments. However, J. T. Dillon does add a caution: There is no guarantee that a higher-level question will elicit a higher-level student response. (Student questioning as a teaching technique is discussed later in this chapter.)

Tips for the Teacher

The implications of these studies for teacher decision-making are many. First, if teachers want their students to develop higher levels of thinking, to evaluate information, to achieve more, and to be more interested, then teachers must learn to ask higher-level questions. Second, teachers must encourage their students to ask more questions—and more thought-provoking ones—if they desire greater student involvement in the process of learning. We should add that the type of questions to be used is the teacher's decision.

Another important consideration for teachers who desire to stimulate critical thinking is the use of textbooks. Teachers should be aware of the advantages and disadvantages of their textbook materials. To attain the objective desired, the teacher may have to supplement the materials provided. For example, Cheryl G. Fedje and Ann Irvine (1982) prepare lesson plans with key questions that require students to observe, compare, contrast, group, order, or determine cause and effect.

It should be noted that you can use questions to: (1) diagnose student

TABLE 6–1 Seven Questioning Hierarchies and Classification Methods

Sequential Hierarchies		
Benjamin Bloom et al. (1956)	Norris M. Sanders (1966)	Hilda Taba (1967)
To know	Memory	Form concept
To comprehend	Translation	Interpret concept
To apply	Interpretation	Apply concept
To analyze	Application	*Harold L. Herber (1978)*
To synthesize	Analysis	*Literal comprehension*
To evaluate	Synthesis	*Interpretative comprehension*
	Evaluation	*Applied comprehension*

Nonsequential Hierarchies		
Arthur Kaiser (1979)	Richard Smith (1969)	Ronald T. Hyman (1979)
Open	Convergent	Definitional
Closed	Divergent	Empirical
Suggestive		Evaluative
Rhetorical		Metaphysical

Source: Lelia Christenbury and Patricia P. Kelly, *Questioning: A Critical Path to Critical Thinking*. Urbana, Ill.: ERIC Clearinghouse on Reading and Communication Skills and the National Council of Teachers of English, 1983, p. 4. Public Domain Document, NIE 400-78-0026.

progress; (2) determine entry-level competence; (3) prescribe additional study; and (4) enrich an area.

Leila Christenbury and Patricia P. Kelly (1983) collected at least seven different questioning taxonomies or hierarchies. They divided the questioning hierarchies into two general sets: sequential hierarchies and nonsequential hierarchies. These two sets are illustrated in Table 6–1. Observe how there are similarities and also great differences between the sets. Further, one or more of the categories can be used to "analyze" questions or statements and the concomitant student responses. The hierarchy can be selected that best fits your instructional objectives. We present this series in keeping with our concept of teacher decision-making.

Summary

Following is a brief list of findings that summarizes the results of a century of research on questioning.

1. Questioning tends to be a universal teaching strategy.
2. Being systematic in the use and development of questioning tends to improve student learning.
3. By classifying questions according to a particular system, the teacher may determine the cognitive or affective level at which the class is working and make adjustments as professionally indicated.

4. Through systematic questioning, the teacher may determine the entry levels of students for specific content areas.
5. Questions should be developed logically and sequentially.
6. Students should be encouraged to ask questions.
7. A written plan with key questions will provide lesson structure and direction.
8. Questions should be adapted to the students' level of ability.
9. Use questioning techniques that encourage the widest student participation.
10. Use statements rather than questions to promote student reactions.
11. A wide variety of questioning options is open to teachers.
12. No one questioning strategy is applicable to all teaching situations.

In addition to these assertions, which are substantiated by research, we also have assumed that higher-level questions demand greater intellectual activity. The research available to date seems to confirm that assumption. Rather than emphasizing a "right" answer, teachers should use questions to stimulate higher cognitive achievements and to make information more meaningful. In the long run, the quality of the questions being asked should be most important. Finally, Walter Borg, one of the creators of the Far West Lab mini-course, concluded that questioning is one of the most essential functions of teaching (Borg and co-workers, 1970). *If* this generally accepted assertion is valid, *then* teachers must achieve a high degree of sensitivity and awareness to use questions in the most efficacious and appropriate manner.

APPLYING QUESTIONING TECHNIQUES

We suggest that all teachers must become aware of the kinds of questions they ask and the kinds of responses that these questions elicit. Thus our theory states: If *the teacher desires a response at a selected level of thinking,* then *an appropriate question must be framed that will elicit the proper response level from the student.* The simple adoption of the "if-then" strategy gives the teacher the needed awareness of the intellectual level at which the class is being conducted. This strategy also requires concomitant and continued decision-making and evaluation by the teacher and can be applied at *all* levels of instruction and with *all* types of students.

Applying the Taxonomies to Questioning

As shown in Table 6–1, there are several hierarchies or taxonomies from which to select a framework for questioning. The context of the questioning must be taken into account. James Riley (1982) notes that if a teacher desires to instruct at higher cognitive levels, the teacher must develop a questioning hierarchy. The hierarchical list then becomes a plan through which the recitations and discussion are implemented. In short, the hierarchy allows the students to perceive an idea, concept, or issue as being structured into a framework for thinking. Thus the hierarchy becomes a visible blueprint for action. Further, in light of J. T. Dillon's work, a series of declarative statements—rather than questions—should be structured in some hierarchical manner to elicit improved student responses.

Basic Questioning Categories

For convenience to the teacher, all questioning strategies may be classified into three convenient categories: (1) convergent; (2) divergent; and (3) evaluative. This classification is a very slightly modified version of that proposed by James Gallagher and his associates (Verduin, 1967). If the teacher assigns value (affective dimension) to the types of questions that are being asked of the students, then it becomes necessary to have a method by which to verify that the teacher is using specified questioning patterns. Thus some type of classification scheme is needed. The studies previously cited indicated that the three categories would be an efficient method by which to tabulate the kinds of questions being used in the classroom.

Convergent Questions

As the term denotes, the focus of a convergent questioning pattern is on a narrow objective. The teacher uses questions that encourage student responses to converge or focus on a central theme. Convergent questions, for the most part, elicit short responses from students. That is, *if* the teacher has a learning objective that involves manifesting a student behavior consisting of short responses such as "yes" or "no" or very short statements, *then* the teacher should plan to use a convergent questioning pattern. Furthermore, the teacher who uses a convergent questioning pattern must be aware that he or she is focusing on the lower levels of thinking—that is, the Knowledge or Comprehension levels. It should be noted that the use of a convergent technique per se is not to be construed as being "bad." There are many situations in which the teacher decides that the students need to demonstrate a knowledge of specifics; in such cases, lower-level questioning strategies are appropriate.

What this means, then, is that the *appropriateness* of any set of questioning strategies must be judged solely on the objectives that the teacher has specified. Of course, if the teacher justifies the continual use of low-level questions with the commonly heard comment that "I don't think my students can do any better," then the teacher may be replaced with a set of programmed instruction materials supplemented by an audio or video cassette learning system.

Why does the teacher wish to prepare learning objectives that utilize a convergent type of questioning pattern? There are several possibilities for consideration. For example, *if* the teacher uses an inductive teaching style (proceeding from a set of specific data to a student-derived conclusion), *then* the teacher uses a large proportion of convergent type questions. Also, the teacher may wish to use short-response questions as "warm-up" exercises with which to break the monotony of the traditional classroom. These warm-up exercises may follow a "rapid-fire" method, which would be most appropriate when the teacher is building vocabulary skills. Teachers in foreign-language classes may use a convergent, rapid-fire pattern to help develop oral, vocabulary, and spelling skills among students. The use of a convergent, rapid-fire technique also allows for participation by all students. The same method may be used by a science teacher. For example, there is some evidence that a typical high school sophomore biology course has a greater number of "foreign" terms and concepts than the total number of new vocabulary words learned by the average sophomore in any foreign language class! Thus, a biology teacher may wish to use a convergent technique for the first few minutes of the class to maximize participation and to generate constructive verbal motivation among the students.

The use of a convergent, rapid-fire technique focuses on specific learning objectives, skills, terminologies, or short responses. The use of this technique with short answers may be demonstrated in a mathematics class, in which the teacher wishes the students to practice verbalized rapid calculation. A social studies teacher may want to use a pinpoint technique in identifying specific bits of information or facts.

The basic convergent pattern allows the teacher to "dominate" the thinking of the students by asking for short-length, low-level intellectual responses that involve a single answer or a limited number of logical answers. It should be thoroughly understood that a convergent questioning pattern is *not* an appropriate means of stimulating thought-provoking responses or classroom discussions; rather, it stresses Knowledge or Comprehension levels. The convergent technique is an ideal application of "teacher-directed instruction" or *direct instruction,* where all students in class respond *in unison* to teacher-asked questions. Everyone participates.

A list of convergent questions follows. Note that these questions all meet the criterion of limiting student responses to a narrow spectrum of possible options and are more recall-oriented than analytical.

1. In what works did Robert Browning use the dramatic monologue as a form for his poems?
2. Under what conditions will water boil at less than 100°C?
3. What helps bread dough rise?
4. Where did tennis originate?
5. Why do relatively few people live in the deserts of any country?
6. Explain the attitudes that the Romantic poets had toward nature.
7. Where and when did Champlain build the first French trading post?
8. Explain the "Big Bang" theory.
9. Describe how parliamentary governmental systems differ from the type described in the American Constitution.

Divergent Questions

Divergent questions are the opposite of convergent questions: The focus of divergent questions is broad. Rather than seeking a single focus, the teacher, with a divergent questioning strategy, evokes student responses that vary greatly. Divergent questions also elicit longer student responses. Thus, *if* the teacher wishes to evoke several different responses from the class, *then* he or she asks a question that is divergent. The anticipated student reply will be typically longer than a response to a convergent question. In summary, when ideas are being discussed and the teacher wishes to elicit a variety of responses from the students, divergent types of questions are appropriate. This technique is ideal for building the self-concepts of children of minority groups or of lower socioeconomic status, because divergent questions often have few "right" or "wrong" responses.

Eliciting Multiple Responses. *If* the teacher wishes to elicit multiple responses, *then* a multiple-response technique can be used. Basically such a technique is as follows: The teacher decides that more than one student should respond to a particular divergent question. The teacher then asks a question that can be answered with multiple responses. After stating the question, the teacher calls on three or four students and then assumes a passive role in this mini-discussion. Such a technique teaches the students to conduct a classroom discussion—a rather sophisticated teaching strategy when used properly. This technique also sharpens the listening skills of pupils.

Accepting Diversity. In addition to eliciting longer and multiple responses, the teacher must also be prepared to accept diverse responses. When the teacher asks a divergent question, then he or she must expect a multiplicity of responses as well as some creative ones. *If* a goal of the teacher is to allow or encourage novel solutions and creative responses, *then* the divergent method is appropriate. It also must be remembered that if the teacher elicits diverse responses from the students, then *the teacher has the professional obligation to accept* those students' responses. This is a very important concept in the art of asking questions. To reinforce appropriate response behavior, the teacher must demonstrate a high degree of acceptance for the response of each student. This means that the teacher may not use subtle "put down" tactics, regardless of how seemingly outlandish a student's point of view may be or how opposite from what the teacher expected. The rule of thumb is that when divergent questions are asked by the teacher, free responses by the students must be allowed. Again, this is a great technique for disadvantaged students, as they get to become "stars" in the classroom.

Beginning the Sequence. A technique that helps the teacher initially frame divergent questions is to write out the questions prior to asking them. Then examine them to ensure that they are clearly stated and convey the precise meanings intended. The teacher who uses divergent questions for the first time will probably find the initial class experience rather difficult or even disappointing, usually because students are not oriented toward giving longer or higher-level thinking responses.

It takes a good deal of reshaping of student behavior patterns to elicit the proper level and type of student responses with the use of divergent questioning techniques. For thousands of classroom hours, students from grade school to high school have been conditioned to respond with short, low-level thinking responses. The teacher who begins to schedule divergent questions in the classroom questioning periods must also have the patience to inform the students that the level of questions is changing and that the level of their responses will also change quite drastically; it will differ from the level of responses given with the convergent or pinpointing technique commonly used by other teachers.

The teacher who uses a divergent technique of questioning will soon discover that the students will respond in the higher-level thinking categories of the cognitive taxonomy—that is, Application, Analysis, and Synthesis. Also the teacher should develop questions that, over an extended period of time, will gradually progress to other divergent questions that will stimulate analytical and synthetic thinking. This point has been amply demonstrated in classes with large proportions of disadvantaged students. Thus *if* you want your students to be prepared to conduct discussions and to give longer and more diverse oral or written responses, *then* the divergent technique is the appropriate one to use.

The divergent method is appropriate for eliciting multiple responses from students. If this is your intent, then it will be important for you to inform the class that a set of multiple responses is desired and that you want each student to take cues from the other students' responses. This means that a teacher does *not* repeat student responses for other class members. (Obviously there are exceptions to this rule. For instance, if a student speaks in such a low voice that it is impossible for some class members to hear, then the teacher may repeat the student response.) The rationale underlying the technique of not repeating is that if a student knows that the previous student's response will be repeated by the teacher, then most students become conditioned to listening only for the teacher's repetition of the response (which is similar to instant replay on television).

Our prescription for avoiding inappropriate teacher behaviors is to allow all students to present their responses without interference from the teacher. This has a positive effect on the class. However, there may be times, when using debate techniques, when the teacher may interrupt a student. This is a more advanced technique that is used after mutual trust has been established in the classroom. In general, we find that teachers tend to interrupt their students before they have fully explained their positions. If the teacher is sensitive to this behavior, the students will realize that their responses *are* important and that they must take their cues from each other rather than from the teacher. This simple technique reduces the time of teacher's talk in a classroom and increases the "responsibility quotient" of students. In short, students realize that they must now be responsive to each other, and the "attending behavior" of the class will improve. It does little good for the teacher continually to remind the students that they are not paying attention. Such negative reinforcement only makes a class less attentive. By encouraging students to listen to each other, the teacher allows them to participate in a dynamic fashion and, thus, to receive peer reinforcement for positive and constructive classroom behavior.

In summary, *if* the teacher wishes to elicit a set of student behaviors that involve higher-level thinking skills, *then* the teacher will plan for a systematic development of divergent questions. Remember that the emphasis is on systematic development of questions over an extended period of time, with well-conceived and appropriate learning objectives. We cannot overemphasize the amount of time involved; it takes weeks, even months, to incorporate these behaviors into the usual repertoire of school behaviors.

Thus, longer and more diverse responses are the criteria that characterize the divergent questioning framework. The decision to use divergent questions requires that the teacher help the students locate different sources of information so that a variety of viewpoints may be shared in the class. The following list includes selected questions that may be classified as divergent. Note that we have adapted a few of these from the previously presented list of convergent questions.

1. What type of social and cultural development might have taken place if Christopher Columbus had landed on Manhattan Island on October 12, 1492?
2. What would happen in a school if it had no rules?
3. What do you think are other effective methods of organic gardening that are not listed in the textbook?
4. How does the environment affect human behavior?
5. Why would one select arc welding over gas welding in the fabrication of art objects?
6. How has the popularity of tennis had both a social and an economic impact on our society?
7. What kinds of evidence would you seek if you were an opponent of the "Big Bang" theory?
8. How would a government organized according to a parliamentary system have reacted to our "Watergate" incident?
9. What impact will be made on our standard of living if we exhaust our nation's petroleum resources within ten to twenty years?
10. List as many alternatives as you can to an interstate highway system being constructed in a city.

Evaluative Questions

The third pattern of questioning is one that attempts to use divergent questions, but with one added component—evaluation. The basic difference between a divergent question and an evaluative question is that the evaluative question has a built-in evaluative or judgmental set of criteria. When one asks *why* something is good or bad, an evaluation question is being raised. It is possible, however, that an evaluative question may elicit nothing more than a poor collection of uninformed student opinions. Therefore, with evaluative questions, emphasis must be placed on the specificity of the criteria by which a student judges the value or appropriateness of an object or an idea. As with divergent questions, the teacher must accept student responses to encourage students to provide evaluative responses to the teacher's questions.

A major component in the evaluative questioning framework is that the teacher systematically helps students develop a logical basis for establishing evaluative criteria. For example, if the teacher asks a question and a student presents a response that is followed by the teacher's asking, "Why?" and the student replies only, "Because," then the teacher should recognize immediately that the student is lacking in logical perception, may be dogmatic or arbitrary, or simply does not understand how to frame a logical, consistent set of evaluative criteria. Once again, we caution that the teacher must *never* use sarcasm or any other disparaging technique, but must take a positive approach and reinforce the student in an environment that is conducive to a logical development of evaluative criteria. The typical teacher comment, "You're not being logical," gives the student no basis for improvement. The teacher must provide a specific set of criteria from which students may develop their own criteria. In this manner, students will understand why they hold value judgments or opinions. As an introduction to this technique, we recommend a joint writing session, with the teacher and small groups of students collaboratively listing criteria.

Observation will verify that as evaluative questions are presented and student responses elicited, the teacher and the students will want to classify the evaluative responses along some type of continuum that will range from "bad" or "illogical" to "good" or "logically developed."

Note that we have been using the term *responses,* not *answers. Answers* carry the connotation of being final, complete, or the last word. To be sure, convergent questioning patterns may elicit student answers. However, it must be recognized that when divergent and evaluative questions are framed, the students will not be responding with definitive or absolute answers but will be providing responses that will tend to be relative, less than certain, or tentative.

Note also that the term *continuum* has been used to describe a classification scheme. Both questions and responses are not conveniently categorized within the dualistic concept of "good or bad" or "appropriate or inappropriate." Most student responses in the evaluative mode will demonstrate a broad range of thought when based on a set of evaluative criteria. This is precisely what the teacher aims for when using evaluation questions. The teacher then classifies the evaluative responses according to their logical development, internal consistency, validity, and perhaps responsibility. In short, we are suggesting that the teacher once again accept all student responses and, as apparent logical inconsistencies develop, discuss them after the student has had an opportunity for classroom discourse. Thus *if* the teacher wishes to allow students to make evaluations and judgments concerning learning activities, *then* the appropriate teacher behavior is to use the evaluative questioning technique.

The following list provides examples of evaluative questions. Remember that most, if not all, evaluative questions will also be divergent. The one characteristic that separates divergent questions from evaluative ones is that the latter rely on established judgmental criteria. Observe that some examples previously designated as divergent have been converted now into evaluative questions.

1. Why is the parliamentary system of government more responsive to the citizens than is our legislative system?
2. Why is the world a better place because of computers?
3. Why should good teachers strive to be aware of the types of questions they ask?
4. Why will the Court's stand favoring abortion reform affect social and moral attitudes and behaviors?
5. Why is it better to switch to either "gasohol" or "hydrogen" as fuel for our automobiles?
6. Why has the federal system of interstate highways harmed our city environments?
7. Defend the strip mining of coal in eastern Montana.
8. To what extent is the "Big Bang" theory a more viable one than the "Cold Start"?
9. Why have professional sports grown to be so popular in the United States?

You may disagree that there are three major types of questioning strategies and may want to establish other categories of your own. If so, you may produce a series of classification schemes for your own use. Our objective is to provide an efficient and convenient system by which to categorize questions quickly so that the teacher is always aware of the specific questioning strategy being used and may anticipate an appropriate set of responses from the students. The decision to use such a system for self-improvement or professional development is, of course, yours.

MAPPING AS A QUESTIONING TECHNIQUE

Just when it appears that the concept of questioning is clear, we will add another contemporary technique. You will find this technique labeled mapping, webbing, highlighting, story mapping, netting, or drafting. We will call the technique *mapping*. It stems from the innovative and creative work of the Bay Area Writing Project (Gray and Meyers, 1978) and the various projects that evolved from it (Barton and Zehm, 1983; Hays, 1980).

Isabel Beck and Margaret McKeown (1981) adapted the concept of mapping to a "story map," which guides question development so that deeper meaning is constructed from a text. The map is simply a visual plan of the major events and ideas ultimately placed in their logical order. The map begins as a "hub," which is the starting point of the story. Then a list of central events and ideas is made in summary form. These elements, which are student statements or questions, are added as spokes on the hub. A progression of the listed ideas and events becomes the foundation for extending comprehension into higher levels, and a "map" emerges. Additional questions or statements can be used to develop interpretations, themes, use of literary conventions, or relevancy to current issues. (Mapping may also be used to teach basic organizational skills in grades one through nine. The technique is also useful to help high school students improve selected analytical skills.)

Gabriele Lusser Rico (1983) provides examples of mapping under her concept of *clustering*. Her work is an excellent resource for the topic.

THE TEACHER'S APPROPRIATE QUESTIONING BEHAVIORS

To develop a repertoire of questioning skills, the teacher must be aware of a wide spectrum of questioning techniques that may elicit appropriate responses from students. The teacher-behavior questioning skills that follow address specific kinds of problems that can be predicted in any class in which questioning strategies are used. Each skill is discussed so that the teacher may identify and practice that particular skill. Thus, when the decision is made to use the strategy, the teacher will know how to use it and why.

Technical and Humane Considerations

The use of questions in a recitation period, a tutorial period, or an inductive session is always predicated on the assumption that some meaningful or purposeful learning activity will take place, allowing the student to gain another learning experience. For this to happen, questions must be used in a positive reinforcing manner—that is, so that the student will enjoy learning and responding. All students should receive positive reinforcement by virtue of the questions being asked and the types of responses elicited. Our basic premise is that questions should *never* be used for punitive means. The teacher who asks a question to punish the student is turning a learning situation into a negatively reinforcing one. The result is that, rather than creating a friendly atmosphere that is conducive to learning, the teacher "turns off" not only the learner but the learning process as well. This is extremely critical, especially when working with disadvantaged or young students. In short, our philosophy is that questioning must be used only in ways that are meaningful, purposeful, and positively reinforcing.

Framing Questions

How does one frame a question? The logical method is to think through your question plan, just as a quarterback or a coach plans the game strategy *prior* to the playing of the game. As a teacher, you establish goals with objectives to be met *and* the appropriate questioning strategy to reach those goals. Once the initial preparation has been accomplished, then it becomes a matter of implementation: Ask the question and elicit an appropriate response.

The basic rule for framing a question is as follows: *Ask the question; pause, then call on a student.* This rule is grounded in the psychological principle that when a question is asked and then followed by a short pause, all students will "attend" to the communication. The nonverbal message (pause) communicates that any student in the class may be selected for a response. Thus, the attention level of the class remains high.

If the teacher reverses this pattern by requesting a particular student to respond prior to asking the question, then all those students who are not involved have the opportunity "not to attend" to the communication between teacher and student.

Thus, the technique of framing entails (1) asking the question; (2) pausing; and (3) calling on the student. This same question-framing technique can be used even when employing a multiple-response method in which the teacher specifies that several students will be selected to respond. Furthermore, once this technique has been mastered by both teacher and students, the teacher can modify the third element to a nonverbal action by simply pointing or nodding to a student for response. This technique becomes easy with a little practice.

We mentioned that the teacher ought to pause after asking a question. There are several justifications for this teacher behavior. The first is that the pause, or *wait time,* gives the students a chance to think about their responses to the question. This is especially essential when a teacher asks higher-level thinking questions.

A pause after the question also provides the teacher with a little time to "read" the nonverbal cues from the class. With some practice, the teacher can readily observe such nonverbal signals as pleasure, apprehension, fright, excitement, joy, or shame. As teachers become more affectively sensitive to humanistic considerations in the classroom, this dimension of teaching becomes very important.

Finally, when the teacher acquires the habit of pausing after asking a question, the teacher will not dread the wait time. Mary Budd Rowe (1973, 1974, and 1980) discovered that teachers are most impatient with youngsters when asking questions. She measured the wait time of many metropolitan elementary school teachers and found that the wait time between asking a question and answering it before the student does or calling on another student had to be measured in *fractions of seconds!* Is it any wonder then that some students dread to be called on. They know that it will elicit impatient behaviors from the teacher and that they will simply be "in Dutch" again.

In subsequent studies, Rowe (1978) described the results of "wait-time 2." In the first set of studies, the teachers paused (wait-time 1) prior to calling on a student to respond. Rowe then discovered that if a teacher waits to respond to the student after the student responds initially, then students will continue to respond—without teacher prompting.

By using the wait-time 2 technique Rowe found that: (1) lengths of student responses increased; (2) the number of questions asked by students increased; (3) there was a decrease in failure to respond; (4) student involvement in the lessons increased; (5) student reasoning improved; (6) slower students responded more; and (7) student disciplinary actions decreased.

The effectiveness of wait time has been substantiated by J. Mark Honea, Jr. (1982) and many other researchers, who collectively imply that "teacher silence may be golden."

We want you to know that classroom silence is not all bad—even when asking questions. So make the decision to wait—not only once, but twice.

Prompting Techniques

Once the question has been asked and a student has been identified to respond, there is the possibility that the student will either not answer the question *completely* or not answer it at all. When this happens, the teacher should promptly conduct strategies that attempt to clarify the question so that the student can understand it better, should try to have the student amplify the response, or should elicit additional responses from the student so that the teacher may verify whether the student comprehends the material. As the teacher develops prompting skills, there are many rules that can be followed. However, to simplify matters, keep one rule foremost in mind: *prompt in a positive manner*. This means that if a student has not answered the question or has not amplified a response to the teacher's satisfaction, then the teacher should decide to prompt. To do this, the teacher should acknowledge the attempted response but then encourage the student to clarify or amplify it.

The teacher may have to prompt a student many times during a questioning session so that a more complete or logical response may be derived from an inadequate response. Basically, the teacher will always aid the student with positive reinforcement so that the student is encouraged to complete an incomplete response or to revise an incorrect one. In most cases, the student will answer with a partially correct response or, to put it negatively, with a partially incorrect response in addition to a partially correct response. Immediately on hearing a response that fits this category, the teacher begins to prompt the student so that the response can be completed, made more logical, reexamined, or stated more adequately or more appropriately.

The next two examples illustrate prompting or probing techniques.

Example 1

Teacher: What did the English citizens and American colonists think a constitution should be like? (Pause.) Hector?

Student: Well . . . um . . . they figured it was a bunch of laws all written down in one place.

Teacher: That's a good description of the American point of view. Now . . . what did Englishmen think?

Student: They thought the laws should be written down in different places . . . sort of.

Teacher: O.K. . . . that's part of the answer. Now, did *all* of the laws for the English constitution have to be written down?

Student: Some stuff was just rules that had been set up and everybody knew what they were and followed them. But others were written down in many different . . . ah, . . . documents.

Teacher: Fine! Now how about going back and summing up what you've worked out so far?

Example 2

Teacher: American colonists and English citizens both had the highest respect for their constitutions. However, they differed in how they should be interpreted. What is an example of this difference? (Pause.) Angela?

Student: The English thought it should be used to exploit the colonists by taxing really hard.

Teacher: Taxation *was* one of the biggest problems. Good! Now, what made the English think they had the right to tax?

Student: Their constitution said so.

Teacher: That's the basic idea. Can you expand that idea a little?

Student: Their constitution said it was O.K. to tax Americans, so their Parliament made a bunch of tax laws.

Teacher: O.K. Now you've worked out the fundamentals, let's see if someone else can supply additional ideas. (Pause.) Zak?

Handling Incorrect Responses

No matter how skillful a teacher is in motivating students, providing adequate and relevant instructional materials, and asking high quality questions, there will be one continual problem that detracts from the intellectual and interpersonal activities of a classroom questioning session—incorrect student responses.

As was discussed previously, prompting techniques may be used by the teacher when student responses are partially correct or are stated incompletely. Basically, prompting is an easy technique because the teacher can reinforce the positive aspect of a student's response, while ignoring the negative or incomplete component. However, when a student verbalizes a totally incorrect response, a more complex interpersonal situation arises. first, the teacher has little to reinforce positively in such a case. But teacher comments such as "No," "You are way off," or "That is incorrect" should be avoided, as they all act as negative reinforcers and, depending on the personality of the child who responds, may reduce that student's desire to participate in a verbal classroom interaction. This is very critical, especially with non-English-speaking youngsters.

Second, if the teacher responds negatively to an incorrect student response, there is a high probability that the "ripple effect" will occur. This effect, which has been described by Jacob S. Kounin (1970), demonstrated that students who are not themselves the target of the teacher's negative strategy are, in fact, negatively affected by what the teacher does to other class members. There is, of course, a difference between a positive or supportive strategy and a negative or threatening strategy. When an incorrect response is provided by the student, the teacher may attempt to move to a *neutral* prompting technique rather than responding with the usual "No, that is not at all correct."

What, then, should the teacher do? Because the entire approach to this method is to stress the positive, the first decision the teacher might make is to analyze the student's verbal response to determine whether or not any portion of the response can be classified as being valid, appropriate, or correct. Following this split-second decision-making, the teacher must then provide positive reinforcement or praise for that portion which is interpreted as being valid, appropriate, or correct. For example, if the teacher asks a general mathematics question and the student responds with a number for the answer, which is totally incorrect, then the teacher might state, "Your response is in the magnitude of the answer," or "Could you tell us how you arrived at your answer?" "Could you rethink your solution and take another try at it?" These responses are neither entirely negative nor wholly positive; rather they can be considered *neutral*.

If there is one teacher behavior that is crucial in handling incorrect student responses, it is to avoid being sarcastic or punishing. If you use a punishing verbal response as a teacher, then you are in fact using a "put down" strategy. The use of such a strategy tends to produce negative reinforcers and ultimately provides residual effects that cause students to ignore opportunities to respond verbally. Verbal teacher abuse is *never* an appropriate *professional* response.

How can a teacher provide either positive or neutral stimuli and yet elicit an appropriate response from the student? One strategy is to rephrase the question in a different manner so that the onus is at least shifted away from the student. As mentioned previously, *if* any portion of the response is correct or appropriate, *then* the teacher can begin a spontaneous prompting session with that student. The teacher carefully leads the student with a set of convergent questions.

Accompanying this strategy is a point that must be kept in mind: The teacher must be careful that nonverbal cues—such as frowning—do not show that he or she is upset or angry at the incorrect response. Thus, the teacher must maintain congruency between verbal and nonverbal behavior when handling incorrect responses. (Chapter 10 has a list of both verbal and nonverbal positive responses.)

Another strategy for helping a student correct an incorrect response is for the teacher to diagnose immediately the type and level of question that was asked and then ask the student a similar question, but one that is less difficult, without making other verbal comments to the student. This is similar to performing a task analysis on a concept in which simpler ideas must precede the more difficult ones. The latter strategy will be most important where concept learning is being stressed—for example, in social studies, science, grammar, and the humanities. What we are recommending is that the teacher react like a computer programmed with many possible options. This system always allows the student to get another set of opportunities to show that he or she knows some answer.

The human or interpersonal relationships that the teacher experiences with the members of the class are subtle and take time to build. After the teacher has the opportunity to analyze the personality types of each individual in the class, the teacher can use some negative as well as positive reinforcers. It is not uncommon for better students to clown or joke with the teacher or to kid the teacher. When the teacher diagnoses such situations, it can be predicted fairly accurately how a specific student will react, and the teacher can, in turn, humor the student. As a general rule, it is much better to be very *cautious and positive* in handling incorrect responses.

For example, it was one of the authors' unfortunate experiences as a junior in high school to be told to "read between the lines" when analyzing poetry. Such deceitful advice is so blatantly bad that it is not any wonder that some students approach English courses with "avoidance tendencies." If a student makes an error in a written response, unless it concerns spelling or mechanics, then the teacher should provide a set of minimum specifications to guide the student in correcting the error. The following examples are suggestions for handling incorrect responses.

Example 1

Teacher: Could you suggest some reasons why Secretary of War Root advocated the establishment of a General Staff? (Pause.) Peggy?

Student: Well . . . generals were pretty important and they really needed somebody to keep house, wash, cut grass, shine things, and stuff.

Teacher: Can you think about what you just said? I stated "General Staff" not "Cleaning Staff." Would you try again, please?

Example 2

Teacher: What was one of the military reforms instituted by Secretary Root? (Pause.) Manuel?

Student: He increased the size of the army to a million men.

Teacher: Well, you got the increase part right. He did increase the size of the army. You got the number a little too high, though. Why don't you lower your estimate and try again?

Example 3

Teacher: In this house plan, the living room windows face west. Is that a good idea? (Pause.) Isadore?

Student: I think it's great. You can see the sunset straight on.

Teacher: Izzy's answer is a good example of individual priorities in house design. To some people, the advantage of being able to view sunsets is very important. What kinds of weather-related problems might be created, though, Izzy, if the large windows face west?

Example 4

Teacher: Who do you think will be the next President, and what views can you offer in support of your judgment? (Pause.) Inez?

Student: I don't know. I really don't care either because they are all a bunch of liars anyway.

Teacher: That's a pretty strong opinion. Could you tell us why you think all the presidential candidates are liars?

Student: Well, to begin with. . . .

In these examples, the teacher responds in a manner that does not criticize the student. We all know of teachers who insult, ridicule, and degrade students who make incorrect responses. We view such teachers as incompetent professionals. One primary goal of schooling is to provide a positive and stimulating environment in which learning can take place. Learning is blocked by insults or negative teacher responses. The student learns nothing by humiliation—except to despise the teacher and to hate the school. We want you to create an atmosphere in your classes that is supportive—one in which students can react freely without the fear of being attacked for being wrong. Again, you must decide how you will behave.

Interactive Questioning Mechanisms

Promoting Multiple Responses

Teachers typically conduct recitation periods through questioning. The teacher asks one student to respond, then asks another student to respond, and so on. For the most part, the teacher does the talking. Few students, if any, need to listen carefully to their peer responses, because there is a closed communications circuit between the two individuals interacting. We recommend using *multiple-response questions,* to each of which at least three or four students may each provide a response. The key to increasing the number of students who respond to a question is to ask either a *divergent* or an *evaluative* question. In this manner, the teacher can predict that there will be more than one response or that there ought to be a set of responses that will not duplicate each other. Thus, the teacher frames a divergent question, asks the question, pauses, and then identifies three or four individuals to offer responses.

Of course, prior to using the multiple-response technique, the teacher must advise the class that a new method will be used. The technique is explained in detail, after which it is used. The teacher must also caution the students that there will not be teacher repetition *of any student response.* Thus students must listen to their peers' responses, so that they will not repeat any that have been previously stated.

The use of multiple-response techniques is a logical precursor to student-conducted discussions. Student discussions are extremely difficult to use effectively because students do not demonstrate the needed discussion behaviors or skills. By using multiple-response questions, the teacher subtly conditions the students to accept more responsibility to listen to each other and to modify anticipated responses based on previously elicited responses.

The multiple-response strategy also affects the teacher's behavior in that it allows the teacher to speak fewer times during the class. This in itself may be cause for celebration among students. But our concern is that the teacher's verbal interaction with the class be kept to an absolute minimum. It is difficult for the teacher to be an empirical observer of student behaviors, be directing a question-and-answer period, be managing the classroom, and be planning for appropriate questions—all at the same time. By using divergent or evaluative questions coupled with the multiple-response strategy, the teacher has the opportunity to analyze the types of responses that are being given. In short, the teacher has the chance to make a qualitative evaluation of each student's response without doing any other work.

By using these strategies, the teacher can expect longer student responses, student statements delivered in greater depth, and the establishment of greater challenges to all students. A slight modification of this technique can be made, in which the teacher subdivides a class into teams of three, four, or five students to add the motivating factors of small-group solidarity and identification. By varying the seating patterns of the desks, the teacher can facilitate more interaction. Also, any competition that develops within the class will be peer-oriented rather than between teacher and student. Friendly intraclassroom competition is established by adapting some type of "game" situation. This is one means of rewarding a whole spectrum of appropriate responses.

Teachers tend to have one major fault: they are very parsimonious with rewards. Thus, by using some adaptations of the multiple-response strategy, the teacher may reward one group for providing the most novel responses, another for the best responses obtained from an encyclopedia, another for the best nonverbal responses (pictures, cartoons, and the like), and another for the best multimedia presentation. All of these are motivational strategies that help make the classroom an enjoyable, creative, and interesting place rather than a prison to which the student is sentenced for one hour each day for one year.

Examples of Multiple Response

It is possible to make a mundane or pedantic recitation period more dynamic. Rather than asking the usual questions about where or when a big event happened, the teacher may conduct the recitation as follows:

Teacher: Today I'm going to use a new technique that we'll continue from here on. I'll ask a question, pause for a few seconds, and then call on three or four of you for responses. Listen carefully because I'll not repeat the question. Furthermore, listen to your classmates as they respond because I will not repeat any of their responses either. . . . Any questions? O.K.?

Teacher: Where might Christopher Columbus have landed if he had set sail from London and headed due west?

Teacher: (Pause.)

Teacher: Trudy, Raphael, Billy, Tommie.

Trudy: He'd have landed in Canada.

Teacher: (Smiles and merely points without comment to Raphael.)

Raphael: I think he would miss Canada and land near Boston because the Pilgrims landed in that area.

Teacher: (Nods head and points to Billy, but without verbal comment.)

Billy: You're both off. He'd have been blown right back to England or maybe Ireland.

Tommie: That would not happen, either. Christopher Columbus would have been blown by the Gulf Stream winds right down to the West Indies.

Teacher: Those are all interesting ideas. Class, let's check the direction of the Gulf Stream and the air currents. Hermie, will you please get the big map of ocean and air currents from the closet and give us a reading?

Hermie: O.K.

Trudy: Will you . . . ?

Evidence from the Far West Laboratory for Educational Research and Development would substantiate the previous hypothetical case. Students do learn to take cues from each other and to carry on a "mini-discussion" without much verbal guidance—or interference—from the teacher.

Use of the multiple-response technique also can aid in the building of other communication skills. For example, when the teacher begins to use this technique, students can be asked to write one-sentence summaries of each response given by their peers. Think of the implications that this simple teaching act can have on (1) improving listening skills; (2) structuring logical discussions; (3) identifying main points in an oral discourse; (4) enabling students to classify arguments, positions, or statements systematically; and (5) learning to outline. Thus teachers of all classes or grades must realize that they are responsible for helping improve student communication skills. Since questioning is such a widely used communication technique in the classroom, it follows that teachers should attempt to maximize the usefulness of this technique so that it improves other cognitive skills and processes as well.

Again, the use of the multiple-response technique is an excellent way to introduce the class to a discussion period. We recommend that discussions and discussion techniques be postponed until the multiple-response technique is mastered by teachers and students alike.

Concept Review Questions

As teachers begin to develop confidence in both themselves and their students, it becomes necessary to review, in the most efficient manner, previously learned concepts and to relate them to knowledge that will be introduced at a later date. In most cases, teachers tend to schedule a review prior to a summative evaluation. Thus "Review Thursday" tends to be boring for most students—even good ones. It is an ineffective use of student time in that the vast majority of students do not need the review and, for those who do, such an oral exercise is usually fruitless in expanding their intellectual understanding of the concepts that the teacher is trying to teach.

How can the teacher review previously taught concepts while conducting questioning strategies? One successful method is to reintroduce previously discussed concepts in the context of newly presented material. For example, if the teacher is progressing through a unit on transportation, in which modern transportation systems such as air travel and freeways are being discussed, and the teacher wishes to review the topic of the railroads that has already been covered, then the teacher should review the placement of transport terminals in both old and new contexts. That is, most railroad terminals as well as airports were initially built at the edge of a city. Through questioning, which uses concept review techniques, the teacher thus provides opportunities for the students to demonstrate comprehension concerning city growth while noting that transportation terminals become engulfed as a city expands; this, in turn, causes a set of problems that is unique to cities and to the transportation industry.

What we are suggesting, as a viable alternative to review sessions, is constant review. Such a review may be conducted at any level in Bloom's Taxonomy. As students begin to relate previously learned skills or concepts to new ones, they may begin to perceive the interesting relationships between old and new materials. If the teacher truly wishes to use the so-called basic liberal arts approach, then he or she should attempt to relate the ideas of one discipline to those of other disciplines. Rather than telling the students about such subtle interdisciplinary relationships, the teacher also can direct the students to the library so that they may discover them on their own and report them to the class. The latter technique is a meaningful one for those students who are always finished with their work and "have nothing to do"—except disrupt the class.

The concept review technique, therefore, requires that the teacher always be on the alert for instances that allow some meaningful relationships to be established, a previous concept to be reinforced, or a synthesis of knowledge to take place, thereby creating added motivation for the class.

Concept Review Examples

(The class is studying the affective domain.)

Teacher: How does the taxonomy of the cognitive domain, which we studied last month, differ from the taxonomy of the affective domain? (Pause.) Bill?

Bill: The cognitive domain is concerned with the intellectual aspects of learning, while the affective domain is more concerned with emotional outcomes.

Teacher: Good. Could someone give us some examples of these "emotional outcomes"? (Pause.) Mary?

Mary: Attitudes and values?

Teacher: Fine. Now, going back to my original question, how are the two taxonomies similar? (Pause.) Sally?

Sally: Well, because they both are called taxonomies, they both are classification systems, and both are hierarchical in nature.

Teacher: Excellent. What do we mean by "hierarchical" in nature, Bill?

Bill: I think it means that each category builds on the ones below it.

Teacher: Okay, could you give us an example of another kind of taxonomy that would illustrate your point?

Bill: Sure, the taxonomy of the animal kingdom. Each phylum supposedly is related in some evolutionary fashion to the one below it.

Teacher: Good. Does everyone see how that example applies to Bloom's Taxonomy? Okay, let's take a second now and try to relate the module on the taxonomy to previous modules. In other words, how could we use the taxonomy with some of the other ideas we've talked about? (Pregnant silence, which does not last for long.)

Teacher: Let me try to be more specific. How could the taxonomy be used in constructing better lesson plans? (Pause.) Jim? Mary?

Jim: You can use the taxonomy to look at your performance objective and see if your procedure correlates with the terminal behavior.

Mary: (With emotion.) You could also use the taxonomy to kind of judge whether the lesson is worthwhile doing at all.

Teacher: How do you mean, Mary?

Mary: Well, if the lesson consists of nothing more than transmitting a lot of facts, maybe the teacher should ask if these facts are ever going to be used again in one of the higher categories. And if the facts are important, there are more effective ways of having the students master them than by a recitation.

Teacher: Good. Anything else? (Pause.) How about the discussion module? Can you make any connections with the taxonomy? (Pause.) Al?

Al: Kind of going along with what we said about lesson plans, the taxonomy might give teachers some new ideas about discussion topics.

Teacher: Could you elaborate?

Al: Well, sometimes it's easy to get in a rut. Though teachers aren't likely to use discussions with performance objectives at the Knowledge level, they may not be aware of the full range or spectrum of possibilities open for discussion topics.

Teacher: Excellent. Anyone else?

Tina: Also, the taxonomy might be useful in analyzing why discussions bog down.

Teacher: In what respect?

Tina: If the students are attempting thought processes at the higher levels and don't have the background at the lower levels, there's likely to be a lot of confusion because the students don't "know" or "comprehend" what they're talking about.

(NOTE: In this interaction, the following topics were reviewed: (1) affective domain; (2) lesson planning; (3) objectives; and (4) discussions.)

Encouraging Nonvolunteers

In most situations, the teacher will not have much of a problem encouraging students to respond to questions. To be sure, if the teacher carefully tabulates the students who respond to the questions, the teacher will find that a few students dominate the verbal questioning sessions. Further observation of any class tends to illustrate that there are several students who do not volunteer their responses. *If* a goal of the teacher is to encourage verbal responses, *then* the teacher must take the appropriate initiative to encourage nonvolunteers to respond. Such encouragement is most difficult at the beginning of a new term when the teacher is relatively new to the students. As the teacher becomes more knowledgeable about a student's interest, it is easier to prompt a nonvolunteer because the teacher can use a question that will be in that particular student's realm of interest. What, then, are some helpful strategies to motivate nonvolunteers to respond verbally during a questioning session?

The first technique is to *maintain a highly positive approach toward the student.* That is, follow the philosophy that we have been espousing. The emphasis must be on allowing nonvolunteer students to respond appropriately or correctly each time they are called on. This means that the teacher must use questions that foster successful answering by the nonvolunteer. Once the nonvolunteer has responded appropriately, there should be generous positive feedback to encourage the student to continue such behavior. Furthermore, the teacher should inaugurate a systematic plan for devising those questions that require short responses and that lead to those questions that require longer responses. In summary, the teacher progresses from a convergent frame of reference to a more divergent one. Also, the opposite approach will ensure at least some response from nonvolunteers, thus allowing for positive reinforcement. The teacher may even begin by using easy evaluative questions because most students respond to questions that concern judgment, standards, or opinion.

Whatever the reason for not volunteering, the teacher must constantly strive to diagnose the verbal deficiencies and assets of each nonvolunteer. This does not mean that the teacher must play the role of an amateur psychiatrist, but that the teacher should determine whether or not there is an apparent pattern of verbal deficiencies for specific students.

Another method that can be used to increase nonvolunteer participation is periodically to make a game out of questioning. One way is to place each student's name on a card so that the teacher may draw the cards at random, thus creating a condition in which every student potentially can be called on to recite. Also, in situations where numerous hands are raised each time the teacher asks a question, the teacher can politely ask those students who are raising their hands to "hold all hands for the next three minutes" so that other students may have an opportunity to respond. In this fashion, the teacher tends to shape the behavior of those students who are adequately reinforced through verbal participation.

In addition, there is nothing wrong with giving each "nonresponding" student a card with a question on it the day before the intended oral recitation period. Very quietly, hand these students a card and tell them they may review the assignment so that they can summarize their responses for the next class period. At least this method begins to build a trusting relationship between the teacher and the student.

Implicit in this technique is the fact that the teacher observes and systematically notes *who* is volunteering responses in class recitations, and in what class situations. If time permits, it would be even more desirable to make a daily listing of such verbal activities. The teacher can appoint one member of the class to keep a tally each day. At the end of a week, patterns will emerge for each student.

Again, we condemn the use of calling on nonvolunteers as a punishment tactic. Schooling ought to be a positive, enjoyable experience, the affective consequence of which will encourage students to want to learn.

As a general rule, the most effective means by which the teacher may encourage a nonvolunteer to participate is for the teacher to be sincere in treating each student as a human being. Nonvolunteers have learned—sometimes painfully—that it does not pay to say anything in class because the teacher will "put you down." Teachers may not be the nicest people on earth and students in the junior and senior high schools, especially, have learned to recognize this and to play the game accordingly. No one likes to put a hand in a hot fire. No student will volunteer to answer a question if the response is going to be met with sarcasm, witty innuendoes, snide remarks, or hostility. The teacher should be highly considerate and approving at all times.

Developing the Student's Skill in Framing Questions

The previous techniques are all oriented toward improving the teacher's questioning skills. The following technique attempts a reciprocal arrangement—that is, to teach students how to frame their own questions.

For the most part, teachers neither encourage nor teach their students to ask questions. As a matter of record, some teachers are upset when students do ask questions. The typical classroom discussion—or, more correctly, recitation period—is conducted by the teacher, who asks the students questions, not vice versa. However, if we desire to encourage critical or reflective thinking, or thinking of any sort, then it behooves all teachers to develop the student's skill in framing questions. To aid in such a strategy, we refer to the game that was made famous many years ago on radio and is currently on many television stations—"Twenty Questions."

The game of "Twenty Questions" is one in which participants ask questions to identify something. The same mode may be applied in the classroom. The teacher may present a problem or identify some concept that needs to be discovered and will only allow the discovery to take place through student questioning. Initially the teacher will conduct the session, but as the students master the technique and become more proficient in the skills, then they may conduct the entire session, with the teacher merely analyzing the various interpersonal reactions.

J. Richard Suchman (1966) prepared the "Inquiry Development Program," in which the emphasis was to develop student questioning skills. The rule of his game is that, after a problem has been presented to the students, the teacher plays a passive role in the learning and responds only with a "yes" or "no" to a student's question. This means that the students must learn how to ask questions on which they may build a pyramid of knowledge, ultimately leading to a convergent response rather than a series of unorganized questions. When this technique is first used, the students have almost no opportunity to ask the teacher questions, thus causing initial results to be discouraging. However, the teacher should review each lesson and give precise and detailed directions on how the questioning can be improved. As one alternative, if it will not be too slow, the teacher may write each student's question on a chalkboard or on an overhead projector transparency, so that those questions being asked by their peers will have been presented visually to all students. In this manner, the gradual accumulation of information and skills can be accomplished in a systematic manner.

Of course, when developing student skills in framing questions, it becomes imperative that the students understand that each question must encompass numerous specifics. In short, the teacher must give practical application to student skills in deductive logic.

Another alternative method of developing students' skills in framing questions is for the teacher to have students prepare study or recitation questions based on the subject being discussed. In this manner, the teacher may select a few students each day to prepare a series of questions for their peers. The teacher may even share with the students a few secrets on questioning techniques, such as following the rationale of Bloom's Taxonomy for cognitive skills. To be sure, most students will be oriented only toward fact because that is what is mostly reinforced in their learning. But a skillful teacher will continually reinforce those questions that are aimed at higher-level thinking skills and ultimately help each student to prepare appropriate higher-level thinking questions.

You will note that as the teacher begins to encourage the class members to ask questions of each other, there is a subtle shift of responsibility to the students. Teachers usually encourage their charges to accept more responsibility. We believe that, by participating in learning situations, students acquire greater responsibility. This statement implies that responsibility is a "learned behavior" just like so many other behaviors. As a teacher, you owe it to your students to help them become articulate and thinking individuals. A splendid opportunity to do so is afforded by the transferring of more responsibility for classroom questioning techniques from the teacher to the students.

As we stated previously, this method must be explained carefully to the students and then practiced for a few class periods so that the students know how to "play the game." Then, perhaps once a week or more often, the students can conduct the questioning sessions. This method is a prerequisite experience to student-led discussions.

The class and the teacher may generate a set of criteria that provides the standards on which the various student-framed questions are based. The criteria also may be applied to a broader context. Students can be requested to evaluate the kinds of questions that are asked on various television quiz shows as a means of improving the students' own skills in data collection and interpretation.

All the teachers with whom we have worked have been pleased with the results of such techniques. More importantly, these same teachers were amazed at how much they *underestimated* the potentials that existed in their classes. We are not implying that these techniques are simple to implement; they take much work and planning. But the attendant rewards make both teaching and learning more worthwhile.

Teacher Idiosyncrasies: A Caution

One can speculate that all teacher behaviors that may be associated with questioning are positive and encouraging. After all, the teacher is assumed to need only a few tricks and a smile to achieve instant success. Unfortunately, there are teacher behaviors that, when used inappropriately, may interfere with a smooth verbal interaction pattern in the classroom. Briefly, these idiosyncrasies are (1) repeating the question; (2) repeating all student responses; (3) answering the question; (4) not allowing a student to complete a long response; (5) not attending to the responding student; and (6) always selecting the same student respondents. Each of these behaviors is analyzed.

Repeating the Question

A common error often made by teachers is the regular repetition of each question. This habit conditions the students to catch the "replay" of the question instead of "attending" to it—either cognitively or intuitively. This habit causes a loss of valuable time, is redundant, and does not help the teacher to maintain efficient classroom management. To be sure, there are appropriate times to repeat questions: in a very large room with poor acoustics; when the question is multifaceted; when the question is not adequately framed; or when the teacher is dictating a question to the class. We do caution that beginning teachers often have difficulty in framing verbal questions that are understood explicitly by the students. In such cases, the teacher should rephrase the question for added clarity. Repeating a question may be appropriate when one uses divergent questions. However, in most cases, repeating a question should be avoided.

Read the following two sets of repeated questions aloud to friends or colleagues and obtain their reactions.

Teacher: What is the main set of criteria by which to frame questions? In other words, what is the main set of criteria by which to frame questions?

Teacher: What is the population of Boston? What is Boston's population? How many people live in Boston?

How did they respond to the repetitious questions? Listen to teachers or professors in oral discourses to determine whether they repeat their questions. If you have not observed this idiosyncratic pattern, then obtain a tape recorder, tape a simulated version of this pattern, and play it back to a small group of peers. We will wager that after listening to a few of these simulated episodes, your audience will be highly amused. This may make a creative term project for your methods class.

Repeating All Student Responses

An equally distracting and time-wasting technique is to repeat all or nearly all of the student verbal responses. Not only is this a waste of time, but it causes the class to ignore their peers as sources of information and subtly conditions the class to wait until the word comes from the "fount of all wisdom." In short, students either do not attend to the initial student response or wait for the "instant replay" from the teacher. If the teacher is the least bit sensitive to the building of positive student self-images, then he or she will not want to be the center of verbal interaction and will attempt to keep the focus on the responding student. After all, if it is important to call on a student and require a response, then it ought to be equally important that student input be given the same priority as teacher-made statements.

This general rule does not hold for large-group sessions. Most large-group rooms or halls have poor seating arrangements, so that the teacher must almost always repeat student responses so that all can hear. The same is true for students with very soft voices. But in the vast majority of cases, there is no need to repeat student responses. Finally, *if* the teacher wishes to condition the students to pre-discussion behaviors, *then* comprehension of this technique is essential. To put it positively, by allowing students to take cues from each other, the desired attitude will be established, so that introduction of true discussions will be a logical sequence.

Answering the Question

Have you ever observed or participated in a class in which the teacher carefully frames a question, pauses, calls on a student, then quite insensitively answers the question? First of all, this idiosyncrasy is a morale defeater. How can students be encouraged to think when they know that the teacher will hardly allow them to voice their opinions? This behavior also tends to discourage volunteers and causes students to be negatively reinforced. If a question is so complex that no student can answer it, then the teacher should rephrase it, begin prompting, or assign it as a research project. As we mentioned previously, Mary Budd Rowe (1973, 1974) found that teachers usually do not wait for student responses or, worse yet, had wait times that measured in fractions of seconds! These findings are a heavy indictment, to say the least.

Not Allowing a Student to Complete a Long Response

One very distracting, inappropriate, and rude teacher idiosyncrasy is to ask a question and then interrupt the student by completing the response or by adding personal teacher comments without attempting to elicit other student responses. An example follows:

Teacher: What impact did the Vietnam War have on our young people? (Pause.) Arnie?

Arnie: Well, I sure don't trust . . .

Teacher: Right, you kids really don't have the confidence in our government. Why, I can remember when I was in high school . . .

Teachers who suffer from excessive talkativeness frustrate students and, worse, neglect to allow them to develop logical response systems. This interruptive technique discourages most students from even participating in the recitation period.

Not Attending to the Responding Student

When the teacher calls on a student, the teacher should show a courtesy to that student by attending to (that is, listening to, or at least appearing to listen to) him or her. After all, the teacher expects to instill attending habits in the students. This habit should be reciprocated during verbal interactions. After all, how would you feel if you were responding and observed that the teacher was gazing out the window or counting some loose change. We *are* suggesting that teachers often fail to reinforce appropriate student behaviors in the class by simply being insensitive to the feelings of others.

Always Selecting the Same Student Respondents

One frequently heard student complaint is that "my teacher never calls on me" or that "the teacher has a few pets that are always being called on." These statements typify the frustrations of students who recognize partiality when they see it. The biased teacher who calls on only a few (usually highly verbal and successful) students is providing a negative reinforcer to the majority of the class members, is making them disinterested in the subject, and causes serious erosion of the group morale.

If you are skeptical, let us remind you of Ray C. Rist's classic study, which was conducted in a Chicago elementary school. Rist (1970) observed that a teacher in a primary grade was exhibiting great bias in the manner in which students were selected for class recitations. Fewer and fewer individuals were being called on by the teacher until only a select few were identified. To make matters worse, the teacher began to move the responding pupils up to the front seats and the others, the nonrespondents, to the rear of the room. Needless to say, there were tremendous disparities between the educational achievements of the students in the front rows and those of all the other students. The teacher and pupils were all of the same ethnic group, so racism can be eliminated as the basis for bias. This may be an extreme case, but in general such situations exist to varying degrees.

A quick way to determine whether you show bias is to ask a different student each day to list the number of times that you call on each student. A quick tally at the end of the week will provide the data.

It is tempting to call on students who often volunteer and who will give you the "right" answer, so that you will appear to be an effective teacher. But *if* you wish to encourage all your students to be winners, *then* you ought to accord them equal opportunity to do so. One motto is fairly accurate in this case: "Nothing breeds success like success." If students are hesitant about responding verbally, then you as the teacher (who is presumably the most secure individual in the class) must gear the questions to suit the individual students, so that all students can enjoy the feeling of success and positive reinforcement.

Thomas L. Good (1982) summarized a series of studies and concluded that teachers exhibit some strong biases against "academically poorer students." For example, researchers have studied the response of teachers to poor academic achievers and high academic achievers. It was reported that teachers (1) wait less time for low achievers to respond; (2) fail to provide low achievers with feedback; (3) generally pay less attention to low achievers; (4) seat the low achievers toward the back of the room; (5) criticize the low achievers more; and (6) demand less from low achievers.

Throughout this chapter we have implicitly suggested that questions must be clear and understandable. Let us now become explicit. To be an effective questioner, teachers must be able to frame clear, concise, and succinct questions. In this respect, M. L. Land (1980) cautioned against teachers using "uhs," false starts, uncertain pauses, and ineffective transitions between topics. All such verbal behaviors by teachers ultimately cause student uncertainty. Of all the virtues, clarity remains high on the list of criteria for good questioners.

Conclusion

If you perceive that we are attempting to make a "game" of schooling, then you may be absolutely correct. School ought to be a place in which one may have fun or at least have a positive experience while learning. The "Puritan ethic"—that if something is fun it must be bad—is totally inappropriate now, as it was when it was first conceived. If learning can be made meaningful and relevant, then students will enjoy working at it. There is a great deal of research that demonstrates that students have a strong interest in and like those areas in which they are successful. If mathematics is distasteful to students, it is because for the most part students have been unsuccessful in this subject. Such an attitude can be rectified easily by making mathematics or, for that matter, all subjects success-oriented.

All of these questioning strategies provide the teacher with important "tools of the trade." But they are just that—tools. Each technique must be used appropriately and must be congruent with the objective that the teacher has for a specified student, group of students, or class.

Because questions play such an important part in the learning process, we have attempted to provide teachers with a cognitively ordered set of questioning alternatives based on "if-then" logic. Our goal is to increase the number of techniques available to the teacher so that whenever a question is asked, the teacher cognitively and automatically knows what he or she is attempting to do with the students. We also believe that the questioning sessions in school classrooms ought to be constructive and cheerful experiences, in which the students' opinions are respected, their interests stimulated, and their minds challenged.

FORMATIVE EVALUATION
Questioning Skills

A. How well did you master the materials on questioning? Here is a quick "knowledge check" to determine your ability to recall the points presented. If you have any problems, you should reread the chapter.
1. Several studies cited by the critics would indicate which trend?
   (a) Teachers tend to use questions that elicit student responses that can be classified in the Knowledge category.
   (b) Most teachers carefully plan their teaching and questioning.
   (c) Teachers stress critical thinking skills when using classroom questions.
   (d) A combination of items (b) and (c) is the best response.
2. The limited evidence on the improvement of cognitive levels of instruction and high-level questions may be interpreted to
   (a) Show that a positive relationship exists.
   (b) Indicate that there is a negative relationship—that is, high-level questions cause low-level responses.
   (c) Substantiate the idea that there is no need whatsoever for teacher training in questioning, since such training is not very helpful.
   (d) Indicate that teachers will ask what they please and that any technique produces high-level thinking.
3. There is evidence to indicate that in textbooks, a vast majority of questions are at which level (based on Bloom's Taxonomy)?
   (a) Knowledge
   (b) Comprehension
   (c) Application
   (d) Evaluation

B. Here is a list of questions and objectives. Classify each according to whether it is convergent, divergent, or evaluative. (For extra practice, also classify each according to the six major categories of the cognitive taxonomy.)
1. List as many major problems as you can that relate to urban education.
2. Given a model of the human eye, correctly label its parts.
3. From the data presented in Table 1, form generalizations that are supported by the data.
4. Zero population growth should become a governmental priority of the United States. Defend or refute this position.
5. What effect did the withdrawal from Viet Nam have on our nation's international prestige?
6. Discuss the differences between evolution and creationism. Which of the two concepts is the better, as supported by the best empirical evidence? List the evidence.

C. Place an X next to each question that has been properly framed by the teacher. If you do not check a question, briefly explain why.
_____ 1. "On what date did Christopher Columbus discover the Americas?" (Pause.) "Christine?"
_____ 2. "Charlie." (Pause.) "Name the ships that Columbus commanded."
_____ 3. "Nancy, I see you horsing around. Please go to the board and write out problem six."

———— 4. "Why would an Italian sail for the Spanish Crown?" (Pause.) "Albert?"

———— 5. "Who knows the port from which Columbus departed?" (Pause.)

———— 6. "How did the Spanish Crown raise the money for the expedition?" (Pause.) "Alfonso?"

D. Circle the most appropriate response.

1. Read the following teacher-student interaction.

   Teacher: Where does the Ohio River flow into the Mississippi?

   Student: I don't know.

   Which questioning technique should be used?

   (a) Multiple response   (c) Concept review
   (b) Clarification   (d) Prompting

2. You cannot prepare a sequence of questions for prompting before class begins because:

   (a) Generally, the right answer is given.
   (b) It takes too long for a teacher to prepare the list of questions.
   (c) It is nearly impossible to determine the necessity of prompting prior to the lesson.
   (d) Prompting questions are based on specific student responses.

3. A student in your class cries when informed that the response is wrong. Which of the following procedures would you use to help overcome this problem?

   (a) Never call on the student in the future.
   (b) Admonish the student for crying.
   (c) Ignore the crying and proceed.
   (d) None of these is appropriate.

4. One of your better students has given an incorrect response in class. Which of the following techniques should be used?

   (a) Tell the student he or she is right, but correct him or her privately after class.
   (b) Reply with a neutral statement such as "Would you think that through again?"
   (c) Wait for other students to correct the student.
   (d) Ignore the response and proceed.

5. An implied consequence of the multiple-response questioning technique is that

   (a) There will be less student participation.
   (b) The teacher becomes more actively involved.
   (c) It will provide a framework for shaping student interactions.
   (d) None of the above is apparent.

6. Select the multiple-response question from the following list:

   (a) What is the single mineral resource of Georgia?
   (b) List one criterion for good classroom discipline.
   (c) Who was the last Whig President?
   (d) Give sound reasons for the collapse of Chile's economy.

7. A student who is a nonvolunteer is asked to provide a solution to a problem that is being discussed by the class. The response is appropriate but of minimal quality. The teacher should

   (a) Ignore the student because he or she is obviously incapable of contributing to the class.

       (b) Encourage or praise the student for the response and then continue to react with the student.

       (c) Tell the student, "I guess that is about all we can expect from you, anyhow."

       (d) A combination of items (a) and (c) is the best technique.

E. The following statements should be identified as either True or False:

  1. True/False. Maintenance of higher-level student thinking is best accomplished by the use of divergent or evaluative rather than convergent, types of questions.

  2. True/False. When the teacher asks a divergent question, the teacher reserves the right to accept the responses given by the students.

  3. True/False. Under normal conditions, the repetition of student responses by the teacher tends to act as a positive reinforcer to the student.

  4. True/False. Calling on the student prior to asking the question is the best method by which to gain and keep the attention of all students, not just the student being called on.

  5. True/False. Multiple-response techniques tend to place greater student dependence on the teacher for answers and lessens student interactions.

  6. True/False. When the teacher repeats the question prior to selecting a student, it means that the question is really important and alerts the students to think this one out carefully.

F. When would you use a sequential hierarchy and when would you use a nonsequential one?

G. How does the logic of a question affect the responses?

H. How do lawyers, medical doctors, and teachers differ in the use of questions?

I. How could you use "mapping" to stimulate your students to generate questions?

J. Wait-time 1 and wait-time 2 differ in what respects?

K. Prepare a chart illustrating different questioning uses.

RESPONSES
Questioning Skills

A. 1. (a)
  2. (a)
  3. (a)
B. 1. Divergent
  2. Convergent
  3. Divergent
  4. Evaluative
  5. Evaluative
  6. Divergent-Evaluative
C. 1. X.
  2. The student should be identified after the question is asked.
  3. The teacher is using questioning as a punishment.
  4. X
  5. It is better to call on one or a few students rather than hoping for a response.
  6. X

D. 1. (d)
  2. (d)
  3. (d)
  4. (b)
  5. (c)
  6. (b) or (d)
  7. (b)
E. 1. True
  2. False
  3. False
  4. False
  5. False
  6. False
F. through K.
  Discuss with class members in small groups

REFERENCES

Barton, Thomas L., and Stanley J. Zehm. "Beyond Bay Area: A Description of the Washington State University Writing Project." *English Education* 15:1983, 36–44.

Beck, Isabel, and Margaret G. McKeown. "Developing Questions that Promote Comprehension: The Story Map." *Language Arts* 58:1981, 913–917.

Bloom, Benjamin S., ed. *Taxonomy of Educational Objectives, Handbook I: Cognitive Domain.* New York: David McKay, 1956.

Borg, Walter R., et al. *The Mini Course: A Microteaching Approach to Teacher Education.* Beverly Hills, Calif.: Collier-Macmillan, 1970.

Clegg, Ambrose A., Jr. "Classroom Questions." In *The Encyclopedia of Education.* Vol. 2. New York: Macmillan, 1971, pp. 2, 183–190.

Cornbleth, Catherine. "Student Questioning as a Learning Strategy." *Educational Leadership* 33:1975, 219–222.

Christenbury, Lelia, and Patricia P. Kelly. *Questioning: A Critical Path to Critical Thinking.* Urbana, Ill.: ERIC Clearinghouse on Reading and Communications Skills and the National Council of Teachers of English, 1983, p. 4. Public Domain Document NIE 400-78-0026.

Daines, Delva. *Teachers' Oral Questions and Subsequent Verbal Behavior of Teachers and Students.* Provo, Utah: Brigham Young University, 1982. EDRS/ERIC ED 225 979.

Davis, O. L., Jr., and Francis P. Hunkins. "Textbook Questions: What Thinking Processes Do They Foster?" *Peabody Journal of Education* 43:1966, 285–292.

Davis, O. L., Jr., et al. "Studying the Cognitive Emphases of Teachers' Classroom Questions." *Educational Leadership* 26:1969, 711–719.

Dillon, J. T. "Alternatives to Questioning." *High School Journal* 62:1979, 217–222.

———. "Cognitive Correspondence Between Question/Statement and Response." *American Educational Research Journal* 19:1982, 540–551. (a)

———. "Do Your Questions Promote or Prevent Thinking?" *Learning* 11:1982, 56–57, 59. (b)

———. "The Multidisciplinary Study of Questioning." *Journal of Educational Psychology* 74:1982, 147–165. (c)

———. A Norm Against Student Questions." *The Clearing House* 55:1981, 136–139. (b)

———. "To Question and Not to Question During Discussion." *Journal of Teacher Education* 32:1981, 51–55. (a)

Fedje, Cheryl G., and Ann Irvine. "Questions to Promote Thinking." *Vocational Education* 57:1982, 27–28.

Gall, Meredith D. "The Use of Questions in Teaching." *Review of Educational Research* 40:1970, 707–721.

Gall, Meredith D., et al. "Effects of Questioning Techniques and Recitation on Student Learning." *American Educational Research Journal* 15:1978, 175–199.

Good, Thomas L. "How Teachers' Expectations Affect Results." *American Education* 18:1982, 25–32.

Gray, James, and Miles Meyers. "The Bay Area Writing Project." *Phi Delta Kappan* 59:1978, 410–413.

Hays, Irene D. "A Procedure for a Writing Assignment Based upon Current Knowledge of the Revision Process." Richland, Wash.: Battelle Pacific Northwest Laboratories, 1980.

Herber, Harold L. *Teaching Reading in the Content Areas,* 2nd ed. Englewood Cliffs, N.J.: Prentice-Hall, 1978.

Honea, J. Mark, Jr. "Wait-time as an Instructional Variable: An Influence on Teacher and Student." *The Clearing House* 56:1982, 167–170.

Huenecke, Dorothy. "Cognitive Levels of Teacher Objectives and Oral Classroom Questions for Curriculum Guide Users and Non-Users." *Educational Leadership* 27:1970, 379–383.

Hunkins, Francis P. "Analysis and Evaluation Questions: Their Effects upon Critical Thinking." *Educational Leadership* 27:1970, 697–705.

———. "Effects of Analysis and Evaluation

Questions on Various Levels of Achievement." *Journal of Experimental Education* 38:1969, 45–58.

Hyman, Ronald T. *Strategic Questioning.* Englewood Cliffs, N.J.: Prentice-Hall, 1979.

Kaiser, Arthur. *Questioning Techniques.* LaVerne, Calif.: El Camino Press, 1979.

Konetski, Louis C. "Instruction on Questioning." Paper presented at Annual Meeting of the National Association for Research in Science Teaching, March 5–8, 1970.

Kounin, Jacob S. *Discipline and Group Management in Classrooms.* New York: Holt, Rinehart and Winston, 1970.

Land, M. L. "Teacher Clarity and Cognitive Level of Questions: Effects on Learning." *Journal of Experimental Education* 49:1980, 48–51.

McKeown, Robin. "Accountability in Responding to Classroom Questions: Impact on Student Achievement." *Journal of Experimental Education* 45:1977, 24–30.

Orlich, Donald C., Frank B. May, and Robert J. Harder. "Change Agents and Instructional Innovations: Report 2." *The Elementary School Journal* 73:1973, 390–398.

Orlich, Donald C., et al. "A Change Agent Strategy: Preliminary Report." *The Elementary School Journal* 72:1972, 281–293.

Rico, Gabriele Lusser. *Writing the Natural Way.* Los Angeles: J. P. Tarcher, 1983.

Riegle, Rodney P. "Classifying Classroom Questions." *Journal of Teacher Education* 27:1976, 156–161.

Riley, James. "The Answer to the Question Is to Listen to the Answer—An Evaluation of Teacher-Student Interaction During Discussions Preparatory to Reading." *Reading World* 22:1982, 26–33.

Rist, Ray C. "Student Social Class and Teacher Expectations: The Self-Fulfilling Prophecy in Ghetto Education." *Harvard Educational Review* 40:1970, 411–451.

Rodgers, Frederick A. "Effects of Classroom Questions on the Selection of Resources and Responses by Undergraduate and Sixth-Grade Students." *Educational Leadership* 26:1968, 265–274.

Rowe, Mary Budd. "Pausing Principles and Their Effects on Reasoning in Science." *New Directions for Community Colleges* 31:1980, 27–34.

———. *Teaching Science as Continuous Inquiry.* New York: McGraw-Hill, 1973, pp. 338–348.

———. "Wait-Time and Rewards as Instructional Variables, Their Influence on Language, Logic and Fate Control: Part I, Fate Control." *Journal of Research in Science Teaching* 11:1974, 81–94.

———. "Wait, Wait, Wait." *School Science and Mathematics* 78:1978, 207–216.

Sanders, Norris M. *Classroom Questions: What Kinds?* New York: Harper & Row, 1966.

Smith, Richard. "Questions for the Teacher—Creative Reading." *The Reading Teacher* 22:1969, 431.

Stevens, Romiett. *The Question as a Measure of Efficiency in Instruction: A Critical Study of Classroom Practice.* New York: Teachers College Contributions to Education, 1912.

Suchman, J. Richard. *Inquiry Development Program in Physical Science.* Chicago: Science Research Associates, 1966.

Taba, Hilda. *Teachers' Handbook for Elementary Social Studies.* Palo Alto: Addison-Wesley, 1967, pp. 87–117.

Verduin, John R., Jr., ed. "Structure of the Intellect." In *Conceptual Models in Teacher Education.* Washington, D.C.: American Association of Colleges of Teacher Education, 1967, p. 93.

7

DECISIONS ABOUT DISCUSSIONS

SETTING THE STAGE FOR
SMALL-GROUP DISCUSSIONS

One factor that will have a critical impact on how you interact with your students and how they interact with one another concerns *your* decision to use small-group strategies as a regular instructional method. The use of small-group strategies and discussions requires much teacher preparation and preplanning, which will be discussed later. Let us now identify what kinds of *process* objectives are described in this learning episode.

After studying this chapter, you will be able to

1. Distinguish process objectives from performance objectives
2. Understand the rationale for establishing small learning groups as an organizational pattern
3. Differentiate between a discussion and other classroom techniques
4. Identify the prerequisites needed to implement small-group learning techniques and discussions in the classroom
5. Prepare a summary of research that supports the concept of small-group learning techniques
6. Select an appropriate discussion technique from those given for classroom use and defend its application
7. Use checklists to identify various group member roles
8. Identify communication patterns that both facilitate and impede discussions
9. Determine participant and leader roles, responsibilities, and development
10. Plan for the organization, orientation, and initiation of small-group learning experiences
11. Determine the appropriate type of evaluation by which to judge the efficacy of a small-group discussion
12. Defend the use of small-group discussion techniques as a meaningful teaching strategy
13. Conduct a small-group discussion after meeting the conditions for doing so

In addition, we would suggest the following affective behaviors:

1. To be willing to consider using small-group discussion strategies, where appropriate
2. To value interactive teaching techniques
3. To incorporate flexible group management

Using Process Objectives

You have already demonstrated competence in the identifying, writing, and specifying of performance objectives. However, there is another type of objective that may be of equal, if not greater, importance—the *process objective*. A process objective, as the name implies, is an objective in which the learner is required to participate in some technique, interaction, or strategy.

A major difference between performance objectives and process objectives concerns learner outcomes. As discussed in Chapter 2, performance objectives require prescribing the exact learner behavior. With process objectives you do not specify a specific learning outcome; in fact, there could be as many final learner behaviors as there are members of the group. What is prescribed is a learning activity, or process. Many of the outcomes may be unanticipated, or "incidental" learning.

Process building is much more subtle than the specifying of performance objectives and requires that the teacher carefully plan *experiences* for the learners. You have heard that the schools should develop student responsibility. Yet the development of learner responsibility is a process that takes years to accomplish and, in some cases, some individuals never master the process. We submit that if the teacher wishes to develop processes such as writing skills, then the students must be given repeated opportunities to practice their writing. The same logic applies to the process building of small-group discussion skills. It takes practice, planning, and cumulative experience to gain the skills necessary to be successful in these techniques.

You will want to consider the effect on your class when deciding when and how to use small-group strategies. You will, first of all, make some assumptions about the organizational development of the class. Then you will decide on a process that will help the students reach the objectives you have planned.

Preparing for Small-Group Discussions: Establishing Goals

The first component of conducting a successful small-group learning activity is the development of a *long-range* set of priorities. Performance objectives are written for immediate achievement. Process objectives are usually written for the gradual development of skills, attitudes, and strategies. The process of establishing such long-range objectives is important, because it enables you, the planner, to identify the skills that the learners must master before they can achieve the objectives. For example, Figure 7–1 illustrates the skills that *both teachers and students* must develop *prior* to implementing student-led discussion techniques effectively. As Figure 7–1 illustrates, it takes approximately eight weeks to practice all the discussion elements, but it has been done in four weeks.

"Baking is no accident—it's *Occident*" was an advertising slogan for the

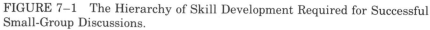

FIGURE 7–1 The Hierarchy of Skill Development Required for Successful Small-Group Discussions.

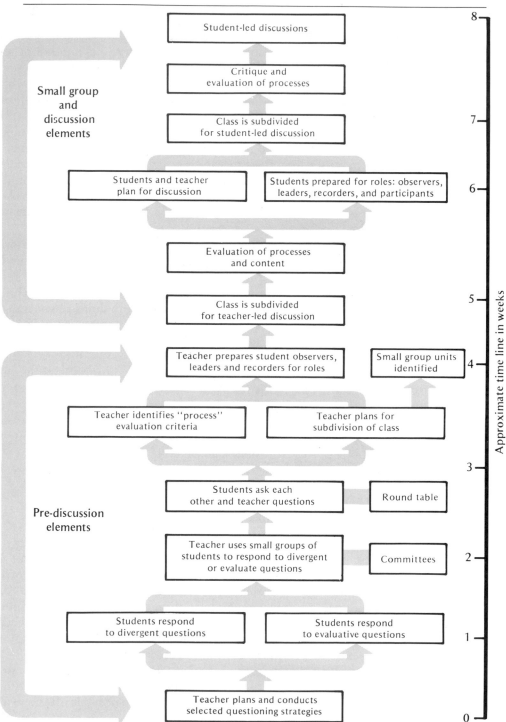

Peavey Flour Milling Company's brand "Occident." The slogan implied that one had to select the right brand of flour to succeed at baking. The same logic may be applied to the use of discussions in the classroom.

The teacher who claims that "discussions don't work; I tried one once during the first week of school and my students wouldn't even participate" demonstrates a lack of understanding about small-group discussions. Effective small-group discussions do not take place accidentally: they are learning activities that develop from carefully structured student behaviors. The teacher thus needs to learn what is involved in conducting successful small-group discussions.

Developing Small Groups

Small Group

It is significant that the first heading in this chapter contains the term *small-group discussions* rather than *group discussions*. Group size is an important variable that influences learner participation levels. There is no absolute minimum or maximum number of persons that must be included in a small group to ensure a successful discussion. An optimal group size generally ranges between six and eight persons. When there are four or fewer individuals involved in a discussion group, the participants tend to pair off rather than interact with all members. Conversely, the likelihood that all members will participate decreases when the group number approaches fifteen.

In our own experiences, we have found that when a group consists of twelve or more participants, student interaction begins to diminish. With larger groups—that is, fifteen or more—a few students tend to remain very interactive, a few appear somewhat interactive, and the majority become silent or passive. It may be appropriate to subdivide the class into groups of twelve or less prior to the initiation of a small-group discussion. We have found through experience that eight people per small group is most effective. This decision will be determined by the topic, the group, and the leader's experience.

Discussion

What is a discussion as it applies to teaching and learning? First, a discussion is *not* merely an informal group chatting in a comfortable corridor. Nor is it a clique-dominated pseudo-discussion conducted by only a few group members. Nor is it the type of activity that is too frequently called a "discussion"; here the teacher tells the class to read certain pages for homework and to be prepared to "discuss" them the following day. Unfortunately, this last situation usually dissolves into a lecture-quiz of textbook facts or into a low-level recitation session. There are times when such recitation of facts formulates a legitimate teaching strategy, but this approach is *not* a discussion and should not be confused with one.

What is the difference, then, between lectures, recitations, and discussions? Obviously, group size is an important distinguishing feature. Lectures can be given to any size group; recitations are more likely to entail one-to-one exchanges; discussions, however, involve high degrees of interaction between all participants.

A lecture may be defined as a series of oral *content* or *process* teacher presentations or speeches that do not necessarily involve student participation. There is wide latitude in lecturing styles. Some lecturers allow for student responses and questions. But the primary emphasis of a lecture is the delivery of a predetermined quantity of material by the teacher. Most—if not all—of the time is spent in teacher talk.

Conversely, a discussion denotes, by definition, an exchange of ideas, with active learning and participation by all concerned. A discussion is an active process of student-teacher or student-student interaction in the classroom. Recitation or lecture methods are more passive in terms of student activity. A discussion also allows the student to discover or state personal viewpoints, not merely repeat those that have already been presented.

For purposes of clarification, and so that the separate parts of the discussion process may be more clearly delineated, a discussion is defined as including the following elements:

1. A small number (four to twelve) of students meeting together.
2. Recognition of a common topic or problem.
3. Introduction, exchange, and evaluation of information and ideas.
4. Direction toward some goal or objective (often of the participants' choosing).
5. Verbal interaction—both objective and emotional.

We will use this definition to distinguish true *discussions* from recitation periods; however, let us expand the rationale for discussions.

Why Use Discussions?

Discussions and small-group learning units are most appropriate *if* you desire to increase teacher-student and student-student verbal interaction in the classroom. Also, by knowing several different techniques or processes, the teacher is adding flexibility to his or her professional skills. If the teacher plans to help students adopt a more responsible and independent mode of learning, then small-group discussion strategies will help in attaining this goal. It is important to note, however, that a systematic and planned set of procedures and experiences needs to be identified and sequenced by the teacher. During the lesson, the students become active participants in the class activities. Through this participation, the learners demonstrate their process skills. During the final stage of the lesson, both the students and the teacher formally evaluate the efficacy and value of utilizing these methods.

The discussion method, because it involves the students, requires the teacher to develop a viewpoint and to tolerate and facilitate the exchange of a wide range of ideas. Discussion is an active process of student-teacher involvement in the classroom environment. Discussion allows a student to discover and state a personal opinion and not merely repeat that which the teacher or text has already presented.

Why should you bother to learn to use the discussion method? When teachers are shown how to use discussion effectively, they welcome the opportunities it offers for classroom interaction. If the teacher wishes to achieve a high degree of student-student-teacher interaction, small-group discussion techniques offer a viable set of alternatives to the usual one-way flow of information.

Another purpose of discussion is to promote meaningful personal interaction and, of course, learning. The learning may be of contents, skills, attitudes, or processes. A widely espoused psychological principle is that people learn best when they are actively involved or participating. Thus, if the teacher wants to promote a wide range of interests, opinions, and perspectives, small-group discussion is one way to accomplish that goal. If the teacher wishes to improve the speaking-thinking-articulating skills of students, then the discussion technique is appropriate. If the teacher desires to have different students doing different tasks or activities at the same time, all leading to meaningful goals, then discussions are suitable. If the teacher wants to practice indirect control of learning, then discussion is the technique to use. If the teacher wishes to impart some informality to the group, then the use of discussion is a means to that end.

Small-Group Discussions for All Disciplines?

Discussions can be held in any classroom, on any subject matter, and at any age or mental level. Students need to learn how to express their ideas effectively and to incorporate these skills as part of their personalities. This learner goal is appropriate not only in subject areas where discussions are easy to conduct, such as in literature and social studies, but also in other areas such as in physics, chemistry, home economics, art, health, foreign languages, and physical education—in all courses in the school. Discussions need to have meaningful purposes, of course. A discussion about the quadratic equation would surely be inappropriate. But a discussion on the methods of proof or the derivations of the quadratic equation could prove to be mind-stretching for the participants.

Study the following list of *purposes* for small-group discussions and form your own *tentative* opinion about the usefulness of this type of teaching strategy in *your* discipline or teaching area.

1. Interest can be aroused at the introduction or the closing of a new topic.
2. Small groups can identify problems or issues to be studied or can suggest alternatives for pursuing a topic under consideration.
3. Small groups can explore new ideas or ways to solve problems, covering either the entire problem-solving cycle or just a phase of it.

4. Discussions provide the opportunity to evaluate data, opinions, and sources of information, and to structure concepts for future application.
5. Small groups can allow students to demonstrate individual strengths.
6. Students can often learn faster and better from each other.
7. Skills in leadership, organization, interaction, research, and initiative can be learned and improved through discussion techniques.
8. Ideas become more meaningful and personal if a student must defend them. Also, flexibility about understanding other viewpoints may be improved.
9. Discussions can provide the students (and the teacher) with opportunities for learning to accept and value other ethnic and/or cultural backgrounds.

After reading these items, reflect on your own discipline or teaching areas. Ask yourself this question: "Based on the nine elements, how many topics in my subject area lend themselves to a discussion?" If you are uncertain about the answer, select a textbook related to your teaching area and peruse the contents. Undoubtedly you will identify easily several topics that can be incorporated into a series of small-group discussions. See Table 7–1 for just a few of the hundreds of discussion topics that can be used in schools.

Now ask yourself: "What kinds of sharing experience do I want for my students?" Some of you probably will respond to this question by immediately focusing on sharing different cultural experiences such as dress habits, playthings and games, family behaviors, and religious practices. You may have thought about the need for students to display and share their unique talents. No doubt some of you may have thought about disadvantaged and handicapped students and of their need to be in a sharing environment.

The two preceding questions are important because most of you will be teaching in mainstreamed classes. Others of you will be involved with gifted and talented classes, and all of you will be faced with the challenge of providing a nonsexist, multi-culturally oriented education for your students. Being adept at using small-group discussions will help you meet the challenge.

Remember that it is the teacher's decision to use this or any other technique. Our goal is to provide enough information about the technique so that when the decision is made, the teacher will know why to use small groups, how to use them, and when to use them. If you decide to use one of the suggested techniques, then you must also set the climate for its most efficient and effective implementation.

Establishment of the Classroom Environment

Possibly the most important criterion for predicting your ability to facilitate small-group discussions is your own set of attitudes and feelings. Mastering small-group discussion methods requires an appreciation of the atmosphere, or emotional setting, of the classroom.

TABLE 7–1 Sample List of Discussion Topics

Topics	Audiences	Grade Levels
Life cycles of cities	Geography; Social studies	4–8
Playground safety	Homeroom	K–3
Community helpers	Social studies	1–4
Ideal office arrangements	Secretarial; Office education	11–12
Effects of colors on moods	Art; Home economics	9–12
Alternative health care plans	Current issues; Family living	10–12
Place value in mathematics	Mathematics	2–6
Explanations of "electrical charges"	Science; Shop	4–9
Options for cardiovascular conditioning	Physical education; Health; Life styles	8–12
Analysis of "popular" advertisements	Speech; General business; Language arts	7–12
Checks and balances in government	Government; History	7–12
Dating etiquette	Family living; Home economics	10–12
Expression, or pizazz in writing	Language arts; English	4–12
Stereotypes and musical preferences	Music; General business	7–12
Successful study habits	All students and teachers	K–12
How to listen	All students and teachers	K–12
Uses of math formulas	Mathematics; Shop	6–12
Impact of science and technology on society	Social problems; Science	8–12

To assess your attitude quickly, respond to the five statements listed here. To what extent do you agree with each of them? Use this three-point scale: Agree (A), Disagree (D), or No Opinion (N).

_____ 1. A student's achievement is highly correlated to the teacher's expectation of the student.

_____ 2. One way to show trust toward your students is to allow them to make suggestions concerning their own learning activities.

_____ 3. Students can conduct their own discussions if provided with the necessary discussion skills.

_____ 4. Students can learn to express their ideas and feelings confidently.

_____ 5. Being supportive and providing positive reinforcement are more conducive to student participation and learning than listing a set of rules.

How did you do? Did you agree with all five statements? If you did, then you have already made an attitudinal adjustment about teaching that often comes after years of experience: you believe that students can be delegated much responsibility, and that the way the leader (the teacher) acts is closely related to the manner in which the followers (the students) respond.

It is the responsibility of the teacher to establish the proper atmosphere in the classroom. As a teacher, you need to develop a "we attitude," an attitude of thinking in terms of "the students and I working together." This "we attitude" will help you in establishing some clear goals that involve teacher-student relationships, student-student relationships, the learning purposes of the classroom, and a supportive emotional climate. The classroom environment needs to be supportive of all persons so that the students will learn to respect all other individuals and their ideas. Such an atmosphere is fostered through small-group learning experiences. But *you* as the teacher must make the decisions that will shape the classroom environment into a supportive learning situation.

There will be themes, topics, chapters, units, or modules of instruction that will absolutely *not* lend themselves to the use of small-group learning activities or discussions. But that is a professional decision for which *you* are responsible. Our intent is to provide a broad spectrum of *means* by which to accomplish those planned, instructional *ends*. The more ideas to which you are exposed, the more options you will have in planning the structure and processes that you want in *your* instruction.

Introducing the Concept of Evaluation

The "Discussion Evaluation Form" (Figure 7–2) is designed to provide some feedback to each person who participates in a group activity. You will note that the preparation of such a form is rather simple. First you ask what the goals or objectives of the activity are and then you identify some criteria that would be applicable for judging each component.

As we continue the development of this chapter, you will observe and perhaps use many more evaluation forms to judge the value of small-group discussion activities. We feel very strongly that, because small-group discussions are process-oriented, the processes should be continually evaluated so that improvement may be noted.

Once the individual has evaluated his or her group activities, it is essential for the group collectively to compile data from each individual so that the group may receive cumulative feedback. To accomplish this aim, it is possible to tally all of the individual responses for each item (as marked on forms such as Figure 7–2) and present the sums to the group. This technique allows each individual to compare the self-rating to that of the group.

Figures 7–3 and 7–4 illustrate alternative methods of tabulating group data. We suggest that these evaluation forms be filed by the teacher so that a determination can be made later regarding the type and direction of growth of each participating individual. Besides, with such baseline and

FIGURE 7–2   Discussion Evaluation Form: Individual Participant Rating

DISCUSSION EVALUATION FORM

Group _____

Participant's name _____

Directions: Rate your own participation in your group by circling one of the numbers in the scales (from 1 to 5) for each of the nine criteria stated at the left.

Criteria	Very Ineffective	Somewhat Ineffective	Not Sure	Somewhat Effective	Very Effective
1. What overall rating of effectiveness would you give this discussion session?	1	2	3	4	5
2. How effective was the background event in getting you interested in the discussion topic?	1	2	3	4	5
3. How effectively did your group seem to be working together by the conclusion of the discussion?	1	2	3	4	5
4. How well was participation distributed among the group members?	1	2	3	4	5
5. How effective were the decisions your group reached?	1	2	3	4	5
6. How effective was the group in considering every idea that you contributed?	1	2	3	4	5
7. How effective was the leader in making it easier for you to say something?	1	2	3	4	5
8. How effective were you in encouraging others to speak or to become involved?	1	2	3	4	5
9. What were the two main good points and the two main problem areas of your small-group discussion?					

A simple form such as this gives each participant some idea of his or her strengths or weaknesses in the group activity. The recorded information can provide a focus for the improvement of small-group discussion processes. Modifications of the form can be made for specific needs.

FIGURE 7–3   A Quick Checklist for Group Discussion

QUICK CHECK POINTS

Your name _____

Directions: To evaluate your group, place an X next to the statement that best describes your reaction to each of the incomplete sentences:

1. I thought that the discussion
   - _____ (a) Gave everyone a chance to participate freely.
   - _____ (b) Allowed nearly everyone a chance to participate freely.
   - _____ (c) Was dominated by only a few.
2. As far as my participation in the discussion is concerned, I
   - _____ (a) Was very involved.
   - _____ (b) Could have been more involved.
   - _____ (c) Was totally uninvolved.
3. The discussion leader
   - _____ (a) Encouraged a wide range of participation.
   - _____ (b) Selected only a few persons to participate.
   - _____ (c) Seemed to dominate the discussion most of the time.

---

long-range data available, the teacher will be able to help students who have not mastered specific discussion skills.

As we previously stated, shorter discussion evaluation forms may be devised. The teacher may decide to help the students become more aware of their own participation by compiling and using very simple evaluation instruments, such as in Figure 7–3.

The teacher may compile group data from such forms to observe the total range of responses. We would suggest that a graph be prepared (by a small group, of course) so that the direction of the groups can be graphically portrayed for instant and easy analysis by the teacher. It also would give the small groups an idea of how they are progressing.

Because the goal of small-group instruction is to increase the participation of each student, it becomes essential to build simple-to-use evaluative instruments so that the progress can be monitored easily and systematically. An alternative method of gathering information about both the amount of participation of specific individuals and the overall pattern of participation for an entire group is illustrated in Figure 7–4. Figure 7–2 may be held by each student and then be tallied for the entire class so that a cumulative evaluation may be determined.

Throughout this chapter, you are exposed to various kinds of techniques that you can use or adapt for small-group situations. Many of the evaluation instruments can be lengthened or shortened to fit specific circumstances. We

FIGURE 7–4   Personal Data Check Instrument

PERSONAL DATA CHECK

Your name _____

Directions: Keep track of the number of times that you participate orally in the small-group activity. Then insert the total number in the place provided in Item 1. After the discussion is over, place an X next to the statement that best describes your reaction to each of the questions.

1. Tally the number of times that you participated verbally in the small-group discussion.
   _____ Your tally.
2. To what extent did you participate in the discussion?
   _____ (a) I really dominated it.
   _____ (b) I participated as much as the others did.
   _____ (c) Not as much as I would have liked to.
3. To what extent would you like to contribute more to the group discussion?
   _____ (a) I'd like to contribute more.
   _____ (b) I'm contributing just about the amount I'd like to.
   _____ (c) I'd like to contribute less.
4. How would you rate the extent to which your group encourages all of its members to participate fully?
   _____ (a) The group encourages everyone to participate fully.
   _____ (b) The group could encourage its members to participate more.
   _____ (c) The group discourages individuals from participating.

have shown some easy-to-use instruments because, as the teacher begins to compile data on process objectives, he or she will want to keep the systems simple and manageable. After many of the early skills are mastered, more complex forms can be used.

A BRIEF REVIEW OF SMALL-GROUP LEARNING PRINCIPLES

Group development and cohesiveness are attained through an evolutionary process. Everyone has experienced, in either large or small classes, how the initial sessions are marked often by a lack of responsiveness and a general climate of anxiety. This phase can be predicted from theories of group development. Effective small-group facilitators (or teachers) understand these theoretical principles and are able to implement the techniques presented in this chapter so as to expedite group development and cohesiveness. Winning coaches have long known and used these principles, often the secret of why they produce winning teams, talent notwithstanding. So let us proceed to those principles that have stood the test of experience.

Instructional Goals or Rationales for Small-Group Discussions

The question we would like to raise now is as follows: Are educators who suggest the use of discussion justified in making claims that it is beneficial to use small-group discussions?

Studies have shown that small-group methods are superior for *selected purposes when conducted under appropriate conditions.* There is evidence that changes in social adjustment and personality can be best facilitated through small-group instructional methods. Students who work together in a small-group discussion are likely to learn more quickly with more accuracy than are students engaged in other learning methods.

This is not to assert that small-group discussions are always more effective than other methods. Exhaustive research done by the Human Resources Research Organization (HumRRO) summarized some of the advantages and disadvantages of small-group methods. Olmstead (1970) had these conclusions:

> A review of existing research concerned with small-group methods leads to the conclusions that the techniques are effective for enhancing motivation to learn, developing positive attitudes toward later use of course material, and improving problem-solving skills. The methods are no more effective than lectures for transmitting information, concepts, and doctrines; however, when used in conjunction with lectures, they are helpful for increasing depth of understanding of course content.

The HumRRO study noted five instances in which it is most feasible to use small-group methods (Olmstead, 1970):

1. To increase depth of understanding and grasp of course content.
2. To enhance motivation and generate greater involvement of students with the course.
3. To develop positive attitudes toward later use of material presented in the course.
4. To develop problem-solving skills specific to content of the course.
5. To provide practice in the application of concepts and information to practical problems.

Teachers can emphasize two process skills in their classes that will increase the effectiveness of the small-group participants. These processes are (1) inquiry skills and (2) cooperativeness. Studies have demonstrated the usefulness of inquiry skills; in fact, many of the newly developed curricula now place a heavy emphasis on an inquiry approach to learning.

In groups that have cooperative members, the quality and quantity of learning are often amazingly high. Conversely, if the group members are competing with each other, both the quantity and quality of learning sometimes decrease. Of course, to reach selected instructional goals, intergroup competition may be desirable if it is not carried to an extreme. Again, that is your decision to make. The overall success of small groups within your classroom depends on a carefully selected blend of discussion modes, some of which require intragroup cooperation and a few that call for intergroup competition, which may be in the form of games or simulations of some kind.

Concepts Concerning Small-Group Interaction

Studies concerned with selected aspects of small-group interaction have resulted in the development of a number of basic concepts that explain phenomena associated with such groups. These concepts have become components of a set of fundamental assumptions concerning small-group interaction processes; these assumptions can be used by teachers to facilitate small-group discussions. These concepts are *interaction, process, structure, role, leadership,* and *group cohesion.* Let us examine each concept in depth.

Interaction

Communication between two or more people is defined as interaction. This communication can, of course, be either verbal or nonverbal or, even more likely, a mixture of both. Astute observation of small-group discussions will reveal both nonverbal and linguistic modes of communication or interaction.

Interaction is the process of persons responding to each other. The essence of the concept is that communication is a reciprocal process between interactors. A group member who says something, but to whom no one listens or responds, is not truly involved in an interaction sequence. Likewise, random body movements are not part of an interaction unless another person notices those movements and verbally or nonverbally responds to them.

Process

Closely associated with interaction is the concept of process. Process may be defined as the aggregate of the interaction. The group facilitator can refer to the interaction process as the communicative actions that occur during the group discussion.

Structure

The interaction process takes place within a structure. Structure can be conceptualized as a pattern of interpersonal relations. Another way to visualize structure is to think in terms of the relative positions of the group members within the framework of the total group. The small-group discussion facilitator will need to remember that the written and unwritten rules of the "school as an institution" may dictate the structure of the group. The institution tends to assign a position or status role to the teacher and different roles to the student. The optimal structure for a small-group discussion in the classroom is one in which the interaction processes are widely and evenly distributed among the members and in which the roles are flexible.

Role

Small-group discussion members can maintain structure because the group members are aware that the particular roles that they play in this setting have certain corresponding expectations. The structure determines the parameters of possible roles. Small-group members can establish expectations that encourage other group members to interact in any given situation. Roles can be associated with sets of expectations. For example, students expect the teacher to give assignments, praise good student efforts, and obey the principal; these functions establish teacher roles.

Group members may be assigned roles, such as teacher or student, or roles may be assumed voluntarily. Each role has specific privileges, obligations, responsibilities, and powers. A role is meaningful only in relation to some other role; thus, roles in such a context are complementary. Although roles are the product of a particular small group's norms, they can be grouped into three general categories. These categories are (1) task roles; (2) maintenance roles; and (3) self-serving roles. In these roles, individuals demonstrate a set of behaviors associated with these functions. No one individual always plays one role. It is the teacher's responsibility to provide each student with opportunities to participate in a wide spectrum of roles.

Task roles include behaviors such as initiating, providing information, seeking opinions, clarifying, elaborating or interpreting, synthesizing or summarizing, and testing for consensus or group commitment. These roles focus on the task of getting the assignment accomplished.

Maintenance roles tend to be management oriented. Maintaining group processes requires that participants help the group be cohesive and productive. An encourager role is played by those who are friendly, receptive, and responsive to others. A norm tester notes the relationships in the group and initiates procedures to see whether the group accepts these relationships. A harmonizer works to reconcile differences. A compromiser yields to a more generally accepted position or encourages others to make concessions to maintain group cohesion. A facilitator keeps communication channels open and encourages others to participate. A recognizer keeps the record up-to-date by giving credit for ideas or actions to the appropriate individual. A standard-setter applies criteria when evaluating group functions or productivity.

Self-serving roles are neither as positive nor as constructive as task roles or maintenance roles. Individuals accepting these roles tend to obstruct a true discussion by serving their own interests. The same individual may play the roles of both a dominator and an aggressor.

A dominator may interrupt, monopolize the discussion, embark on a monologue, establish a position early, provoke action, and/or lead by asserting authority. The aggressor struggles for status, boasts, criticizes, and denigrates others.

A blocker interferes with progress by rejecting ideas, by responding pessimistically and negatively, by arguing unduly, and by refusing to cooperate with the group. A deserter withdraws, becomes inattentive, whispers to others to distract them, and wanders away from the subject.

A recognition-seeker is the person who makes exaggerated attempts to get attention. The recognition-seeker may claim to possess great skills, be petty, call for careful examination of all sides of the question, or depend heavily on personal experience as a basis for an opinion.

The playgirl or playboy tends to lack involvement in the group activity and to distract others by the use of horseplay, inappropriate humor, and/or cynical comments.

Leadership

One of the most important roles in small-group discussion is that of the leader. There are several ways to explain leadership and to theorize about the role of the leader. At least two types of leadership roles—status and functional—are evident in the classroom. The *status leadership* role is fulfilled by the person (the leader) having an official or designated title. The title carries an assumption of authority with it—such as teacher, "assigned student" group leader, or spokesperson.

Functional leadership describes the situation in which any group member who performs a function that helps the group move toward accomplishing its task fulfills a leadership role, if only for the duration of the one behavior. Functional leadership is a key concept for those facilitators who subscribe to the "democratic" theory of leadership—that leadership should be shared among the group members.

Group members will be more satisfied with the group if they feel that they have some influence on group decisions. Group facilitators need to be sensitive to the fact that the group members want to feel involved and influential in both the process and product areas. The teacher may be the status leader, but in group work the leadership role should be shared with the group members. The teacher is responsible for providing an opportunity for each student to become a leader.

Group Cohesion

The concept of cohesion is best understood if one examines its three crucial elements—unity, attraction, and purpose. The cohesive group displays evidence of the "we attitude" (unity); its members express a strong desire to belong to the group (attraction); and its members can define group goals and activities (purpose). In the vernacular, a cohesive group is one that "has its act together."

Group cohesion is not a desirable end in itself. For instance, the situation in which students are cohesive but rebel against or exclude the teacher may make learning impossible. It is crucial that the teacher be a part of the "we." However, the "we" must not be so strong that it fosters too much conformity and ignores the value of individualism.

Developmental Stages of Groups

The development of small groups that are cohesive and productive is a demanding and long-range task. It requires a teacher, or facilitator, who is flexible and has a great deal of organizational skill. Another skill that is needed is the ability to analyze group interaction and then prescribe ways to help the group to evolve through its developmental stages.

Richard A. Schmuck and Patricia A. Schmuck (1971), in their book *Group Processes in the Classroom,* examined three theories of group development and, from those theories, synthesized four stages of group development. Suggestions for positive teacher behavior are included in our discussion of each stage.*

Stage 1: Acceptance-Inclusion-Membership-Trust

A person normally reveals a little about himself or herself to the group when making first contact with the group. The higher the level of self-confidence, the faster this revealing process occurs and the quicker the person is accepted into the group. Some students may need a great deal of self-concept development before they can fully accept their place in the group and, in turn, trust the group process.

When students do not feel accepted, group development is retarded and there is likely to be both social and academic withdrawal. Discipline problems may also increase because, if a student does not trust the group, that person will not accept and comply with the group norms. During Stage 1, each person tries to determine his or her place in the group. The student is likely to try to present his or her "best behavior" but will still have inward self-doubts as well as misgivings about relating to others. The teacher should be careful to accept every person and to show confidence and trust in the group, while helping any student to overcome fears of personal inadequacy. Relationships should be honest and the lines of communication need to be open; indeed, emotions as well as cognitive learnings have a place in the classroom.

*From Richard A. Schmuck and Patricia A. Schmuck, *Group Process in the Classroom, 1971*. (Dubuque, Iowa: Wm. C. Brown Co., 1971). Used with written permission of Wm. C. Brown Co.

Stage 2: Influence Patterns—Task and Maintenance Communication

During Stage 2, influence patterns are developed by the group. Some participants are influential academically, and others keep the group cohesive through emotion and social interactions. A pattern of decision-making usually appears during this stage. A one-way communication pattern must be avoided, because it is observed that, in general, group members wish to communicate with a power-based person rather than with those with little or no influence. Communication between and among students should be encouraged. The teacher must realize that, at times, frustrations will be evidenced as groups attempt to complete their tasks. A great deal of time will often be spent by participants in tending to the social-emotional needs of one another.

Stage 3: Productivity—Goal Attainment

The teacher must work *with* the students in establishing goals and in setting procedures for reaching the goals. Evaluation of group efforts should be done on a regular basis so that the processes may be integrated at appropriate times. It is probable that if the teacher sets the boundaries of behavior, the group will handle its own problems within that framework. Unless the group has passed through Stages 1 and 2, it is unlikely that it will progress to the third stage: productivity. Some individuals may produce in academic terms of productivity. But the teacher must give ideas, aid in planning, and be available with information or directions so that persons who are not productive may be prescribed achievable group objectives.

Stage 4: Flexible Norms—Self-Renewal

The final stage represents the maximum level for both individual learning and group productivity. The group has developed in maturity and trust so that it can analyze its own problems and then prescribe appropriate corrective actions. It is crucial for the teacher to recognize the legitimacy of emotional expression within the group setting and to help the group deal with feelings naturally and openly. Groups that have reached Stage 4 are flexible enough to allow each individual to function with a particular learning style while encouraging quality group work. Figure 7–5 illustrates the evolution of these four stages.

Figure 7–5 indicates that each stage is contingent on reaching the preceding one. This is much the same way that Gagné arranges his concept of hierarchies. Stages 3 and 4 seem to develop only because the teacher takes the time and makes the effort to plan for experiences that allow the students to demonstrate growth in terms of accepting responsibility and to evaluate their individual participation. The attainment of these later stages cannot

FIGURE 7–5 Adaptation of the Schmuck and Schmuck Model of Group Development

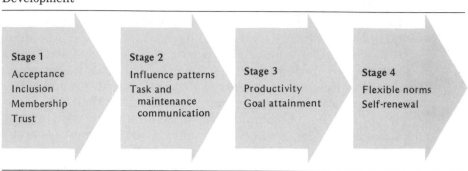

Source: Adapted from Richard A. Schmuck and Patricia A. Schmuck, *Group Processes in the Classroom, 1971* (Dubuque, Iowa: William C. Brown Company, 1971). Adapted with written permission of William C. Brown Company.

be guaranteed by the teacher simply announcing that "today we'll have a discussion on. . . ."

Behaviors for Teachers

The four stages of group development, as synthesized by Schmuck and Schmuck, need attendant and appropriate teacher behaviors in order to be implemented in the classroom. Here is a summary of a set of applicable teacher behaviors that seem essential to implementing discussion techniques. Each stage is identified and shows the teacher how to monitor progress and to interact positively.

Stage 1: Acceptance-Inclusion-Membership-Trust

The teacher behaviors that are essential for this stage include the showing of interest, trust, and confidence in each student's opinions and abilities. The teacher must accept and allow expressions of doubt or fear. In many cases, the teacher will direct the activities of each group but with an air of spontaneity.

Stage 2: Influence Patterns—Task and Maintenance Communication

The desired teacher behaviors to implement Stage 2 are indirect methods that stimulate students. As teacher, you should ask questions that encourage extended student responses. Your goal is to stimulate two-way communication, or even three-way communication—that is, student-student-teacher. To encourage those "quiet" people, you should direct questions and tasks in their direction.

Observe how the behaviors associated with Stage 1 tend to integrate easily and smoothly with those needed in Stage 2. Throughout your experiences with these or other teaching decisions and techniques, you will observe that there is usually a smooth blending of methods rather than an abrupt insertion of them. How you behave and react to situations and how you make those interactive decisions are extremely essential for success with any teaching method. Planning ahead for these decisions increases the probability of success.

Stages 3 and 4, particularly the latter, will probably be reached faster in the elementary grades. In these grades, the same teacher and students will usually spend several hours together daily, thus making it possible to move through Stages 1 and 2 rather quickly. The middle and secondary school teachers who only see a group of students for one period daily should expect that Stages 3 and 4 will not be reached early in the year.

Stage 3: Productivity—Goal Attainment

Productivity and goal attainment are closely associated with evaluation. Prior to the beginning of this stage, there must be consistent evaluation of each group's progress. Encourage the students to complete evaluation forms such as those illustrated in Figures 7–2, 7–3, and 7–4. By conducting planning and evaluating sessions with the groups, you may collect data as shown in Tables 7–2 and 7–3. Note that these tables are constructed from

TABLE 7–2   Interactions of Seven-Member Group Led by Mr. A

Interaction Categories (Functions)	Group Members						
	T	2	3	4	5	6	7
Shows solidarity—seems friendly	6	0	0	0	0	0	0
Shows tension release—dramatizes	2	2	0	1	0	0	0
Agrees	21	1	1	4	0	1	1
Gives suggestion	22	0	0	0	0	0	0
Gives opinion	15	13	4	10	10	6	7
Gives information	21	10	5	4	3	6	0
Asks for information	8	1	0	1	0	0	0
Asks for opinion	43	0	0	0	0	0	0
Asks for suggestions	2	0	0	0	0	0	0
Disagrees	1	0	0	2	0	0	0
Shows tension	0	0	0	0	0	0	0
Shows antagonism—seems unfriendly	0	0	0	0	0	0	0

Source: From R. A. Pendergrass, "An Analysis of the Verbal Interaction of Small Group Discussion Members in Secondary Social Studies Classes" (Ph.D. diss., Washington State University, Pullman, Washington, 1973).

Note: Under the head "Group Members," "T, 2, 3, etc." are given. Each of these represents a separate individual, with the teacher being identified as "T" and the students as numbers 2 through 7. The numbers listed in the table body refer to the number of times that each group member spoke. The "Interaction Categories" list the kinds of interactions that occurred.

TABLE 7–3   Interactions of Eight-Member Group Led by Mr. B

Interaction Categories (Functions)	Group Members							
	T	2	3	4	5	6	7	8
Shows solidarity—seems friendly	0	0	1	0	0	0	0	0
Shows tension release—dramatizes	0	0	0	0	0	0	0	0
Agrees	2	0	1	0	0	0	1	1
Gives suggestion	4	0	0	0	0	0	0	0
Gives opinion	4	0	7	0	0	1	1	6
Gives information	9	0	3	0	0	0	0	1
Asks for information	5	0	0	0	0	0	0	1
Asks for opinion	4	0	0	0	0	0	0	1
Asks for suggestions	0	0	0	0	0	0	0	0
Disagrees	0	0	0	0	0	0	0	1
Shows tension	0	0	0	0	0	0	0	0
Shows antagonism—seems unfriendly	0	0	0	0	0	0	0	0

Source: From R. A. Pendergrass, "An Analysis of the Verbal Interaction of Small Group Discussion Members in Secondary Social Studies Classes" (Ph.D. diss., Washington State University, Pullman, Washington, 1973).

Note: Under the head "Group Members," "T, 2, 3, etc." are given. Each of these represents a separate individual, with the teacher being identified as "T" and the students as numbers 2 through 8. The numbers listed in the table body refer to the number of times that each group member spoke. The "Interaction Categories" list the kinds of interactions that occurred.

"real" high school situations. Examine the interactions of each group, then continue reading the text.

The evaluations noted in Tables 7–2 and 7–3 describe interactions by two different groups. The teachers were active in both groups. Teacher A (Table 7–2) participated in every interaction category except "shows tension" and "shows antagonism." Teacher B was not as deeply involved but still tended to be the leader of the discussion. Use of such evaluation tables will enable the teacher to determine when to seek methods that involve every student in the discussion group.

The more you involve the students in establishing meaningful goals and in specifying clearly attainable objectives, the greater will be the success of the groups. Remember that you must help the groups to find operating procedures for achieving goals and objectives.

Stage 4: Flexible Norms—Self-Renewal

It is implied in the fourth stage that the class groups possess the internal influence, control, and skills needed to solve the various difficulties that arise. A positive and supportive attitude by the teacher will help classes mature into groups that are able to diagnose problems of leadership, inclusion, norm-building, and communication. As a group develops, it will need less guidance from the teacher.

In many cases, the students may exhibit unfriendly feelings and make criticisms. When these occasions arise, the teacher and the group should be at the point of personal, emotional, and group growth to be able to discuss the conditions that have caused the negative feelings and should attempt to resolve the disagreements.

The more mature the group, the more open will be the feelings about tasks, norms, or objectives. The final level reached in using small-learning groups is the self-renewal stage—the apex of ideal organizations.

Considerable planning, effort, and class time are needed to achieve all these stages. The process may be accelerated by more flexible class schedules and longer time blocks. Furthermore, the types of materials being studied must be appropriate for this technique.

SEVEN BASIC SMALL-GROUP DISCUSSION TYPES

From among the seven basic discussion techniques that we will present next, our goal is to provide you with at least one discussion type that will fit your teaching style. To be most helpful, the creative teacher must master several teaching styles and techniques, including the subject of small-group discussions.

If you as a teacher plan to use a small-group discussion, then you should be able to choose from among many styles. The basic contingency for selection will be the state of preparation of the students. The teacher who can organize and facilitate several different types of discussions will be able to design more varied learning activities than the teacher who knows only one or two types. To increase your effectiveness as a discussion-oriented teacher, seven kinds of small-group discussions are introduced. As you are exposed to this wide spectrum of small-group methods, you should seek out fellow students with whom to practice each of the types. In this manner, you will acquire first-hand experience.

One method by which to classify (and remember) discussion types is to use the variable of control or domination. When facilitating a small-group discussion, the teacher makes decisions regarding the amount of teacher or leader control that is desired. The teacher can dominate almost totally the activities of any group, can act in an egalitarian manner, or can choose not to participate at all. The last situation can be observed in small-group discussions in which interaction is controlled totally by the students. Table 7–4 illustrates the seven basic types of discussions viewed along a control continuum.

Although the element of controlling a discussion is one dimension of planning, there are three other important concepts that must be identified when choosing a discussion type for a particular situation. These are (1) the desired or anticipated process or skill; (2) the desired or anticipated product; and (3) the combination of process and product in a problem-solution type. Group work always has a goal, such as the completion of a given task. This

TABLE 7–4   A Taxonomy of Discussion Groups

Types of Discussions	General Instructional Purposes	Orientation	Knowledge, Skills, and Control Continuum
Skill Building			
Brainstorming	Creativity Stimulation Generate ideas	Processes	Lowest need of discussion skills and moderate probability for teacher control
Phillips 66	Role-building Leadership Responsibility Listening Evaluating	Processes	↑
Task Building			
Tutorial	Individual Skills Questioning Basic Competencies	Processes and products	
Task Group	Delegation of responsibility Initiative Achievement Planning skills	Product and processes	
	Group learning Affective consequences Accomplishment Evaluation	Product and processes	
Role-Playing	Clarifying issues Evaluation	Processes	
Panel	Debating ideas Reflective thinking Group consensus Values analysis Presenting information	Processes	
Problem-Solution Building			↓
Inquiry group	Inquiry Evaluation Analysis Synthesis Evaluation Student initiative	Processes and product Processes	Highest need of discussion skills and lowest probability for teacher control

goal is the *product*. How the members interact with each other during the discussion is the *process*. These two objectives must be taught to the students so that they will know how to "play" the game. Let us now proceed to those seven basic techniques.

Two Skill-Building Techniques

Brainstorming

A very simple and effective type of technique to use.when a high level of creativity is desired is "brainstorming." Any number of students can become involved in a brainstorming activity. The shorter the period of time for discussion, the fewer should be the number of group participants, so let time dictate the size of the group, which should fall within a five-to-fifteen-person limit.

The brainstorming session is started by the leader, who briefly states the problem under consideration. The problem may be as simple as "What topics would the group like to consider this semester?" or as complex as "How can an office of secretaries and junior executives be arranged to maximize efficiency?" Every school subject has some elements that require students to do some free-wheeling thinking. This is when you want to use a brainstorming group. Refer to Chapter 6 to review the topic of *mapping,* as it is effective when combined with brainstorming.

After the topic is stated and before interaction starts, it is crucial to select a method of recording the discussion. It can be taped, or one or two students who write quickly can serve as recorders. The leader should stress to the group that *all* ideas need to be expressed. All group participants need to realize that *quantity* of suggestions is paramount.

There are some very important rules to follow when using the brainstorming technique. (Different writers have slightly different views on some of the minor techniques. You may want to peruse the bibliography for these variations.) Although all the students will be oriented to the rules, make sure that the student leader enforces these procedures. The following rules seem to be especially important.

1. All ideas, except for obvious jokes, should be acknowledged.
2. No criticism is to be made of any suggestion.
3. Members should be encouraged to build on each other's ideas. In the final analysis, no idea belongs to an individual, so encourage "piggy-backing."
4. Solicit ideas, or opinions, from silent members. Then give them positive reinforcement.
5. Quality is less important than quantity, but this does not relieve the group members of trying to think creatively or intelligently.

Brainstorming is an initiating process and must be followed up with some other activity. One way to follow up would be to use the ideas generated in the brainstorming session as the basis for another type of discussion. *After the brainstorming session, it is important that ideas be evaluated and as many of them as possible be used by students in follow-up activities.* Brainstorming can lead to the arranging of the elements in order of priority—for example, when the teacher wishes to evaluate a series of suggested topics according to their importance, so that they can be used for future study.

The evaluation of a brainstorming session should not be lengthy and it should be nonthreatening for the participants. Remember that you want everyone to contribute, regardless of their current level of academic capability. You may want to make some private assessments about academic levels, levels of inhibition, the pecking order, who is bored in class; but all public evaluations must be highly positive in nature.

Phillips 66

The "Phillips 66" discussion group, which involves exactly six students, was developed by J. Donald Phillips of Michigan State University. Such a group is established quickly and does not require pre-orientation of students; also, students do not have to be highly skilled in group interaction for this type of discussion to work effectively. In fact, the Phillips 66 technique is most appropriate as an initial mixer activity.

The class is divided into groups of six (this can be done by the teacher or on a volunteer basis). The groups then have one minute in which to pick a secretary and a leader. At the end of one minute, the teacher gives a clear and concise statement of the problem or issue for discussion, worded so as to encourage specific single-statement answers. The time limit for the discussion is then imposed, and students have exactly six minutes to come to an agreement as to the best solution for the problem. After the discussion is over, you may want to point out to students that leaders can keep the group focused on the task. The Phillips 66 method is also a good training technique for future group leaders, recorders, and evaluators.

When using the Phillips 66 group in the primary grades, you may decide to eliminate the role of secretary. We would encourage you still to consider the benefits of having one of the students summarize the group's solution. Listening and summarizing are important skills for group work.

The Phillips 66 discussion group can be very useful as the set induction activity for a concept formation-attainment lesson or as the set inducer for a new unit. You should consider using the Phillips 66 technique for some of the times when it would be beneficial to focus the students' attention on, and quickly create interest in, a problem or concept.

The teacher's role is very simple. You decide on the topic, arrange the groups, start the discussion, and then just observe. Figure 7–6 illustrates five spatial arrangements for the Phillips 66 discussion groups. How many other spatial configurations can you suggest?

FIGURE 7–6   Some Configurations for the Phillips 66 Technique

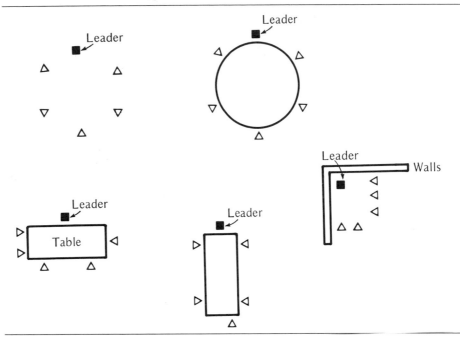

Four Task-Building Techniques

Tutorial

The tutorial discussion group is most frequently used to help students who have experienced difficulties in learning or progressing at a satisfactory rate. The group has only a few students (usually less than five) and focuses on a narrow range of materials. Teachers of such subjects as reading, mathematics, home economics, art, and business often use the tutorial group for remediation of basic skills. In the social studies, language arts, and sciences, the tutorial group is used to help students grasp a concept, again with the purpose of remedying a learning difficulty. Physical education and primary grade teachers employ a tutorial mode frequently in the area of motor development. It is an excellent way to facilitate the handling of manipulatives, to demonstrate and evaluate motor activities, and to help students understand the relationships between movement-exercise and body function.

The selected discussion leader has three major functions to perform when the tutorial mode is used: (1) questioning the students to pinpoint the exact problem that has blocked learning; (2) providing the feedback or skills to facilitate learning; and (3) encouraging the students to ask questions and to seek answers among themselves. Lest you have serious reservations about the tutorial technique, it has been demonstrated that students often learn better from each other than from the teacher!

FIGURE 7–7   Spatial Arrangements for Tutorial Groups

We caution, however, that prior to using student tutors, a teacher must be satisfied that each potential student tutor has mastered the necessary competencies—such as the skills of questioning, giving positive reinforcement, and analyzing work tasks. Many school districts currently use student tutors and are finding them to be invaluable resources for the classroom teacher.

Although remedial work will probably be used most often to improve student learning difficulties, the tutorial discussion group is an excellent method by which to encourage independent projects or advanced learners. Many gifted students will find it a challenge to try and explain their project to other students.

The person who leads the tutorial type of discussion will need to have developed some skills in the area of human relations. The leader must be patient and provide both feedback and warm encouragement. The leader must also keep the group moving toward its product, accept the inputs from others who learn slowly, and prod those group members who are slow to contribute. (It may even be a good idea to give your student leaders a brief review of those questioning techniques that you studied.)

Figure 7–7 illustrates two excellent spatial arrangements for participants of a tutorial group. Note that in either case the arrangements provide easy "eyeball-to-eyeball" contact. Such visual contact helps facilitate the flow of communication between all persons. Also note that the leader is clearly identified and plays a somewhat dominant role in the group process.

Tutoring that combines feedback and formative evaluation, writes Benjamin S. Bloom (1984), is such a powerful instructional technique that tutored students can gain 98 percent more than students in conventional classes, as measured by achievement tests. This critical finding validates the instructional efficacy of the tutorial. No other instructional variable—homework, advance organizers, conventional classes—surpasses tutoring. Bloom also reports that a tutorial is equally effective with a small group of two or three students participating.

Task Group

One of the least complex discussion types is that of the task group. As the name implies, students are involved in some kind of work or activity in which significant contributions can be made by each group member. A prerequisite to using the task group is the specification of clearly defined tasks to all group members. The task group is very similar to a committee and probably, under most circumstances, would be classified as a student committee. As in a committee, a task group has clearly defined goals and clearly identified individual assignments and roles. Also, it may be beneficial for the teacher to establish a work schedule and a system for internal monitoring of achievements, and initially even to provide all of the learning resources that may be necessary to accomplish the identified tasks. We recommend the latter.

Task groups tend to be teacher-dominated, in that the teacher usually selects the tasks and assigns each class member to accomplish a specific role. This discussion type can be used very efficiently during the early part of the semester when the teacher is attempting to prepare students with specific process competencies. Furthermore, the teacher may observe how selected students work with each other and how responsibly they tend to accomplish the assigned task.

A cautionary note must be added. Despite the fact that the teacher gives a specific assignment to each task group member, it may *not* be assumed that the task will be carried out completely. Students must learn how to accept responsibilities, *but* it is the teacher's job to provide appropriate goal setting, motivation, and consistent monitoring of each person's activities to help all students achieve their assigned goals.

Role-Playing

Role-playing is a process-oriented group technique that may include almost any number of participants, although we suggest that seven to ten is ideal. This type of group probably should not be used until you are well acquainted with role-playing techniques. Students also need some coaching in the three aspects of the role-playing group: the briefing, or the establishing of the situation; the drama or role-playing; and the follow-up discussion. A thorough preparation will help them enjoy the process and experience of the role-playing episode and not be overly concerned about interactions that may, in other situations, be perceived as personal attacks.

To repeat, the role-playing technique should not be used until all students know each other, because early use of the technique can stereotype certain students unfavorably and thus foster a rigid perspective when students view each other. Role-playing can work in almost any situation or subject matter. It is usually the spontaneous acting-out of a situation or incident to portray a problem that is common to group members or to give a common background to all members. The construction is free, with no script, but considerable briefing and planning should precede the role-playing scene. An episode lasts no more than five to ten minutes, and it is important for the activity to approximate reality.

A large-group discussion or debriefing should follow the final scene of any role-playing episode. The debriefing usually lasts up to fifteen minutes. It is at this point that the class analyzes the group process. During the analysis, the leader or teacher should strive for identification of the values and behavior of the characters and the consequences of their interactions.

The benefit of role-playing will be increased if the participants understand the differences between sociodrama and psychodrama. Role-players and all students who participate in the follow-up discussion should not be allowed to psychoanalyze anyone or to pretend that they are psychologists. Such analytical activities exemplify psychodrama and should be reserved for psychologists and other professionals with considerable expertise in the area of interpersonal relationships. In sociodrama, or role-playing, as we are using the term, the emphasis is not on the psyche of any character, but on re-enacting or dramatizing a *real situation* and demonstrating how the different characters react to the situation.

It is difficult to suggest how you should evaluate this type of group discussion because each role-playing group discussion is a unique experience. Some of the elements that you may assess are as follows: Did some of the students who are usually quiet or in the background take a more active part? Did the situation that prompted the discussion seem to be better understood by the participants? Was the situation resolved (if it involved classroom problems)? Did the role-players take their roles seriously? Did the participants avoid self-serving roles during the discussion phase?

Many advocates of role-playing have shown a special concern for low-achieving students, or those who are sometimes referred to as being educationally "retarded." For these students, role-playing can be the bridge between talking and action. Role-playing provides a safe yet dynamic setting for trying out, or practicing, social skills. In the multiethnic, mainstreamed classroom, the role-playing discussion group can be a powerful teaching tool; however, as with most powerful tools, it must be used wisely.

Role-playing can be applied to all levels of academic achievement and to all levels of school. L. Gerald Buchan (1972), in his book *Roleplaying and the Educable Mentally Retarded,* has suggested the use of role-playing in secondary schools to help students learn about job interviews, purchasing intangibles such as loans and insurance, and establishing personal relationships. Teachers in skill areas and vocational areas can easily use role-playing groups to help assess competency levels.

Panel Discussion

The panel discussion is designed to allow students to be productive and to have a meaningful exchange of ideas on *relevant* issues. It is most appropriate when you want students to do high-level thinking and when the discussion topic can be legitimately viewed from different perspectives. Panel discussions can be useful in helping students develop tentative or divergent alternatives to controversial issues. The panel is an excellent approach but we must stress that the group members will not necessarily reach the same solution or conclusion.

The topic for a panel discussion should be identified well in advance. The best topics are obviously oriented to student issues and concerns *relative* to your instructional goals. The topics should involve the students intellectually and emotionally; that is, students should care about the potential solutions. You may want to use a brainstorming session to generate possible topics for the panel discussion groups.

Students need to be well prepared for the panel discussion. Everyone needs to have some basic understandings (knowledge and comprehension) of the topic to be discussed—through lectures, readings, films, or interviews prior to the discussion. In addition, the students who will actually be the panel must conduct more extensive research into the topic. Probably two or three is the ideal number to be on the panel. A total group of up to fifteen students should listen or interact, although a full class could also listen to the issues and then prepare individual position papers on the topic. At times outsiders may be panel members because of their expertise in a particular area. In these cases, be sure to stress that this will be a *discussion*, not a guest lecture or a debate. It would be helpful to share the following with them.

A moderator begins by introducing the topic and the panel members and by reminding the total group to use their discussion and listening skills. The panel members then present rather short statements of three to five minutes representing various viewpoints. These statements should be provocative and present strong points or arguments. They should *not* be summarizing statements—those can be made at the end of the discussion.

Following the opening statements, the moderator facilitates a free and open discussion. The moderator's goal is to get the total group involved in the give-and-take and yet to give the panel members periodic opportunities to add new information or to clarify previous statements. It is the moderator's responsibility to conduct the discussion so that it does not become an argument between any two people, degenerate to a gab session, or stray to other topics. As you may infer, the panel discussion works much better *after* the students have learned or practiced some discussion skills.

A good way to end the panel discussion is to ask each panelist for some general conclusions or summaries, stated in terms of tentative solutions to the issue being addressed by the panel. The quality of these solutions will aid you in evaluating how well the students have mastered the topic.

The process of the panel discussion should also be evaluated. Students who had special roles as well as the group as a whole should receive feedback on how they performed during the discussion. The assessment form shown in Figure 7–8 may be used for this evaluation. (This form is also appropriate for use with the task group; you may modify any form to fit the particular group and situation.) Figure 7–8 shows a very thorough evaluation of the processes that may have taken place during a small-group discussion. This form would serve as a final or summative process evaluation and would conclude the small-group work or at least one major phase of it. This form also can be modified so that an observer may tabulate other selected

FIGURE 7–8   Comprehensive Evaluation of the Environment in Which a Small-Group Experience Took Place

---

TEST FOR ATMOSPHERE

Scale	Very Low	Low	Needs Improvement	High	Very High
	1	2	3	4	5

Using this rating scale, insert a number from 1 to 5 next to each of the items below to rank your feelings regarding the atmosphere created during the conduct of this small-group experience.

_____   1. How free are the participants to state their real opinion?

_____   2. How free are the participants to choose to work on areas of their own concern?

_____   3. How free do I feel to interact with the teacher?

_____   4. How positive do participants feel toward the work in which the group is engaged?

_____   5. How productive has this small-group experience been?

_____   6. How well has this learning experience been progressing?

_____   7. How do you feel about [Here you insert some concern, etc.]?

_____   8. How well do you feel this class has used its participant (human) resources?

_____   9. Do people seem to help each other?

_____   10. How does this experience compare to the "typical" course activities?

Comments _____

_____

_____

---

behaviors as they occur—unless videotape playbacks are used. In this case, an entire group could evaluate the playback.

A Problem-Solution Building Technique

Inquiry Group

If the teacher wishes to emphasize problem-solving, or discovery teaching, then the *inquiry discussion group* is extremely valuable. Any number of students may be in the discussion group, but we suggest that six to ten students per team would be ideal for this technique.

The purposes of inquiry group discussions are easily identified: (1) the stimulation of scientific thinking; (2) the development of problem-solving skills; and (3) the acquisition of new facts. It is possible that the teacher may be the leader of this type of group. However, if you have a student who has demonstrated good questioning skills and who understands the concept (facts) under consideration, then allow that student to be the leader.

J. Richard Suchman (1966) has long encouraged teachers to establish responsive environments wherein inquiry development is used to stimulate students to become *skillful askers of questions.* At the first stage of the Suchman model, students are presented with a problem that demonstrates a principle. Following the exhibition of the problem, a technique for introducing inquiry is used in which the students ask the teacher a specific question to which the teacher can only answer "yes" or "no." Suchman then proposes another procedure wherein the teacher allows the students to test their hypotheses so that they may determine, by direct experiences, whether they are valid. The inquiry group discussion is most appropriate for those disciplines that lend themselves to problem-solving—science and social science.

It must be realized that, prior to using inquiry discussions, students should have mastered observing, question-asking, and inferring behaviors. The teacher then encourages these behaviors by having students ask questions based on selected observations of phenomena, by having them collect data, and by having them summarize and draw conclusions. After the problems are identified by the teacher and the class, the students are subdivided into small groups to complete the investigation of each problem.

The inquiry group can be used most effectively when students are studying about the general subject of "rights" in the social sciences. For example, a group can role-play an episode in which a civil right has been violated and then, through inquiry discussion, can isolate the specific aspects of the violation or solve the problem in other ways. To make the inquiry group most meaningful, the teacher must plan for an activity that has some degree of authenticity. Furthermore, student hypotheses should have a testable quality. Real-life situations would appear to be most relevant.

We would even consider the use of inquiry discussions in the field of language arts, especially English. This may be the one opportunity for students to show creativity when posed with a problem, such as an unfamiliar literary device.

The "what" to evaluate concerning the inquiry group is fairly obvious. What you need to know, and what the students need to know, is how well they ask questions. Were they able to ask higher-order questions that could lead to hypothesis-making and testing? Of course, you also will want to know whether they learned the concept being discussed.

The "how" is more difficult to evaluate in the inquiry group. How the students ask questions may be tabulated by using the form in Figure 7–9. Note that there are five categories of higher-order questions, one category of lower-order questions, one category of formal hypothesis stating, and one

FIGURE 7–9   Tabulation Form for Inquiry Discussion Questions

Type of Question or Statement	Students									
	1	2	3	4	5	6	7	8	9	10

Observer _____

Teacher _____

Time _____

1. Knowledge

2. Comparison

3. Cause and effect

4. Inference

5. Application

6. Evaluation

7. Hypothesis

8. Other

Comments _____

category for miscellaneous statements. We suggest that the evaluation be accomplished in one of three ways: (1) The teacher maintains a continuous checklist as each person comments during the discussion. (2) The discussion is taped (preferably videotaped) and the student evaluated during the playback. Videotaping has the advantage of allowing the teacher to discuss questioning skills with the students, as well as pointing out some academic aspects that may have been overlooked or misunderstood. (3) Another teacher may do the tabulation during the discussion session. This method may be adapted to allow a trained student to perform this task.

We would suggest that modifications of this form be made for specific classes or topics. Also, it may be very useful to assign two or more observers to use this form to evaluate the discussion. In this manner, each observer could tabulate certain types of questions or statements, or each observer tabulates all questions or statements. The critique of the group is then made jointly by the committee of reviewers.

More About Inquiry Groups: Buzz Groups

The *buzz* group is a simple variation of an inquiry group. Regardless of the label that you attach to this kind of group, there are two definite thoughts to keep in mind. First, the inquiry group is best suited to a small number of students who are, or can be, fairly self-directed. Second, the teacher will be mainly an outside observer, although it is permissible to provide resource help if the group asks for it.

The students in an inquiry discussion group create a free and uninhibited environment in which they can discuss a topic that they select. So a buzz group, in particular, is one that is totally student-managed and is oriented to student issues or topics. The major factor in determining the size of the group is student interest. As many as six students who are interested in the topic can participate in each group. The length of time will also vary with each discussion session, and no absolute time guidelines can be given; however, it is often wise to end the discussion when it seems appropriate. Thus, relatively short, time-limited problem-solution discussions maintain interest for the next discussion period because students know they will have another opportunity to express themselves.

The topics are best selected, written, and identified before the discussion begins. The students decide which group to join and then leaders, recorders, and researchers may be assigned their roles in advance. The teacher may wish to meet privately with the leaders to discuss leadership roles and functions. (We strongly recommend all these procedures.) All students should have an opportunity to be a group leader. But if you as teacher attempt to influence the group's selection of leaders, they may feel that you are trying to dominate them. Thus, you may want to point out quietly that "Sally hasn't had an opportunity to lead this year," or you may want to use the other discussion types to provide leadership practice for all students.

The inquiry group is aimed at allowing the students to be productive and to have a meaningful exchange of ideas on *relevant* problems. The student leader should initiate the discussion and should try to keep the group members performing maintenance and task functions. The greatest pitfall of the inquiry group is that it may degenerate into a gab session and lose its intellectual or analytical status. Because each student must be familiar with various group discussion roles before using this technique, problems that arise should be analyzed by their respective group to identify and remedy the role deficiencies. The teacher must not become the arbitrator or the boss of the group. If the group cannot analyze the behavior process that seems to cause the group to degenerate, then the group can be given some additional experiences in role-playing or can be allowed to carry out task and maintenance functions. As another alternative, a videotape may be made for group analysis by using the form shown in Figure 7–9. This additional experience can be directed by the teacher, who may then allow the group to again try an inquiry discussion after their group skills have improved.

It should be kept in mind that inquiry groups are designed to produce high-level thinking. They are not spontaneous episodes, nor are they used merely to kill time—for example, on a Friday afternoon, the teacher may be tempted to just let the students discuss anything until the bell rings. Students need time and resources to prepare for inquiry sessions. Group leaders, with help from the teacher, should encourage each student to be emotionally and academically equipped for the discussion.

Using an inquiry discussion with physical education, Annemarie Schueler (1979) reports how she effectively incorporates an inquiry model of student-led discussions. Schueler begins the class with a provocative question. For example, the question, "Should girls box?" is one that causes students to probe, clarify, and examine various perspectives. Six processes are integrated into these inquiry discussions: (1) orienting the issue, (2) building hypothesis, (3) defining terms, (4) exploring alternatives, (5) finding supportive evidence, and (6) generalizing. Schueler finds such discussions to be thought-provoking, stimulating, and student-involving.

We suggest that all evaluation forms be maintained over a long period, so that changes in behavior and growth patterns may be determined by the group.

Summary

There are several questions that can be asked that will help the educator to decide which of the seven types of discussion groups is desirable for a given class situation. These are some of the questions:

1. How much control of the group's activities needs to be exerted by the teacher or group leader? Has the group developed its own norms so that little external control is needed? Does the group still need some assistance from the adult leader to function smoothly?
2. Does the objective of the discussion require more emphasis on the *process* or on the *product?*
3. Are the students familiar with the categories of roles and functions, and have they had pre-discussion experiences in filling selected roles? Will they receive feedback concerning functions they performed during the current discussion?
4. If skillful leadership qualities and a good academic background are needed for a discussion, is the teacher the only one with these skills or can a student handle the discussion?

Once these questions are answered, then meaningful discussion sessions can be planned.

FORMATIVE EVALUATION
Small-Group Discussions

1. Next to each of the following terms, insert the letter of the statement that best defines it.

_____ Task group   _____ Inquiry group
_____ Phillips 66   _____ Panel discussion
_____ Tutorial group

   (a) A type of discussion in which the teacher acts as a questioner or responder. The typical way to begin such an activity is to pose a question that is either divergent or evaluative.
   (b) Students are involved in some type of activity in which there are clearly defined tasks.
   (c) Emphasizes inquiry-to-discovery teaching in which students have to become skillful askers of questions.
   (d) Small-group discussion in which the primary purpose is to reach a consensus quickly.
   (e) Used to emphasize individualized instruction.
   (f) Used to discuss various viewpoints toward a topic. Usually emphasizes higher levels of thinking.

2. Which of the following is true of the brainstorming technique?
   (a) Judgments are made on each idea.
   (b) Only notes practical and logical ideas.
   (c) Piggybacking on someone else's idea is encouraged.
   (d) Quality is the most important feature.

3. Task groups
   (a) Are one of the more complex types of discussion.
   (b) Are similar to a committee.
   (c) Tend to be teacher-dominated.
   (d) Are both (b) and (c).

4. An inquiry group is
   (a) Teacher-dominated.
   (b) A less complex type of discussion.
   (c) A problem-solving approach.
   (d) Only appropriate in science.

5. Panel discussions
   (a) Require previous research or study.
   (b) Are those in which the teacher decides on the topic.
   (c) Are spontaneously generated.
   (d) Require simple skills on the part of the students.

RESPONSES
Small-Group Discussions

1. (b) Task group   (a),(c) Inquiry group
   (d) Phillips 66   (f)   Panel discussion
   (e) Tutorial group
2. (c)
3. (d)
4. (c)
5. (a)

ENCOURAGING SMALL-GROUP LEARNING

The preceding text provided you with an orientation to the world of small-group learning and urged you to employ small-group discussions for *meaningful* learning experiences. Perhaps at this point you are convinced of the use of small groups as a distinctive teaching-learning method. But how does one get organized to do it? Throughout this chapter, we reiterate that the teacher must systematically build pre-discussion skills that culminate in true small-group discussion processes. Let us now address issues related to the building of appropriate small-group environments.

Two major problems that are encountered when using small-group discussions in the schools are: (1) teachers tend to talk too much; and (2) some students will not talk at all. The results of Pendergrass's study (1973) indicated that teachers made approximately 51 percent of all verbal interactions during small-group discussions. (These were discussions—not lecture presentations.) More than one-half of the students accounted for less than 13 percent of the interactions. Pendergrass also observed that male students were significantly more active in the discussions than were female students. With this introductory statement, a few valuable hints are provided on how to increase student participation in small-group discussions.

The concept of the "facilitator" is useful in explaining the role of the teacher in developing and maintaining effective small-group discussions. The kind of development and cohesiveness that we describe in the chapter cannot be "decreed" by the teacher; it must be facilitated. In other words, the teacher makes it possible for the students to develop an effective group by making them feel free to express themselves. This occurs most often when the teacher allows for the development *(facilitates* the development) of classroom norms that are conducive to student participation. Such conditions foster the students' belief that *"it is okay for me to express my opinion; it is okay to interact with my peers and with the teacher; my opinion has value."*

Cohesiveness and involvement are most increased by the development of two specific norms: (1) a norm of self-disclosure (for example, I think or I feel . . .); and (2) a norm of present concrete observations (for example, I like what you're saying . . .). These norms, when created, do help to facilitate cohesiveness and sharing. These qualities are important in some instances, but not in others. A task group, for example, will not, and perhaps should not, have the same cohesiveness as an inquiry group. At some time, the facilitator may give way to the more *directive* teacher.

This cautionary note has been added to summarize a very important aspect of small-group discussion behavior. What follows now are some other general suggestions that help to create an atmosphere that is conducive to student participation.

Developing Listening Skills

Being a good listener is partly a matter of attitude and partly a matter of skill, so you and your students have two things to practice—positive attitudes and listening skills. From our work with students and from the work of Thomas J. Buttery and Patricia J. Anderson (1980), and Joseph L. McCaleb (1981), we have gathered tips that can help you become systematic and thorough in fostering listening in the classroom.

Begin by modeling excellent listening habits for your students. Pay attention to your nonverbal behaviors, such as eye contact, facial responses, and gestures. Observe yourself: do you lean forward, make eye contact, and seem really interested in the students? Or do you fidget, look away, show boredom, or walk around the classroom? The former behaviors are indicators of listening. You must give the students nonverbal feedback when they talk to you: your nonverbal posture is the only way that they have of determining if you really heard and *understood* what was said. Also observe if you reinforce students for listening to one another.

Follow up the modeling tips with these tips on instructional practices. First, use *short* and *simple* directions. Children in the early grades can usually remember only one or two directions. Even older students forget if you give long directions or a series of directions. (Write detailed sets of directions on paper and hand out to the students.) Second, do not keep repeating and explaining the directions. Expect the students to listen the first time. Three, to help the students develop into listeners, check to see that unnecessary noises, such as teacher talk and equipment noises, are reduced.

Some enjoyable activities can also be meaningful learning activities. One example is to have a discussion in which all classroom managing is done nonverbally; no one calls on anyone *verbally,* yet everyone has to say something. Another example is to make up or borrow a page of directions that students must follow exactly. For example, if a classroom microcomputer is available, have the class examine the programming manual, which is usually full of explicit details. The manual conveys the idea of following directions *precisely.*

When students know that there are some purposes for listening they will improve. If you give them practical listening experience, some of what they learn will show up in their discussion activities. Raising the quality of students' listening skills can affect their learning positively in all subject areas. Yvonne Gold (1981) reminds us that listening is a learned behavior; that is, it helps establish skills that aid in academic achievement, especially all disciplines that focus on language arts. Gold also cautions that it is the teacher's attitude that illustrates to the student that listening is important.

How can you teach attentive listening? We have already presented a few tips. Here is a series of techniques that teachers have told us work:

- Prepare a short, well-organized lecture. Have the class outline the lecture. Then review the lecture to identify main topics and main points.
- Ask a question. Have students paraphrase the question and recite these paraphrases in class.
- Conduct oral tests frequently.
- Limit or avoid repetition of directions, questions, and comments.
- Allow students to conduct some recitations.

- Paraphrase television programs that are observed in the classroom.
- List good speaking habits (i.e., at the end of each class, each student could list one good speaking habit).
- Post a bulletin board display that relates to listening skills.
- Appoint a class recorder who provides a summary of the day's recitations or discussion activities.
- Appoint one or two students to listen for any grammatical errors spoken in class.
- Ask a student to paraphrase a previous student's response to a question.

As Mortimer J. Adler (1983) observed, speaking and listening are companion skills. Discussions require groups to speak. Listening is a prerequisite skill to discussing. The more effectively you build those skills, the more effective will be your small-group discussions.

Arranging the Room

The best possible spatial arrangement for small-group discussions is a small seminar room in which the participants can sit either at round tables or in a circle and where everyone can have eye contact with one another. While observing classroom discussions, the authors have noticed that, even in this type of room, the teacher often tends to sit several feet away from the group, and group communication basically is limited to teacher-student exchanges initiated by the teacher or to those initiated by the group members. There is very little communication between the students themselves. It is preferable for the teacher or the leader to sit within the boundaries of the group and to encourage interaction between the students.

Probably the second best room arrangement consists of "discussion centers" within a large room. The centers can be partially isolated from the rest of the room by using bookshelves or folding room dividers, or by merely turning the seats so that the group participants face each other and are not distracted by activities taking place in the rest of the room. Students will normally block out noise from the other groups if each circle is enclosed so that eye contact is made only with members of the same group. By converting the room into "centers," the teacher can conduct several types of activities simultaneously without disruptions.

Circular or semicircular seating arrangements offer at least four advantages to encourage small-group interaction (Hoffman and Plutchik, 1959). They:

1. Reduce the authority role of the teacher
2. Provide the ideal that everyone is equal
3. Reduce the possibility that a student is ignored by the group or withdraws from it
4. Help create a responsible setting that encourages listening and contributing to the discussion

John W. Keltner (1967) suggested using seating arrangements with alternate shapes that work equally well—for example, square or triangular shapes. He observed that a rectangular shape is less desirable because of the tendency for people to sit in a "line-up," thus creating comparatively long distances between participants. A "T" formation is popular among adult groups, but it may create a somewhat undesirable status at the center and also may make it difficult for some members to see the others.

Because personal interaction is the key to successful discussion-leading, Keltner suggested that at least three formations be avoided. Note that each of these three formations tends to retard the interaction that is so important to the discussion process (Keltner, 1967).

1. Students should not be seated so that they are unable to face each other.
2. Students should not be seated in rows with their backs to each other.
3. Concentric circles should be avoided; instead, separate circles should be formed elsewhere.

Although reported research studies concerning optimal group arrangements have produced conflicting evidence about the superiority of one formation over another, it has been noted that people tend to talk to persons sitting across from, or immediately next to, them rather than to persons sitting at angles to them. Thus, the crucial point is that the group leader needs to be sure that he or she talks to everyone in the group and that the other group members are encouraged to talk to everyone else and to avoid talking only to those across from, or next to, them.

Some persons feel more comfortable when sitting behind an object such as a table or a desk. During the initial phases of discussion-building episodes, it may be advantageous to encourage the group to sit around tables or to move students' desks into a tablelike arrangement. Once students feel at ease with discussions, they may simply choose to sit in a circle on the floor or in a circular configuration made up of chairs.

Charting Interaction Patterns

Small-group interactions can be improved if you have some discrete data about the interaction patterns. These patterns can be determined easily by the use of simply constructed grids. One such grid is illustrated in Figure 7–10. Observe that by mapping a discussion configuration and then simply drawing lines with arrows, the directionality of a discussion may be determined. A one-way straight arrow shows that a comment was aimed at one individual. A wiggly arrow indicates that a comment was directed at the entire group. A double arrow shows a dialogue pattern.

Such grid networks can be sketched on a minute-by-minute (or longer) time frame to determine group interaction or the lack of it. In the example given in Figure 7–10, it may be noted that nearly all interactions took place between persons seated next to, or directly across from, each other. Knowl-

FIGURE 7–10 Grid Network to Determine Interaction Patterns

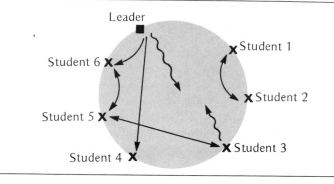

edge of such spatial interactions allows the leader to keep the discussion less cliquish and more open.

Figure 7–11 illustrates an even simpler adaptation of the grid. For each episode of some specified time frame, an observer lists first the name of the person who initiates an interaction, followed by the names of those who join it. By examining the interaction patterns, a group leader, or the entire small group for that mattter, will be able to determine whether the group is being dominated by only a few individuals.

As you may note from these two examples of grids, interaction patterns may be identified easily in an objective and systematic manner. Such tabulations are designed not to chastise the students but to help them to improve in the processes.

You have already examined some forms concerning interaction patterns that small-group participants can complete. Figure 7–12 illustrates just

FIGURE 7–11 Simple Small-Group Interaction Form

Date _____

Episode _____

Topic _____

Group _____

Observer _____

Interaction 1: Ann, Al, Ann, Cy, Tom, Ann, Wanda (time: four minutes)

Interaction 2: Ann, . . . Ann [indicates a long response or speech]

Interaction 3: Ann, Tom, Al, Ann, Wanda, Al, Wanda, Al, Wanda, Al (time: four minutes) [Al and Wanda entered into a dialogue that reduced all other inputs]

FIGURE 7–12   Individual-Response Form

Date _____

Group _____

Directions: Place an X next to the response that best describes your reaction to each of the following questions.

1. Do you think that your time is being used effectively in the discussion group?
   _____ (a) Not at all
   _____ (b) About right
   _____ (c) Very much
2. Is there sufficient discussion between you and your group members?
   _____ (a) Not at all
   _____ (b) About right
   _____ (c) Very much
3. Is the work being done in your small group informative enough?
   _____ (a) Not at all
   _____ (b) About right
   _____ (c) Very much

Suggestions or comments _____

_____

_____

how simple it is to prepare an instrument for checking opinions about the satisfaction gained from participating in a given small group. The type of continuum to be used is contingent on the objectives of the specific discussion episode. By tabulating the group responses, the observer can quickly prepare a master list that will show how each group member feels about his or her respective interactions. Note that we allocated this job to the observer, not to the teacher. The teacher must learn to delegate most of the tasks to the students, because the teacher simply will not have the time to do all the work. The teacher's main role is as the organizer, who will examine the data and then make new decisions on how to continue.

Selecting a Lively Topic

The topic may be determined by the teacher's wish that certain phases of class work be discussed in depth, or it may be generated from the students' responses to, and interest in, a selected area. The usefulness of the discussion depends in large part on the ability and willingness of students to define the nature of the problem. At times even we have been surprised and pleased by the willingness of students to deal realistically with both academic and social problems. (Social problems will be discussed further in Chapter 10.) Examples of such student initiative and ability include (1) a "low-ability" third-grade group successfully handling the topic of uses and misuses of drugs; (2) a small group of multihandicapped deaf students discussing Adolf Hitler or John F. Kennedy and the man's influence on society (Pendergrass and Hodges, 1976); or (3) a third-grade group building a thinking machine.

The topic chosen should be dual in nature: it should be pertinent to classroom material and study, and it should be on a subject chosen for maximum interest to the students. Such a discussion topic should be short and worded in a lively manner. If possible, and it usually is, let the students do the wording for the topic being discussed. We also suggest that the students ultimately take full responsibility for the conduct of the discussion once they have learned the essential skills.

The problem to be discussed should be presented in the form of a question, because the discussion should be an inquiry into matters, and not simply the proving or disproving of some assertion as in a debate procedure. For example, a discussion topic in a home economics course may be: "All boys should have a course in home economics." This may then be converted into questions such as: "What benefits can home economics have for boys?" or "Why should boys be taught to master home skills?"

The question should be rewritten until it is free of ambiguous terms that may have various meanings to various members of the class or until the group establishes some limits on the meanings it wishes to consider. One question may read: "To what extent should the high school course work be liberalized?" The word *liberalized* could suggest several interpretations: Should more courses be added, and what kind? Should the present courses be changed to emphasize their liberalizing values? Should the amount of homework be reduced? Should all students be able to determine their own course requirements regardless of school policy? *Liberalized* in this context, then, is so ambiguous that the discussion would lead to a series of tangents. Each person would react to what he or she thought was meant.

The question should be worded impartially so that any decision or judgment reached is a result of the discussion and not of the possibly emotion-laden phrasing of the question (Howell and Smith, 1956). The following questions are worded poorly and influence judgment before the discussion even opens: "Should the United States adopt the Communist-inspired plan of socialized medicine?" and "How can the present deplorable public taste in reading material be improved?" These questions may be reworded objectively to read: "Should the United States adopt socialized medicine as it applies to the aged in Great Britain?" and "What can be done to change public taste in soft-cover novels?" or "What is the current public taste in paperbacks and magazines sold in newsstands?"

The issue should be sufficiently difficult to sustain interest and should require serious and creative thinking. In short, the topic must have relevance to those discussing it. The issue also must have sufficient information available to class members in the event that it becomes necessary to research the topic for more meaningful discussion.

Amos Dreyfus and Ronit Lieberman (1981) observed that science classrooms provide a rich arena for lively discussions. They suggested using both teacher-initiated and student-initiated topics. Preplanning for the discussion, they noted, was essential for success.

A beginning teacher or preservice intern can identify those issues that have a high probability of becoming successful discussion topics. One element will be fairly certain: most students do not have the skills that are essential for conducting or participating in true discussions. This should be a challenge to the teacher, who will experience a feeling of accomplishment as he or she succeeds in helping the students acquire and master these skills. Again, we are not proposing the indiscriminate use of discussion techniques, but we do suggest that these skills be developed systematically.

Developing Student Skills and Responsibilities

Students need to be made aware of the skills that they are expected to employ and develop as they learn discussion techniques. They will be expected eventually to combine critical thinking abilities with human-relations responsibilities.

Students also need to be cautioned against fallacious reasoning and propagandistic techniques. The many errors that are committed in discussion groups should all be identified as techniques that are inappropriate for rational discourse. For example, there is the broad class of "ignorance" statements that appear to reflect hate, fear, superstition, or rationalization; these statements are persuasive but illogical. Then there is the appeal to "authority," which is an intimidation tactic. Also, clichés and colloquial words, when used, should be analyzed to show how they distort meaning or have no real meaning.

Along the same lines, it must be shown that analogies are appropriate as examples but are never permissible as evidence. Skills such as inferring and concluding must be taught so that students are cognitively aware of their own thinking processes. Through the use of audio recorders or videotape recorders, each small group can be helped by observing examples of both good and bad techniques.

Encouraging Development of Leadership

When beginning the use of small-group discussions, the teacher may choose the first student leaders on the basis of leadership abilities already observed in class situations. These leadership abilities may include such considerations as personal popularity, academic standing, temperament or sociability, thinking ability, and speaking ability.

Ideally, leadership will develop spontaneously in the groups, but it is wise to discuss with the class early in the semester what qualities a leader must have *to help the group work together*. Leadership is a learned and practiced skill, so that in order for several students to gain experience, the teacher may appoint leaders arbitrarily by rotation or may select two leaders for each discussion—one a strong leader and the other weaker—until the weaker one shows evidence of growing ability and confidence. It is the *responsibility of the teacher* to help students develop the desired leadership behaviors and competencies. For example, some time must be scheduled for teaching and learning questioning skills, how to report a summary, how to involve nonvolunteers, and how to restrain the dominating volunteers without using aversive techniques. Ultimately every class member should have an opportunity to be a leader and to develop the same skills.

The leading authorities on small-group behavior and organizational development, such as Matthew B. Miles, emphasize five main functions of the small-group leader that all students can practice at any time during the discussion, even though the performance burden rests primarily with the leader. These functions are as follows:

1. *Initiating:* keeping the group moving when it is bogged down or off on a dead-end tangent (such as clarifying certain statements or asking questions that call for more than a yes or no answer)
2. *Regulating:* influencing the pace of the discussion (such as summarizing or pointing out time limits)
3. *Informing:* bringing information to the group that no one else may know; never lecturing
4. *Supporting:* making it easier for members to contribute (such as harmonizing opposing viewpoints, voicing group feeling, varying place in group, helping group get acquainted)
5. *Evaluating:* helping the group to evaluate process goals (may test for consensus or note the group progress in some facet)

Not all of these functions *must* be performed by one leader, but the person who is leading should provide whatever is missing from the discussion process. Sometimes the teacher may want a leadership team: one student provides the vocal leadership; the other silently records and summarizes, when necessary, the main points made by the group.

A sophisticated discussion group of considerable strength and ability may function well under a nondirective leader whose principal value lies in the fact that he or she lets the group develop the greatest amount of self-control and self-administration. Such a situation is ideal but extremely difficult to implement—almost impossible with inexperienced leaders and participants in the secondary school classroom. Initial discussions should be conducted with as simple a format as possible. As the students (and the teacher) gain experience, more complex activities can be added.

Providing Positive Feedback

Each of the previous activities in which you participated contained provisions for evaluating the small-group discussion that was specified in the activity. In addition, several ideas for evaluation formats were presented with the seven types of discussion groups. It will be very beneficial if you think of evaluation as *feedback* and not as *grading*.

Why use positive feedback? First, positive feedback increases responses, and we know that many students do not respond because they are afraid of giving an incorrect reply and then of being subjected to a negative teacher reaction. If a partially correct response is given, some positive feedback will usually motivate the student to try again. Peer approval, or feedback, is considered by many students, especially at the secondary level, to be even more important than teacher approval.

Second, students need to learn to be cooperative and to be supportive of others. Students *can* and *will* learn to give positive feedback to one another. But they probably will not do so if the teacher is always giving feedback. Thus, the teacher can gradually shift to the group members the responsibility of providing feedback. This is one area in which a desirable quality of leadership can be developed—if we believe that the leader should promote activity and harmony within the group.

Third, the teacher, or group leader, and each student need to assess individual progress. At first, this evaluation may be merely a matter of how many responses the student makes during the discussion session, or some general impressions of that person. Later it may focus on specific functions that the student needs to master and, at the highest level, on how the student can get other students to be cohesive group members. Remember that the teacher cannot abdicate the responsibility of helping each student in the class. At times, the group may not be having a positive influence on a particular student. When this occurs, the teacher must bear the responsibility of correcting the student's behavior while working with the group to shape long-term behavior goals.

Evaluation should be nonthreatening and varied. Students need to know, prior to the discussion, what they are being evaluated on. Evaluation should be based on the objective. If you are seeking a variety of ideas, it is totally unfair to put a grade on quality or on any other standard. If students know that evaluation is to be used for diagnostic purposes in some cases, they will feel freer about discussing and participating in the evaluation activities.

In summary, the evaluative processes should accomplish three tasks: (1) provide feedback to the group concerning progress in discussion skills and processes; (2) inform the teacher about how the group is progressing in relation to process objectives and group goals; and (3) allow the teacher and each student to assess individual progress.

Motivating Toward Participation

There are no surefire means of motivating students to participate in group discussions. You will undoubtedly have students who monopolize the discussion as well as those who are hesitant to volunteer. We believe that the following ideas will help you facilitate small-group discussions but, as always, we encourage you to use your creativity in trying new methods. (We would also appreciate your sharing your successes with us.)

1. Choose Relevant Topics

The more students are interested, the higher will be their motivation for participation. As much as possible, let the students help you to choose the discussion topic. Reword the topic problem or question until it is stated in terms that are used by the students. Many discussions are ruined because no one can understand what the problem or question is.

2. Place Students in Different Small Groups

The teacher initially may allow the students to group together with friends until the students learn not to feel threatened by group work. Be sure that each group has the skills needed to complete the task.

3. Encourage Direction Toward Goals (Either Teacher-Set or Group-Set)

If the goal has many divergent elements, work on all of them. If it involves coming to a decision or solving a problem, aim for that. Train the groups in the procedures for arranging activities and setting schedules; teach them how to acquire the necessary resources, divide labor, and make reports.

4. Foster a Congenial Environment

Help a friendly atmosphere to prevail, in which disagreement is permitted objectively but not emotionally or in a hostile form. Help the students distinguish between disagreeing with an idea and disagreeing with the person who has the idea. Expect the students to joke and kid around somewhat. Do not try to force them to be serious always and to work on the task every minute of the time (even the best of us do not).

5. Get Voice Contact from Noncontributing Members

The methods used to elicit responses from nonvolunteers are limited only by the creative resources of the teacher. For example, the leader can throw an inflated beach ball to a student whenever the leader wants that student to speak. This is also a good technique to employ in a group that is dominated by a few constant talkers.

Another method is to call on Student B by name and to ask him or her to paraphrase (to Student A's satisfaction) what Student A has just said and then to add his or her own ideas. Student C must then paraphrase Student B's response to Student B's satisfaction, and so on throughout the period.

The paraphrasing, besides encouraging listening and focusing on thinking, gives the student a chance to say something on a one-to-one nonthreatening basis before giving any ideas to the group.

All of these suggestions have been tested by teachers and have been reported in the literature. To be sure, the use of discussions as a systematic way of learning takes a great deal of planning and encouragement by the teacher. But if you want to promote learning, then we suggest that you try systematic discussions with small groups. The decision is yours.

FORMATIVE EVALUATION
Small-Group Discussions

1. Place an X next to each statement that would likely increase student participation and make small-group discussions more effective.
   - _____ (a) The teacher models good listening habits.
   - _____ (b) The group leader does not try to get quiet members to talk.
   - _____ (c) Teacher and students determine relevant topics.
   - _____ (d) Feelings or emotions are not permitted in the discussion.
   - _____ (e) Keep students in the same small groups.
   - _____ (f) Help students learn leadership skills.
   - _____ (g) Any form of disagreement must be permitted.
   - _____ (h) Evaluation is nonthreatening and varied.
   - _____ (i) Students learn to infer, conclude, and summarize.
   - _____ (j) The teacher encourages direction toward goals.
   - _____ (k) Develop a plan for getting nonvolunteers to respond.
   - _____ (l) Repeat directions over and over until everyone listens.
2. There are several ways to evaluate or measure the interaction processes of small-group discussions. Select any two of those presented and field-test the instruments to observe how they work for you. (We suggest that you work in dyads or pairs to complete this task.)

RESPONSES
Small-Group Discussions

1. (a) X   (g)
   (b)   (h) X
   (c) X   (i) X
   (d)   (j) X
   (e)   (k) X
   (f) X   (l)

REFERENCES

Adler, Mortimer J. *How to Speak: How to Listen*. New York: Macmillan, 1983.
Bloom, Benjamin S. "The 2 Sigma Problem: The Search for Methods of Group Instruction as Effective as One-to-One Tutoring." *Educational Researcher* 13(6):1984, 4–16.

Buchan, L. Gerald. *Roleplaying and the Educable Mentally Retarded.* Belmont, Calif.: Fearon, 1972.

Buttery, Thomas J., and Patricia J. Anderson. "Listen and Learn!" *Curriculum Review* 19:1980, 319–322.

Dreyfus, Amos, and Ronit Lieberman. "Perceptions, Expectations and Interactions: The Essential Ingredients for a Genuine Classroom Discussion." *Journal of Biological Education* 15:1981, 153–157.

Gold, Yvonne. "Teaching Attentive Listening." *Reading Improvement* 18:1981, 159–164.

Gorman, Alfred H. *Teachers and Learners: The Interactive Process of Education.* Boston: Allyn and Bacon, 1969.

Hoffman, Randall W., and Robert Plutchik. *Small-Group Discussions in Orientation and Teaching.* New York: Putnam, 1959, p. 57.

Howell, William S., and Donald K. Smith. *Discussion.* New York: Macmillan, 1956, pp. 36–37.

Keltner, John W. *Group Discussion Processes.* New York: Longmans, Green, 1967, p. 113.

Litsey, D. M. "Small-Group Training and the English Classroom." *English Journal* 58:1969, 920–927.

McCaleb, Joseph L. "Indirect Teaching and Listening." *Education* 102:1981, 159–164.

McGehee, Louise, and R. A. Pendergrass. "Facilitating Group Interaction Among Hearing Impaired Children." Unpublished paper.

Miles, Matthew B. *Learning to Work in Groups.* New York: Bureau of Publications, Teachers College, Columbia University, 1959, p. 20.

Olmstead, Joseph A. *Theory and State of the Art of Small Group Methods of Instruction.* Alexandria, Va.: Human Resources Research Organization, 1970, pp. vii, 36, and 79.

Pendergrass, R. A. "An Analysis of the Verbal Interaction of Small Group Discussion Members in Secondary Social Studies Classes." Unpublished dissertation, Washington State University, Pullman, Washington, 1973.

Pendergrass, R. A., and Marlis Hodges. "Deaf Students in Group Problem Solving Situations: A Study of the Interactive Process." *Annals of the Deaf* 121(3):1976, 327–330.

Sadow, Stephen A. "Creative Problem-Solving for the Foreign Language Class." *Foreign Language Annals* 16:1983, 115–118.

Schmuck, Richard A., and Matthew B. Miles, eds. *Organization Development in Schools.* Palo Alto, Calif.: National Press Books, 1971.

Schmuck, Richard A., and Patricia A. Schmuck. *Group Processes in the Classroom.* Dubuque, Iowa: William C. Brown, 1971.

Schueler, Annemarie. "The Inquiry Model in Physical Education." *Physical Educator* 36:1979, 89–92.

Suchman, J. Richard. *Inquiry Development Program in Physical Science.* Chicago: Science Research Associates, 1966.

8

DECIDING TO USE INQUIRY

Traditionally, teachers at all levels emphasize bodies of knowledge, the content of which becomes both a *means* and an *end* in education. Is it any wonder then that hundreds of thousands of students get bored by the routine lectures or recitations? We would like to offer you an alternative teaching technique that is not new but centuries old. The generic term for the technique is *inquiry*. You may find it referred to in the literature as *inquiry, enquiry, discovery, problem-solving, reflective thinking, inductive teaching,* or several other terms. We will discuss these techniques and point out the major differences among them. But first, what should you learn from this chapter? After completing this chapter, you should be able to

1. Recognize and describe at least five different inquiry techniques
2. Observe the role of questioning in inquiry
3. Prepare a set of inquiry materials for your own discipline or grade level
4. Justify the use of specific inquiry instructional techniques for selected concepts
5. Understand that inquiry processes are carefully taught (or learned) by systematic planning and instruction

In addition, the following affective objectives are offered for your own attitude adjustments—as needed. We would like you to

1. Appreciate instructional styles or techniques that tend to be "open" rather than closed
2. Be willing to incorporate elements of inquiry teaching in your teaching
3. Value the goal of "thinking" by systematically using instructional techniques that will help students learn how to think
4. Become an advocate for inquiry-related teaching

UNDERSTANDING THE CONCEPT

The concept of inquiry is rather difficult to define in nonoperational terms—that is, without giving precise examples of teacher strategies and the concomitant student behaviors. As we develop a spectrum of inquiry-teaching options, we will demonstrate their operational meanings by example. Inquiry processes require a high degree of interaction among the learner, the teacher, the materials, the content, and the environment. Perhaps the most crucial aspect of inquiry is that, as it is defined in the dictionary, both student and teacher become persistent askers, seekers, interrogators, questioners, and ponderers and ultimately pose the question that every Nobel Prize winner has asked: I wonder what would happen if . . . ?

Of course, we do not expect *all* of you to make internationally significant discoveries, although we would like to see a few of your students do so. What is important is that *you* as the classroom teacher set the stage for the process of inquiry to take place. In short, *you* make the difference. *You* decide how much time will be spent developing the many processes associated with inquiry behaviors. *You* make the decision to try another method of teaching units of instruction that lend themselves to inquiry processes. *You* are the one who systematically will teach *your* students how to ask questions.

Questioning plays a crucial role in both the teaching and learning acts associated with the inquiry mode of learning. Questions lead to investigations that attempt to solve a well-defined aspect of the question. Such investigations are common to *all* areas of human endeavor. The investigative processes of inquiry involve the student not only in questioning, but also in formulating the question, in limiting it, in deciding on the best methods to use, and then in conducting the study.

The emphasis on inquiry instruction seems to be a twentieth-century phenomenon. Perhaps the prime advocate for its wide acceptance is none other than John Dewey. This may surprise you, for in most textbooks and lectures and in the common press the late John Dewey seems to be blamed for every conceivable ill that has befallen our society, with the exception of earthquakes. We explore the contributions of Dewey as they pertain to problem-solving. You may be surprised to learn that it was Dewey's ideal that became popularized in a conference of scientists, leading to the publication of Jerome S. Bruner's (1960) now classic *The Process of Education*. This brief historical background on the inquiry process is essential to avoid the same fallacious thinking that thousands of teachers have been guilty of because they were not fully aware of the foundations of inquiry.

As we mentioned, inquiry is an old technique. The distinguished trio of ancient Western culture—Socrates, Aristotle, and Plato—were all masters of the inquiry processes. One can argue that the processes they used have since affected the way most people in our Western civilization think. That heritage has given us a mode of teaching in which students are vitally involved in the learning and creating processes. It is through inquiry that new knowledge is discovered. It is by becoming involved in the process that students become historians, scientists, economists, artists, businesspersons, poets, writers, or researchers—even if only for an hour or two in *your* class.

Basic Processes of Inquiry

What then are the basic processes of inquiry? Briefly, they are observing, classifying, using numbers, measuring, using space-time relationships, predicting, inferring, defining operationally, formulating hypotheses, interpreting data, controlling variables, experimenting, and communicating.

The above-mentioned basic processes, thirteen in all, are found in every learning episode that involves inquiry. We submit that even poets use most of them. The main point that we are developing is that inquiry is not simply the asking of a question; it is a process of conducting a thorough investigation (see Fig. 8–1 on p. 260). A similar chart can be constructed easily for selected aspects of literature, art criticism, homemaking, first aid, and many other nonscience subjects.

It is extremely important that *you* understand that each of those processes associated with inquiry must be carefully developed and practiced in a very systematic manner. This requires that the teacher decide how much of each lesson will be devoted to cognitive-skill building and how much to process building—just as with the process of building small-group discussions.

Finally, both the teacher and the students must become aware that the processes must be learned, practiced, demonstrated, and assimilated into the *students'* learning styles. Of course, the teacher must know the processes and must know how to establish learning situations that will aid in their application. The inquiry processes are most effective when they are internalized by each and every student. We do imply that *every* student can learn the fundamental processes of inquiry, although this does not mean that every student will demonstrate the same quality of inquiry. In our experiences, we have observed that the "slow" students enjoy using the inquiry processes as much as the very "best" students.

As one more way to learn, inquiry provides a dimension to the classroom environment that no other teaching method can—the excitement of learning something that just might not be in the textbook.

Thinking and Inquiry

Before we discuss inquiry and its related techniques, we must discuss the topic of thinking. As a nation, we want our schools to teach *thinking.* Nearly every statement on goals has some reference to the "goal of the school is to teach critical thinking." This goal was articulated forcefully by Ronald S. Brandt (1983), executive editor of *Educational Leadership,* when he observed that high-technology industrial leaders thought that it was less important to provide a great deal of technical training in the schools than to develop the student's ability to think and solve problems. To develop thinking and problem-solving skills, the teachers must make the decisions to promote thinking: the schools must provide *experiences* in thinking and problem-solving. To think, a student must learn to be actively involved with issues, data, materials, topics, concepts, and problems.

Is there a problem in teaching how to think? An analysis of how well seventeen-year-old students performed on the 1973 and 1978 National Assessment of Educational Progress (NAEP) examinations suggests that the schools fall short in teaching young adolescents the skills for examining ideas (Gisi and Forbes, 1982). The NAEP test results indicate that students are taught to be superficial in interpreting information and cannot extend the interpretations to comprehension or evaluation skills.

You may recall our strong plea in Chapters 4 and 6 for structuring learning to include comprehension, application, analysis, synthesis, and evaluation. These cognitive skills are the traits of thinking. We also report that both textbooks and teachers tend to question predominantly at the Knowledge or lowest cognitive level. Thinking and reflection in most school rooms are obviously missing elements of instruction. We would like to change that.

What does it mean to teach thinking? Lynn Grover Gisi and Roy H. Forbes (1982) of the Education Commission of the States (the group that administers the NAEP examinations) compiled a list of basics for the schools. Their list noted that students in kindergarten through grade 12 should acquire the following basic skills:

1. Evaluative and analytical skills
2. Critical thinking
3. Problem-solving
4. Organizational and reference techniques
5. Synthesis
6. Application
7. Decision-making
8. Information-processing
9. Communication
10. Creativity

In short, Gisi and Forbes have added "thinking skills and processes" as a basic for all students.

To teach thinking skills, a teacher must emphasize the use of knowledge. Further, a student must be taught global skills, such as perceiving data carefully, enjoying work that demands precision, interpreting situations or data, and feeling positive about education—that school is helpful to one's individual life goals. (These skills are all affective objectives, which we mention to illustrate the subtle link between affective and cognitive objectives.)

To teach thinking, teachers carefully *sequence* (see Chapter 3) and *plan* (see Chapter 5) for systematically prescribed learning activities and experiences. Arthur Whimbey (1977) illustrated how teachers may help all students, including so-called low-aptitude students, to begin thinking in systematic and higher-order reasoning and comprehending fashions. Whimbey cautioned that both students and their teachers tend to make their evaluations too quickly without conducting the necessary intermediate steps. He then provided two techniques to teach thinking. First, the teacher must explain and demonstrate the skill. Second, the students must practice the skill. By carefully and slowly guiding the students, teachers will achieve success in their goal of helping students learn how to think.

Thus, to teach thinking, you must plan and organize for incremental learning. You will not teach students how to think in one or two lessons: To teach thinking requires months or even years of patience. If every teacher were to begin today, it would not take long to observe results on test scores—and in many other areas of life.

INDUCTIVE INQUIRY

Let us begin with a caveat: There is no pure inductive-inquiry teaching mode. Basically there are elements of the inductive method that prevail with all inquiry strategies. But note well that inductive teaching methodologies may or may not be true extensions of "discovery." What then constitutes inductive inquiry? Induction or inductive logic is a thought process wherein the individual observes or senses *a selected number* of events, processes, or objects, and then constructs a particular pattern of concepts or relationships based on these limited experiences. Inductive inquiry, then, is a method that is used by teachers when they present sets of data or situations and then ask the students to infer a conclusion, generalization, or a pattern of relationships. It is a process that allows the student to observe specifics and then to infer generalizations about the entire group of particulars.

Inductive inquiry may be approached in at least two different ways: (1) guided; and (2) unguided. Lee S. Schulman and Pinchas Tamir (1973) provided an easy-to-use matrix illustrating that *if* the teacher wishes to provide the basic elements of the lesson—that is, the specifics—but wants the students to make the generalizations, *then* the teacher is conducting a *guided* inductive lesson. If the teacher decides to allow the students to provide the cases and to make the generalizations, the process may be labeled *unguided* inductive inquiry. Such a distinction between guided and unguided inductive inquiry is very essential. In most cases, the teacher will begin to build the processes of induction through a set of guided experiences. In this manner, the teacher knows that there is a fixed number of generalizations or conclusions that can be reasonably inferred. The teacher can then go about helping various students to make the observations that lead to these conclusions. In our experiences with inductive inquiry, the guided method provides an easy transition from expository teaching to that which is less expository.

Inductive inquiry is appropriate at all levels of instruction, from preschool to university graduate schools. Obviously the kinds and quality of induction will vary considerably. An important aspect of inductive inquiry is that the *processes* of observation, inference, classification, formulating hypotheses, and predicting are all sharpened (or reinforced) by the experiences.

Guided Inductive Inquiry

The use of pictures is usually the easiest way to introduce the initial elements of guided inductive inquiry. As one example for younger children, different pictures of the same scene are shown to the class. The teacher selects these based on the fact that they illustrate some of the differences associated with the seasons. Thus, four typical or even stereotypical pictures are used to show spring, summer, autumn, and winter.

Before beginning the lesson, the teacher will arrange to have all of the necessary materials so that the children are all given materials from which to have similar experiences. In conducting this lesson, the teacher will make extensive use of question-asking skills (which were learned previously in Chapter 6). The teacher will ask the children to make observations about what they see in the pictures. As the children venture their responses, the teacher must be careful to distinguish between statements based on observations and those based on inferences. When an inference is stated, the teacher should simply ask, "Is that an inference or an observation?" (Of course, the lesson should begin with the concepts or processes of observations and inferences presented in the simplest manner.) As the class progresses, the teacher will prepare a simple chart or will list on the blackboard the actual observations and the accompanying inferences. Each process will be built slowly and carefully with many such examples.

The pattern that the child observes should be stated by the child as some type of generalization that can apply whenever that pattern is repeated. The process of inductive thinking is developed gradually. Each teacher should plan to conduct some guided inductive-inquiry exercises whenever the occasion arises. The teacher should use simple questions such as: "What could cause this type of track in the snow?" and "Where have we seen this before?" These are the kinds of questions that require the child to do the generalizing rather than the teacher to simply present the generalizations.

In guided inductive inquiry, the teacher cannot expect the students to arrive at particular generalizations unless the learning activities, classroom recitations or discussions, learning materials, and visual aids are all arranged so that everything is available to the learner to make the generalizations. Perhaps these initial experiences can even utilize some small groups, such as task groups.

At all levels, the teacher should ask each student to write down the observations and, beside them, the inferences. In this fashion, the student will gain the habit of becoming systematic. This method also helps the teacher to check the observations that were the bases for any inferences.

Inferences are generalizations about certain objects or events. James G. Womack (1966), a social studies educator, suggests the following steps to be used in arriving at generalizations through guided inductive inquiry.*

1. Decide on the generalization(s) the students should discover from a particular unit of study.
2. Organize the learning activities and materials in a manner which exposes the strands or parts of the generalization(s) to the students.
3. Ask the students to write a summary of the content which contains the generalization(s).
4. Ask the students to identify the sequence of the pattern of events comprising the content, omitting any reference to any particular people, places, or times.

*From James G. Womack, *Discovering the Structure of the Social Studies* (New York: Benziger Brothers Publishing Company, 1966), p. 13. Used with the written permission of the Benziger Brothers Publishing Company.

5. Ask the students to synthesize the various parts of the pattern of events into one complete sentence which purports to be a generalization.
6. Ask the students to offer proof that their statement is, in fact, a generalization by citing examples that it existed and operated in other periods, places, and among other people.

We should note that the sixth step of Womack's process actually approaches the "hypothesis-building" and "testing" stages of the inquiry process. The decision to use step 6 is contingent on the teacher's judgment that students are ready to proceed to that point.

The Time Involved

When you initially utilize any type of inquiry activity in your classes, you must plan to spend at least twice the amount of time on each lesson than you would normally expect. Any inquiry activity takes much time to initiate and complete. This greater time use is spent on in-depth analysis of the content by the students. Furthermore, the use of inquiry methods requires greater interaction between the learner and the materials. There is also greater interaction between the teacher and the students. However, there is a small amount of risk involved for the students. They will not have an authority or book to cite, but must rely on their own data or observations. You will find that most children and adults approach inquiry activities with a great deal of caution—if not apprehension. But as the inductive-inquiry activities become a part of the ongoing procedures of the class, learner apprehension diminishes.

Another caveat is required: When you use an inquiry method, the amount of material covered is actually reduced. The reason is that you are using more time to develop thinking processes and reducing the time spent on memorization of fact or content. You cannot maximize thinking skills and simultaneously maximize content coverage. If you wish to build the so-called higher-order thinking skills, then you must reduce some of the content and substitute processes instead (see Chapter 1). In fact, you are not sacrificing anything. You are providing important instruction and experiences that are a part of the function of understanding the structure (epistemology) of the disciplines. The decision to follow this approach is yours. *Your* role is therefore very important.

In lower grades or when conducting initial experiences, the final generalization(s) may involve an oral summary or review of the concepts, a listing of the ideas presented, and finally, the eliciting of the learners' own views as to what constitutes a meaningful generalization. As the learners provide such input, the teacher should use such questioning techniques as probing, concept review, and prompting.

The testing of the generalizations can be accomplished by having the class apply the statement to different times, places, peoples, objects, or events. A major limitation of the testing will be the backgrounds and experiences of the learners.

Another technique that may be used with guided inductive inquiry is to write down a series of events on cards or on some other manipulative medium. Then ask the learners to place the events in the "proper" sequence, without any reference to the order being right or wrong. This activity can follow a reading assignment. When the sequence of events is completed, ask the students to observe the pattern of events and to state the pattern in just one sentence. This sentence will be the generalization. Other members of the class can be asked to test the generalization by examining it for significant exceptions.

These suggestions provide some tested models that help students to think inductively—that is, infer generalizations. Such models are adaptable to all levels of instruction. The efficiency of the learners—and of the teacher—will improve with practice.

Analysis of Guided Inductive Inquiry

As you read the previous presentation, you probably noted that we did not have any set prescription or rules to follow. The model illustrated in Figure 8–1 shows six major steps in that inquiry system: (1) identifying the problem; (2) developing tentative research hypotheses or objectives; (3) collecting data and testing the tentative answers; (4) interpreting data; (5) developing tentative conclusions or generalizations; (6) applying or retesting the conclusion; revising original conclusions. Implied in such a model is that the student finds the problem, or at least recognizes it, and then follows the six steps to attempt to resolve it.

These steps usually are needed for introductory guided inductive lessons. Recall that the process objectives are to observe, to infer, and to conclude. The problem, if it can be called one, is to determine a meaningful pattern in an array of events or objects. This process is *not* simply the allowing of wild guesses to take place. All inferences must be supported by some evidence—that is, observations or data. The latter may be obtained from some standard reference source such as the *United States Statistical Abstract,* or from almanacs, yearbooks, reports, or encyclopedias. The data become the focal point of the inquiry session and thus serve as a common experience for the entire class.

Guided inductive inquiry includes the following characteristics:

1. The thought processes require that the learners progress from specific observations to inferences or generalizations.
2. The objective is to learn (or reinforce) processes of examining events or objects and then to arrive at appropriate generalizations.
3. The teacher controls the elements—the events, data, materials, or objects—and as such, acts as the class leader.
4. The student reacts to the specifics of the lesson—the events, data, materials, or objects—and attempts to structure a meaningful pattern based on his or her observations and on those of others in the class.

FIGURE 8–1   A General Model of Inquiry

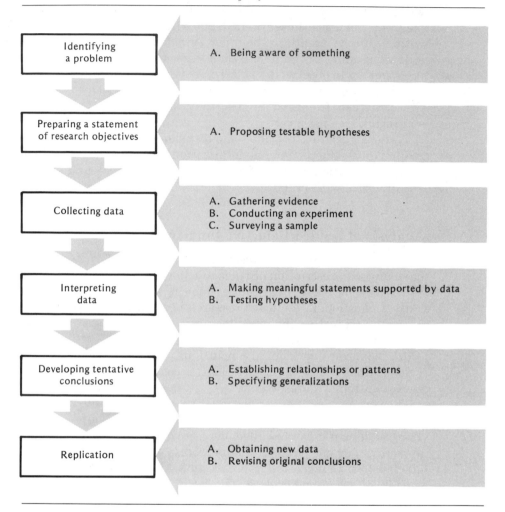

5. The classroom is to be considered a learning laboratory.
6. There is *usually* a fixed number of generalizations that will be elicited from the learners.
7. The teacher encourages each student to communicate his or her generalizations to the class so that others may benefit from individual perceptions.

The use of guided inductive inquiry may or may not be "creative" in the sense of allowing the learners the opportunity to "discover" something new. It can be argued that the process of discovery should be reserved for that which is truly unique in our culture. But such a situation would limit discovery to only the U.S. Patent Office. In schooling, the term *discovery* can mean that (1) the student has, for the very first time, determined something unique to that individual; (2) the student has added something to a discussion about a problem that the teacher or other students had not known before; or (3) the student has synthesized some information in such a manner as to provide others with a unique interpretation—that is, the student has demonstrated creativity.

Unfortunately, such a variety of definitions causes disagreements about discovery in the schools. Purists tend to support the third definition. Teachers usually accept the first definition. We tend to defend the position that discovery should be reserved for those situations in which problems are being solved and possible solutions or alternatives have not yet been stated. Thus, we support the second definition.

Models of Guided Inductive Inquiry

Two models of guided inductive inquiry are presented here. The first model was initially used in Pasco, Washington, when one of the authors was an instructor on a teacher-aide project. The aides were given the challenge of determining the patterns observed when using the compound microscope so that they would be familiar with one of the most commonly used pieces of scientific equipment. This exercise has since been used widely at several grade levels. Note how simple such an exercise can be.

The second model, a clever guided inductive device, allows students to learn about the mixing of colors from their own observations. In this model, note how easy it is to adapt elements of guided inductive inquiry to the fine arts. Another aspect of Model 2 is that it readily lends itself to the use of the overhead projector. Later in this chapter, we will discuss the use of transparencies in stimulating group instruction in an inquiry mode.

Although we have made a strong case for individual work during inquiry sessions, there is nothing wrong with the teacher also presenting the stimulus to the entire class. If the teacher decides to use this technique, then he or she should require that each student write down his or her own observations, inferences, and generalizations, rather than having an oral recitation period. This technique helps each learner to become more self-reliant. In this manner, each individual can develop his or her own logical framework, which may not be the case during oral recitations. In a group mode, it may even be wise to prepare a handout for the students so that they may record their observations and opinions in a guided, systematic manner.

After examining the two models of guided inductive inquiry, try to develop a similar lesson for your teaching area or discipline. Do not make the mistake of saying, "It can't be done for my subject." More than 2,000 students or teachers in our classes, with majors ranging from art to zoology, have all prepared either a guided or an unguided inductive inquiry lesson.

| **Model 1** | **An Inductive Approach to the Compound Light Microscope*** |

Biology and general science students are usually introduced to the compound microscope through a general discussion or lecture on nomenclature, microscope care, proper use of focusing knobs, lens systems, and the like. They are then given a microscope, a set of slides, cover slips, and other materials needed to complete observation exercises, and are expected to prepare suitable drawings for the teacher's examination.

NOTE: Students are seldom aware that the objects they view are inverted, upside down, or reversed—despite knowledge that movement of the slide causes a reverse action. Furthermore, they are unaware that the focal area is in a plane and that by continual focusing, new planes come into view.

This report describes an exercise needed to give students a better understanding of the compound microscope than they usually acquire through traditional means of presentation. Using an inductive approach, it allows students to make "discoveries" and generalizations about the microscope for themselves. The materials involved are simple and can easily be permanently mounted for classroom use.

Exploring the Compound Light Microscope

Objectives. The purpose of the exercise is to allow students to arrive inductively at the following three generalizations:

1. Objects appear inverted and reversed left to right.
2. The field of observation is inversely related to the power of the lens being used. As the magnifying power of the lens increases, the area of the observed field decreases.
3. Materials can be viewed as three-dimensional objects and are arranged on distinct planes.

Use. The exercise is presented here as it was developed and used for a class of teacher aides. However, it is readily adaptable for use with high school students.

Part 1. For the first phase of the exercise—to help students realize the inversion of objects under the microscope and their reversal left to right—several words and other symbols were typed on sheets of cellophane paper, using carbon ribbon to make a dark impression. Initially, one line of typed material was mounted on a posterboard slide having a quarter-inch slit to expose the typed line (see Fig. 8–2).

Students were asked to observe the line of characters, especially the question mark, and to draw exactly what they observed under low power, medium power, and high power. When all students had completed their drawings, they were asked to state generalizations concerning what they had observed.

Sample Results. Interestingly enough, during the period several students observed that the object being viewed was upside down. However, these students proceeded to reorient the slide on the microscope stage to give them a "corrected" image! Other students drew the figures as they appeared through the eyepiece—that is, inverted. When asked to make generalizations regarding this phenomenon, all agreed that the objects had been reversed or upside down.

---

*From Donald C. Orlich, *Science Teachers' Workshop* (West Nyack, N.J.: Parker Publishing Company, 1970), p. 13. Reprinted with written permission of the Parker Publishing Company.

FIGURE 8-2   Slide Used to Determine Field Area of Magnification and
Inversion of Objects

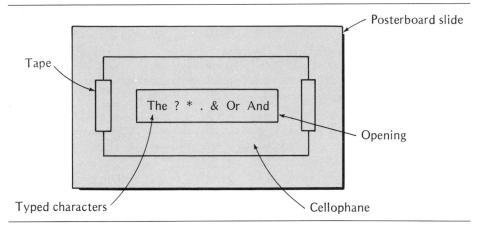

One participant who had recently completed a college biology course was as-
tounded to realize that she had never made this observation in a full quarter of
biology lab work. She stated that the slides she had used were either stained or
unstained and unprepared but that at no time had she realized inversion took place,
and that no one had ever mentioned this in class—including the instructor.

Part 2.   The second part of the exercise, seeking generalizations relating field size
to the magnifying power of the lens, was difficult for many students to comprehend
immediately. However, on repeated observation, without the instructor telling them
what they should observe but with leading questions, those who had difficulty were
able to state that "you cannot 'see' all of the letter under the highest power that you
can see under the lowest power."

Part 3.   The third objective—to have students observe that the field is arranged in
planes—was achieved by using overlapping pieces of cellophane with type-on letters and other symbols. The letters on one sheet were typed with a red ribbon, those
on the other with a black ribbon, so that each plane of focus would be observable
even though the planes overlapped (see Fig. 8–3).

NOTE: While students can obviously be "told" about these phenomena, telling
students is not as meaningful as helping them to make the "discoveries" themselves
using an inductive method similar to that described here.

Model 2 | Color Wheeling and Dealing

The usual approach to teaching the color wheel tends to be rather mechanical,
requiring little discovery on the student's part and, most of the time, involving only
memorization of concepts and principles. A more inquiry-oriented approach would
be to allow the students, through a guided inductive inquiry experience, to observe
visually what happens when primary colors are mixed.

This model uses a simple device that is prepared by using three sheets of transparency film. The three sheets are in the primary colors of blue, yellow, and red. They

FIGURE 8–3   Side View of Slide Illustrating Two Viewing Planes

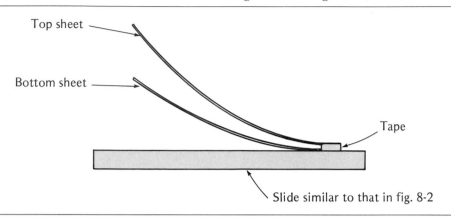

Top sheet

Bottom sheet

Tape

Slide similar to that in fig. 8-2

first are identified and then are arranged in a circle so that each third of the circle contains one of the three transparency films. The teacher then displays them on an overhead projector and defines them as the primary colors. A separate set of blue, yellow, and red wedges are prepared so that the teacher may direct student observations that help them to learn about color mixing.

What Happens When Primary Colors Are Mixed?

Objectives.   This device is designed to allow students, through observations, to arrive at the following conclusions:

1. Blue + Yellow = Green
2. Blue + Red = Purple
3. Red + Yellow = Orange
4. Orange + Blue = Brown
5. No other color combinations will produce the secondary colors.
6. The lightness of a color is a function of the thickness or concentration of the overhead transparency film.

Procedures.   The teacher prepares a color circle that contains the red, yellow, and blue transparency films. These films are then shown to the students so that they will know that they represent the three primary colors. The students are then asked to predict what might happen if the red and yellow films were superimposed on each other and to write down their responses. The teacher then lays the red strip on the yellow strip, or vice versa, and the students observe the resultant orange color.

The teacher next asks the question, "Does it make any difference whether the red or yellow transparency is on top of or under the other?" The students make predictions, and the teacher places the red film on the yellow, and the yellow on the red. The students then generalize that it makes no difference which color is placed on which, since orange is always produced when red and yellow are mixed.

The teacher repeats the procedure using blue and yellow and asks the students to make predictions. The teacher lays a blue strip of overhead transparency film on a yellow strip and, of course, the result is green. The teacher reverses the order, superimposing a yellow strip on a blue strip. The students are again asked to predict the color. Again, it is shown to make no difference which strip is placed on which, for the resultant color is always green. The teacher does the same operation using blue and red transparency film wedges, with the resultant color being purple.

The teacher then displays the orange color, which was made by mixing the red and yellow strips of film, and asks the student to predict what would happen if blue were superimposed on it. After the predictions are made, the teacher lays the blue strip on the orange color, producing a brown color. The teacher then proceeds to mix various transparency colors so that from the primary colors the secondary colors of orange, violet, and green are created. During the entire procedure, the teacher repeatedly asks, "What would happen if we mixed these colors?" The students make predictions, make observations, and change their predictions based on their observations.

The full color wheel may be impossible to make unless a complete set of overhead transparency films is available. However, a very close approximation of a color wheel can be made to show complementary colors.

The important aspect of this guided inductive device is that students are given an experience that requires them to make observations and to change their predictions based on these observations. Furthermore, the students will observe that the amount of light coming through seems to be reduced as the colors are mixed. The teacher may ask for explanations for this phenomenon (that more light is absorbed with darker mixes). The relationship between the amount of light and the darkness of a mix, as well as the relationship between the amount of light and "concentration," may be discussed.

Another procedure that can be tried is to use solutions of water and food coloring to demonstrate the three primary colors. The water, contained in separate small glass dishes, may be placed on the stage of an overhead projector. The teacher may then drop the food coloring into the water, or the students may be asked to mix the colors. The teacher can set up an experiment in which concentrations of the food coloring may be one variable and the amount of water the other. In this case, sets of identical containers will have varying depths of water but the same number of drops of food coloring. The students are asked to arrange the containers in some type of observable pattern, and then to explain by what variable the containers are arranged. The expected response will be that the darkness or lightness of color is the variable used. The teacher then asks the students to try to match the darkness or lightness of the colors. The students then prepare different sets of solutions with varying color darknesses. In all cases, the students will collect data concerning their observations and the techniques being used.

Depending on how the teacher wants the color-mixing inductive technique to be conducted, students will probably make a chart that will show the following: (1) the number of drops of food coloring in a specific volume of water; and (2) the number of drops of food coloring in different volumes of water. The students will then begin to discover the concept of concentrations being based on the operational definition of lightness.

This model of guided inductive inquiry can be controlled entirely by the teacher, or the students can be involved in conducting all of the trials. The essential elements of inquiry are integrated into the lesson, and the students become more active in a topic that usually does not require involvement. The students can even suggest additional "experiments." However, the teacher has the choice of using either a dry medium (that is, transparency paper) or a solution, depending on the medium being used by the class. But in either case, the students will have learned a useful inquiry technique while "color wheeling and dealing."

Questioning and Guided Inductive Inquiry

We have noted that teacher questioning plays an important role in inquiry, because the purpose of inquiry is to pursue the "search," the "investigation." To accomplish this purpose, the teacher becomes a question-asker, not a question-answerer. Teachers who are masters of guided induction inquiry will state that they spend their time interacting with the students but provide very few answers.

What kinds of questions should a teacher ask? Dr. James M. Migaki, a science educator and master of the technique, has categorized several "stems" or lead-in questions for teachers who want to have a more inquiry-oriented class environment. Of course, what makes Migaki's set of stems so interesting is that they are especially suitable for use in social studies, science, and mathematics. But they are usable in *any* class in which the teacher wants to stress the process of inquiry.

If you are conducting an experiment, collecting data, examining cause-and-effect relationships, or analyzing events, then the following set of question stems are very appropriate for challenging the student to think.*

> What is happening?
> What has happened?
> What do you think will happen now?
> How did this happen?
> Why did this happen?
> What caused this to happen?
> What took place before this happened?
> Where have you seen something like this happen?
> When have you seen something like this happen?
> How could we make this happen?
> How does this compare with what we saw or did?
> How can we do this more easily?
> How can you do this more quickly?

Note that this list is oriented to dynamic situations. You may even think of a few more questions to add for your own specialty or grade level. These stems are probably best classified as prompting questions, similar to those described in Chapter 6.

If you are examining more static living or nonliving objects, the following stems will prove very useful.

> What kind of object is it?
> What is it called?
> Where is it found?
> What does it look like?
> Have you ever seen anything like it? Where? When?
> How is it like other things?
> How can you recognize or identify it?

---

*The two sets of question stems are reprinted with the written permission of James M. Migaki.

How did it get its name?
What can you do with it?
What is it made of ?
How was it made?
What is its purpose?
How does it work or operate?
What other names does it have?
How is it different from other things?

Again, note that these prompting questions help the student to understand better all kinds of interrelationships—one of the desired goals of inquiry teaching.

To supplement the role of questioning and process-building, the teacher of younger students can use a series of pictures about where people live. This guided inductive-inquiry project would be ideal in a social studies class. The materials would consist simply of pictures of various "typical" houses of the world, which can be obtained from magazines. If you have no sources of such pictures, just ask the students to bring in old magazines from their homes or from the neighbors. In no time, you will have accumulated a lifetime supply.

There are several ways you can approach this lesson. The first may be to select houses that all have some similar trait—for example, steep roofs, flat roofs, white paint. The objective is to get the students to observe patterns, similarities, and differences.

As a preliminary activity, you can conduct a recitation involving the whole class. (Later, we would prefer you to subdivide the class into groups of eight, so that you may practice those discussion skills you learned in Chapter 7.) Have the students observe the pictures while you list their observations on the chalkboard or, better yet, on newsprint. By using the latter, you can tape the newsprint to a wall and place the pictures on a table next to it, thus allowing the students who did not seem to master the process of inductive logic to practice more on their own. But let us return to the lesson.

You may need to ask a series of questions about the houses, the land, and other observable elements in the pictures. Then you begin to build toward a general statement regarding all the pictures being studied. When this statement is made *by the class,* successful guided inductive inquiry is demonstrated. The lesson can be reinforced by using other objects such as leaves in the fall, old buttons in the winter, mittens, whether or not the children wear mittens, the children's feet, their hands, their earlobes—any objects that can be classified, sorted, counted, or contrasted. It is essential to keep reinforcing the learning wherever possible simply by asking, "What do we observe here?"

Norris M. Sanders (1966) presents an interesting guided inductive device in his book, *Classroom Questions: What Kinds?* He uses data from the economic sector—such as the gross national product and the public debt—that are presented over a period of several years. Again, the students make generalizations and present hypotheses that explain the various fluctuations.

The teacher with any initiative can use this type of lesson at higher grade levels. For example, junior high students can determine the relative standards by which houses are built in different areas of the world and the reasons for the discrepancies. High school students can be challenged to compute the energy costs of heating or cooling systems and the effectiveness of insulation in conserving energy. The teacher is thus the organizer and expediter of guided inductive inquiry, while the students are the active thinkers and doers.

Unguided Inductive Inquiry

In the preceding text concerning *guided* inductive inquiry, you noted that the teacher played the key role in asking the questions, prompting the responses, and structuring the materials and situations, and in general was the major organizer of the learning. Guided inductive inquiry is an excellent method by which to begin the gradual shift from expository or deductive teaching toward teaching that is less structured and more open to alternative solutions. If the teacher senses that the class has mastered the techniques of guided inductive inquiry, then the teacher ought to introduce situations that are still predicated on inductive logic but are more open-ended in that the students must take more responsibility for examining the data, objects, or events.

The basic processes of observation, inference, classification, communication, prediction, interpretation, formulation of hypotheses, and experimentation are all a part of *unguided* inductive inquiry. The teacher's role is minimized, which causes a concomitant increase in the students' activity. Let us briefly summarize the major elements of unguided inductive inquiry.

1. The thought processes require that the learners will progress from specific observations to inferences or generalizations.
2. The objective is to learn (or reinforce) the processes of examining events, objects, and data and then to arrive at appropriate sets of generalizations.
3. The teacher controls only the materials and simply poses a question such as: "What can you generalize from . . . ?" or "Tell me everything that you can about 'X' after examining these. . . ."
4. The students interact with the specifics of the lesson and ask all of the questions that come to mind without further teacher guidance.
5. Meaningful patterns are student-generated through individual observations and inferences, as well as those generated by others in the class.
6. The materials are essential to making the classroom a laboratory.
7. There is usually an unlimited number of generalizations that the learners will generate.
8. The teacher encourages a sharing of the inferences so that all students communicate their generalizations with the class. Thus, others may benefit from one individual's unique perceptions.

Unguided inductive inquiry provides a mechanism for greater learner creativity. Also, the learners begin to approach a genuinely authentic discovery episode. For, as Kenneth A. Strike (1975) has argued, discovery learning is approached when learners find out something by themselves and come to know that fact. Strike refers to this process as *relative discovery*—that is, the event may have been known to others prior to the time the learner discovered it by himself or herself.

When the teacher begins to use unguided inductive inquiry, a new set of teacher behaviors must come into play. The teacher must now begin to act as the "classroom clarifier." As students start to make their generalizations, there predictably will appear gross errors in student logic, too broadly stated generalizations, too much inference from the data, the assigning of single cause-and-effect relationships where there are several, and assigning cause-and-effect relationships where none exist.

Thus, the teacher patiently examines the learner in a *nonthreatening* manner to verify the conclusion or generalizations. If errors exist in the student's logic or inferences, these should be pointed out. But the teacher should not tell the student what the correct inference is, for this would defeat the purpose of any inquiry episode.

We suggest that during initial unguided inductive experiences, the students should work alone. In our experiences, we have noted that when students work alone they tend to do most of the work themselves. When they work in pairs or triads, one in the group usually takes the leadership role and dominates the thinking of the group, so that there is only one participant and two observers. When students demonstrate the aptitude to use the inductive method successfully in an unguided fashion, then small groups can be assigned to work together.

Techniques for Unguided Inductive Inquiry

What are some tested ideas that can be used as prototypes to encourage teachers to seek appropriate inductive learning experiences that can be incorporated into an ongoing lesson?

Dr. S. Samuel Shermis of Purdue University uses two very inexpensive devices to aid students in understanding the culture of different parts of the United States and of the world. The first device is the telephone directory. Shermis simply gives his students copies of worn-out, discarded, or obsolete telephone directories and then says, "Tell me all you can about Gary . . ."—if the directory happens to be that of Gary, Indiana, of course. The students begin to examine the contents and to jot down notes about the city such as the number of people, industries, services, and organizations. A good problem is to give some members of the class directories from different geographical regions, such as Boston, Tulsa, Nashville, and Salt Lake City, and to ask them to compile a set of generalizations about those cities' religious preferences, by "letting their fingers walk through the Yellow Pages."

To obtain those directories, send a letter to the superintendent of schools in the cities that you select and ask them for the old editions. Or go to the manager of the Directory Department of your local telephone company and ask for some of the obsolete volumes. When big business knows that it is helping the schools, it is usually happy to provide materials.

A second technique that Shermis uses to introduce an unguided inductive inquiry is to distribute a set of postcards from any city, state, or country and then to pose the question: "What do you think this city considers to be important?" He does the same thing with travel brochures obtained at no cost from any travel agent.

Cancelled postage stamp collections provide an excellent medium to develop inquiry and thinking skills. Lloyd H. Barrow and William Moore (1976) illustrated how observing, inferring, classifying, and estimating skills can be extended. Students are given a pile of old postage stamps. They are asked to divide them into groups based on a single property. For example, students are asked to (1) infer values from the stamps, (2) design a stamp, (3) examine a stamp under magnification, (4) count the number of perforations on an edge, and so forth.

Along the same line, Willis J. Horak and Virginia M. Horak (1981) suggested using old mail-order catalogues as the material by which to develop inquiry skills. Students are asked to observe the placement of items; the number of pages devoted to specific categories (i.e., men's and women's clothing); cost of merchandise; placement of merchandise by cost on the page; colors being used; and how the index is used and placed. Students are then encouraged to generate questions for the class.

You may use the local newspaper as an inquiry laboratory. In one such experience you can challenge the students to find examples of bias or news that is slanted. In general, newspaper bias can be classified into eight major types.

1. Bias through selection and omission
2. Bias through placement
3. Bias by headline
4. Bias by photos, captions, and camera angle
5. Bias through use of names and titles
6. Bias through statistics and crowd counts
7. Bias by source control
8. Bias by word selection and connotation

Over time, students will be able to identify these eight sources of bias—by using unguided inductive inquiry techniques. All you have to do is bring in the laboratory materials and provide some time. This laboratory could even take the form of a "learning activity center" located in the corner of the classroom. By establishing a learning activity center, students may work on the material at their own pace and own time.

The important point in these various activities is to require that students analyze and evaluate. Require that all students provide concrete evidence for any generalization; in this manner, comprehension and analytic skills are reinforced. Using these techniques will help your students progress far beyond simple Knowledge skills.

Note how very much open-ended these experiences are in that there is ample "learning space" that will allow everyone in the class to participate. The "slowest" to the smartest students can all make meaningful contributions.

The authors have had fun using data taken from the U.S. Decennial Census. By arranging the census data in five-year increments, by age, for any one or more years, one can build a "population pyramid." The students are asked to discuss in small groups the question: "What can you generalize from this Figure?" Virtually hundreds of generalizations are offered. Observe the selected pyramids in Figures 8–4 and 8–5 and the data in Table 8–1. How many questions or problems can *you* pose from each of these simple presentations of data. Students always note the "dent" in the pyramid indicating a decrease in the population. Their explanations for the "dent" are interesting. A few examples follow: "The people were killed in World War II"; "they died of starvation during the Depression"; "they died from epidemics"; and "people just had fewer kids."

The advantage of these explanations, or hypotheses, is that they can all be tested. The students are sent to the library to do research to verify their hypotheses. They soon realize that their hypotheses are untenable. The reality dimension of such inquiry exercises helps to develop logical processes in the child's method of looking at nature.

These data inquiry challenges can be great stimulators of classroom discussions. Data exist for every grade level experience and for every possible subject, ranging from art to zoology. It is also possible to present data in such a way that students must either interpolate (predict what should have come earlier) or extrapolate (predict later outcomes). Teachers can control the flow of data (information) so that predictions may be made and justified. Evidence, facts, and their interpretation all become more meaningful to the students instead of being merely words in a book.

We are suggesting that any teacher at any level has some information that poses questions for which there are no answers. By providing this information to the students, the teacher initiates unguided inductive inquiry. To be sure, we do not assign exercises just for the sake of having the students do them. Exercises must be correlated with the learning objectives or goals that *you* have selected for the unit, chapter, or module. Some topics lend themselves easily to inductive inquiry while others do not. *You* must decide on these topics.

For example, Russell M. Agne (1969) of the University of Vermont uses original data in the teaching of earth science. He presents radiosonde data in tabular form, providing learners with the barometric pressures for various altitudes on one-kilometer increments. The learners are given both guided and unguided exercises to complete. Other original data provided by Agne include temperatures at varying altitudes, solar radiation data, mean annual temperatures, and other "real" data.

FIGURE 8–4   U.S. Population by Age and Sex: 1900–1960

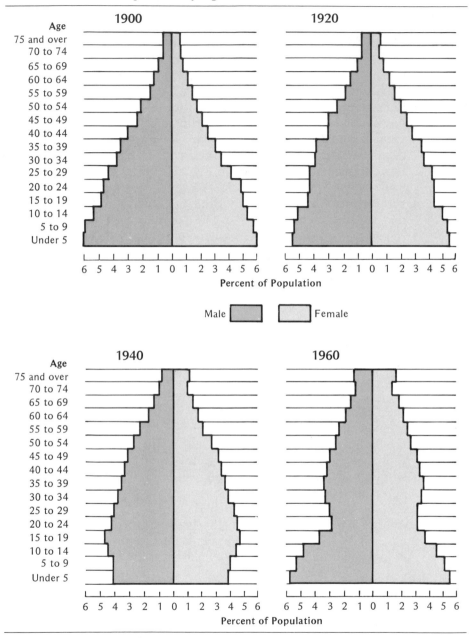

Source: Executive Office of the President: Office of Management and Budget, *Social Indicators, 1973* (Washington, D.C.: U.S. Government Printing Office, 1973), Chart 8/8, p. 250.

FIGURE 8–5   U.S. Population by Age and Sex: 1960–1980

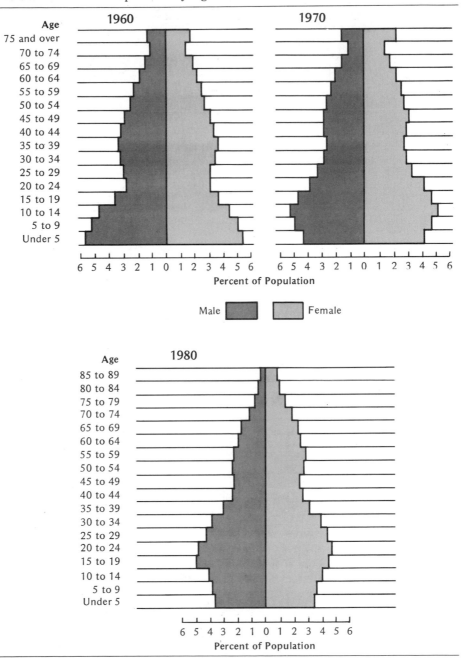

Source: 1980 Pyramid, *Age, Sex, Race, and Spanish Origin of the Population by Regions, Divisions, and States:* 1980, PC80-51-1, Bureau of the Census; 1970 and 1960 Pyramids, Executive Office of the President: Office of Management and Budget, *Social Indicators, 1973* (Washington, D.C.: U.S. Government Printing Office, 1973), Chart 8/8, p. 250.

TABLE 8–1 U.S. Population, by Age and Sex: 1920–1980

Age	1920 Male	1920 Female	1940 Male	1940 Female	1960 Male	1960 Female	1970 Male	1970 Female	1980 Male	1980 Female
NUMBER OF PERSONS (thousands)										
All ages	54,086	51,935	66,350	65,815	88,331	90,992	98,912	104,300	110,032	116,473
Under 5 years	5,880	6,738	5,379	5,210	10,330	9,991	8,745	8,409	8,360	7,984
5 to 9 years	5,771	5,663	5,444	5,291	9,504	9,187	10,168	9,788	8,538	8,159
10 to 14 years	5,383	5,285	5,980	5,820	8,524	8,249	10,591	10,199	9,315	8,926
15 to 19 years	4,687	4,767	6,209	6,173	6,634	6,586	9,634	9,437	10,752	10,410
20 to 24 years	4,544	4,761	5,728	5,917	5,272	5,528	7,917	8,454	10,660	10,652
25 to 29 years	4,552	4,560	5,482	5,664	5,333	5,536	6,622	6,855	9,703	9,814
30 to 34 years	4,147	3,950	5,095	5,186	5,846	6,103	5,596	5,835	8,676	8,882
35 to 39 years	4,090	3,710	4,767	4,813	6,080	6,402	5,412	5,694	6,860	7,103
40 to 44 years	3,301	3,067	4,435	4,379	5,676	5,924	5,819	6,162	5,708	5,961
45 to 49 years	3,132	2,651	4,221	4,055	5,358	5,522	5,851	6,265	5,388	5,701
50 to 54 years	2,546	2,203	3,765	3,511	4,735	4,871	5,348	5,756	5,620	6,089
55 to 59 years	1,887	1,671	3,021	2,838	4,127	4,303	4,766	5,207	5,481	6,133
60 to 64 years	1,587	1,402	2,406	2,335	3,409	3,733	4,027	4,590	4,669	5,416
65 to 69 years	1,082	990	1,902	1,913	2,931	3,327	3,122	3,870	3,902	4,878
70 to 74 years	707	689	1,274	1,300	2,185	2,554	2,315	3,129	2,853	3,944
75 to 79 years	421	437	725	781	1,360	1,694	1,561	2,274	1,847	2,946
80 to 84 years	186	217	360	416	665	915	876	1,409	1,018	1,915
85 years and over	91	119	157	208	362	567	542	968	681	1,558

TABLE 8–1 Continued

Age	1920 Male	1920 Female	1940 Male	1940 Female	1960 Male	1960 Female	1970 Male	1970 Female	1980 Male	1980 Female
PERCENT OF TOTAL POPULATION										
All ages	51.0	49.0	50.2	49.8	49.3	50.7	48.7	51.3	48.58	51.42
Under 5 years	5.5	5.4	4.1	3.9	5.8	5.6	4.3	4.1	3.7	3.5
5 to 9 years	5.4	5.3	4.1	4.0	5.3	5.1	5.0	4.8	3.8	3.6
10 to 14 years	5.1	5.0	4.5	4.4	4.8	4.6	5.2	5.0	4.1	3.9
15 to 19 years	4.4	4.5	4.7	4.7	3.7	3.7	4.7	4.6	4.7	4.6
20 to 24 years	4.3	4.5	4.3	4.5	2.9	3.1	3.9	4.2	4.7	4.7
25 to 29 years	4.3	4.3	4.1	4.3	3.0	3.1	3.3	3.4	4.3	4.3
30 to 34 years	3.9	3.7	3.9	3.9	3.3	3.4	2.8	2.9	3.8	3.9
35 to 39 years	3.9	3.5	3.6	3.6	3.4	3.6	2.7	2.8	3.0	3.1
40 to 44 years	3.1	2.9	3.4	3.3	3.2	3.3	2.9	3.0	2.5	2.6
45 to 49 years	3.0	2.5	3.2	3.1	3.0	3.1	2.9	3.1	2.4	2.5
50 to 54 years	2.4	2.1	2.8	2.7	2.6	2.7	2.6	2.8	2.5	2.7
55 to 59 years	1.8	1.6	2.3	2.1	2.3	2.4	2.3	2.6	2.4	2.7
60 to 64 years	1.5	1.3	1.8	1.8	1.9	2.1	2.0	2.3	2.1	2.4
65 to 69 years	1.0	0.9	1.4	1.4	1.6	1.9	1.5	1.9	1.7	2.2
70 to 74 years	0.7	0.6	1.0	1.0	1.2	1.4	1.1	1.5	1.2	1.7
75 to 79 years	0.4	0.4	0.5	0.6	0.7	0.9	0.8	1.1	0.8	1.3
80 to 84 years	0.2	0.2	0.3	0.3	0.4	0.5	0.4	0.7	0.4	0.8
85 years and over	0.1	0.1	0.1	0.2	0.2	0.3	0.3	0.5	0.3	0.7

Note: Data do not include Armed Forces overseas.

Sources: Bureau of the Census, 1920 Census of Population, Abstract of the Fourteenth Census of the United States; 1940 Census of Population, Vol. IV, Part 1; 1960 Census of Population, Vol. I, Part 1; 1970 Census of Population, Vol. II, Part 1; and unpublished data. Executive Office of the President: Office of Management and Budget, Social Indicators 1973, Washington, D.C.: U.S. Government Printing Office, 1973, p. 255; and Bureau of the Census, 1980 Census of Population, Supplementary Reports, "Age, Sex, Race, and Spanish Origin of the Population by Regions, Divisions, and States: 1980," PC80-S1-1, p. 3.
The authors thank Annabelle Cook, Department of Sociology, Washington State University for her help in supplying the 1980 data.

In the humanities and the arts, the teacher is the *only* limiting factor. If you really know your discipline, you also know its "structure"—that is, its epistemological basis. By collecting materials from your area of expertise, you can build a file of appropriate items, objects, events, or artifacts that can be used to supplement the usual classroom instruction.

Planning for Inquiry

Again, a word of caution to future teachers: You do not suddenly begin to use inquiry without preparation. You plan for experiences that are meaningful and relevant. For language arts classes, the local newspaper is one of the finest and cheapest resources for raw data. Have the students examine the editorial pages and the front-page news stories of the local "scandal sheet" as well as those of various cities around the state or country. Let them make generalizations about such matters as editorial positions, the use of propaganda and persuasive techniques, and the ways of slanting (or biasing) stories.

Weekly, biweekly, and monthly magazines are gold mines of inquiry activities. Junior high school teachers in the language arts have long used advertisements in magazines to illustrate various communication principles. Art classes also can use these materials to illustrate communication techniques as well as to examine the artistic principles being used.

Even physical educators can use inductive inquiry techniques with selected skill-building activities. Students can be allowed to determine various moves, stances, balance points, and the like through guided inductive inquiry.

Poets use inductive logic to a great extent, especially when developing such elements as characters, images, and themes. The readers must infer the meaning or determine the pattern that is being built. It can be fun when poetry is employed—if it is appropriate to the objectives of the lesson—to teach students how to use inductive logic while attempting to analyze meanings. (Of course, the authors are well aware of John Ciardi's [1979] criticism that teachers tend to overanalyze poetry to the point of *reductio ad absurdum*.)

Along the guidelines suggested, the eighth-grade history program in Northampton, Massachusetts, was totally restructured to incorporate historical interpretation, analysis, and evaluation as basic skills—along with knowledge of history. Students were provided with materials and reprints from early newspapers dating back to 1754. Students determined the effects of selected governmental decisions on the merchants, landowners, and other groups. Students created a play about one of the periods in the town's growth. The students did the research, wrote the script, and made the costumes.

As the local history was studied, story boards and time-lines were created so that a historical perspective could be gained. Incidents were linked to other historical events. Social concepts such as justice, prejudice, development of laws, government, politics, and group dynamics were examined. Compare this exciting course with the one you had in eighth grade.

If you want to develop some initial inductive skills, offer the class a challenge: how is the national zip code organized? One of the authors of this text has developed a "zip code game" that uses inductive and unguided inquiry techniques. Students receive the challenge and a blank map of the United States. Cards with state capitals and their zip codes are distributed and as the exercise progresses, patterns of zip codes begin to emerge. The national areas are identified and zip codes are predicted for states, territories, and islands in the Atlantic and Pacific Oceans. This experience helps develop pattern-building, inference, prediction, and classification skills. Further, it reinforces geographic areas, names and locations of states, and knowledge of the zip code.

Students are then challenged to compare the zip codes of the United States with the postal codes of Canada and other countries. Similarities and differences are then identified. The processes of inquiry are nicely reinforced with the content.

Although we have not emphasized the process of classification in the inquiry modes, we wish to mention that, as humans, we constantly classify everything in our lives—such as people, objects, baseball games, suits, houses, cars, movies, and TV shows. One of the generalizations that will quickly emerge as you use inductive modes is that there is no one way to classify anything. Your students will arrive at usable classification schemes that you may not have thought existed.

One of our favorite classification exercises involves the "old button box" device. Obtain as many buttons as you can from a "scavenger hunt" and place them in a bag. Then ask each class member to establish a classification scheme for the buttons that he or she has. We guarantee that you will be surprised at the number of characteristics that the students will observe as being useful in classifying their buttons.

Classification exercises can lead to some elements of evaluation as we know it in Bloom's Taxonomy. Evaluation, as you recall, is conducted using explicitly stated criteria. But how does one classify or evaluate the criteria? Utility has to be one consideration. There are others, but allow the students to determine them for themselves. Table 8–2 presents some topics appropriate for inquiry.

About the Inductive Method

Perhaps you have been taught that the inductive method of inquiry is "the method of science." If so, you have been led astray. To be sure, scientists use inductive methodologies. But detailed analyses of scientific thought by Karl R. Popper (1959; originally published in 1934) and, more recently, by Thomas S. Kuhn (1962) show that modern science is characterized more by *hypothetico-deductive* reasoning than by pure inductive logic. However, inductive logic is a basis for inference building, and scientists typically rely on

TABLE 8–2   Topics Appropriate to Inquiry by Discipline

Discipline	Topics
Art	Color wheels
	Drawing: what happens to movement
English	Symbols in a masterpiece
	Mapping for writing
History	Bias in recorded history
	Life in the Great Depression
Family living	Properties of different textiles
	Family interactions
Industrial arts	Commonalities of period design
	Hardware choices
Languages	Cultural differences in prefixes
	Comparing similar objects, e.g., tickets, maps, advertisements
Music	Infer style and moods
	Establish patterns from different composers
Physical education	Disease control
	Athletic injuries
Science	Animal communications
	Chemical reactions
Social studies	Demographic trends
	Cultural geographical similarities and differences
Theater arts	Social impact of playwright
	Symbolism in set design

theories or working hypotheses on which to base their "inductive experiments." This means that modern-day empiricism is undergirded by theoretical propositions. Actually, Popper argues that there is no such thing as theory; there are only testable hypotheses. The longer a hypothesis stands the tests of experimentation and predictability, the more it gains "respect" in the scientific community. Emerging social science fields such as sociology, psychology, and anthropology, to list three, are now developing substantial bodies of tenable theory—that is, working hypotheses. The worth of any theory or hypothesis is its ability to predict future events. The so-called hard sciences—chemistry and physics—have had a long tradition of hypotheses that have stood the rigors of experimentation and prediction. Physicists and chemists proudly state that without the strong theoretical commitment those disciplines have, they would be unable to function in the laboratory to conduct systematic research.

Compare this position to teaching or education. In our field, there are few tenable hypotheses that can help the teacher to teach better. Thus, the state of the art for education is far behind that of the other social sciences. Perhaps you have complained that education courses "have too much theory." We argue that you have been exposed to too much inductive logic in the form of classroom anecdotes, without the necessary theoretical structure.

PROBLEM-SOLVING

A curricular model that should have had a greater impact on the schools than it did was one advocated by John Dewey, a major writer who published extensively from 1884 to 1948. Among his major educational contributions was his advocacy of a curriculum *based on problems*. He defined a problem as anything that gives rise to doubt and uncertainty. This theory is not to be confused with the "needs" or "interest" theories of curriculum. Dewey did have a definite idea of the types of problems that are suitable for inclusion in the curriculum. The problems that Dewey promoted had to meet two rigorous criteria: (1) the problems to be studied had to be important to the culture; and (2) the problems had to be important and relevant to the student.

It is very apparent that many curriculum projects developed between 1958 and 1970 in science, mathematics, and social studies tended to be based on Dewey's problem-solving approach. Most contemporary curricula and a large majority of textbooks suggest "problems" to be solved by students. Some of the curricula that you may encounter will stress elements of inquiry, discovery, or problem-solving. Contemporary curricula, especially interdisciplinary ones such as environmental studies, rely heavily on the two criteria that were first suggested by Dewey. If you assign "research reports" to be prepared by your students, you will be using elements of problem-solving. Again, we caution that the use of this technique, like any inquiry method, requires careful planning and systematic skill-building.

Implicit within the framework of problem-solving is the concept of "experience." This concept assumes that activities that students attempt under the school's direction will produce certain desirable traits (or behaviors) in those individuals, so that they will be better able to function in our culture. Furthermore, the experiences provided by the schools should articulate the *content* and the *process* of knowing. Both knowing what is known and knowing how to know are important objectives for the learner.

The Teacher's Role

When using problem-solving with learners, the teacher must constantly play the "great clarifier" role. The teacher must always help the learners to define precisely what it is that is being studied or solved. Problem-solving methodologies focus on the systematic investigation of the students' problems. The students set up the problem, clarify the issues, propose ways of obtaining the needed information or data to help resolve the problem, and then test or evaluate the conclusions. In most cases, the learners will establish written hypotheses for testing. We cannot overemphasize the fact that students need continual monitoring by the teacher. Problem-solving demands that the teacher continually receive "progress reports" from those students engaged in the investigative process.

Students are not simply allowed to follow their whims. Problem-solving requires the building of close relationships between students and teacher. It also involves a systematic investigation of the problem and the proposing of concrete solutions. Let us present two case histories of real problems that took place in a Boulder, Colorado, high school and in a Massachusetts elementary school.

Examples of Real Problem-Solving

Boulder, Colorado, is situated on the eastern terminus of the great Rocky Mountain Range. The picturesque setting has all the natural beauty that is shown in scenic books and chamber of commerce brochures. Cascading down the mountains is Boulder Creek. It enters the city of Boulder as an uncontaminated, clear, cool stream. Unfortunately, it does not leave in the same state. *Awareness* of this condition prompted a group of high school students to raise the question: "What are the contributing causes of this problem?" Thus the group went to work in setting up a plan of investigation.

It soon became apparent that the class had to seek help from the chemistry teacher, for if a group is to determine what types of pollutants are present, the water must be chemically analyzed along several points of the creek. This development presented the need for cooperation—that no one person could complete the total investigation alone and that others had to be brought in for "expert" advice. While the chemical analyses were being conducted, another group took a series of temperature readings and depth soundings to determine the temperature fluctuations along the creek's course as it flowed through the city. Other small groups attempted to locate users of the creek's water.

Thus, a *heuristic* approach, in which students learn by their own investigations, was used. The larger problem was subdivided into specific or more manageable components. The authenticity of the problem was apparent, so the teacher did not have to establish the credibility of the study. Furthermore, all student hypotheses could be tested in the real world. The group proposed the ways of obtaining information and then evaluated the worth of the data that had been collected.

To conclude this case study, these students found out that the major polluter of the creek was, in fact, the University of Colorado's maintenance department. The university would simply flood the lawns on the campus to irrigate the lawns in the most economical manner. The only trouble with that system was that it raised the temperature of the water and contributed the nitrates and phosphates that were used to fertilize the lawns. When the final report was duplicated, one copy was presented to the president of the university and another was sent to the local paper. Needless to say, the university changed its watering methods, and the creek was less polluted than before.

In a similar vein, children in a Massachusetts elementary school collected data and presented it to their local school board showing that at a major intersection there was a grievous safety problem. The students then showed how an overpass walk could be constructed and even contacted architects to obtain estimates of the cost of such a structure. The school board was impressed and so was the city council, for the walk was constructed later just as the elementary school children had proposed.

These are just a sample of case studies of students using problem-solving in the real world. Such examples are a bit dramatic, although they do not all have to be. For instance, a class may observe problems in the immediate school environment—parking, lunch lines, locker rooms, or noise—and may begin to investigate these problems with the idea of creating alternatives to the existing situations.

Some Steps in Solving Problems

Problem-solving implies a certain freedom to explore the problem and to arrive at a possible solution. One tackles a problem to achieve objectives and not simply to use the process of inquiry per se. The following steps are associated with the problem-solving technique:

1. Becoming aware of a situation or event that is labeled a "problem."
2. Identifying the problem in exact terms.
3. Defining all terms.
4. Establishing the limits of the problem.
5. Conducting a task analysis so that the problem may be subdivided into discrete elements for investigation.
6. Collecting data that are relevant to each task.
7. Evaluating the data for apparent biases or errors.
8. Synthesizing the data for meaningful relationships.
9. Making generalizations and suggesting alternatives to rectify the problem.
10. Publishing the results of the investigation.

Obviously, if *you* decide to use a problem-solving episode in your classes, you must realize that it will last for a period of days or even weeks. During that time, other learnings may be accomplished as well—for example, using reference books, writing for unavailable information or data, interpreting data, presenting progress reports to the class, and taking responsibility for the conduct of a task.

If the problem allows for other independent study, that also may be arranged. The teacher may be able to conduct both the problem-solving episodes and the elements of the "regular" class lessons. In many cases, there are time lapses between phases of the problem-solving procedures. The teacher should make appropriate use of such time so that it will not be wasted.

The students will experience a sense of accomplishment in problem-solving. We suggest that the teacher plan for a systematic evaluation of the episode. You can adapt the evaluation forms presented in the treatment of discussions in Chapter 7. In this manner, both the teacher and the learners will be able to benefit from the experience. Problem-solving, then, is one more inquiry technique that is available for making schooling a more memorable experience.

DISCOVERY LEARNING

Who really discovered America? Leif Ericson seems to have been the first European to visit our shores. However, Christopher Columbus gets the credit for the discovery simply because he announced it first, while the territory is named for Amerigo Vespucci because he knew he had landed on a brand new continent and not in India. Thus the defining of *discovery* is difficult.*

Dictionary definitions of *discover* carry connotations that go beyond the denotations. For example, examine the following definition quoted from *Webster's New Collegiate Dictionary:***

> **dis·cov·er . . . 1 a:** to make known or visible; EXPOSE **b** *archaic:* DISPLAY **2:** to obtain sight or knowledge of for the first time: FIND ~ the solution of a puzzle) ~ *vi:* to make a discovery— . . .
> **syn 1** see REVEAL
> **2** DISCOVER, ASCERTAIN, DETERMINE, UNEARTH, LEARN *shared meaning element:* to find out something not previously known to one
> **3** see INVENT

With all these connotations for one term, it is not surprising to observe so much confusion in the use of the word in the field of education. This is not to be construed as derogating the technique of discovery; it is merely meant to show the possibilities attending the state of the art.

The terms *discovery learning* and *inductive methods* are often used in place of the same generic term of *inquiry*. We shall differentiate among these so that each method will be better understood. Induction is a method of logic, while discovery is a method by which thoughts are synthesized to perceive something that an individual has not known before. In this vein, Kenneth A. Strike's (1975) comprehensive analysis of methods associated with discovery learning may be of immediate use. Strike establishes two categories of discovery: *absolute* discovery and *relative* discovery. Absolute discovery is that attributed to those classic firsts—the discovery of the DNA molecule's reproduction mechanism, America, new planets, theories, or synthetic materials. Relative discovery means that an individual has learned or found out something for the first time.

Strike also presents four modes of discovery: (1) knowing that; (2) knowing how; (3) discovering that; and (4) discovering how. Finally, he provides a basic criterion that is essential for any act to be labeled a discovery. The discoverer must communicate both the *what* and the *how* to others. Thus, if

---

*We thank Kenneth A. Strike (1975) for the idea.

**By permission. From *Webster's New Collegiate Dictionary* © 1979 by G. & C. Merriam Co., Publishers of the Merriam-Webster Dictionaries.

you do discover the "Lost Dutchman Mine" in Arizona and do not tell a single individual, you have not made a discovery.

The four modes of discovery that Strike presents are very consistent with the thirteen major processes that we described earlier (p. 253). Communicating is a major inquiry process and is very much a part of discovery. Also, the model that Strike describes implies that learners must "know" something before they can "discover" something. Content, knowledge, fact, and processes are all very much a part of the discovery strategy.

Although there is much luck involved in discovery, it must be remembered that "chance favors the prepared mind." Even though there is a trial-and-error element associated with discovery, the most important discoveries made by scientists—including social and behavioral scientists—are the result of careful observation and systematic research. Discovery makes use of the same processes and skills that were described for inductive inquiry and problem-solving. This should come as no surprise because we have already emphasized the idea that inquiry, by its very epistemological nature, requires systematic conduct, not haphazard bungling. (Note: The method by which knowledge of a field is determined, as well as the limits and validity of that knowledge, constitute the science of epistemology. Inquiry-related techniques are based on the epistemology of empiricism. Observations, experiences, experiments, and replications are the techniques of empiricism—and of inquiry.)

Examples of Discovery Learning

The Black Widow Spider and Other Insects

Judith Miles of Lexington, Massachusetts, wondered how spiders would spin webs under the effects of weightlessness. The subject of her curiosity was one of nineteen Skylab Student Projects conducted in the National Aeronautics and Space Administration (NASA) earth-orbiting space station in 1973. The Skylab Project placed three astronauts above the earth for 28 days. Judith's experiment demonstrated that a black widow spider was initially "confused" and did not spin the appropriate web pattern. But within a relatively short time, the spider did, in fact, spin the appropriate web!

Is this an example of problem-solving or discovery? We think that it fits in the category of *absolute* discovery because it was the first time that anyone had communicated the problem and had completed the research. Her science teacher, J. Michael Conley, had encouraged Judith to submit her idea in a contest sponsored by the National Science Teachers Association in conjunction with NASA. This demonstrates the partnership that develops when learners and teachers share in the excitement of inquiry.

Similarly, Todd Nelson, a student from Adams, Minnesota, designed an experiment for the third mission, March 1982, of the space shuttle Columbia. Nelson suggested that Columbia's crew videotape the behavior of selected flying insects—velvetbean caterpillar moths, honey bees, and common houseflies—to determine the effects of a gravity-free environment. Todd's experiment was selected along with those of Ph.D. research botanists to determine the same effect on pine tree, oat, and Chinese bean sprouts. Again, this experiment demonstrates absolute discovery—and by high school students, too.

Mystery Island

Not all discovery learning needs to be as dramatic as the NASA experiment. One technique that is commonly used to generate the fun and discipline accompanying the conduct of inquiry or discovery is to utilize the overhead projector and to present an event that requires student analysis. Jack Zevin (1969) reported on how to make use of a set of overlays that depict an unnamed island. The stimulus—the overhead projector—is presented in a group mode. The initial projectile shows the outline of an island. The map contains some standard clues to the island's general world location such as topographical symbols, rivers, and latitude and longitude symbols. This device is used primarily to focus the learner's attention on the event or to motivate inquiry.

The episode usually begins with the children being told that the island is uninhabited and that they are going to be the first persons to land on it. Their task is to choose where they will settle and to justify their choices. Ultimately the children are given other tasks such as to find the places that may be the best for farming, industries, railroads, harbors, airports, resorts, and the like. Inferences concerning rainfall, winds, deserts, and other natural phenomena can all be generalized by the students.

One can argue that mystery island is simply an inductive exercise. To be sure, induction is used; so is problem-solving and the application of previously learned skills and content. This stimulus does allow children to know "that" and "how" and to discover "that" and "how." The use of this device has unlimited opportunity for student inquiry.

Assumptions About Inquiry

Perhaps this topic should have been the very first in the chapter. However, if we gave the rules first, followed by the activities, we would be using a deductive approach rather than an inductive one. In Chapter 9, we treat extensively the use of deductive modes of inquiry. But it must be thoroughly understood that all inquiry exercises are predicated on selected assumptions about both learning and learners.

Several writers who have addressed the assumptions about inquiry learning include Arthur A. Carin and Robert B. Sund (1971), Louis I. Kuslan and A. Harris Stone (1968), Mary Budd Rowe (1973), and J. Richard Suchman (1966). The following list is a synthesis of their collective views as well as those of the present authors.

1. Inquiry requires that *the learner* develop the various processes associated with inquiry, which include those basic thirteen processes that were presented earlier in this chapter (p. 253).
2. Teachers and principals must be supportive of the concept of inquiry teaching and must *learn* how to adapt their own teaching and administrative styles to the concept.
3. Students at all ages and levels have a genuine interest in discovering something new or in providing solutions or alternatives to unsolved questions or problems.
4. The solutions, alternatives, or responses provided by the learners are *not* readily located in a textbook. Reference materials and textbooks are surely used during inquiry lessons, just as real scientists use books, articles, and references to conduct their work.
5. The content of inquiry is often *process*. In many instances, the product or solution will be relatively unimportant compared to the processes that were used to arrive at it.
6. All conclusions must be considered relative or tentative, but not final. Since inquiry depends mainly on empirical epistemology, the students must also learn that, as new data are discovered, conclusions tend to be modified.
7. Inquiry learning cannot be gauged by the clock. In the real world, when people think or create, it is not usually done in 50-minute increments.
8. The learners are responsible for planning, conducting, and evaluating their own efforts. It is essential that the teacher play a supportive role, but not the active role of doing the work.
9. Students have to be taught the processes associated with inquiry in a systematic manner. Every time that a "teachable moment" arrives while the class is being conducted, the teacher should immediately capitalize on it to further the building of inquiry processes.
10. The work of the teacher is usually increased owing to the many interactions that may emanate from inquiry teaching/learning.

This set of assumptions is presented so that you will understand better the theoretical bases on which inquiry rests. The more of these assumptions that your classes measure up to, the closer will your classes approach becoming learning laboratories in the truest sense of the term.

THE SUCHMAN INQUIRY MODEL

Not supported by the National Science Foundation, J. Richard Suchman was one of the few curriculum researchers to develop a program designed entirely around the concept of inquiry. His early works (1961) ultimately led to the development and publication of the Inquiry Development Program (IDP) in 1966. Basically IDP is a junior high school–oriented program with a physical science emphasis specifically designed to (1) stimulate and sustain inquiry by students, and (2) develop the basic processes associated with inquiry.

Inquiry Stimuli

The basic feature of the Suchman model is to present some problem-focusing stimulus to the students, which portrays an event actually taking place. The original stimuli used by Suchman were short, silent, color, loop cartridge films. Each film showed something happening and usually contained some "discrepant event." This term meant that the viewing students would observe an event taking place that was contradictory to what they had anticipated. Thus, a problem or question was generated by the filmed presentation.

Suchman designed the discrepant events so that the questions or problems would be real to the learner. He believes that the processes of inquiry are more "productive" if the inquirer perceives problems that are "real" in the sense that the inquirer can identify with the problems, based on previous experiences. Thus, the Suchman model extends one step further the hypothesis from current learning theory—that when a learner is bothered or puzzled by some problem, more effective learning takes place. It shows that the more relevant the problems are to the students, the more readily they will learn.

After the film is viewed, the teacher asks the class for suggestions about what has transpired. If the class does not perceive any problem, the teacher can either reshow the film or ask some probing questions concerning the illustrated event. Teachers who have used the IDP films have had almost *no* trouble in getting the children to respond and to raise their own questions. In addition to the films, IDP presented several other demonstrations that acted as stimuli. As one example, a bi-metallic knife was heated and bent up in one instance and down in another. Actually, the teacher simply rotated the device 180° to confuse the students. Thus, all stimuli were single-concept oriented, and the discrepant event was identified through student observations.

Suchman presented a prototype mechanism by which teachers could portray events to students with or without the materials specifically developed by the publishers (Science Research Associates). With some imagination, teachers at any level can create events modeled after the IDP materials and can use them in social studies, literature, reading, art, science, or any course that has an element of the unknown associated with it.

Conducting Suchman's Inquiry Sessions

Once the problem has been established, the *students* construct reasonable hypotheses that explain the event. Usually students hypothesize by simply guessing. But guessing is not enough. Once a hypothesis has been presented, it is the students' responsibility to gather data to support or refute that hypothesis, just as scientists do.

Students as Questioners

In the Suchman model, all questions concerning the events or data are raised by the students and answered by the teacher. However, the teacher does not act as the authority, for all questions are simply answered by the teacher with a "yes" or "no." The students quickly learn how to frame questions that conform to this ground rule. In one sense, this type of question-asking resembles the game of "Twenty Questions," but in the Suchman model, the student has the right to ask as many questions as he or she wants without being interrupted by other class members. This rule is enforced so that the students can have the freedom to establish a long-range pattern of questions that help in solving the problem.

Suchman also believes that students need time to develop their logic and problem-solving strategies without having the effectiveness of the thinking session impaired. Suchman asserts that if the learner is allowed as much time as necessary, he or she will be under less pressure, will be more relaxed, and will tend to be more creative.

Another rule that is a part of the IDP strategy is that the teacher will not respond to any student questions that focus on statements of theories or that attempt to gain the teacher's approval of a student-originated theory or hypothesis. With such a rule, the students are placed in the position of having to formulate their own hypotheses, to collect their own supporting or refuting data, and to draw their own conclusions.

We suggest that students be allowed to conduct any reasonable tests or experiments to establish the validity of their suggested hypotheses. In an IDP classroom, you will observe students working independently on experiments, evaluating data in small groups, reexamining the stimulus film loop, engaging in mini-questioning sessions with the teacher, and being involved in a host of other activities often associated with independent learning styles.

The Learning Environment

The IDP model requires a responsive and helpful learning environment. While the teacher should provide some of the information to help the student solve the problems, each learner is also encouraged to seek data without help from the teacher. The classroom should contain the necessary materials with which the learner can test all hypotheses by conducting experiments. Even though the IDP classroom will have the appearance of a "three-ring circus," it must be emphatically stated that the activity is *meaningful, relevant,* and *purposeful.* Such an environment fosters self-confidence, initiative, and responsibility.

We add one caution: not all stimuli and materials need be as dramatic as the loop film events. You can generate just as much inquiry by using pictures from newspapers, magazines, or posters; case studies that are "open-ended"; charts with comparable data or graphs, resource persons who have had experiences that may be considered unique; or problems raised by the learners themselves. All of these elements are part of the environment. Furthermore, you can encourage your students to create their own materials to be shared with other class members.

Evaluating IDP Strategies

Evaluation of inquiry instruction should be a continuous process and should not simply be based on intuition. Evaluation of learner behaviors can be based on the quality of task accomplishment and of product outcome.

Suchman suggests that students be evaluated according to the kinds of questions they ask.

He grouped student questions into four categories: verification, experimentation, necessity, and synthesis. Verification questions are those asked to substantiate a fact or event. Experimentation questions are those asked by students to verify hypothetical solutions. Necessity questions are used to determine whether a particular aspect of a given event is necessary to the problem's outcome. Synthesis questions are utilized to determine the validity of an idea.

Four subgroups of data are events, objects, conditions, and properties. Events are those observable experiences that happen. Events have a time dimension—a beginning, an ending, and a duration. Objects are those separate components of an event. Conditions refer to the "state" of the objects. Properties are the characteristics of the objects, which do not change with time and which give objects their identity.

Analysis of the Suchman Model

Suchman offers a clearly defined model for presenting problems that spark student interest. By using his suggested model, the teacher will begin to develop creative thinking, to encourage critical analysis, and to stimulate active participation in the learning activities. Suchman's evaluation system can be modified so that any number of attributes or behaviors can be identified at the teacher's discretion. The learner is involved in the activity and must verify his or her own hypotheses. This model approaches the hypothetico-deductive method used by most scientists.

All of these elements of an inquiry lesson already have been discussed in this chapter. What is unique about the Suchman model is its use of discrepant events, which requires that a student begin to define and to sharpen those skills associated with logical thinking. One of the major problems in the schools is that there are very few opportunities for students to be truly logical in the presentation of information. This is most valid in those classes in which the teacher decides to emphasize rote learning and to be unconcerned about information processing.

The Suchman model can be modified to fit any situation or teacher style. Perhaps the only problem that may arise is the repeated use of one inquiry method. Your decision is simply to use any model at the most opportune time to achieve the inquiry process objectives. The authors have presented a series of inquiry models so that you can choose those that will best achieve your intended teaching goals.

Other Uses of Inquiry

Inquiry techniques may easily be applied to foreign language instruction, observed Diane W. Birckbichler and Judith A. Muyskens (1980). They stress that a student should read foreign language literature for interpretation and evaluation. They also state that inquiry may be developed by ranking statements, completing items, and role-playing.

The Physical Education Teaching Laboratory is an inquiry-based environment at the University of Calgary. Joan N. Vickers and Gary D. Sinclair (1982) wrote that the laboratory is an inquiry-related center to apply psychomotor skill acquisition.

Fred Hartford (1982) uses the hypothetico-deductive technique to stimulate high school students enrolled in his chemistry class to design research experiments. However, the students are required to list as many questions as they can that relate to the experimental variable.

It takes between ten and forty hours to complete an analytical reasoning course that stresses thinking, analyzing, and solving problems, reported Nancy J. Vye and John D. Bransford (1981). What is novel about their approach is that the skills are focused on adolescents who have been labeled retarded or learning disabled.

To make social studies more exciting, Barry K. Beyer (1982) integrates writing and five inquiry processes. He has his students applying social studies content by (1) inventing testable hypotheses; (2) generating new knowledge of the content being studied; (3) developing concepts and generalizations from the content; (4) reinforcing previously studied materials; and (5) developing empathy for the group. Observe the mixing of cognitive, affective, and process skills.

Robert F. Bibens (1980) provides an excellent set of tips for those who desire to "experiment" with inquiry techniques. As a teacher, you should

1. Focus on the students and the content.
2. Pace the instruction, but do not expect to have students master any set number of concepts on a specific schedule.
3. Accept student responses; if responses are off the track, guide the students back through questioning.
4. Be sure that all steps of inquiry are conducted by each student, even if a solution has been formulated early on.
5. Encourage every student to search for implications beyond the immediate solution.
6. Respond to student solutions with the question, "Why?" In this manner the student must review all the steps used to determine a solution.

Finally, Bibens agrees with our position: inquiry teaching takes time and much teacher energy. In our collective experiences, we have never seen teachers sitting at their desks when teaching through inquiry—they are on the go, and so are their students.

In summary, our main intent has been to illustrate a general technique that has long been considered the exclusive domain of science teachers. We wish to clarify this false assumption; inquiry strategies, in fact, belong to all disciplines and to all grade levels. The only real limitation to the technique is the teacher's initiative.

Complete the formative evaluation and proceed to Chapter 9, where this general topic is expanded further.

FORMATIVE EVALUATION
Inquiry

Identify the response that *most* correctly completes the statement or answers the question.

1. An inquiry technique on the use of some instruments would help to bring out the idea that
   (a) A lecture demonstration should always be given before students touch the instruments.
   (b) Students should memorize the rules for handling the instruments before using them.
   (c) An inductive approach helps the students to make discoveries and generalizations that can be remembered.
   (d) The instruments are so complex that extensive lesson plans and learning techniques must be prepared.
2. To stress thinking skills properly, the teacher should emphasize which of the following:
   (a) Making observations is rather unimportant.
   (b) Learning from theory is more important than learning by doing.
   (c) Systematic book learning only should be required of everyone.
   (d) Students should participate in selected activities.
3. Which questioning technique would be appropriate for most problem-solving or inductive lessons?
   (a) As teacher, you ask no questions.
   (b) Use questions requiring only memory responses.
   (c) Involve each student in the questioning process as much as possible.
   (d) Seek out those students who are interested in the problem, so that only highly motivated students conduct the lessons.
4. There is some evidence to show that inquiry
   (a) Is always inferior to other types of learning techniques.
   (b) Is always superior to other types of techniques
   (c) Is superior to other types for selected purposes when conducted under appropriate conditions.
   (d) Is inferior to other types, since small-group learning tends to ignore teacher-student planning.
5. A big story breaks in your local newspaper. You want to use the headline as an inquiry device. You might begin by

(a) Explaining what you believe to be the underlying causes.
(b) Asking the class to infer connotations and denotations from the headline.
(c) Describing the background of the story as you know it.
(d) Showing the headline and then asking for a volunteer to read the story to the class and interpret the meaning.

6. Following are four activities associated with inquiry. In what hierarchical order should they be introduced so as to develop student inquiry skills in the most systematic and logical manner?
   A. Students design and conduct their own experiments.
   B. The class observes teacher-led demonstrations and recitations.
   C. The teacher begins to use guided inductive strategies.
   D. Students learn to ask questions that are appropriate to the topics being taught.
   The most logical order for these four steps is
   (a) A, B, C, D.
   (b) C, D, B, A.
   (c) C, A, D, B.
   (d) B, C, D, A.

7. In the Suchman model, all questions concerning events or data are
   (a) Asked by the teacher and answered by the students.
   (b) Answered by the teacher in detail.
   (c) Raised by the students and answered "yes" or "no" by the teacher.
   (d) Limited to two questions per student.

8. If you decide to use inquiry strategies in your teaching, you will assume that
   (a) Inquiry teaching will require less time to achieve the instructional objective than does expository teaching.
   (b) Inquiry teaching requires about the same amount of time to achieve the instructional objective as does expository teaching.
   (c) Inquiry teaching requires a greater amount of time to achieve the instructional objective than does expository teaching.
   (d) None of the above.

9. When using *unguided inductive inquiry*
   (a) The objective is to arrive at one generalization.
   (b) There is usually a limited number of generalizations.
   (c) Materials are not essential to the success of the experience.
   (d) There is usually an unlimited number of generalizations proposed by the learners.

10. How would you use the following or similar short statement as an inquiry stimulus?

Agent Orange

Agent Orange is the U.S. military name for a mixture of two chemicals: 50% 2,4-dichlorophenoxyacetic acid and 50% 2,4,5-trichlorophenoxyacetic acid. These chemicals are defoliants, meaning that they cause trees and bushes to lose their leaves. A by-product formed when the chemicals are synthesized is "dioxin," which has been shown to cause cancer and birth defects.

During the Viet Nam War, from 1965 to 1971, approximately 12 million gallons of Agent Orange with its dioxin contaminant were sprayed in South Vietnamese jungles to expose Viet Cong troops. The U.S. says this made our troops less vulnerable to ambush. Some 2.5 million U.S. servicemen in South Viet Nam were exposed to Agent Orange, as well as much of the indigenous population of South Viet Nam.

Following the Viet Nam War many veterans have complained that exposure to Agent Orange has caused birth defects in their children. The Veteran's Administration's stand on the issue is that "There is no medical evidence to establish that exposure to Agent Orange has caused birth defects in the children of Viet Nam veterans."

Now a recently released study of 40,000 Vietnamese families shows a high correlation between a man's exposure to Agent Orange and birth abnormalities in his children. A U.S. government study of Viet Nam veterans is "years away from completion," according to the National Veteran's Law Center.

RESPONSES
Inquiry

1. (c). The emphasis is on participation.
2. (d). Thinking strongly stresses activity.
3. (c). The technique requires much student interaction.
4. (c). As with any technique, inquiry must be used under the appropriate conditions.
5. (b). It is preferable to get the entire class involved.
6. (b). This is the most logical order, as it progresses from a simple pattern to a more complex one.
7. (c). This technique is described in the text.
8. (c). Undoubtedly, inquiry techniques require great amounts of time.
9. (d). With unguided inquiry, there is a tendency for an unlimited number of generalizations to be proposed.
10. The essence would be to locate *evidence* to support or refute any statement.

REFERENCES

Agne, Russell M. "A Comparison of Earth Science Classes Taught by Using Original Data in a Research-Approach Technique Versus Classes Taught by Conventional Approaches Not Using Such Data." (Ph.D. diss., University of Connecticut, 1969).

Barrow, Lloyd H., and William Moore. "Phenomena for Inquiry—Postage Stamps." *Science and Children* 14:1976, 40.

Beyer, Barry K. "Using Writing to Learn Social Studies." *The Social Studies* 18:1982, 100–105.

Bibens, Robert F. "Using Inquiry Effectively." *Theory Into Practice* 19:1980, 87–92.

Birckbichler, Diane W., and Judith A. Muyskens. "A Personalized Approach to the Teaching of Literature at the Elementary and Intermediate Levels of Instruction." *Foreign Language Annuals* 13:1980, 23–27.

Brandt, Ronald S. "Teaching for Thinking." *Educational Leadership* 40:1983, 3, 80.

Bruner, Jerome S. *The Process of Education.* Cambridge: Harvard University Press, 1960.

Carin, Arthur A., and Robert B. Sund. *Developing Questioning Techniques: A Self-Concept Approach.* Columbus, Ohio: Charles E. Merrill, 1971.

Ciardi, John. "Manner of Speaking." *Saturday Review*, passim; and telephone interview, April 27, 1979.

Dewey, John. *Democracy and Education.* New York: Macmillan, 1916.

———. *Experience and Education.* New York: Macmillan, 1938.

Gisi, Lynn Grover, and Roy H. Forbes. *The Information Society: Are High School Graduates Ready?* Denver: Education Commission of the States, 1982.

Hartford, Fred. "Training Chemistry Students to Ask Research Questions." *Journal of Research in Science Teaching* 19:1982, 559–570.

Horak, Willis J., and Virginia M. Horak. "Using Catalogs to Develop Inquiry Skills." *Science and Children* 18:1981, 30.

Kuhn, Thomas S. *The Structure of Scientific Revolutions.* Chicago: The University of Chicago Press, 1962.

Kuslan, Louis I., and A. Harris Stone. *Teaching Children Science: An Inquiry Approach.* Belmont, Calif.: Wadsworth, 1968, pp. 138–139.

Popper, Karl R. *The Logic of Scientific Discovery.* New York: Harper & Row, 1959.

Rowe, Mary Budd. *Teaching Science as Continuous Inquiry.* New York: McGraw-Hill, 1973.

Sanders, Norris M. *Classroom Questions: What Kinds?* New York: Harper & Row, 1966.

Shulman, Lee S., and Pinchas Tamir. "Research on Teaching in the Natural Sciences." In *Second Handbook of Research on Teaching,* Robert M. W. Travers, ed. Chicago: Rand McNally, 1973, pp. 1098–1148.

Strike, Kenneth A. "The Logic of Learning by Discovery." *Review of Educational Research* 45:1975, 461–483.

Suchman, J. Richard. *Inquiry Development Program in Physical Science.* Chicago: Science Research Associates, Inc., 1966.

Suchman, J. Richard. "Inquiry Training: Building Skills for Autonomous Discovery." *Merrill-Palmer Quarterly of Behavior and Development* 7:1961, 147–169.

Vickers, Joan N., and Gary D. Sinclair. "The Physical Education Teaching Laboratory: Theory to Practice on the Campus." *Journal of Physical Education, Recreation, and Dance* 53:1982, 16–18.

Vye, Nancy J., and John D. Bransford. "Programs for Teaching Thinking." *Educational Leadership* 26:1981, 26–28.

Webster's New Collegiate Dictionary, 8th ed. Springfield, Mass.: G. & C. Merriam, 1979, p. 326.

Whimbey, Arthur. "Teaching Sequential Thought: The Cognitive-Skills Approach." *Phi Delta Kappan* 58:1977, 255–259.

Womack, James G. *Discovering the Structure of the Social Studies.* New York: Bensiger Brothers, 1966, p. 13.

Zevin, Jack. "Mystery Island: A Lesson in Inquiry." *Today's Education* 58:1969, 42–43.

9

MORE DECISIONS ABOUT INQUIRY AND SIMULATIONS

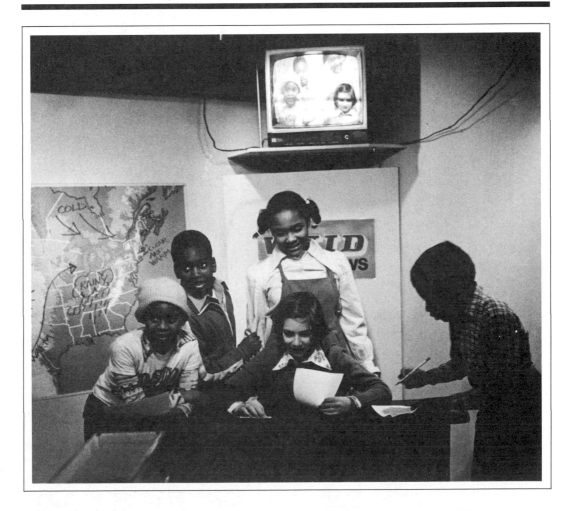

In Chapter 8, we introduced you to the general concepts, rationales, and strategies usually associated with inquiry teaching and learning. Now we want to expand those ideas to include an additional set of teaching techniques that educators often do not realize are inquiry-oriented. On completing this chapter, you should be able to

1. Use at least one system of deductive inquiry
2. Determine the necessary parts of a deductively oriented inquiry lesson
3. List the elements needed to prepare a simulation (or game)
4. Determine the educational uses of classroom microcomputers
5. Synthesize the findings of studies related to inquiry teaching
6. Prepare an evaluation device that can be used to judge the effectiveness of an inquiry-related lesson

Further, we would encourage you to

1. Organize your lesson planning to include deductive inquiry when possible
2. Appreciate how the classroom microcomputer can aid inquiry or simulation
3. Commit some of your free time to studying the applications of the microcomputer for your respective area or specialization
4. Be willing to try one or more of the strategies illustrated in Chapter 9

DEDUCTIVE MODES OF INQUIRY

What do the terms *deductive, didactic,* and *expository* have in common? These terms all suggest a process of instruction; however, they are not synonymous, as we will now demonstrate.

The deductive approach to teaching implies that the structure of the content or the processes proceeds from general statements toward the application of specific cases. In other words, the teacher states a rule (provides a generalization) and then expects the learners to apply it (to test the rule with specific cases).

Didactic or expository instructional methods encompass a broad spectrum of teaching styles including lecturing, rule giving, conducting recitations, demonstrating, using inductive logic, using deductive logic, and using elements of problem-solving. In short, the terms *didactic* and *expository* tend to be "catch-all" terms often used without specific operational definitions. However, the term *deductive mode* is defined as a method of instruction in which principles or generalizations are presented initially and then are followed by the application or testing of these principles or generalizations.

Why do we consider appropriately used deductive modes of instruction as a form of inquiry? We do so because schools and the materials used in schools have for centuries been organized according to the basic tenets of deductive logic. Most students—perhaps worldwide—are familiar with the commonly used method of instruction: to provide the rules for a problem being solved and then to have the students apply them to the practice problems in order to learn them. Rote, or memorized learning, may or may not be a part of the method. As we carefully illustrated in our previous discussions of inductive inquiry and problem-solving, if one learns the solution to a problem by rote, then there is clearly no inquiry taking place. The same statement is valid for deductive inquiry.

Meaningful Verbal Learning

This heading is taken directly from David P. Ausubel, a proponent of deductive learning as an alternative to discovery or inductive strategies. In *Educational Psychology: A Cognitive View* (1968), Ausubel argues that much of the empirical framework that supports discovery learning strategies is based on conducted research, which compares discovery modes with rote modes. Differentiating between rote learning (memorization), problem-solving, and meaningful verbal learning, Ausubel maintains that, through careful structuring of materials and learning experiences by the teacher, the learner will be able to translate newly learned content into something meaningful to him or her.

Ausubel's Deductive Learning

The deductive mode of inquiry, according to Ausubel, includes three basic components: (1) *advance organizers;* (2) *progressive differentiation;* and (3) *integrative reconciliation.* His model also requires a body of knowledge that can be organized hierarchically. The purpose of Ausubel's model is to provide students with a structure so that they understand *each part of the hierarchy of knowledge* in the lesson as well as the relationships among *all parts of the knowledge hierarchy.*

An Ausubel lesson begins with the *advance organizer.* This is a broad term that encompasses those elements that the learner will be required to master in the lesson. The English teacher starting a unit that includes metaphor, simile, and personification will want to start the lesson with a definition or generalization about figures of speech. The teacher will follow a very simple hierarchy chart like the one shown in Figure 9–1.

If the advance organizer is understood by each student, it will provide a frame of reference for the lesson, so that each part of the lesson can be more easily understood. Also, the organizer provides an "ideational scaffold" that

FIGURE 9–1 Hierarchy Chart for Figures of Speech

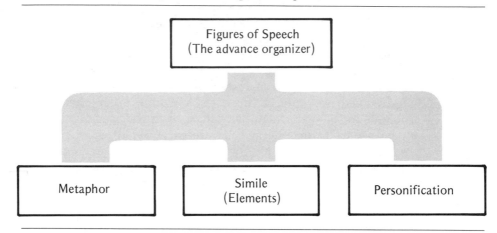

enables the learner to relate the lesson material to previous knowledge. The teacher's task is to develop an abstract statement that *encompasses* all aspects of the lesson and that the student can relate to previously learned material.

The advance organizer is usually a *generalization* or a *definition*. For example, the authors have found that using the structure of sentences as a hierarchy chart is an effective way to teach grammar. An illustration of a partially developed hierarchy chart on figures of speech can look like the one shown in Figure 9–1.

The teacher has considerable latitude in organizing and developing the lesson. Therefore, two teachers using the same advance organizer, such as sentence structure, may develop and teach the lesson quite differently, whereas lessons on figures of speech will tend to be more similar because the subject is based on a conceptual hierarchy. A practical note is helpful here: write the advance organizer on a transparency or large sheet of paper. This allows students to refer to it throughout the lesson and it provides direction and focus for the lesson.

After the advance organizer has been presented and the teacher is assured that it is understood, the second phase of the model begins. This phase, *progressive differentiation,* is the process by which the content is subdivided into more complex ideas. The English teacher can start a lesson on metaphors with the statement: "A metaphor is *one* kind of figure of speech. The primary characteristics of a metaphor are . . ." The teacher has taken a broad abstract concept (figure of speech) and narrowed it to a smaller, more complex concept (metaphor). Progressive differentiation is the procedure of isolating each idea, concept, generalization, or skill within a hierarchy of knowledge, so that it can be learned as an independent piece of knowledge. Highlighting the unique and discrete characteristics of an element makes the information easier to learn.

The third component of the Ausubel model is *integrative reconciliation.* It is in this phase that a deliberate attempt is made to help students to understand similarities and differences among the components of the hierarchy of knowledge and to reconcile real or apparent inconsistencies between the ideas presented. In our English lesson example, the teacher makes certain that the students understand the relationship between figures of speech and metaphor, which is a case of vertical reconciliation, and that they comprehend the differences and similarities between a metaphor and a simile, which is an example of lateral reconciliation.

The basic purpose of integrative reconciliation is to ensure that the material is comprehended in a meaningful way. In this phase, the teacher makes certain that the relationships among all parts of the hierarchy are understood by the students.

In summary, the Ausubel model is a deductive model designed to teach organized bodies of content. The advance organizer provides the students with an overview and focus; progressive differentiation provides the students with items of information that can be more easily understood; and integrative reconciliation provides meaningful learning by helping students to understand the relationships among the elements of the content being taught.

Although the three components are presented as sequential, in reality they are interactive, especially progressive differentiation and integrative reconciliation. If the comparison and differentiation discussion develops the students' understanding of a specific concept or generalization, the teacher should not hesitate to use the two steps concurrently. As with any teaching model, the teacher should use the model and its components so that they help the students to learn. The model should be applied with flexibility, and not used as a straitjacket.

Be careful not to confuse deductive thinking with lecturing. Often lectures are neither deductive nor inductive. A deductive lesson can contain as much teacher-student or student-student interaction as an inductive lesson. According to Ausubel, after the advance organizer is presented, the teacher can hold the students responsible for progressive differentiation and integrative reconciliation. In this instance, the teacher becomes the facilitator of the learning process much in the same manner as in an inductive lesson.

One can argue that Ausubel has developed a model for guided and sequenced deductive inquiry. The degree of guidance provided by the teacher may be the criterion according to which various modes are classified. For example, Table 9–1 presents Lee S. Shulman's (1970) interpretation of four inquiry possibilities.

Another Ausubel Example

Assume that the class is studying about government and the concepts associated with the institution of government. The class has already studied about different basic forms of government. The teacher may introduce the lesson with the following advance organizer:

TABLE 9–1   Classification of Inquiry-Expository Learning Modes

Rule	Solution	Type of Teacher Guidance
Given	Given	Exposition
Given	Not given	Guided discovery (deductive)
Not given	Given	Guided discovery (inductive)
Not given	Not given	"Pure" discovery

Source: Lee S. Shulman, "Psychology and Mathematics Education," in *Mathematics Education*, The Sixty-Ninth Yearbook of the National Society for the Study of Education, Part I, Edward G. Begle (ed.). Chicago: The University of Chicago Press, 1970, p. 66. Used with the written permission of the National Society for the Study of Education.

Government is but one of the institutions serving society. The state or government is essential to civilization and yet it cannot do the whole job by itself. Many human needs can be met by the home, the church, the press, and private business.

With the presentation of the advance organizer, the teacher is ready to proceed with the progressive differentiation component of the lesson. Materials are made available to the students so that they may begin their investigations on the human needs that are met by different institutions. Prior to beginning the study, the teacher and the class prepare a list of different problems that can be studied. As an alternative, they list the steps that should be taken to identify the areas in which the various institutions serve the society and in which institutional functions overlap. Functions that are not covered by any institution would also be listed. In the true "Ausubelian" sense, the teacher utilizes some guided discovery techniques in conducting the class. As the material is gathered by students and presented to the class, the teacher leads the students in the progressive differentiation and integrative reconciliation processes. The result is an interactive, deductive lesson.

How successful is this mode of instruction? Based on at least one recently completed study in Australia, the students perform better with this method of instruction than simply with textual materials that do not have the necessary advance organizers. John A. Clarke (1973) reported that his class in science, which applied Ausubel's Cognitive Field Learning Theory by using expository and comparative organizers, performed significantly better than those students who used the standard textbook format. We recognize that one study does not validate an instructional theory, but this study illustrates that instructional materials may be prepared to test a theory of instruction.

G. Hermann's (1969) review of discovery learning studies (which is discussed in greater detail later in this chapter) provides much evidence that deductive-inquiry instructional strategies or simply deductive modes of instruction are about as effective as inductive or discovery modes of instruction. Obviously, the teacher must decide which mode of instruction is most efficacious for the materials being studied. Some materials, types of content, or processes just do not lend themselves to any inquiry at all.

The lesson plan in Table 9–2 was prepared by Cathy Valencsin Duffy and used with her permission. It illustrates the three elements of an Ausubelian lesson.

TABLE 9–2   An Ausubel Lesson Plan About Verbs

Advance Organizer

1. Review sentence elements to conclude that the subject is one of the two basic elements of a sentence.
2. What is the function of the subject in a sentence?
3. After we have a subject, what is the second basic element of a sentence?
4. Usually, there are more than only two words in a sentence. But we will concentrate on these two most basic sentence elements because they are necessary in writing a sentence.

Progressive Differentiation

5. Today, we will talk specifically about verbs.
6. What is the primary function of a verb?
7. There are many types of verbs, but today we will want to focus specifically on action verbs.
8. Why is it important that we use action verbs in our writing?

9. Administer list of verbs to determine how much the students might already know about verbs. Tell them to circle action verbs.
10. Ask students to read those verbs that they did not circle.
11. Tell students that these verbs are called "forms of the verb *to be*" and are used to show being or existence.
12. If teachers have ever told the students that their writing was lifeless or dry, it could be that they were not using enough action verbs.

Integrative Reconciliation

13. A verb is one of the two basic what?
14. How is a verb related to a subject?
15. When can one of these basic sentence elements be left out of a sentence but the sentence still be considered correct? (Awareness of inconsistencies.)
16. Put a box on the table. Ask the students to list at least three actions that can be done to the box, or that the box performs.
17. Review importance of action verbs in writing.
18. Give the next day's assignment—to write a paper that describes the student's favorite sport and that uses ten action verbs.

General Deductive Model

The general deductive model to be presented here is similar to the Ausubel model in that both are deductive. However, they are different in that the general deductive model is not as dependent on an organized body of knowledge or a hierarchy of knowledge as is the Ausubel model. The model developed by Paul D. Eggen, et al. (1979) attempts to provide teachers with a broad, generic approach to deductive teaching.

The first of four steps in the model is the *presentation of the abstraction*. The lesson starts with the presentation of a concept or generalization to the students. The abstraction should be presented visually so that the students can concentrate on understanding it. Where possible, the teacher should link the abstraction to previously learned material, as in the technique of "concept review" discussed in Chapter 6.

The second step is *classification of terms*. The purpose of this step is to ensure that the abstraction is meaningful to the students. To accomplish this, the teacher must make certain that the students understand all concept characteristics and all terms used within the generalization. Asking the students to provide examples of the concept or generalization is one way for the teacher to ascertain whether or not the students understand the abstraction.

The third step is the *presentation of illustrations*. Often the teacher thinks the lesson is complete if the students are able to restate the concept or generalization. Actually, this only proves that the students have good memories. In a lesson on metaphors, the students should be presented with examples of metaphors. In a lesson on the executive branch of the government, the students should be given illustrations of how this branch of government operates. More specifically, if you are teaching the concept of "proper noun" and have discussed its definition—"the name of a person, place, or thing"—you should provide the students with examples such as "Sally is the name of a girl next door; therefore, Sally is a proper noun" and "Volkswagen is the name of a German car; therefore, Volkswagen is a proper noun." It may be useful in this step to provide examples of concepts that may be confused with the concept being taught. For example, for the concept of "proper noun," the teacher may want to present examples of a "common noun" so that students will understand the difference.

The fourth and final step in the general deductive model is *the generation of examples by the students*. This step gives students the opportunity to relate the new material to their own experiences and provides feedback to the teacher as to how well the students have learned the new material. Students should be encouraged to relate their examples to the concept or generalization.

Teaching Deductively

In Chapter 8, we presented a series of statements summarizing the basic tenets of inductive teaching. We now offer a series of similar principles for deductive teaching—but without reference to any individual's theory of instruction.

1. The teacher develops the lesson or aims for the learning objectives by moving from a general concept toward specific cases that may be subsumed logically within the general concept.

2. The emphasis of the process is on testing the principle, applying the principle, or discovering the relationship among the content elements in specific cases, examples, situations, or problems. Since the generalization is already known, the learners should be guided by the teacher to refer continually to it as learning experiences are accomplished. In this way, the deductive mode of instruction provides "verification" episodes for the learners. We must again emphasize that *deduction is not necessarily rote learning.* Deduction is a logical process of thinking and of processing information. Rote learning may or may not be logical in development; usually it is not.

3. The teacher acts as the information coordinator and, through the use of expository or comparative advance organizers, presents the major themes, principles, abstractions, or generalizations.

4. The students are not actively engaged in determining the generalization. They are active in testing the generalization, in collecting information, or in applying this information to specific examples. (Note well here that we do *not* consider passive lecturing to be the *only* method of deductive instruction.)

5. The deductive method of inquiry is probably less time-consuming than inductive inquiry because of its focus on content.

6. The teacher has a broad spectrum of materials and means of presentation available. The classroom may appear to be a laboratory as should be the case in inductive inquiry classes.

7. Deduction can be used as a method by which to organize data, test processes, generate content, make predictions and extrapolations, and conduct experiments.

RESEARCH FINDINGS ON INQUIRY: SOME GENERALIZATIONS

Our detailed treatment of the various aspects of inquiry may have led you to wonder whether or not this method is widely used in the schools. Initially, we had planned to prepare a comprehensive survey of the related literature and research on the use of this technique; however, it soon became apparent that such a survey would easily fill another book. Thus, we are providing a very selective review of empirical studies on the topic. Our intent is to be objective and realistic. We realize that research findings alone do not encourage teachers to use inquiry. Attitude, locale, school, personality, and preparation also influence the teacher's decision.

In a very comprehensive analysis of published research studies, G. Hermann (1969) presented the following points, among others, as "tentative" conclusions regarding inquiry and deductive learning modes.

1. Students tend to retain information better through the rule, or deductive, mode of learning.
2. Discovery learning, which includes most forms of inquiry, results in better transfer of learning—that is, students can use the knowledge or processes in different situations from those in which it was learned.
3. Discovery learning seems to be more effective when the transfer tasks become more difficult.
4. When one is determining what is learned and is testing a transfer task, discovery learning is relatively more effective over a long time span.
5. Discovery learning modes are effective when the students have a rather limited background of the subject.
6. "Low" ability groups seem to benefit more from discovery learning modes than do "high" ability groups.
7. Guided discovery seems to be more effective than none at all.

These seven generalizations from Hermann's analysis of inquiry strategies can all be tested—that is, verified, modified, or refuted—by further research.

In a very comprehensive analysis of various curricula and their effects on student learning, Decker F. Walker and Jon Schaffarzick (1974) concluded that the new or innovative curricula are superior "only in their own terms." They went on to state: "More precisely, these studies showed that students using different curricula in the same subject generally exhibited different patterns of test performance, and that these patterns generally reflected differences in content inclusion and emphasis in the curricula."

The Walker and Schaffarzick study could be summarized thus: If you decide to teach something by using certain techniques, you will obtain concomitant types of results and the supporting research should come as no surprise.

Let us digress for a moment to restate a generalization previously made. You cannot maximize two variables simultaneously. When you stress inquiry skills, you forego some learning of content. If you stress the learning of content, then you cannot achieve a high proficiency in process skills. Our main emphasis is that you must provide an appropriate blend of content and processes. Processes need content and content is made useful by processes. This is an almost cyclical phenomenon.

In an extensive review of research, Lee S. Shulman and Pinchas Tamir (1973) illustrated that not all studies favor inquiry teaching. Evidence to support this statement was also presented by Hermann (1969) and by Walker and Schaffarzick (1974). Yet these investigators did provide evidence to support the conclusion that inquiry teaching does affect learner outcomes in ways that are compatible with the entire concept of inquiry teaching-learning.

Two of the present authors were involved in a three-year study to improve elementary school social studies by adapting inquiry techniques to instruction (Orlich et al., 1972, 1973). Although the results of the study are inconclusive, we did observe that teachers changed their teaching techniques to reflect those skills associated with inquiry. One unreported development that resulted from our studies was that the school district adopted an inquiry- and activity-oriented elementary science curriculum, and the teachers are now attempting to adopt in its entirety a social studies curriculum that is similar in methodology and philosophy to the science program.

We would even generalize, cautiously of course, that once teachers become accustomed to and comfortable with inquiry techniques, they will use them more and more in their teaching. Concomitantly, these same teachers will become more dissatisfied with expository teaching (lecturing or simply using recitations). The latter statement reflects one of the present authors' experiences while implementing inquiry techniques in elementary science programs between 1970 and 1976.

In one of the more compelling statements, Ted Bredderman (1983) documented the overall effectiveness of inquiry-oriented elementary science programs when compared to textbook science programs. Bredderman found that the inquiry programs were activity oriented and had the students involved with "sciencing." Students in these programs did noticeably better on tests that measured process skills than did students using textbook programs or teacher-made programs. Further, economically disadvantaged children achieved more process skills in inquiry programs than in traditional programs. Activity programs also resulted in children with better attitudes toward the subject and more creativity than children in traditional programs.

Kenneth T. Hensen (1980) listed some apparent advantages and disadvantages of inquiry (discovery) learning. Documented advantages show that students (1) gain greater motivation; (2) increase learning and retention; (3) focus attention on concepts; and (4) score better on higher-level thinking questions on examinations. Disadvantages of inquiry reflect that students (1) are required to do more work and thinking; (2) must adjust to the uncertainty of inquiry activities; (3) do not compete for grades; (4) do not "cover" the quantity of information.

Hensen also noted that there is both much work and much enjoyment for teachers who use inquiry techniques.

Obviously, the evidence is not totally conclusive. However, if you wish to modify the methods by which you teach, then inquiry—or deductive inquiry, to be more specific—affords you additional instructional alternatives. One such alternative that develops both skills and processes is simulation or educational game playing. Simulation provides another mode of interactive instruction that can help you to make your school an institution that deals with the problems of reality, but without the possible risks associated with reality.

SIMULATIONS

While inquiry has been stressed as a viable instructional method for at least most of the twentieth century, *simulation*—an adaptation or application of inquiry—is relatively new to the educational scene. Simulation—or gaming, as it is often called—has been used for entertainment for decades in the private sector. For example, the world famous game of Monopoly is one such simulation that is used for "enjoyment" by innumerable people.

But why do educators find games to be of instructional value? There are many reasons. Games and simulations are very useful to the classroom teacher because they can be used as application devices for the expression of previously learned principles, concepts, or facts. In other words, simulations have a definite place in the instructional spectrum as a *planned* learning episode. As a teacher, you make decisions about what children will learn in school. If your objectives lend themselves to the use of simulations, then you are about to add one more tested technique to your already full "bag of professional skills."

What Is Simulation?

Simulation is the presenting of an artificial problem, event, situation, or object that duplicates reality, but removes the possibility of injury or risk to the individuals involved in the activity. Simulation provides a model of what exists or might exist in a set of complex physical or social interactions. Simulation is a representation of a manageable real event in which the learner is an active participant engaged in learning a behavior or in applying previously acquired skills or knowledge.

Clark Abt (1966), long associated with the preparation of simulation materials for the private sector, divides simulation into its three major components: (1) models; (2) exercises; and (3) instruction.

Typically, models tend to be *inactive*—that is, they do not interact with the participants. They remain static but do resemble some dimension of reality. Globes of the world, physical models of the solar system, and some case studies are examples of the inactive simulation model. However, computer-controlled models that provide active patterns of interaction with the users are now being used at various instructional levels. These models are just now becoming available to the public schools, as their costs are now within the schools' budgetary limits. In the not-too-distant future, these models may be commonplace in most schools. Models need not always be physical replicas of the real objects. Pictures, drawings, sketches, and maps can all be classified as models of inactive simulation.

Exercises are activities designed to allow the learner to interact with someone in either a physical or a social manner. Coaches have long utilized exercises as they plan for an upcoming game with the next opponent. Trade and industrial teachers, in setting up equipment that needs to be adjusted or checked (trouble shooting), allow the learners to interact with machines.

Instructional simulations involve the learner in various functions. Paul A. Twelker (1968), a designer and early advocate of instructional simulations, suggests that instructional simulations can perform three functions. They can (1) provide information to the participants; (2) create situations in which the learner demonstrates some skill or knowledge, since the simulation elicits a response; and (3) assess the performance of the participant by measuring it against an already established standard.

Richard Maidment and Russell H. Bronstein (1973) stress that simulations provide games that are based on existing social theory and, through the interactions that result from playing the games, the learners validate the various aspects of social theory.

While simulations have long been used in the military, in business, in medicine, and in administrative planning units, their introduction into the schools is a more recent event. However, the latter part of this statement should be qualified, as teachers have for years used play stores and school councils, as well as other interaction methodologies, as instructional devices to reflect selected dimensions of reality.

Purposes of Simulations

There appear to be at least ten general purposes for the use of simulations and games in education. The following list is synthesized from the works of several researchers (Chapman et al., 1974; Girod, 1969; Maidment and Bronstein, 1973; and Reese, 1977) and is provided as a quick checklist of purposes. Simulations or educational games are designed to

1. Develop changes in attitudes
2. Change specific behaviors
3. Prepare participants to assume new roles in the future
4. Help individuals to understand their current roles
5. Increase the student's ability to apply principles
6. Reduce complex problems or situations to manageable elements
7. Illustrate roles that may affect one's life but that one may never assume
8. Motivate learners
9. Develop analytical processes
10. Sensitize individuals to another person's life role

Each of these ten purposes, we must warn, *cannot* be obtained from any one simulation device. You select simulations or games that are appropriate for a specific learning objective. One of the desired developments that result from simulation is that the learners will be stimulated to learn additionally from the exercise by demonstrating independent study or research. Furthermore, as students engage in relevant simulation exercises, they may begin to perceive that knowledge learned in one context can become valuable in different situations. This is, of course, the well-known concept of "transfer" that keeps psychologists so perplexed.

In our own use of simulations, we have observed that students become immersed in the activities almost immediately. Games and simulations are great "icebreakers" for diverse groups of students. There is also an element of risk-taking for all players. Even though there is no penalty for the participants, each individual tends to view the simulation from a serious, personal perspective. We made this observation, especially in case studies that required the participants to make simulated decisions concerning the espousal of critical human values. In the "bomb shelter" simulation (in which you are under nuclear attack and can only allow five persons in your shelter and must decide who gets in), we observed students who refused to participate because this value decision went too much against their own moral commitments. Of course, we do not suggest that all simulations involve such personal intensity. We cite this example merely to demonstrate the intense personal involvement that can occur with simulations.

Types of Simulations

Robert Maidment and Russell H. Bronstein (1973) identified three major types of simulations: (1) human simulation, which includes role playing; (2) person-to-computer simulation, which is slowly increasing in use; and (3) computer-to-computer simulation, which is the most sophisticated and complicated type and is currently used to generate global or whole earth models. The third type of simulation may be used by your students when they enter the professional world as researchers or business leaders.

Educational games currently available to the schools tend to use two basic patterns, as Alice Kaplan Gordon (1972) reported. The first is the *game board,* which resembles commercially prepared games such as the classic Monopoly. In the elementary school game of "Neighborhood," students develop a geographical area, shown as a grid on a board, by placing tokens that represent people, factories, stores, and the like on the grid. The objective of the game is to learn how complex interactions take place in neighborhood development. As the game progresses, the board becomes filled and the players must accommodate their communities as best they can. By the end of the game, the players observe the final course of the development as graphically portrayed on the board.

The second format identified by Gordon is the *role-play* game. The roles of such formats are designed to teach selected social processes—for example, human relations, negotiations, bargaining, compromise, and sensitivity. These simulations usually have a scenario and character profiles so that the conditions, persons, and consequences of all collective actions may be charted. This format is used to a great extent in a curriculum called the High School Geography Project.

Regardless of the format, all simulations and games have rules that establish their objectives, the types of roles that the players are to assume, and the types of actions that are allowed or disallowed.

Is there a difference between a game and a simulation? One distinction is that games are played to win, while simulations need not have a winner. In some simulations, it is difficult to determine whether or not there are winners and losers, and which players belong to which category. For example, in a simulation of a legislature, the issue is whether to raise taxes. Students are provided with character profiles and a scenario describing the various conditions of the issue. After the arguments are made, a vote is taken. In this simulation, it is difficult to say who has won.

Simulations seem to be more easily applied to the study of issues rather than of processes. The principal purpose of a simulation is to encourage students to express, in their own words, the basic arguments for the various sides of an issue. Games, however, try to get students to make more intelligent decisions as they learn the processes represented in the game. Obviously, the distinctions are not clearcut. Purists may find that any labeling of these activities may be a matter of semantics.

Predominant Problem Orientation or Probable Learning Outcomes

The predominant problem orientation of a simulation-type activity establishes the probable learning outcome of that activity. The two terms— *problem orientation* and *learning outcome*—are synonymous. Learning outcomes are either affective (attitudes and values) or cognitive (intellectual skills and abilities). Simulation-type activities that require personal involvement with a role (role-play and simulation-game emphasizing role-playing) tend to be affectively oriented.

Primary Role Definition

Primary roles can be qualitative or quantitative. Qualitative roles usually involve the participant in interpersonal interactions and in positions of advocacy or persuasion. Quantitative roles tend to involve the participant in controlling resources, planning and forecasting, and calculating alternative trade-offs. Although roles often have both qualitative and quantitative aspects, primary role definitions are distinguishable. Role definition is related to problem orientation in that role-playing usually has an affective learning outcome.

Complexity of Activity

The complexity of an activity is determined by the amount of information generated by the activity. Role-play tends to have one main activity. It has a narrowly defined focus and deals with immediate issues and consequences. Little or no chance enters into role-play. In fact, it is not very complex. Simulation exercises, simulation-games, and games, on the other hand, often involve long-term planning and complex analyses. In these activities, which tend to be more realistic, people pursue different goals by various means, and time is often simulated. In some simulation activities, chance plays no part, while in games, the outcome is based entirely on chance. These simulations tend to be more complex.

Problem-Solving Mode

The problem-solving mode seems to be partially characterized by the amount of information shared by the players. When there is little information about other players' strategies, extreme competition and lack of trust often result. This is typical of pure games, in which players from the start see one another as having opposing interests. When more information is shared, players begin to perceive common interests and are more likely to build alliances and trusting relationships.

The amount of information-sharing that occurs depends on the amount and style of negotiation allowed. There appear to be two kinds of negotiation styles. The first is formal-rule behavior, in which players talk to each other because the rules dictate it. The second is informal-rule behavior, in which responses to problems are neither forbidden nor required by the rules. While formal-rule behavior usually results in bargaining activity, informal-rule behavior may lead to cooperation through shared interests.

Another element in the problem-solving mode is goal orientation. If winning is a goal, then the efforts to win tend to be more intense. In noncompetitive activities, such as role-playing and many simulation games, cooperation tends to develop because the objectives are more open-ended (Chapman et al., 1974).

While we acknowledge that there are several elements in the model by Chapman et al., we do not wish to confuse you with concepts, terms, and definitions. Our intent is to illustrate how simple or complex a simulation may be. Furthermore, there may be few distinctive characteristics by which to differentiate among models, exercises, or instruction in this model. Purists may prefer to make a clear distinction between simulations and games. We will try to blend the concept of "simulation" with "game" while illustrating how these two overlap with instruction.

Role-Play

In Chapter 7 we discussed role-playing as a discussion technique that tended to develop selected skills. Simulations that use role-playing are based on the discussion technique. For example, L. Gerald Buchan (1972) provides a series of role-playing episodes for educable mentally retarded children in the schools. He presents a specific problem on which the children must focus. In one episode, there are four children who act out academic and behavioral problems, while one child plays the role of teacher. Initially, the students are given "prompts" to set the stage for the episode. After conducting the role-playing experiences, the real teacher critiques the entire happening with the group of five children. This is done to develop more appropriate behaviors in the children.

We find Buchan's presentations about role-playing to be very timely, especially with the passage of PL 94-142, which is discussed at great length in Chapter 1. Role-playing as a simulation technique for children with learning disabilities of any kind may help both anxious teachers and handicapped students to cope better with the children's problems. When this technique is used, an affective dimension is added to the program of studies.

Simulations: Examples

Simulation requires the participants to be involved as active players. A book may provide impetus for classroom simulations: take for example Joel Garreau's *The Nine Nations of North America* (1981). Garreau analyzed the social, economic, and geographic components of North America, then creatively subdivided the continent into nine new nations that each reflected a major trait. The nine new nations he designated were New England, The Foundry, Dixie, MexAmerica, The Empty Quarter, Ecotopia, The Breadbasket, The Islands, and Quebec.

Students could use these nine nations as means to simulate national interests, such as a model United Nations, trade, money exchanges, defense, and natural resources. This type of simulator addresses the higher level of Bloom's Taxonomy combined with elements of problem-solving.

Tom G. Denison (1981), concerned about the costs of welding instruction in high schools, devised a simulated arc welder that he calls the "Blue Streak Welding Simulator." Denison's research indicated that students working with the simulator could achieve the needed initial skills in one-half the time that it took with a real arc welder. This case illustrates a shop teacher's desire to improve instruction and decrease costs.

The editors of the *Music Educator Journal* (Vol. 65, February 1979) devoted an article on simulation techniques that could help music teachers improve instruction. Two of the simulations being used by contributing music teachers were (1) clapping hands in code to generate stresses, rhythm, or interpretations; and (2) snapping fingers, whistling, and stamping. These simulations are fun, and their purpose is to involve the students in activities that lead directly to the music objectives.

A very common simulation, which may be more real than simulated, is the "student school corporation." Numerous papers have been published that describe the organization of student-managed corporations that manufacture and sell some product. Skills in economics, marketing, sales, mathematics, English, and language arts—and pride in work—are all outcomes of these simulations. James Gruber (1979) discussed how his students actually simulate a business enterprise as part of the school's business education curriculum.

Along the same vein, but on a broader scale, Ronald R. Rosenblatt (1982) described a simulation for that business of businesses—"The Stock Market Game." William Bennett and co-workers (1979) have a project in which schools subscribe to a service that provides the students with general knowledge about the operations of the stock market. When a class understands the operations, they are given a prescribed number of simulated "dollars" to invest. Each week the class receives a printout of their investments. Teachers who participate in these classes find that this simulation generates a great deal of enthusiasm—especially when the class selects winners on the big board.

More importantly, students begin to understand the importance of research, of the monetary system, and of one element of the free enterprise system. With simulation, economics becomes a real issue as opposed to just a subject in the traditionally taught economics class. Students learn how to write reports, predict costs, and compute complicated ratios. Application of principles, analysis of trends, synthesis of information, and evaluation of alternatives are all cognitive objectives (remember that these processes are the higher levels of the cognitive domain). Students are involved in the manipulation of data and information. Not many teachers in social studies can make that claim. Is the simulation used? As of 1985, 10,000 students in the Philadelphia public schools were learning with it.

Health educators can break up the usual classroom tedium by adapting one of television's game techniques. Jon W. Hisgen (1981) reports that he adapts the game show "To Tell the Truth" in his health classes. This simulation has an announcer and five panelists, all members of the health class. The contestants introduce themselves and their health-related occupations. The panel members must then distinguish the "real" health professional from the imposter. Prior to the game, students are busy learning facts and information about the topic to be "aired." Again, this device illustrates a novel attempt to make cognitive learning a bit more interesting.

The providing of experiences in decision-making and analyzing information is the real pay-off, observes William R. Thames (1979). Thames advocated the use of classroom simulations that help students learn how to analyze and generalize. Further, he noted that a "postgame analysis" is of critical importance so that the concepts, skills, or applications may be evaluated.

You can "teach with a newspaper." The local newspaper offers a wealth of information not only for discussions and inquiry, but also for simulations. The latter is most apparent for career education. Careers can be identified in the community. More importantly, the education, training, or experience needed as entry levels to careers will be eye-opening to most of your students.

Also from a newspaper, students can be taught how to proofread, as nearly every local newspaper provides generous numbers of typographical errors. "What's a Headline Have?" is another game that you can devise (in this game, "verbs" are what headlines have). Or newspaper games are an excellent way to reinforce grammar and its impact on communication.

Let us examine four more examples of using simulation. Our first is from the area of English or language arts. David Sudol (1983) found that sophomore literature can be a very frustrating experience for teachers and students alike. But Sudol found that literary concepts could be successfully taught by involving the students in the plot being studied, having students develop characters and then developing the plot. Thus, a simulation technique allowed the students to have an experience in an area in which student experiences are usually confined to reading. Similarly, you could select some classic quote, for example, the opening paragraph from *A Tale of Two Cities* by Charles Dickens, "It was the best of times, it was the worst of times," and ask the students to simulate a plot, a story line, characters, and a location. Use the current year. How closely do you think the students might parallel Dickens? After this simulation, *A Tale of Two Cities* could be read for both knowledge and comparison to the student outlines.

An article on games to be used in foreign language instruction was written by Alice C. Omaggio (1982). Any teacher of foreign languages from kindergarten to graduate school will be intrigued by the wealth of activities, games, simulations, and student involvement techniques that are presented in this one paper. Omaggio clearly illustrates student learning objectives may be easily translated into existing formats that help students learn and apply their second language.

Janet Olson (1982) presented a questioning game guide that can be applied to art appreciation, especially at the elementary school level. But, in our analyses, her techniques could be applied wherever you examine any picture. Basically, one begins the game by asking the viewers, "What do you see?" Then, questions are asked from the affective domain, for example, "How do you feel about this character?" Students are asked to identify clues to support their feelings. Then a series of process questions are framed to elicit divergent and evaluative responses. Interpretations, themes, and aspects of design all become apparent to the students from this art appreciation game. We would suggest forming small groups and having the groups prepare questions for other groups. The student could be rotated among stations, just as one does when using the "county fair" technique. The materials remain at one station—a table—and the students rotate between the stations. Olson's ideas seem to apply most appropriately to the area of simulations.

Let us close this section with a mystery simulation. Janet A. Harris (1982) wrote "Chemically Speaking . . . Who Done It?" in which a mystery format (simulation) is used to excite and introduce her students into the world of science careers. She provides simulations on crime-solving applications of chemistry. They use extensive analytical and deductive logic skills in the solving of the simulated crimes. Students learn about chemistry, science processes, and career education. Harris skillfully integrates learning activities with motivational techniques.

Collectively, there are thousands of ways of incorporating games and simulations into classrooms. With a little thinking, we know that you could list a dozen such strategies from your own field of specialization. If you need a few sources, then the next section provides several excellent ones.

Conducting Games or Simulations

There are several procedures that have proved to be successful and should be noted as you decide on the role that games or simulations will play in your teaching styles. These procedures are described in the following passages that are adapted from Gordon (1972).

The Teacher

The optimal way to learn about a selected game or simulation is to gather a group of teachers together and to play the game. This assures familiarity with the basic rules. In many cases, the teacher must prepare handouts, materials, and other objects. All pre-game arrangements can then be made in advance of the actual classroom use of the game.

In role-playing games or simulation, the teacher must be knowledgeable about roles, rules, and conflicts. Also, it may take from two to four traditional class periods to complete some of the more lengthy games or simulations. The teacher must be willing to devote that much time to the activity. Generally, one *cannot* appreciably reduce the time needed to complete a game or simulation.

The Class

Once the teacher is prepared, the class must be briefed on rules, roles, scenario, conditions, and options. This should be accomplished prior to conducting the exercise. Bear in mind that students learn the rules of the game not by reading about them but by practicing them. The roles can be assigned by drawing lots, or the teacher may give major roles to students who do not perform well in conventional classroom activities. If the teacher uses simulations regularly, the method of assigning student roles should be rotated.

Once the game is begun, the students usually require a "referee"—the teacher. Much adjudicating will be required with initial experiences. The teacher should clarify rules, interpret situations, or answer questions. The teacher should be careful in responding so that one player does not gain an advantage over another because of the teacher's maturity or experience.

During any simulation, there will be much activity and "meaningful noise." The principal and your colleagues in neighboring classrooms should be warned about the game ahead of time, so that they may plan accordingly. This is not to imply that your classroom will be in chaos but there will be more movement, activities, interactions, and noise than usual.

During the course of a simulation or game, the teacher should constantly move about observing the roles of the players and perhaps even systematically noting various reactions so that a critique may be made when the game is finished. If possible, we suggest that some type of form be used for tabulating student behavior, such as those illustrated in our treatment of discussion in Chapter 7. In some cases after your evaluation, you may decide to modify a selected game based on an initial experience of the class.

Figure 9–2, from Maidment and Bronstein (1973) illustrates a general cycle associated with both the design and use of games or simulations in the classroom.

Designing Your Own Games

As illustrated in *Voilà*, prepared by Melaine J. Jones Libey, a former undergraduate student of ours, it is easy to design your own simulation or game. There are about ten steps involved. The general design rules, as presented by Alice Kaplan Gordon (1972), follow:*

1. Define design objectives.
2. Determine the scope of the game in terms of the issues to be examined, its setting in time, and its geographic area.
3. Identify key actors in the process, whether individuals, groups, organizations, or institutions.
4. Define the objectives of the actors, in terms of wealth, power, influence, and other rewards.
5. Determine the actors' resources, including the game information each receives.
6. Determine the decision rules, or criteria, that actors use in deciding what actions to take.
7. Determine the interaction sequence among the actors.
8. Identify external constraints on the actions of the actors.
9. Decide the scoring rules or win criteria of the game.
10. Choose form of presentation (board game, role-playing) and formulate sequence of operations.

Other Considerations

Our brief introduction to the use of classroom games or simulations must surely have caused you to ask yourself the question: Will they work for my area? The answer depends on what your goals or objectives are. If you want to build processes associated with decision-making, then games and simulations provide alternatives to the usual classroom routines. If you wish to promote human interactions, then simulations and games are appropriate. If you intend to provide experiences that students may not have in the routine application of learning skills or principles, then you should use games or simulations that will achieve this end.

Examine the following game, *Voilà*, to observe how, with some ingenuity, knowledge of your subject, initiative, and imagination, *you* too can design a simple game or simulation.

---

*From Alice Kaplan Gordon, *Games for Growth*. © 1970, Science Research Associates, Inc. Reprinted by permission of the publisher, pp. 123–131.

FIGURE 9–2 A Design and Use Cycle for Games or Simulations

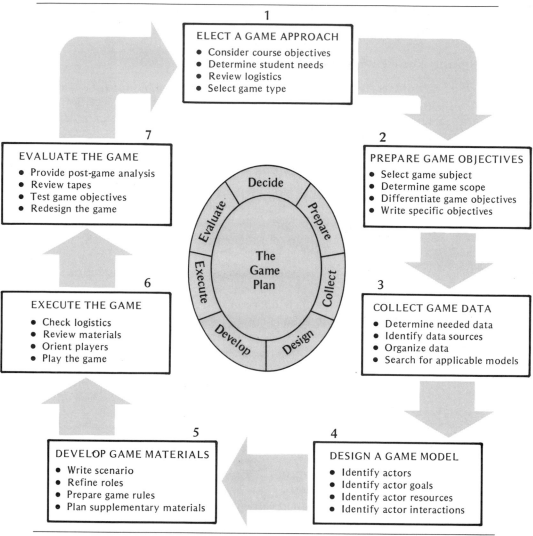

Source: Robert Maidment and Russell H. Bronstein, *Simulation Games: Design and Implementation* (Columbus, Ohio: Charles E. Merrill Publishing Company, 1973), p. 57. Used with the written permission of Charles C. Merrill Publishing Company.

Voilà: The Educational French Game

Teachers often think of the "unteachable moments" of class as those last five minutes before the bell rings or perhaps the entire day before any holiday or major school event. But teachers seldom regard the first day after vacation as an almost equally difficult time to motivate students academically. It may be contended that many students merely trudge through that day and absorb the bare minimum of the lesson as they daydream about the wonderful time they had outside of school.

Voilà has been developed to make any "unteachable day" meaningful for the French student. The objectives of the game are to revive student thinking in French, to utilize game theory, and to do it all painlessly. To compensate for the students' memory loss over the vacation, learned nouns and their genders are stressed. A small number of new words are introduced to challenge the alert, prepared student.

Voilà is played on a board, or card, similar to that used in Bingo (see Fig. 9–3). Each letter of the word *Voilà* has its own column of five squares, each containing a picture representing a single noun. The gender of the noun is stated in the upper left-hand corner of the square. Since colors are basic to vocabulary, they also are included. In the center of the board, there is the "question" space, though it cannot be equated with the "free space" in Bingo. Like any other picture, the center square must be called before it can be covered, but this can occur with greater frequency as there is more than one "question" card in the drawing pot. Each board is numbered for teacher reference. The boards may be identical or different, depending on the goals of the teacher and the experiences of the students.

Other elements of the game include small black squares with which to cover the pictures that are called and call cards for every picture. The game procedures follow.

1. All conversation during the game is in French.
2. Each player begins with a blank card and a pile of black squares.
3. The leader calls out the article and name of the picture and the column heading under which it is found.
4. The player covers only the picture called.
5. IMPORTANT: A player *must* ask for the meaning of any words that are not understood. One may not simply guess and cover the picture; the player must be sure. Even those words not on the card must become familiar to the player. Other players and the leader may give as many clues as necessary to accomplish this goal.
6. At any time during the game, the leader or the player may ask a person the meaning of any word called out. If that person cannot answer correctly, one point is lost. (Negative point totals are allowed, though not encouraged.)
7. When a player has covered any five spaces in a straight line, either horizontally, vertically, or diagonally, the response is, "*Voilà!*"
8. The player must then substantiate the *Voilà* by reading back the five covered squares in French. If the player is unable to do this, the *Voilà* is forfeited, as is the unidentified picture that cannot be recovered.
9. Two points are given for each correct *Voilà*.
10. Play continues until everyone has achieved at least one *Voilà*.
11. The winner is the player with the greatest number of *Voilà*'s. In the case of a tie, the victor is the first to achieve an initial *Voilà*.

Voilà can be developed in any of several directions. To stimulate creative thinking, the student may be encouraged to make up a sentence using the five words in *Voilà* to get an additional point. To incorporate writing skills, the student may be required to jot down the components of *Voilà* and to turn them in correctly spelled the next day, with the meanings written down in French. The student may even be asked to compose a paragraph involving the words found on the board. The student may be given a few verbs, adjectives, and adverbs to develop further the paragraph or short story. For still more variety, the student may separate the words into three lists, according to whether there is a horizontal, vertical, or diagonal *Voilà*. These innovations will enhance the educative potential of the game, which will be a welcome change in assignment from the traditional textbook-oriented task.

FIGURE 9–3   One Model of *Voilà* Game Card

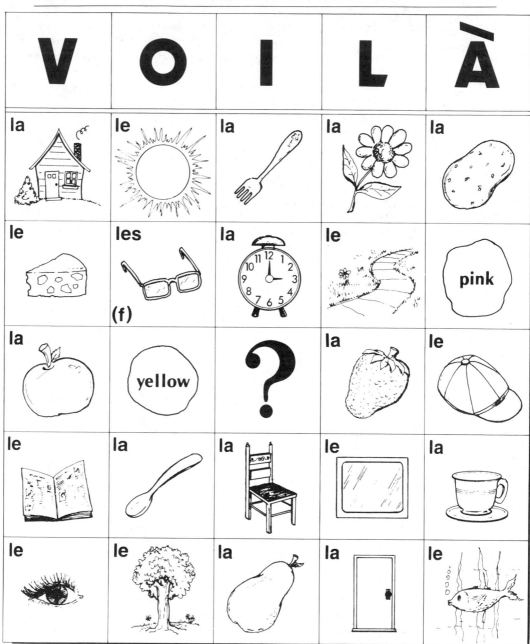

This type of expansion is also beneficial as it fulfills the ultimate objective of *Voilà*—that of refocusing the student's attention on academic pursuits. The next day, after the teacher reads aloud several of the papers prepared by the students or follows up the assignment in some manner, the student is asked to tackle the rudiments of grammar as presented in the typical textbook.

Voilà, as presented initially, consisted of forty-two distinct words, with twelve possibilities under each column (some words are used in more than one column). The words ranged from those used every day to those that are moderately uncommon. With few exceptions, they all could be found in both first- and second-year textbook vocabularies. In this limited form, the game demanded at least 20 minutes for one playing and not less than 10 minutes for the first *Voilà* to be achieved. Thus, it already had been demonstrated to be very workable and complete without further development.

One of the greatest advantages of this game, however, is its endless possibilities for variation and expansion. It is readily adaptable to different group sizes, to varying facets and levels of instruction, and even to other languages.

Voilà can be played in both large- and small-group situations. Used with a complete unit involving the entire class, it can be a fun way of reviewing. Questions originating from the students allow for some student-student interaction and positive competition, as long as the game maintains a lighthearted overtone, with emphasis on the group working together as a whole and helping each other with unknown words. In a small-group situation, students may experience more interaction because of reduced inhibitions in a more informal setting. To add variety, the students can take turns acting as the leader. In this case, call cards should be slightly revised so that they consist of only the pictures, with or without the genders, depending on the degree of difficulty desired. For example, this variation may be too complex for a first-year class but may be a needed challenge for second-year foreign language students. Another advantage of the small-group situation is that this game can be played while many other games are also in progress in the room.

Several variations of this game can be played in a small-group situation. One cluster of students can play Number *Voilà* (the same as Bingo); one group, Translation *Voilà* for verbs or adjectives/adverbs (the English words are called and the French words are on the card); one group, Conjugation *Voilà* (the tense and person of the verb is called in French and the student looks for the correct form); and another group, the regular *Voilà*. For some of these variations, the question space is probably changed to the traditional free space.

To compensate for varying levels of French proficiency, this game lends itself easily to modification. Any aspect of the language can be made challenging yet can be simplified for more inexperienced students. Without being altered, *Voilà* can vary in complexity merely by the amount of emphasis given to knowledge of genders or perhaps to spelling.

Voilà can be used in any language if the genders are removed entirely from the cards and a five-letter word in that language is superimposed on the word *Voilà* at the top of each card. For each language, call cards can have a distinctive color.

All variations obviously cannot be used by every class; however, a combination or modification of these ideas can provide the right form of *Voilà* for any French class. Best of all, there no longer need be "unteachable moments" that extend for more than a few minutes, especially preceding or following a vacation.

Voilà was prepared and fieldtested by Melaine J. Jones Libey when she was a junior in a teaching methods class at Washington State University. She continues to use the game and adapts it to her French classes. Used with her written permission.

Research Findings on Simulations

The research on simulations is quite voluminous. Gerald R. Girod (1969) and Alice Kaplan Gordon (1972) provide both evidence and case studies that support the use of simulations to improve the cognitive and affective skills and attitudes of the players. Hubert J. Klausmeier and R. E. Ripple (1971) report that games, role-playing, and simulations are effective means of cultivating desirable school-related attitudes.

The review of games and simulations by F. L. Goodman (1973) regards such activities as excellent student motivators. Karen C. Cohen's (1970) work shows that a group of previously unmotivated and apparently disinterested truants were persuaded to attend school by enticing them with the "Consumer Game." We agree that the use of simulations and games does increase student interest in the subjects being studied.

James M. Migaki, one of our colleagues at Washington State University, has long used his own creation, "The Pancake Game," as an end-of-semester activity for junior-year university students in his methods class. The amount of interaction, interest, and application of skills and knowledge is tremendous. Students who interact very little during the regular class periods begin relating to each other as if they are old friends. Thus, if you wish to increase the interactions within your groups or classes, you should use a game that requires interpersonal contacts.

Games and simulations are devices that can help to establish a supportive environment that is conducive to learning. Teachers have reported that the use of simulations and games seems to help many "quiet" students to participate more in class activities. Jay Reese (1977) suggests that simulations may be good learning motivators. He adds that there is a need for a discussion or debriefing session at the culmination of any simulation activity. The debriefing helps the students to determine the implicit or explicit learnings to be gained from the experience.

Analyzing the concept of simulations, Katherine Chapman et al. (1974) believe that simulations and educational games tend to promote logical reasoning and decision-making. In addition, these authors state that simulations provide a steady source of feedback to all participants. By learning how to use the feedback, the players learn how to process new knowledge and to modify previously made decisions. Such activities tend to provide a more complex learning environment than that usually found in the classroom. Thus, a major advantage of games and simulations is that they teach students how to establish a strategy and how to modify it through rational means.

Games also produce affective consequences, or feelings. In the "Ghetto Game" or in "Woman and Man," one group always has a built-in advantage over the other. Assigning students to the group that has less control over its fate is a powerful means of evoking feelings of despair.

Simulations also can be levelers of ability. Children who are judged to be poor students can participate on a near equal, if not totally equal, basis as the better students. More importantly, having a chance to compete or participate with others helps to build students' morale and makes the classroom a more enjoyable place in which to learn.

When does one integrate a simulation into the curriculum? Chapman et al. (1974) suggest that "folk wisdom" provides teachers with at least five possible instances when it would be appropriate.

1. After a unit or as the culminating or generalizing activity
2. As rewards to students who complete assignments
3. For a change of instructional pace
4. To introduce a unit or to motivate students to learn
5. To help meet the instructional learning objectives

Simulations are excellent devices with which to develop value clarification sessions. Elliot Carlson (1969) suggests three topics that are most appropriate for simulations: (1) business practices; (2) politics; and (3) crises. We believe that business practices, politics, and environmental issues may often be controversial topics for the class. Yet, by inventing a simulation with which to examine the issues in question, the teacher provides the students with a safe place in which to reflect on their personal values and on those of society.

We have visited excellent high schools and have found that the mathematics centers in the classroom stock games and simulations of all kinds to be used as stimulators and motivators in mathematics instruction. Along the same lines, Laymen E. Allen et al. (1966) report that the game of "Wff'n Proof" in junior and senior high school did improve problem-solving skills for those students who played the game for 45 to 60 minutes per day for six weeks.

Simulations have been used by nearly every teacher who has included an "activity corner" in the classroom environment. In many cases, the games can be developed by teachers in cooperation with professional game designers. Some teachers purchase the games, while others recruit older students to create games by simply giving them the objectives, materials, and the basic plan, such as that shown in Figure 9–2. Alan J. McCormack (1978) challenges teachers who wish to stress creativity to use simulations, inquiry, and problem-solving. He also recommends that teachers have available a lot of materials that can be used by children to build their own "Incredible Banana Split Machine," the title of his article.

Mary Anne Symons Brown (1977) discusses the use of games as mechanisms that allow students to set their own academic goals, pace, and practices. She also observes that sensitive or more serious subjects can be made a bit lighter through simulation activities. In addition, she uses games as a means of reviewing previously taught concepts, which is a more dynamic method of accomplishing a usually routine task.

Terry Armstrong and Michael Heikkinen (1977) suggest that the teacher offer an open-ended challenge to the class. Although they are discussing inquiry in general, their suggestion also applies to simulations, especially those involving educationally disadvantaged youth. The main advantage of an open-ended challenge is that it allows a whole spectrum of appropriate responses. This is one sure way of improving the self-images of young people who have not had much of a chance to be winners. As the teacher, you can reward or reinforce a wide variety of responses—the most original idea, the best technique, the neatest paper, the toughest project, or the greatest number of alternatives. There is no limit to the number of positive school-related rewards that can be given to students.

Thomas Popkewitz (1977) suggests using the community as an inquiry device if you want to develop inquiry in social studies subjects. In addition to using the community at large, students can use their own school to study social structures and social interactions. Personal involvement is the key to Popkewitz's concept of inquiry, as it is to ours.

Locating Sources About Simulations

Although the distribution of simulations is rather widespread, we wish to suggest some excellent sources of simulations for your use. Robert E. Horn (1977), David W. Zuckerman and Robert E. Horn (1970), Robert E. Horn and Anne Cleaves (1980), and Jean Belch (1974) provide references and information about simulations that are easy to use. They describe thousands of simulations so that you may make the most appropriate selection for your class and your learning objectives.

Robert E. Horn (1977) and David W. Zuckerman and Robert E. Horn (1970) provide a list and brief descriptions of almost 1,000 simulations and games. Sixteen different descriptors are listed for each entry. These descriptors include information about copyright, age level, number of players, playing time, supplementary materials, special equipment, preparation time, descriptions, roles, objectives, decisions, purposes, user report, editor's comments, costs, and producer. By referring to the works of these authors, you can quickly determine the status of published and unpublished simulations.

Jean Belch (1973) provides an eleven-point system of descriptors similar to those just listed. She also supplies valuable cross-referencing by subject, author, and producer. Additional sources of simulations are typically listed in books and articles on the topic.

Richard D. Duke and Cathy S. Greenblat (1979) published *Games-Generating-Games,* an interesting interactive book on game building. One does not read this book, rather one interacts with it to design or to build your own game. John L. Taylor and Rex Walford's (1979) *Learning and the Simulation Game* describes the evolution of simulations, a set of representative simulations, and a directory of more than 300 currently available games.

A very handy source for simulations is Ken Jones' (1980) *Simulations: A Handbook for Teachers.* Henry I. Ellington et al. (1980) published *Games and Simulations in Science Education,* which focuses on simulations especially for British science teachers. Lynton Gray and Ian Waitt (1982) edited a rather detailed work on the topic, *Perspectives on Academic Gaming and Simulation Seven: Simulation in Management and Business,* which is a good reference about the management and business, especially business administration. Finally, at the more esoteric level, there is the work edited by Lance A. Leventhal (1982), *Modeling and Simulation on Microcomputers.*

We wish to stress one last point. Games, simulations, or inquiry devices should be incorporated into the ongoing instructional goals. These techniques are *not* entertainment mechanisms, although they may prove to be incidentally so. The most important use of inquiry-related techniques is to support the instructional goals and objectives of the school. You as teacher must decide how best to achieve these goals. Teaching through inquiry is not simple; it requires a well-prepared teacher to do an effective job. However, the rewards far exceed those found in the traditional classroom.

THE COMPUTER REVOLUTION AND YOU

In the late 1970s, the first successful and reasonably priced microcomputers entered the marketplace. It is doubtful if anyone could have predicted the immediate and overwhelming positive response to this technological triumph.

We view the microcomputer as one additional piece of educational technology that will help teachers meet the challenges that always confront any labor-intensive industry. How to integrate that technology into an ongoing operation, make the necessary role changes, and improve the total instructional effort are the major tasks we face today. We assume that microcomputers will be widespread in their adoption and implementation and that they will *not* replace teachers, books, films, libraries, or schools.

How can you use microcomputers? From the flood of publications, advertisements, and papers, we identify four basic classroom functions. In Chapter 5 we introduced the microcomputer as a tool able to (1) manage noninstructional teaching functions; (2) expedite drill and practice activities; (3) provide tutorials; and (4) promote simulation and inquiry activities. The current circumstances of simulation and inquiry strategies lead us to predict that nearly every field of study will have high-quality stimuli by which to meet the criteria set forth in Chapters 8 and 9 for the entire spectrum of inquiry. Coupled with interactive videodiscs, school inquiry activities will assume a real-life dimension never before possible.

Uses of the Microcomputer

If the advertisement of Verbatim Corporation in early 1983 is any indication, we will observe a flurry of activity by computer software companies to create ready-made programs. Verbatim announced a competition with cash prizes and personal computers for teachers who write imaginative instructional software, including games, inquiry activities, and general challenges to students of various ages.

Carolyn Barnato and Kathy Barrett (1981) suggested that when teaching biology, two important concepts—populations and pollution—can be presented most effectively through microcomputer simulations. These two teachers used a combination of brainstorming and computer simulation to determine alternative solutions. The manipulation of data and decision-making were important processes in their two programs.

Using a microcomputer to aid in French instruction was the subject addressed by Glyn Holmes and Marilyn E. Kidd (1983). They cite that computers can be used effectively to display information; to provide feedback to students; and to aid in developing skills in grammar, vocabulary, translation, and comprehension. Holmes and Kidd observed two major limitations: the computer cannot analyze compositions and it cannot analyze oral aspects of foreign language instruction. They did predict that the latter would be corrected through use of videodiscs.

Frederich Weber (1983) views using the microcomputer as one method by which to improve human relations skills of students. In most cases, students must share the machine, share ideas, and even prepare reports cooperatively. Weber observed that the closeness of such a situation helps students both become more friendly and shape values.

Several educators use microcomputers to teach communication skills. Charles Moran (1983) is an English teacher who has his students draft, compose, and prepare their papers on word processors. He notes that revisions and proofing may be made easily. Writing in the same area, but from a vocational viewpoint, were Orville F. Boes and Ray Bernardi (1982). They state that business students must be trained to use computers as future employers will assume that they know how. They emphasize the business letter in their training.

Learning-disabled students can also benefit from computer-aided instruction. Marley W. Watkins and Cynthia Webb (1981) found that young children in grades one through six were able to gain more through computer-aided instruction than were similar children who did not have access to computers.

It is clear that the computer acts as a motivating mechanism. Students want to "beat the beast"; thus they apparently spend more time on computer tasks than they normally do on traditional work.

Anticipated Problems with Microcomputers

Although the technology is new, we have already amassed observations about the microcomputer. Rather than providing a lengthy discussion of the problems, we simply provide a list of problems (instructional planning and decision-making) that must be solved *before* the microcomputer arrives.

• Exactly where will the computer be located?
• Will student traffic patterns need to be rerouted?

- How many stations are available each class period?
- Will an adult be available to supervise?
- Will all microcomputers be stored centrally?
- How will computer usage be assigned?
- Will the computer be an integral part of the class or an enrichment component?
- Will peripheral equipment be required?
- Are the classrooms free of dust?
- How will the microcomputers be secured (i.e., safe-guarded against theft)?
- Where will the software be stored?
- How many microcomputers will each teacher have?
- Will the entire classes have access to computers simultaneously?
- How will independent student study or practice be scheduled?
- Will computers be available before and after school hours?
- How long will any one student have access to the computer?
- Will your school stock entertainment games for students to use?
- Will there be a computer course to teach students how to use the hardware and software?
- How will the noise of computer usage affect the class?
- Will the computers have excessive maintenance problems when the school is chilled (closed?) during vacation periods?
- Must every classroom have a computer whether it is used or not?
- What plans have been made for routine maintenance?
- What happens to the computers during the summer vacation?

The problems are not insurmountable, but the questions must be raised and answered before the equipment is purchased. In approximately four years, we will all know if the microcomputer revolution was "for real" or a "simulation."

EVALUATING INQUIRY AND SIMULATION ACTIVITIES

We saved the toughest problem until last. As this book is being written, educators seem to be pressured into being "accountable." The term, as used in the context of education, has no set definition; its interpretation is arbitrary. Indeed, over two-thirds of the state legislatures in the country have defined it in their own different ways. It is irrelevant to argue here about the suitability of the legislation passed in each state; the important point is that accountability is a reality. You, as teachers, must use some method or technique to show parents, patrons, administrators, school trustees, and even the students that some kind of learning progress is being made and that you are, indeed, evaluating the students' efforts. To achieve this, we refer you to Chapter 7, in which we provide numerous evaluation instruments that can be used to document evidence of process growth. Also, as we discuss in Chapter 2, if you have written process-oriented performance objectives, you will have criteria that can be used to measure the students' success.

There is at least one more alternative that can be used to evaluate student progress: Prepare a report form that relates directly to your subject area. Figure 9–4 illustrates one form that is in use in the Spokane, Washington, public schools. At the time this form was devised, Spokane had no formal process instrument. This record was produced by a committee of educators and is oriented directly to Spokane's elementary science program, Science Curriculum Improvement Study (SCIS).

In this form, observe that every element is behaviorally oriented. Classify each of the criteria according to Bloom's six categories. You will discover that, surprisingly, there are no Knowledge-level criteria. The criteria used are all at the Comprehension, Application, Analysis, or Synthesis levels—all involving higher-level cognitive behavior. You will also observe a few affective qualities as well as one or two criteria involving psychomotor activity.

In addition to subjective teacher evaluations, you may use student rating scales during, or when completing, a game or simulation. For example, you can ask the participants to respond to the following types of questions by inserting a check mark where appropriate:

1. To what extent do you think that participating in the simulation was an effective learning experience?
   ( ) Very effective.
   ( ) Effective.
   ( ) Ineffective.
   ( ) Very ineffective.

2. How much do you like participating in simulations as compared to other instructional techniques?
   ( ) I like simulations much better.
   ( ) I like simulations a little better.
   ( ) I like all instructional techniques equally.
   ( ) I like other instructional techniques a little better than simulations.
   ( ) I like other instructional techniques much better than simulations.

3. To what extent did you conscientiously participate in the simulation?
   ( ) Very conscientiously.
   ( ) Somewhat conscientiously.
   ( ) Somewhat unconscientiously.
   ( ) Very unconscientiously.

These three examples illustrate how the evaluative question is framed and is then followed by a continuum of responses. We have not developed other questions to ask the participants, but we have provided you with several sets of response continua as shown in Figure 9–5. All you have to do is generate the questions.

FIGURE 9–4   Pupil Evaluation Record for Elementary Science Program

(NOTE: Teacher retains in file—records grade on report card each quarter.)

Name of Pupil _____

Grade _____ **School Year** _____

Teacher _____

Key: 4 = Demonstrates great proficiency
             3 = Demonstrates proficiency
             2 = Demonstrates some proficiency
             1 = Demonstrates little proficiency

Directions: Insert *number* in box provided for appropriate quarter.

EVALUATION CRITERIA

	First Quarter	Second Quarter	Third Quarter	Fourth Quarter

I. Curiosity
   A. Uses several senses to explore organisms and materials.
   B. Asks questions about objects and events.
   C. Investigates circuits and other systems actively.
   D. Shows interest in the outcomes of experiments.

☐ ☐ ☐ ☐

II. Inventiveness
   A. Uses equipment in unusual and constructive ways.
   B. Suggests new experiments.
   C. Describes novel conclusions from observations.
   D. Proposes original models to explain observations.

☐ ☐ ☐ ☐

III. Critical Thinking
   A. Uses evidence to justify conclusions.
   B. Predicts the outcome of untried experiments.
   C. Justifies predictions in terms of past experience.
   D. Changes ideas in response to evidence or logical reasons.
   E. Points out contradictions in reports by classmates.
   F. Investigates the effects of selected variables.
   G. Identifies the strong and weak points of a scientific model.

☐ ☐ ☐ ☐

FIGURE 9–4 *Continued*

IV. Persistence

	First Quarter	Second Quarter	Third Quarter	Fourth Quarter
A. Continues to investigate materials after novelty has worn off.	☐	☐	☐	☐
B. Repeats an experiment in spite of apparent failure.				
C. Completes an activity even though classmates have finished earlier.				
D. Initiates and completes a science project.				

Average—Each Quarter:

	First Quarter	Second Quarter	Third Quarter	Fourth Quarter
	☐	☐	☐	☐

Quarter Letter Grade:
(Translate number average to letter grade.)

	First Quarter	Second Quarter	Third Quarter	Fourth Quarter
	☐	☐	☐	☐

**Transfer letter grade to report card
for appropriate quarter**

Teacher Notes (include dates):

Source: Spokane, Washington, School District No. 81. Used with permission.

By systematically conducting a series of brief evaluations, you will be collecting the kinds of evidence that form the basis of an accountability system. A combination of this type of evaluation instrument and others previously mentioned will be adequate for fulfilling the need for accountability. This can be your opportunity to improve student performance in thinking.

In Conclusion

Our conclusion, in part, comes from one of our undergraduate students, Thomas M. Cools. In summarizing a report about inquiry, he concluded his paper with the following paragraph:*

Inquiry is the most natural method by which to identify that which nature "hides" from us. In most disciplines, inquiry is beneficial and satisfying pre-

*Used with the permission of Thomas M. Cools.

FIGURE 9–5   Response Continua for Evaluation of Simulations

Very adequate	Almost always valid
Adequate	Usually valid
Inadequate	Usually invalid
Very inadequate	Almost always invalid
Strongly agree	Very important
Agree with reservations	Somewhat important
No opinion	Undecided
Disagree with reservations	Somewhat unimportant
Strongly disagree	Very unimportant
Very clear	Almost always supportive
Somewhat clear	Usually supportive
Somewhat unclear	Usually unsupportive
Very unclear	Almost always unsupportive
Greatly encouraged	Very satisfactory
Encouraged	Satisfactory
No opinion	Undecided
Discouraged	Unsatisfactory
Greatly discouraged	Very unsatisfactory
Strongly favor	Very good quality
Tend to favor	Good quality
No opinion	Uncertain
Tend to disfavor	Poor quality
Strongly disfavor	Very poor quality

Modified from Donald C. Orlich, *Designing Sensible Surveys*. Pleasantville, N.Y.: Redgrave Publishing Co., 1978, p. 55. Reprinted with written permission.

cisely because the human mind proceeds from the particular to the universal— that which is first known by humans, to that which nature knew first. It is no wonder that inquiry works so well. Inquiry develops the mind to think and satisfies our natural curiosity. Learning through inquiry is not a new discovery but one well known to the early Greeks. However, the early Greeks sought to know "truth." Modern people tend to view truths as being more relative. Yet we're finally learning; we hope that with more inquiry in the schools, all of our educational programs will improve.

We stress once again that the more you know how to teach and interact with your students, the more likely it is that you will discover a teaching style that each and every one of them will like. Getting students to like school is a basic principle. As teachers, you owe it to your students to motivate them in some way to be successful. As Benjamin S. Bloom so dramatically noted in his paper on mastery learning (1968), *interest* is a function of *success*. For too many years, we have operated schools according to the converse of the Bloom formula—success is a function of interest. In other words, if you want students to be interested in learning and in its related activities, then—most important of all—students must be successful in school. B. F. Skinner, the noted behavioral psychologist, repeated Bloom's point in an article titled "The Shame of American Education" (1984).

With inquiry, you can generate enthusiasm among the students in your classes. You can inspire individuals to discover, to question, and seek. You can break the monotony of dull classes by using interactive simulations or games. You control the learning environment. Structure this environment so that everyone in it will be highly motivated and successful in learning. It is the very least you can do or, perhaps, . . . the very most!

FORMATIVE EVALUATION
Inquiry, Games, and Simulations

Place an X next to the response that most appropriately answers the question.

1. Educational games are often different from entertainment games because educational games
   - _____ (a) Pertain more to real life, and competition is not so important.
   - _____ (b) Give little personal success to the winner.
   - _____ (c) Place greater emphasis on game competition than on the game process.
   - _____ (d) Put little emphasis on board formats or role-play formats.
2. The use of small groups in problem-solving techniques produces best results in
   - _____ (a) Acquisition of very specific information.
   - _____ (b) Development of psychomotor skills.
   - _____ (c) Promoting individual creative talents.
   - _____ (d) Working together to attain a general goal.
3. All but one of the following are characteristic of discovery learning involving student interaction and an emphasis on discussions.
   - _____ (a) Student involvement in decision-making.
   - _____ (b) Teacher checking of lessons to determine right and wrong answers.
   - _____ (c) Probing analysis of concepts and issues.
   - _____ (d) Shifting leadership roles among the participants.
4. The greatest value of simulation activities lies in
   - _____ (a) Enhancing the acting skills of talented students.
   - _____ (b) Permitting ego gratification on the part of some students.
   - _____ (c) Promoting the creative instincts of students.
   - _____ (d) Deepening insights and understandings relative to the issues.
5. Which of the following is *not* a characteristic of educational games?
   - _____ (a) They are active and responsive.
   - _____ (b) They are goal-directed.

_____ (c) The object of winning is initially a motivating factor.

_____ (d) They are remembered because they distinguish a particular person as winner.

6. A student of yours sends an idea to the National Science foundation (NSF). From this idea, a new process for making paper is generated that cannot be copied by Xerox, IBM, or 3-M copiers. This discovery would be classified as

_____ (a) Absolute discovery.

_____ (b) Binary discovery.

_____ (c) Relative discovery.

_____ (d) Simulated discovery.

7. Citing his criteria for problem-solving, you argue that John Dewey had sound theories regarding the subject. These criteria would include which _one_ from the list below?

_____ (a) Problems are relevant _only_ to the students.

_____ (b) Problems are relevant _only_ to the teachers.

_____ (c) Problems should be significant to the culture.

_____ (d) Problems are unimportant; it is the process that is important.

8. Which statement below is _not_ an assumption about deductive inquiry teaching?

_____ (a) Teachers should be antagonistic to the responses of their students as this stimulates student initiative.

_____ (b) Students must be taught processes associated with inquiry.

_____ (c) Students at all levels of learning can benefit from inquiry experiences.

_____ (d) Solutions to the problems are not easily found in textbooks.

9. The major justification for helping students to develop skills of group processes through simulations is

_____ (a) The inclusion of speech in the language arts curriculum.

_____ (b) The failure of parents to accept responsibility for teaching these skills.

_____ (c) The necessary response that such activities proceed from the more cognitive aspects of the instructional program.

_____ (d) The prevalence of group activity and human interaction in everyday life and experience.

10. The microcomputer can best perform all the functions _except_ which one?

_____ (a) Record keeping.

_____ (b) Theme analysis.

_____ (c) Vocabulary building.

_____ (d) Testing.

11. David Ausubel would probably approve of which techniques as fitting his deductive schema?

_____ (a) Outlining a lecture before delivering it.

_____ (b) Asking students to generate questions from a lecture.

_____ (c) Videotaping a lecture, then analyzing it.

_____ (d) Using computers as classroom entertainment.

12. What trait do inquiry, simulations, games, and microcomputers have in common?

_____ (a) They are all inductively sequenced.

_____ (b) They all require decision-making.

_____ (c) Each requires individualized instruction.

_____ (d) They all require close teacher supervision.

RESPONSES
Inquiry, Games, and Simulations

1. (b)	7. (c)
2. (d)	8. (a)
3. (b)	9. (c)
4. (d)	10. (b)
5. (d)	11. (a)
6. (a)	12. (b)

REFERENCES

Abt, Clark. Address presented at the "Man-Machine Conference" in Portland, Oregon, November 26, 1966.

Agne, Russell M. "A Comparison of Earth Science Classes Taught by Using Original Data in a Research-Approach Technique Versus Classes Taught by Conventional Approaches Not Using Such Data." Unpublished doctoral dissertation, the University of Connecticut, 1969.

Allen, Laymen E., Robert W. Allen, and James C. Miller. "Programmed Games and the Learning of Problem Solving Skills: The WFF'N PROOF Example." *The Journal of Education Research* 60:1966, 22–26.

Armstrong, Terry, and Michael Heikkinen. "Initiating Inquiry through Open-Ended Problems." *Science and Children* 14:1977, 30–31.

Ausubel, David P. *Educational Psychology: A Cognitive View.* New York: Holt, Rinehart & Winston, 1968.

Barnato, Carolyn, and Kathy Barrett. "Microcomputers in Biology Inquiry." *The American Biology Teacher* 43:1981, 372, 377–378.

Belch, Jean. *Contemporary Games, Vol. I, Directory.* Detroit: Gale Research Co., 1973.

————. *Contemporary Games, Vol. II, Bibliography.* Detroit: Gale Research Co., 1974.

Bennett, William, et al. *The Stock Market Game, Players Manual.* Manhattan, Kansas: Kansas State University Center for Economics Education, 1979.

Bibens, Robert F. "Using Inquiry Effectively." *Theory Into Practice* 19:1980, 8–9.

Bloom, Benjamin S. "Learning for Mastery." *Evaluation Comment* 1:1968, pp. 1–4.

Boes, Orville F., and Ray Bernardi. "Using the Computer to Teach Specific Communication Skills." *Business Education Forum* 36:1982, 14–15.

Bredderman, Ted. "The Effects of Activity-based Elementary Science on Student Outcomes: A Quantitative Synthesis." *Review of Educational Research* 53:1983, 499–518.

Brown, Mary Anne Symons. "Games Can Make You a Winning Teacher." *Forecast* 23:1977, 19.

Buchan, L. Gerald. *Roleplaying and the Educable Mentally Retarded.* Belmont, Calif.: Fearon, 1972.

Carlson, Elliot. *Learning Through Games.* Washington, D.C.: Public Affairs Press, 1969.

Chapman, Katherine, James E. Davis, and Andrea Meier. *Simulation/Games in Social Studies: What Do We Know?* Boulder, Colo.: Social Science Education Consortium, Inc., SSEC Publication No. 162, 1974. (U.S. Office of Education Grant No. OEC-0-70-3862.)

Clarke, John A. "Ausubel and ASEP: An Application of Cognitive Field Learning Theory to an ASEP Unit." *Australian Science Teachers Journal* 14:1973, 92–97. ERIC EJ095 139.

Cohen, Karen C. "Effects of the 'Consumer Game' on Learning and Attitudes of Selected Seventh Grade Students in a Target-Area School." Report No. 65 of the Center for the Study of Social Organization of Schools. Baltimore: Johns Hopkins University, 1970. ERIC ED038 733.

"Consumer." New York: Western Publishing, 1969.

Denison, Tom G. "The Effectiveness of Simulated Practice for Teaching Welding" (Ph.D. diss., Washington State University, Pullman, Washington, 1981).

Duke, Richard D., and Cathy S. Greenblat. *Games-Generating-Games.* Beverly Hills: Sage, 1979.

Eggen, Paul D., Donald P. Kauchak, and Robert J. Harder. *Strategies for Teacher Information Processing Models in the Classroom.* Englewood Cliffs, N.J.: Prentice-Hall, 1979, pp. 131–141.

Ellington, Henry I., Eric Addinall, and Fred Percival. *Games and Simulations in Science Education.* New York: Nichols Publishing Co., 1981.

Gagné, Robert M. *The Conditions of Learning,* 2nd ed. New York: Holt, Rinehart & Winston, 1970.

Garreau, Joel. *The Nine Nations of North America.* Boston: Houghton Mifflin, 1981.

"Ghetto." New York: Western Publishing, 1969.

Girod, Gerald R. "The Effectiveness and Efficiency of Two Types of Simulation as Functions of Level of Elementary Education Training." Final Report, Project No. 9-I-055. U.S. Department of Health, Education and Welfare, Office of Education, Bureau of Research. Pullman, Washington, September 1969.

Goodman, F. L. "Gaming and Simulation." In *Second Handbook of Research on Teaching,* Robert M. W. Travers, ed. Chicago: Rand McNally, 1973, pp. 926–939.

Gordon, Alice Kaplan. *Games for Growth.* Palo Alto, Calif.: Science Research Associates, Inc., 1972, pp. 123–131.

Gray, Lynton, and Ian Waitt, eds. *Perspectives on Academic Gaming and Simulation Seven: Simulation in Management and Business.* New York: Nichols Publishing Co., 1982.

Gruber, James. "Students Learn to Begin a Business." *Business Education Forum* 33:1979, 20–22.

Harris, Janet A. "Chemically Speaking . . . Who Done It?" *The Science Teacher* 49:1982, 43–44, 49–50.

Hensen, Kenneth T. "Discovery Learning." *Contemporary Education* 51:1980, 101–103.

Hermann, G. "Learning by Discovery: A Critical Review of Studies." *The Journal of Experimental Education* 38:1969, 58–72.

Hisgen, Jon W. "To Tell The Truth: A Classroom Gaming Procedure." *Health Education* 12:1981, 32–33.

Holmes, Glyn, and Marilyn E. Kidd. "Second-Language Learning and Computers." *Canadian Modern Language Review* 38:1983, 508–516.

Horn, Robert E., ed. *The Guide to Simulation/Games for Education and Training,* 3rd ed. Lexington, Mass.: Information Resources, Inc., 1977.

Horn, Robert E., and Anne Cleaves, eds. *The Guide to Simulations—Games for Education and Training,* 4th ed. Beverly Hills: Sage, 1980.

Howe, Robert W., and Gregor A. Ramsey. "An Analysis of Research on Instructional Procedures in Secondary School Science, Part I: Outcomes of Instruction." *The Science Teacher* 36:1969, 62–70.

Jones, Ken. *Simulations: A Handbook for Teachers.* New York: Nichols, 1980.

Klausmeier, Herbert J., and R. E. Ripple. *Learning and Human Abilities: Educational Psychology.* New York: Harper & Row, 1971.

Leventhal, Lance A., ed. *Modeling and Simulation on Microcomputers.* Lajolla, Calif.: The Society for Computer Simulation, 1982.

Maidment, Robert, and Russell H. Bronstein. *Simulation Games: Design and Implementation.* Columbus, Ohio: Charles E. Merrill, 1973.

McCormack, Alan J. "The Incredible Banana Split Machine." *Instructor* 87:1978, 54–57.

"Monopoly." Salem, Mass.: Parker Brothers, 1935.

Moran, Charles. "Word Processing and the Teaching of Writing." *English Journal* 72:1983, 113–115.

Olson, Janet. "Think of the Possibilities." *School Arts* 82:1982, 31–35.

Omaggio, Alice C. "Using Games and Interaction Activities for the Development of Functions Proficiency in a Second Language." *The Canadian Modern Language Review* 38:1982, 517–546.

Orlich, Donald C. *Designing Sensible Surveys.* Pleasantville, N.Y.: Redgrave Publishing Co., 1978.

Orlich, Donald C., F. B. May, and R. J. Harder. "Change Agents and Instructional Innovations: Report 2." *The Elementary School Journal* 73:1973, 390–398.

Orlich, Donald C., et al. "A Change Agent Strategy: Preliminary Report." *The Elementary School Journal* 72:1972, 281–293.

Popkewitz, Thomas. "Social Inquiry and Schooling." *The Educational Forum* 27:1977, 315–320.

Reese, Jay. *Simulation Games and Learning Activities Kit for the Elementary School.* West Nyack, N.Y.: Parker Publishing Co., Inc., 1977.

Rosenblatt, Ronald R. "You and the Investment World: Teaching and Learning About the World of High Finance." Paper presented at the Kansas Council for Social Studies, Wichita, October, 1982.

Shulman, Lee S., and Pinchas Tamir. "Research on Teaching in the Natural Sciences." In *Second Handbook of Research on Teaching,* Robert M. W. Travers, Ed. Chicago: Rand McNally & Company, 1973, pp. 1098–1148.

Skinner, B. F. "The Shame of American Education." *American Psychologist* 39:1984, 947–954.

Sudol, David. "Creating and Killing Stanley Realbozo or, Teaching Characterization and Plot in English 10." *English Journal* 72:1983, 63–66.

Taylor, John L., and Rex Walford. *Learning and the Simulation Game.* Beverly Hills: Sage, 1979.

Thames, W. R. "The Game Is the Least Important Thing." *Social Studies* 70:1979, 122–124.

Twelker, Paul A. "Simulation: What Is It? Why Is It?" Paper presented at the conference, "Simulation: Stimulation for Learning," sponsored by the Commission on Education Media of the Association for Supervision and Curriculum Development, NEA, San Diego, April 1968.

Unpublished materials from the Walla Walla, Washington, Public Schools, Title III, ESEA, Social Studies Project, 1969–1971.

Walker, Decker F., and Jon Schaffarzick. "Comparing Curricula." *Review of Educational Research* 44:1974, 83–111.

Watkins, Marley W., and Cynthia Webb. "Computer Assisted Instruction with Learning Disabled Students." *Educational Computer* 1:1981, 24–27.

Weber, Frederich. "The Microcomputer: A Human Relations Resource." *The Clearing House* 56:1983, 378–379.

Zuckerman, David W., and Robert E. Horn. *The Guide to Simulation Games for Education and Training.* Cambridge, Mass.: Information Resources, Inc., 1970.

10

DECIDING HOW TO MANAGE A CLASS

The classroom is a center for a dynamic system of interactions. Hundreds, if not thousands, of individual verbal and nonverbal behaviors and a multiplicity of possible combinations occur in every classroom. The more enthusiastic the teacher is, the greater is the likelihood that the number of interactions will increase. Enthusiasm and interaction are essential to the learning process. However, while enthusiasm and interaction can promote learning, if not carefully monitored, they also can sabotage and ultimately destroy the fragile balance between them, causing students to move from productive to nonproductive behaviors. The management of the classroom and the balancing of the interactions within it will be the focus of this chapter.

The text that follows will help you to achieve the following objectives:

1. To comprehend the concept of "classroom management"
2. To understand the concepts of "norms," "power," and "awareness"
3. To determine the applicability of desist strategies
4. To understand the uses of reality therapy
5. To understand the use of behavior modification in the classroom
6. To understand the use of referral resources
7. To develop a rationale toward corporal punishment, suspension, and drug or alcohol abuse management
8. To evaluate classroom management systems and to be able to select appropriate options to fit specific situations

Additionally we would like to encourage you to incorporate the following attitudes:

1. Perceive the role of classroom management from student's and adult's perspective—simultaneously
2. Analyze any classroom management system for its value to student learning
3. Keep an open and unbiased mind as you begin to manage your own classes

THE ROLE OF DISCIPLINE

George H. Gallup (1984) reported in his annual poll of public attitudes on education that, for fifteen of the last sixteen years, discipline is viewed as a major problem for the schools. With or without data from national polls, teachers, administrators, parents, school patrons, and students know that there are many discipline problems in the schools. And it comes as no surprise that the students cause most of the behavioral problems; however, some discipline problems are caused by teachers themselves. Indeed, this is a serious indictment against the teacher.

What discipline means to the average person is not entirely clear. However, discipline is usually perceived as the preservation of order and the maintenance of control. These are traditionally the outcomes of classroom management techniques; however, we feel that this view of discipline is far too simplistic. Teachers must make on-the-spot, split-second decisions and must react spontaneously when using management techniques to solve problems that arise in the classroom. Classroom management principles must be understood and developed in light of appropriate social and instructional outcomes as determined by *teacher-student-situation* factors. The attitudes that students develop in formal classroom situations are influenced by the classroom management skills of a teacher.

Some of the most difficult situations encountered by both student teachers and teachers involve *classroom management issues.* Why are management issues of such concern? First, most persons have never been charged with establishing and enforcing guidelines for behavior. Until faced with classroom management, the vast majority of college students have had responsibility for only themselves. As a teacher you are being asked to become responsible for the management of others, namely a group of precocious and energetic students.

Your ideas about what the classroom should look like and how it should function will determine classroom atmosphere. Very few people who enter a new field have thought much about the day-to-day happenings of their chosen profession. Many assumptions—some correct, some incorrect—fill the void of knowledge, but a teacher must test these assumptions and act upon them immediately.

Student-teaching experiences tend to resolve some management questions, but most individuals focus their primary attention on subject matter preparation. Precious little time is left to think consciously about management. Thus, many new teachers follow in the footsteps of their own teachers until such time as a personal management style evolves. However, we prefer to provide you with a variety of management strategies for your review. Your task will be to read and understand them, sample their ideas in classroom practice, and measure your classroom observations of teachers against the strategies detailed here. You will need to prepare yourself for a successful classroom experience by formulating a management program. We want you to succeed where many others have failed because they were not prepared for classroom management. You are responsible for your own success. The knowledge and background are available; you only need to think and respond adequately to the task ahead.

A Few Historical Insights

Prior to the late 1950s and early 1960s, the major emphasis in teacher preparation involved classroom control. Control differs from management in one major respect. The former implies order and obedience, while the latter suggests that there are activities and rules. The theory of "mental discipline," physical punishment, order, and obedience all tended to provide educators with a rather consistent frame of reference.

Schools began to shift more of the burden for classroom climate and conduct to the teacher. While this shift in responsibility was occurring, the results of relevant studies of discipline by social and behavioral scientists began to be applied in the schools. The shift of teacher responsibility, combined with social and behavioral research, set the stage for "democratic discipline." At least two teaching principles emerged from democratic discipline that could be applied to classroom management.

1. As the adult member of the class, the teacher must add the rational dimension to the rule-making capacities of the group.
2. Rules administered by the teacher should reflect the wisdom and fairness of a judge who participates in a trial as an impartial observer and arbiter.

No longer would the teacher be described in terms that implied superior or subordinate status. Thus such words as *facilitator* and *learner* emerged in the jargon of educational practitioners.

Classrooms began to change even more dramatically during the 1970s and 1980s. First, families have become very mobile. It is not uncommon for even a rather stable school to show 25 percent student turnover and for others to range between 35 and 70 percent. The mobility factor simply means that classrooms tend to be relatively unstable social systems.

The second phenomenon focuses on the so-called breakup of the family. More students now live with single parents than at any other time in our educational history and this number is increasing.

Third, there tends to be a prevailing student ethos that school is a place to "get through." It is harder to motivate most students.

Finally, urban schools have different problems when compared with suburban or nonurban schools. One simply cannot compile a list and expect it to apply to all schools. Julie Sanford and associates (1983) noted that a productive working environment in which students know what is expected of them is a trait of successful classroom management. Another of those traits is providing a safe and positive school climate. Teaching during the 1980s and 1990s will be affected by classroom management problems not encountered in previous decades.

Our definition of classroom management implies a humanistic orientation toward the classroom environment. Young minds and attitudes are being shaped by overt and covert teacher behaviors. The most successful teachers are those who knowingly make decisions based on sound principles of social psychology. The following text is a discussion of three concepts that are central to the principles of classroom management and social psychology: norms, power, and awareness.

The Influence of Social Psychologists

The concepts of social standards and democratic discipline in the educational literature closely parallel those developed by social psychologists. Social standards are synonymous with norms, and discipline is a special kind of power.

Norms

Although this concept is central to social psychologists, there has been much confusion and ambiguity in the use of the term. A norm is usually defined as a behavioral rule accepted to some degree by most members of a group. The members feel some obligation to adhere to the behavioral rule, as it introduces a high degree of regularity or predictability into their social interaction. Norms are not recorded like the laws of a country. However, there exists in the minds of the group members an ideal standard for how each member ought to behave under specific conditions. Deviation from the norm usually results in some kind of punishment by the group.

Norms are functionally valuable to social relationships because they reduce the necessity for exercising direct, informal, and personal influence. Adherence to norms provides for the control of individual and group behavior without any one individual overtly exerting power.

Power

Teachers tend to control tightly the transmission of skills and knowledge, which provides them with one form of power. The teacher's power is increased to the extent that these skills and experiences are not replaceable. Yet you should bear in mind that teachers are not the sole custodians of knowledge. Television, motion pictures, travel, families, and work all contribute to an individual's store of knowledge.

By virtue of role position in the classroom, the teacher has superior power. Unrestrained use of that power creates insecurities and resistance among the class members, which can adversely affect the attainment of learning objectives. While the administrative organization of schools keeps students in a relatively powerless position, students can nonetheless retaliate against the teacher who overuses power by forming coalitions, by creating irritating disturbances, and by intellectual sitdown strikes. In order to be an effective classroom manager, the teacher should learn to exercise the least amount of power necessary to accomplish the desired result.

Awareness

A class is constantly giving the teacher verbal and nonverbal cues. This communication occurs between the teacher and individual students and between the teacher and the class as a whole. How does the teacher respond to this network of communication?

Initially, the teacher must determine how the class is presenting these cues. The teacher who says, "My class was particularly lousy today," says nothing in terms of effectively dealing with the input received. This teacher must define with some precision what is meant by the term *lousy*. What behaviors did the class exhibit that led to the inference that the class was "lousy"? Have the students recited inappropriately, not paid attention, or not accomplished the work requested? Whatever the reason, the teacher must know how to specify what behaviors are being alluded to when the class is identified as "lousy."

In the following section, two classroom management principles will be described.

Principle 1

If acceptable standards of class behavior are not established and the teacher wants the student to behave according to a specified set of standards, then the teacher must use a strategy to establish acceptable standards. *Standards,* like *norms,* are regularized, predictable forms of social behavior.

One of the findings that has come from the study of effective schools reinforces Principle 1. Proponents of the effective school movement maintain that the very first day of school is critical in the establishment of standards. Further, one technique is to distribute the behavioral expectations as a printed handout and immediately—the first day of class—begin instruction. This action signals that learning is important.

Principle 2

If the teacher wants all class members to behave in a specified manner, and one individual misbehaves, then the teacher should use a procedure that is firm, courteous, and rational to change the inappropriate behavior.

A Continuum of Management Systems

All teachers need to decide very early in their professional careers what classroom management systems they intend to implement. One cannot implement a system on "the spur of the moment." Systems are studied and analyzed. Yet, whatever the circumstances, teachers are faced with choosing along a continuum of management strategies between self-discipline and imposed discipline. Self-discipline implies a system of organized behavior designed to promote self-interest while contributing to the welfare of others. Imposed discipline suggests a code of conduct prescribed for the best interests of the individual and of the classroom or the society in which he or she lives. Between self-discipline and imposed discipline are numerous choices.

FIGURE 10–1   A Continuum of Classroom Management Systems

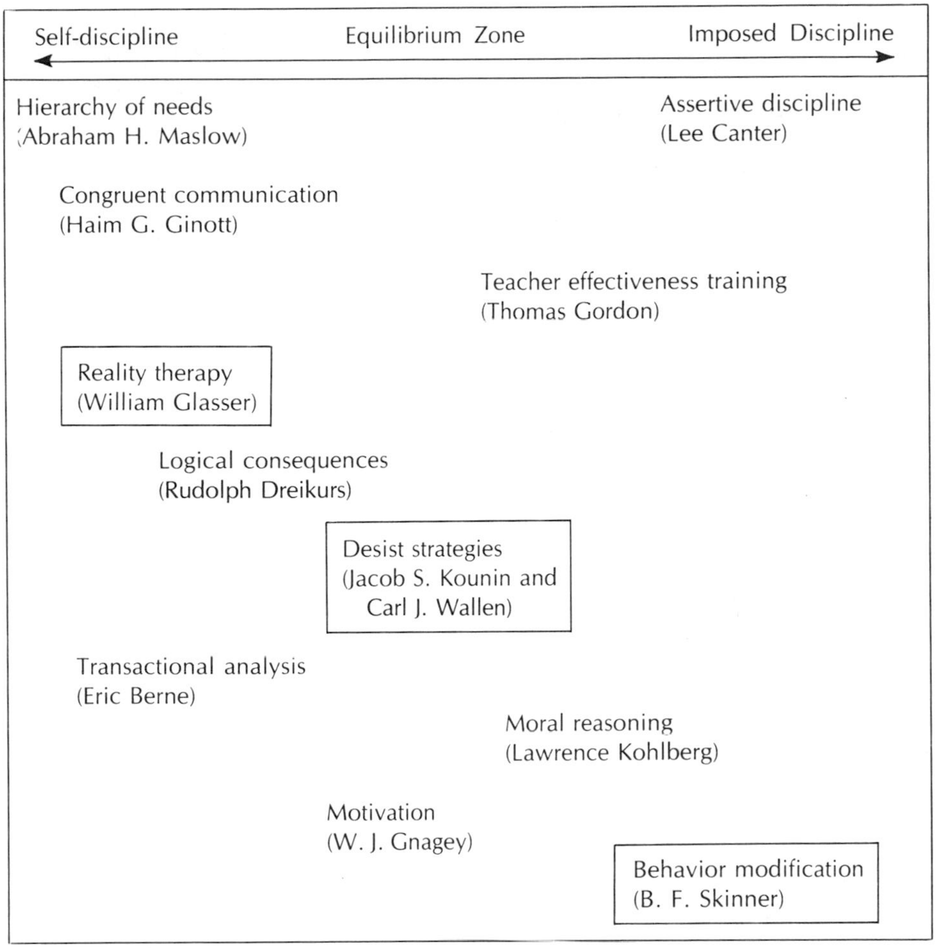

| Self-discipline | Equilibrium Zone | Imposed Discipline |

Hierarchy of needs
(Abraham H. Maslow)

Assertive discipline
(Lee Canter)

Congruent communication
(Haim G. Ginott)

Teacher effectiveness training
(Thomas Gordon)

Reality therapy
(William Glasser)

Logical consequences
(Rudolph Dreikurs)

Desist strategies
(Jacob S. Kounin and
Carl J. Wallen)

Transactional analysis
(Eric Berne)

Moral reasoning
(Lawrence Kohlberg)

Motivation
(W. J. Gnagey)

Behavior modification
(B. F. Skinner)

Hundreds of books have been written on the various classroom management choices that teachers have. To provide you with a quick look at some of them, we show (Figure 10–1) a continuum with self-discipline and imposed discipline as the two extremes. We do not discuss eight of the current systems; however, three management strategies that lie between the two end points are discussed in depth. These strategies are desist strategies, reality therapy, and behavior modification. Desist strategies and behavior modification focus on imposed discipline, and reality therapy is a self-discipline approach. We select these three systems for fuller development because they tend to be "generic" (i.e., other systems have been initiated or developed from them).

If you are interested in any system we do not discuss, please refer to the reference list at the end of the chapter.

DESIST STRATEGIES

Of the three classroom management techniques we shall discuss, the desist strategy is the most traditional. (The term is derived from "desist techniques" suggested by Jacob S. Kounin and Paul V. Gump [1959].) The technique of desist strategies is a means of systematically communicating the teacher's desire to stop or alter the behavior of a student. The communication may be accomplished by a command such as "Stop that!" or by a glance or by a movement made near the student.

The application of desist strategies is related to the teacher's power and authority. The teacher's power resides in the definition of the role of teacher, which is traditionally determined by the expectations of various segments of society. Accordingly, the teacher's authority is defined as the legitimate use of power as recognized by society—the parents, the school administration, the courts, the legislatures, and the students. However, not everyone will recognize the teacher's authority all the time. There always will be occasional instances when the teacher's authority is not respected. In such cases, the teacher's authority is often characterized by the power to reward and punish.

Desist strategies offer a systematic framework for applying the teacher's authority to maintain group norms. The technique of desist strategies involves two basic concepts. First, there are three levels of force dimension—low, moderate, and high. Second, there are two types of communication-of-force dimension—public and private. It is also important to note that desist strategies require quick decision-making.

In dealing with classroom management problems, it is usually best to use a low rather than a high level of force, and it is always better to use a private rather than a public form of communication. However, there will be occasional situations in which a high-level, public dimension is the most appropriate. A classroom fight may be an example of such a situation. However, in the vast majority of cases, the teacher will find it best to use *low-level, private* forms of desist strategies to handle the "normal" classroom management problems. Desist strategies are further explained in Tables 10–1 and 10–2, which present sets of operationally defined terms and their appropriate teacher behaviors.

The concept of "desist strategy" is summarized in two principles that were first described by Carl J. Wallen in 1968. They are as follows:

Principle 1

If a classroom activity is about to occur and standards of student behavior and teacher expectations have not previously been established, the teacher should specify expectations and behavioral standards prior to beginning the activity.

TABLE 10–1 Examples of Desist Strategies

Level of Force Dimension		
Level of Force	Definition	Desist Strategy
Low	Nonverbal, a signal or movement	A glance, shaking of head, moving over to child unobtrusively in the instructional activity
Moderate	Verbal, conversational, no coercion	Appeal to child to act reasonably, remove disturbing objects, command the child to stop
High	Verbal and nonverbal, changed voice pitch, may use coercion	Raise voice and command child to stop, remove the child from group, threaten, punish, physically restrain

Public-Private Dimension		
Type	Definition	Desist Strategy
Public	Intended to be noticed by most of the children in a class	Acting and/or speaking in a way which commands attention
Private	Intended to be noticed only by small groups of children	Using unobtrusive actions or moving close to a child when speaking

From Carl J. Wallen, *Establishing Teaching Principles in the Area of Classroom Management* (Interim Report, Project No. 5-0916). Monmouth, Oregon, Teaching Research, January, 1968, Appendix A, p. 15.

Principle 2

If in a continuing activity a student or group of students behave in a manner contrary to specific expectations, the teacher should use a desist strategy aimed at reaching the level of expectations while causing the least possible disruption to the classroom setting.

It is important for the teacher to specify the behavior that students should exhibit during a particular activity. During a test, for example, the teacher may decide that the students should speak out if they raise their hands and are called on. During a construction period, the students may be permitted to speak quietly. The verbal statement of the appropriate social behavior is the social standard or norm. The social standard may be established directly by the teacher telling the students what is expected of them, or the standard may be established indirectly by the teacher leading a discussion on the appropriate behavior for a specified activity.

TABLE 10–2   Desist Strategies in Combination

Desist Strategies in Two Dimensions: Level of Force and Public-Private

1. Glance

Low Level—Private (Glance)	*Low Level—Public (Glance)*
Teacher shakes head so only one or two other children notice the action.	Teacher shakes head dramatically so most of class notices the action.

2. Appeal

Moderate Level—Private (Appeal)	*Moderate Level—Public (Appeal)*
Teacher moves close to child, asks child to act reasonably, and uses voice and manner so only one or two other children notice the action.	Teacher asks children to act reasonably in a manner which most of the class notices.

3. Threat

High Level—Private (Threat)	*High Level—Public (Threat)*
Teacher moves close to child, tells what will happen if misbehavior continues, and uses voice and manner so only one or two other children notice the action.	Teacher tells what will happen if misbehavior continues, uses a loud and commanding voice which most of the class notices.

From Carl J. Wallen, *Establishing Teaching Principles in the Area of Classroom Management* (Interim Report, Project No. 5-0916). Monmouth, Oregon, Teaching Research, January, 1968, Appendix A, pp. 15–16.

Classroom Regulations

With the principles of desist strategy used as guidelines, five elements have been identified as important when establishing classroom regulations. First, students are, for the most part, reasonable human beings who are anxious to make their classrooms cooperative and pleasant places in which to learn. By enlisting student aid in the formulation of classroom regulations, the teacher helps to prevent classroom management problems in two ways: (1) students tend to have a greater interest in the maintenance of these regulations when they have had a part in generating them; and (2) they have a greater understanding of the need for and the meaning of regulations when they help to develop them.

Second, classroom regulations must be stated with as much clarity as possible so that the students are not confused about what the regulations are or what they mean.

Third, classroom regulations must be maintained with justice by the teacher. If the regulation was worth establishing, it should be worth maintaining with consistency for each student throughout the school year.

Fourth, classroom regulations should be used to establish a classroom routine. When regulations are stated with clarity and maintained with fairness, students soon realize what is expected of them in the classroom without being constantly reminded and nagged by the teacher. When a routine is established in the classroom, deviations from the routine are more obvious and, therefore, more controllable in terms of classroom management techniques.

Fifth and finally, the teacher and the class should make as few regulations as possible.

Desist Strategies: Another Look

We should not leave the topic of desist strategies without including a short summary of one of the more important works on the topic. Jacob S. Kounin, as we mentioned previously, coined the term *desist* as a teacher action that stops or alters the behavior of a student. In 1970, Kounin published the results of several experiments that related to group management. He reported that over half (55.2 percent) of the teachers' perceived student "misbehaviors" could be categorized as talking or noise behaviors. In addition, nontask misbehaviors—for example, gum chewing—accounted for 17.2 percent of the total, and all other deviations—being late, not having homework, moving about the room without permission—accounted for the remainder of the misbehaviors (27.6 percent). According to Kounin's categories, the bulk of student misbehaviors would be rated as "low" level in significance.

Yet, when teachers were given the options of punishing, providing a suitable desist, or prescribing another form of productive activity in reaction to these misbehaviors, over half of the teachers' reactions were classified as high-level, public-dimension desists (see Table 10–2). The interesting, or perhaps sad, finding in Kounin's study is that in 92 percent of the cases, the teachers could give *no reasons* why the student misbehavior was perceived as being bad. Furthermore, in 95.6 percent of the cases, the teacher never provided the class with any knowledge of the expected standards (Kounin, 1970). This, of course, is an indictment of the teacher, not of the students.

The "Ripple Effect"

In another study, Kounin noted the effects on the class of the way in which teachers either punished students or provided desists when a student or group misbehaved. After observing students in kindergarten through college, he collected data based on experimental conditions to illustrate that the manner in which the teacher provided a desist had, in fact, an accompanying effect on all of the class members. This Kounin called the "ripple effect." As students observe the teacher confronting a student for apparent misbehavior, there is a tendency for all other class members also to be adversely affected. Kounin reported that the nature of the angry desist did not motivate the other students to behave better or to attend to the task; rather, the other students became anxious, restless, and uninvolved.

Lest it seem that all is lost because of teacher insensitivity, Marvin L. Grantham and Clifton S. Harris, Jr. (1976) reported that an entire elementary school faculty in Dallas* decided to improve student discipline by determining that they, the faculty, were part of the problem. The faculty took action and decided on a course of inservice education. Within one year, a marked *decrease* in discipline problems resulted, while some student gains in standardized tests were being achieved.

In summary, the use of desist strategies is predicated on prudence and wisdom. When dealing with classroom management problems, it is usually best to use a low rather than a high level of force, and it is generally better to use a private rather than a public form of communication. However, there will be occasional situations in which a high-level, public dimension is the most appropriate. A classroom fight or other life-threatening situations are examples of such a use. In the vast majority of cases, the teacher's use of low-level, private desists will handle the classroom problem. The indiscriminate use of power will render any classroom management technique ineffectual.

REALITY THERAPY

The theories behind desist strategies are well documented and are based on the research of social scientists. The principles are widely used by the typical teacher, although many teachers may never have heard of the term *desist strategy*. Reality therapy, the second classroom management strategy, is also familiar to educators. In brief, reality therapy is *an approach that helps individuals to take responsibility* for solving their own problems. As humans, we have the ability to determine our own personal destinies. We are not uncontrolled victims of circumstances. Glasser (1965) wrote that reality therapy is a "therapy that leads all patients toward reality, toward grappling successfully with the tangible and intangible aspects of the real world." As a technique, reality therapy requires positive, genuine, human involvement in which persons recognize their own realities and begin to reshape their own behaviors to meet selected needs.

Basic Principles

Now that we have discussed the rationale of reality therapy, let us turn to the principles of the technique as they apply to classroom management. A basic tenet is that teachers must avoid labeling inappropriate behaviors with some interesting-sounding tag—for example, paranoia, schizophrenia, or character behavior disorders. Also, examination of family history or of past case histories is unessential. The main premise is that an individual must perceive his or her own failures and must be personally responsible for becoming successful.

---

*Dallas as a city has been known, in educational circles, to mete out tough corporal punishment. See "Bottoms Up in Big D," *Newsweek,* May 17, 1971, p. 99.

Principle 1

The first principle of reality therapy is human involvement. All the other principles of reality therapy are derived from the basic concept of involvement. Essentially, Glasser (1965) notes that we are always involved with other people—at the very minimum, one and, ideally, with many more. At all times in our lives, there must be at least one person who cares about us and for whom we care. The concerned teacher's objective is to be involved enough to give the pupil the confidence needed to make new and lasting self-involvements both with the teacher and with others.

In the classroom setting, the strategy involves devising a structure that facilitates teacher-student and student-student involvement. Management problems can then be resolved in ways that express care and concern, primarily on the part of the teacher, with direct student involvement.

Principle 2

The next step is to examine current behaviors. The traditional form of psychotherapy involves a detailed examination of past behaviors and of feelings about current behaviors. This activity is irrelevant in reality therapy, which holds that people avoid facing present behavior by emphasizing past experiences that have caused the behavior or their feelings about their current behavior. While reality therapy does not deny emotions and their importance, successful therapy depends on focussing on current behaviors—on what the student *is doing now.*

To apply the second principle, the teacher should ask a misbehaving student what he or she is doing. Typically, teachers tend to recapitulate previous activities, such as in the comment: "Well, that is the seventh time today that you've interrupted without raising your hand." Rather, the teacher should ask, "What are you doing?" Note that the emphasis is on the *you,* so that there can be no misinterpretations as to who is responsible for the misbehavior.

Principle 3

Reality therapy requires the student to examine his or her current behavior, to evaluate it, and to make a determination that the current behavior is not beneficial or appropriate for self-needs. In terms of classroom management problems, this means that the student who is constantly misbehaving must be made to discuss his or her current behavior and to come to the conclusion that another type of behavior would be more beneficial or appropriate. Also, the student is simply labeled as responsible or irresponsible if he or she does not come to grips with inappropriate behavior. This point is very important. The teacher does not evaluate decisions or label the behaviors as good or bad but, without moralizing, simply indicates whether they are appropriate or inappropriate.

Principle 4

Once a student makes a self-judgment about his or her behavior, the teacher must assist that student in making realistic plans to change that behavior. A failing person not only needs success but also needs to take small, individually positive steps to attain success.

For example, a student who never studies should not be expected to study two hours a night. Realistically, fifteen-minute sessions a few times a week are more appropriate. Be certain that the remedial plans are realistic in terms of the individual who makes and must implement them. This is a particularly important principle for teachers, because reality therapy, as applied to the classroom situation, involves an emphasis on student contracting. The student, with the help of the teacher, develops a plan to help meet personal or educational goals; the student individually and responsibly implements this plan under the teacher's guidance. It is essential that the teacher take great care in helping the student to develop realistic plans that will allow small, individual steps that can be successfully completed.

We must reemphasize the fact that success is essential for reality therapy to be effective. In far too many classrooms, the teachers are not fully aware that success leads to success. Many teachers tend to be negative toward their students—that is, they do not expect their students to succeed—and, true to expectations, their students do not. Reality therapy requires a positive perspective, even though some failures may occur when the technique is used.

Principle 5

Reality therapy demands a commitment from the student. After a reasonable plan has been devised, it must be carried out. In terms of the classroom setting, Glasser's reality therapy most frequently requires that the student prepare a plan in writing and sign it as a means of increasing personal motivation to maintain and fulfill the plan. This kind of commitment intensifies and accelerates the behavior of the student, and it offers the student a concrete way of demonstrating his or her commitment to a change in behavior. It also helps to provide a means of measuring success and individual responsibility.

Principle 6

There are no excuses when the student fails to change in behavior. The student has expressed a commitment in the form of a written plan and cannot be excused for not fulfilling the plan. However, it is essential that both the teacher and the student be willing to reexamine the plan constantly and to renew or change the commitment if the original plan is in some way inadequate. This does not mean that the teacher excuses the failure of the student. When failure occurs, it must be mutually recognized that the responsibility lies with the student either for not having fulfilled the plan or for not having planned appropriately in the first place.

Note well that this technique places the onus of responsibility on the student and not on the teacher. Too often we believe that it is the teacher's responsibility to make students "behave." The tenets of reality therapy reverse this role. The teacher must be a helper to the student; the teacher's praise of student success increases the involvement between the teacher and the student and leads to more responsible student behaviors (William Glasser, *Impact,* 1972).

Principle 7

The final principle in reality therapy is the absence of punishment. Glasser believes that punishment hinders the personal involvement that is essential between the teacher and the student. The purpose of punishment is to change an individual's behavior through fear or pain. Glasser observes that punishment has proved ineffective; if it had been effective, we would not have so many failures in our present society.

Reality Therapy and the Entire Class

Thus far, the emphasis has been on reality therapy as an individually oriented management technique. However, reality therapy also may be applied to an entire class through the use of classroom meetings. These are discussed so that you may observe a logical extension of the technique to large groups.

Social Problem-Solving Meeting

As the name implies, this is a meeting that basically is concerned with the students' social school behaviors. To implement this type of meeting, the teacher should observe the following guidelines:

1. All group and individual problems in the class are eligible for discussion.
2. The session focuses on solving the problem, not on finding faults or specifying punishment.
3. Meetings are conducted with all individuals positioned in a tight circle to foster interaction.

Glasser (1969) provides the following illustration of such a social problem-solving meeting.

Students in an eighth grade class were truant at an increasing rate as the warm days came in the spring term. A social problem-solving meeting was called and the teacher asked if everyone was there. In discussion, the class admitted that eight of thirty-five were absent. The class was then asked why they were absent. Most student responses included terms such as *dull* and *boring*. With the "problem" exposed, the teacher then pressed for a solution.

The students were asked to make value judgments on the worthiness of school. They were asked to sign a statement promising to come to school the next day. Only one-third of the class would sign. Next they were asked to sign a paper stating that they would not sign the promise. This was to cause the students to make some type of commitment. Once again, one-third of the students would sign, leaving one-third who would sign nothing. This last group was then asked to allow their names to be placed on a paper stating that they would not sign anything, and to this they agreed. There was little improvement in truant behavior as a result of this meeting; however, the problem became a principal topic of general class discussion and set the stage for additional meetings that eventually resolved the problem. In this particular case, the general class discussion eventually may focus on the teacher's responsibility for stimulating student interest through a variety of teaching strategies and materials. Would a written promise or contract on the teacher's part be appropriate according to the principles of reality therapy?

There are many individual and group techniques that teachers can use in implementing a program of reality therapy. However, there is one requirement that is essential to all of these techniques: being involved to the degree demanded by reality therapy. Although it is not easy to function according to the principles of reality therapy, it can be done. It takes training, patience, and, above all, perseverance on the part of teachers.

Teacher Involvement

As Glasser (*Impact,* 1972) wrote, "We begin and end with involvement."* Most teachers would immediately retort, "We're involved up to our ears." The problem with the latter type of involvement is that the teachers really mean that they interact with the class members but usually do not get involved. This is because it is generally much easier to send a student who appears to need help to a counselor or to the vice-principal. In this manner, the teacher avoids involvement as it applies to reality therapy.

To encourage a sense of involvement and responsibility, the student who is removed from the class because of inappropriate behavior is helped to return by having him or her follow a definite procedure. The student is required first to identify the exact personal behaviors that were the cause of exclusion from the class. Next, the student is asked to develop a written plan to get back into the class. If the student has trouble developing this type of plan, the teacher or administrator helps with an acceptable plan. This is a very important step that teachers traditionally and inappropriately avoid with such glib remarks as, "Well, it's up to you!" Finally, the student is required to take the written plan back to the class meeting and to ask the class for help in reaching a workable solution. According to Glasser, this step is a nonpunitive, problem-solving approach that allows the student

---

*Used with written permission of William Glasser.

to settle grievances in a nonthreatening way while easing interpersonal tensions and enhancing involvement.

What then is teacher involvement? First, it is wanting to work in a personal manner with the individual on behavioral or academic problems. Second, it requires that the teacher remain in a "teacher role," for the teacher is not the student's peer, but a mature and responsible adult. The teacher helps the student to make plans, to carry them out, to revise them, and to strive continually for success. Third, involvement means that the teacher helps the student to become more responsible for individual behavior by having the student constantly state what he or she is doing.

Involvement also means meeting with parents, if possible, and seeking their cooperation. Furthermore, teachers can set up short interviews with other teachers in the school to discuss the welfare of certain students. How many teachers have ever gone to the locker room to talk with the coaches about helping a young man or woman to become more responsible? Involvement means helping the student in every possible way. Does it require too much effort? The answer lies with the teacher, who must decide whether to tolerate inappropriate student behaviors or to try to improve them in a systematic manner.

In conclusion, the basic principle of reality therapy is that each individual is personally responsible for his or her own behavior and improvement. With regard to classroom management, if student behavior is to change, the previously outlined seven principles of reality therapy, which require positive human involvement by both teachers and students, should be followed. As with any management plan, the success or failure of the outcome rests with the teacher's willingness to become involved. Too often we believe that it is the teacher's responsibility to make students "behave." The tenets of reality therapy reverse this role. The teacher must be a helper to the student: the teacher's praise of student success increases the involvement between the teacher and the student and leads to more responsible student behaviors (Glasser, *Impact,* 1972).

BEHAVIOR MODIFICATION

Behavior modification is an imposed-discipline approach to managing both individual and classroom behaviors. We will examine some of the underlying principles of this approach, which has gained support from parents, clinicians, psychologists, counselors, and teachers.

Technically, behavior modification refers to the use of modern learning principles in the design and improvement of educational practice. For our purposes, behavior modification is defined as an approach to education in which instructional procedures are planned, implemented, and modified according to the student's progress toward identified educational or behavioral goals.

Before addressing the principles behind behavior modification, it is important to clarify several issues for the prospective teacher. First, behavior modification, with all its formats, procedures, and contingencies, is often attacked because of its "excess baggage." As teachers often state, "It's just not realistic; it asks too much of the teacher." Indeed, teachers, without help, will not be able to implement the extensive charting and interventions that we detail in this chapter. However, experienced teachers will adapt many of the procedures listed here to suit the conditions and constraints of their situations. In other words, if this approach works for you, use it; if parts of it work for you, adapt it; and if none of it works for you, drop it.

Second, the neophyte teacher who goes into the teachers' lounge and announces that he or she is trying behavior modification on a particular student will quickly learn that *all* good teachers have been using this approach for years without benefit of the label. With these ideas in mind, we will move on to the procedures and principles of behavior modification.

The use of behavioral principles necessitates that a rather well-prescribed format be defined. Generally this involves four phases: (Phase 1) obtaining baseline information; (Phase 2) using an intervention phase when the contingencies are changed or manipulated; (Phase 3) conducting a reversal state when the original contingencies are reinstated; and (Phase 4) returning finally to the intervention condition.

Phase 1: Charting Baseline Behaviors

During the baseline period, observations and tabulations of the target behavior (the behavior to be changed, or increased or decreased in frequency) are recorded. At this stage, information is provided on how often the target behavior occurs, when and under which classroom conditions it occurs, and whether or not the problem actually exists. Many times systematic observation reveals that a student who has been labeled as "disruptive" does not exhibit the disruptive behavior more often than do his or her peers.

Data collected during the baseline period are used to determine the effectiveness of the intervention stage that follows. All data are identified and tallied so that an established "rate" may be determined. (See Figure 10–2, which illustrates one example of charting.)

In collecting these data, units of time are employed. The units that are chosen depend on the frequency of behavior. For example, if a response occurs very infrequently, it is not worthwhile to use very short time intervals when determining the frequency of its occurrence. For behaviors that occur frequently, a time sampling of a period of a few minutes can be used. Again, the time intervals depend on the situation. In this type of approach, the observer records the occurrence of the behavior during an established time interval. For example, if the time interval chosen is 10 seconds, the observer takes note during each 10-second period and records the behavior that occurs. The observer also records the consequences of the target behavior. A code system can be utilized so that the recordings can be listed rapidly. For example, you can use codes such as Ti (talking at inappropriate

FIGURE 10–2   Typical Chart Illustrating Student's "Turning in Homework" Behaviors During Four Phases of Behavior Modification Paradigm

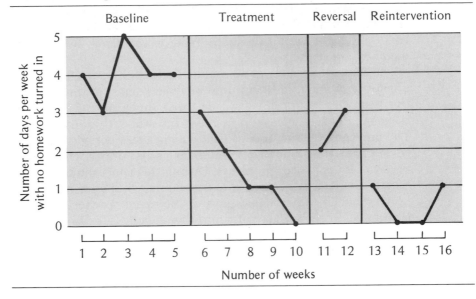

times) and At (attention from the teacher). When these codes are combined, a Ti and At indicate that the student talked and the teacher responded with attention. This type of systematic data collection provides the teacher with information about the frequency of the behavior and the contingencies that produce or maintain it.

For example, assume that the teacher has a student in class who is perceived as having numerous behavioral problems. In such a case, it is difficult and sometimes seems impossible to deal with the situation. The teacher's first step is to choose one target behavior from those identified and to focus attention on it. In this instance, the student talks to his or her neighbors during class activities, and this behavior appears to be excessive and to interfere with the attending behaviors of the other students involved. It can be assumed that the student is not talking out of turn all of the time, so the teacher's task is to determine the exact amount of talking time involved and how much of the time is spent in this inappropriate behavior.

The teacher begins by constructing a chart and simply records on it each time the behavior occurs within a predetermined time span, such as 10 minutes. If the time spent in the actual behavior is important, then an indication in seconds or minutes should be made. This, of course, requires more observer attention plus the use of a watch. The chart may be divided into 5- or 10-minute periods or into class periods, whichever is more convenient for recording and analyzing the behavior.

The chart should show a pattern of when the defined behavior occurs at the end of three or four days. The chart should be studied carefully because the behavior may be demonstrated only at specific times during the day. In our example, the chart may show that the student talks out of turn most frequently during the study period when the class is required to do silent reading. The problem, then, is limited to a specific behavior at a specific time and is now much more readily corrected by various behavior modification strategies.

The chart also serves as a baseline that will help in choosing an appropriate strategy and in determining the effectiveness of the strategy chosen. If the behavior occurs only two or three times during silent reading, the teacher may select ways to increase the student's ability to read silently. The day can be structured so that during these periods the teacher is positioned near the student to administer verbal praise when the appropriate behavior (silent reading) occurs. During this time, the teacher continues to record the student's behavior to determine whether or not the intervention is effective. If, after a few days of increased teacher attention, there is a decrease in the number of times the student talks to neighbors during a silent reading period, the teacher can assume that the strategy is having a positive effect.

Phase 2: Intervention or Experimental Phase

Once the specific behaviors have been identified and their frequency charted, a plan is then devised for changing the behaviors in some desired direction. In most cases, the teacher will try to reinforce an appropriate behavior while ignoring or not responding to the inappropriate ones.

Often, student problem behaviors are followed by more attention than usual from the teacher or peers; if a student shows isolate behavior, for example, the teacher may attempt to cajole or persuade that student to cooperate with other class members. During the intervention phase, the teacher can test the reliability of the strategy by reversing the contingencies. This means that the subject will no longer receive attention for working in isolation but will be given attention only when there is observable interaction with others. If the strategy is correct, the subject will show an increase in interaction and a decrease in isolate behavior.

The results of an initial strategy will be shown to be valid or invalid during the intervention phase of the behavioral model. Sometimes verbal reinforcers are adequate to modify the subject's behavior. The teacher often must experiment in order to determine the appropriate set of reinforcers that requires the least effort to change the subject's behavior. In some cases, there must be visible or material reinforcers such as stars on the student's papers, the student's name on the class "honor list," tokens, pencils, or special privileges given to the student. Whatever the reward, it is absolutely imperative that it follow the appropriate behavior immediately.

The use of reinforcers is a critical component for behavior modification. Teachers often use the same set of reinforcers over an extended period of time and then find that they lose their efficacy. After studying this problem,

Roger Addison and Donald T. Tosti (1979) compiled a system and a list of reinforcers that can be applied with various motivational strategies in an education environment. The reinforcers are

1. recognition
2. tangible rewards
3. classroom learning activities
4. classroom and school responsibilities
5. status indicators
6. incentive feedback
7. personal activities
8. social activities
9. relief from aversive policies or procedures
10. relief from aversive classroom environments

Addison and Tosti cautioned that reinforcers are very personal, and a teacher may have to try various reinforcers with a specific student before finding the most powerful one. Obviously there is no one universal reinforcer.

Phase 3: Reversal Phase

For most teachers, there is no further class manipulation once the appropriate reward or reinforcer is determined. However, to follow the behavior modification paradigm completely, the teacher should revert from phase 2 conditions to those that took place during original baseline conditions. This requirement is often resisted by teachers, since it means returning to the original undesirable condition. But how else will one know whether or not the condition instituted in phase 2 is really effective? By reverting to the previous phase, data are obtained to demonstrate whether or not the change in behavior is due to the intervening action.

As with phases 1 and 2, in phase 3 data are consistently tabulated so that the behavioral patterns are quickly discernible. Phase 3 usually is conducted only long enough to effect a reversal of behavior to the baseline type. When such behavior has been observed, it is time for phase 4.

Phase 4: Reinstating the Intervention Conditions

The final stage reinstates the conditions used during phase 2. If the intervention caused a change in behaviors during the second phase, it should do so again during this final phase. However, if there is no change toward the desired behaviors, then it means that you were just lucky in phase 2, and you will have to start all over again.

One variation that may be applied in lieu of moving to phases 3 and 4 (reversal and reinstatement) is to use a multiple series of baselines. This technique follows the same format as noted above, but does not use the reversal and reinstatement components. Instead the student is "charted" in several or possibly all classes, e.g., math, science, physical education, art. The intervention or reinforcement is applied in only one of the classes while baseline data collection is maintained in the remaining classes. If a change in behavior takes place in the reinforced, but not in other classes, then the other teachers might begin that intervention to change behavior in their classes also. However, if there is a change (in the direction desired by the teachers) in behavior in all classes, it may be concluded that reinforcement in the one class was adequate enough to alter the student's behavior.

Intervention may also be applied to other inappropriate behaviors. The math teacher might reinforce the completing of assignments; the science teacher might simultaneously reinforce "attending" behaviors. With the participation of the key people with whom the student interacts (other teachers, counselor, parents), the identification and implementation of a plan of reinforcement is assured.

Reinforcement. When using behavior modification in the classroom the teacher will be faced with the problem of deciding what reward or reinforcement to use. Teachers in the elementary grades can use extra recess time, library time, or simply some form of "do what you like" to reward individual or class behavior. These techniques have been widely cited. But a teacher in the usual middle school or senior high school does not have the flexibility in scheduling students because of fixed time frames in which teachers operate—the 55-minute period being the common one. This means that many of the rewards or reinforcers must be intrinsic rather than extrinsic. Given these restrictions, the following studies may suggest several general principles for the selection of reinforcement strategies.

In his 1959 study, David Premack observed that the individual's or group's preferred activities can be used to reinforce their less preferred activities. This means that if the less preferred act is completed, then the student is permitted to perform the more preferred behavior.

Examples of the principle are: (1) allowing students to talk to each other for the last 2 or 3 minutes of the class period after the entire class has been quiet or attending for some specified period of time; and (2) allowing students to play "rock" music on Friday for 15 minutes *if* all of the specified work is accomplished in both quantity and quality by Wednesday of the same week.

In summary, then, the teacher observes individuals and the class to determine the kinds of activities that are most preferred by the students. (We assume that school work, school behaviors, and the like are less preferred by them.) Then the teacher systematically uses the more preferred activities to reinforce the less preferred activities.

Charles B. Schultz and Roger H. Sherman (1976) also warned teachers that the preference for a reinforcer should be made "separately for each individual rather than by the a priori judgments of the experimenter." Schultz and Sherman analyzed studies that concerned the selection of student reinforcers by persons who used the social class status of the student as the primary criterion. Teachers, they cautioned, tend to think that lower socioeconomic class students need material things as reinforcers, while middle and upper class students respond better to nonmaterial reinforcers. Their study showed this generalization to be erroneous!

These techniques have been developed because traditional methods of dealing with children have been relatively ineffective. S. H. Herman and J. Tramontana (1971), for example, found that instructions alone were ineffective in controlling behavior. Instructions were found to be good for prompting students for very specific behaviors, but reinforcement was needed to maintain it. The findings of Margaret L. Cooper et al. (1970) suggest that for effective classroom management, teachers need some experiences in reinforcement techniques.

Principles for Effective Classroom Management

There are several general principles that can help the teacher to apply behavior modification in a classroom situation.

Accentuate the Positive

Schools have been criticized for being too "unpleasant," and teachers, for being far too negative toward students. To change this image, the teacher must praise students, even if it is for the most inconsequential matter. Admittedly, it may be very difficult to be supportive of a student who continually disrupts the classroom, but it has been frequently demonstrated that simply admonishing a student will not reduce the inappropriate behavior. Praising some positive aspect of the student's behavior is more likely to bring about change.

How does the teacher use different forms of praise or social reinforcement? There are verbal, nonverbal, and tactile reinforcers. For example, there are positive verbal praise terms such as:

All right	Far out	Marvelous	Right on
Awesome	Fine	Mighty fine	Royal
Beautiful	Great	Neat	Splendid
Boss	Heavy	Nice work	Super
Clever	Ideal	Nifty	Terrific
Darn good	Just great	Oh, boy	Unreal
Dynamite	Keen	Pleasurable	Very interesting
Excellent	Keep it up	Quite nice	A winner
Fabulous	Lovely	Really great	Wonderful
Fantastic			Wow

Nonverbal praise can be provided by the following actions:

Laughing	Nodding approval	Signaling by
Looking with interest	Pointing with a smile	lifting palms
Moving toward student	Raising the eyebrows	Smiling
		Winking

Identify Productive Behavior for the Class

Praise not only reinforces the student at whom it is directed, but also helps to provide the entire class with an explicit model of what is expected. To be sure, public praise can be embarrassing as well as reinforcing. The teacher must learn what technique reinforces each student.

Starting Small

In most cases, adolescents view major changes in behavior as being unachievable. If a student hands in about 25 percent of the required homework, there is little chance that reinforcement will cause him or her to produce 100 percent of the work right away. Given this situation, the teacher should establish a definite contingency schedule and should make a behavior contract with the student. The student may complete two of five assignments in the first week. If so, the teacher should move up the requirement to three of five assignments for the next week. In terms of successive approximations to the desired behavior, it is important to remember that the student probably did not reach the present level of academic deficiency in just one giant step. Therefore, the teacher should not expect to remedy the problem in one great leap. Small initial steps should be followed by an increase in the quantity or the quality until the student reaches the criterion measure agreed on. This requires patience on the teacher's part and constant positive feedback to the student.

Being Consistent

As the teacher begins to use some form of behavior modification in the classroom, whether on an individual or group basis, teacher behaviors should be modified so that they are consistent and predictable. If teachers remain consistent in their responses to student stimuli, then the probability of predicting the reactions of class members will increase.

Contingency Contracting

In many cases, the teacher and students may decide to work out a formal agreement in a negotiated "contingency contract." The teacher establishes the work standards (or behaviors to be shaped), while the student prepares a written statement. Both the performance and the reward are specified. "Get twenty-five of the problems correct in the next three assignments and you'll be able to listen to your pocket radio with ear plugs for 5 minutes during the study portion of class each day."

The contract should be agreed on by both the teacher and the student. Such contracts are limited only by the participants' ingenuity. University courses are taught with great success by contingency contracting, as are courses at all levels of the education continuum.

Ignoring the "Rabbit Ears" Syndrome

In the sports world, performers at all levels, from the little league to the big leagues, are subjected to ridicule from the fans. Players who get upset by snide comments are said to have "rabbit ears." The same term can be applied to the vast majority of school teachers. They respond to almost every nonproductive comment made by the students. As a matter of record, students test nearly every teacher to determine whether or not they can annoy him or her. Although it is very difficult to do so initially, ignoring behavior that does not threaten the learning environment (for example, quiet chatter, a passed note) in the classroom can be a very effective way of discouraging such behavior.

Specificity and Clarity of Directions

The giving of directions is a critical part of the teacher's function. Whether the directions primarily concern instructions or classroom management, it is essential that directions be given clearly and succinctly and, most importantly, that their orientation be positive. Directions given to disruptive students—such as "Stop that" or "Cut that out"—omit the most important part of the teacher's objective: *What is the student to do after he or she "stops" or "cuts out" the behaviors that are disruptive?* It is much more accurate and meaningful to give directions to students in a positive form. It makes much more sense to stop disruptive behavior by providing the student with a constructive alternative. For example, the teacher may suggest that the student return to work or may provide some instructionally related activity that replaces the disruptive behavior. This approach both changes behaviors and directs students to a positive activity.

Applying the Technique: Group Management

Techniques used to help individuals to demonstrate more appropriate behaviors can be applied to class groups as well. One of the most comprehensive classroom applications of behavior modification has been instituted in the "programmed learning classroom" at Rainier School in Washington State (Birnbrauer et al., 1965). The classroom was established for two purposes: (1) to develop programmed instructional materials in academic subjects; and (2) to develop procedures based on reinforcement principles to promote and strengthen motivation, good study habits, cooperation, perseverance, and concentration.

Eight boys were selected as members of the "programmed learning classroom." Their chronological ages ranged from 9 to 13 years, and all students had extremely low academic achievement scores. The teachers were instructed to ignore instances of inappropriate behavior and to reinforce desired behavior or approximations of it. Praise and token stars were used to reinforce good school work. The stars were saved in booklets and exchanged for various gift items or privileges. Within five months, the researchers found that seven of the eight boys could be described as good students. They learned to study independently for longer periods and accomplished more work. In addition, disruptive behaviors were virtually eliminated.

S. I. Sulzbacher and J. E. Houser (1970) reported success in eliminating one undesirable behavior in the classroom—the use of the "naughty finger." This behavior disrupted the class, since students laughed and continued to make verbal references to the incident. The entire class was involved, so the teacher used a group contingency approach. The teacher announced a time reward system, whereby free time would be reduced every day by 1 minute whenever the behavior occurred or if anyone mentioned it. The frequency of the behavior decreased drastically.

The advantage of group contingency methods is that group pressures to reduce deviant behaviors are exerted by peers. Positive reinforcement no longer accompanies the occurrence of the inappropriate behaviors. In fact, such behaviors are subsequently discouraged or negatively reinforced by other students.

We have already illustrated how this technique can be applied to non-attending class behaviors. With this technique, the class is rewarded if every member attends to the task for the specified period. If one student displays disruptive behavior, then the entire class loses the reward. But when all students display the desired behavior, then the entire class shares the reward. It is important in these situations that the duration of the behavior required to be rewarded is short enough at first to ensure success. Furthermore, the behavior must be within the limits of the individual's ability. The requirements should be made progressively more difficult with time. This approach can be highly successful, especially if the teacher explains it to the class in a positive manner. Often, the problem student will begin to receive praise from his classmates and to feel important. In many instances, a group consequence technique, in which the individual earns rewards for peers as well as personally, is more effective than self-consequences, in which only the individual is rewarded, in controlling a student's disruptive classroom behavior.

Summary

Behavior modification is a viable alternative with a set of strategies that can be used in establishing effective classroom management. Many teachers, principals, and counselors are outwardly hostile to the behavior modification model because it is allegedly "unhumanistic." To be sure, there is behaviorism and there are behaviorists. They are not one and the same. The classroom teacher may select components of the behavioral approach to classroom management, yet retain a humanistic rather than behavioristic approach to learning and students. If the ultimate goal of classroom management is to change behavior and if behavior modification will accomplish the goal with the least amount of effort, then behavior modification is a very humane contribution to the mental health of all concerned.

We recall the story told by Albert Rosenfeld (1974) about a junior high school in Visalia, California. The teachers were complimenting one of the special education teachers on the great job that had been done in improving the behavior and scholarship of the problem students. Finally, the special education teacher confessed that he had taught his charges to use behavior modification on their teachers. The students used positive reinforcement to shape teacher behaviors and they, in turn, received higher quality teaching and better treatment from the teaching staff. Maybe that is the answer—teach the students how to apply behavior modification.

TEACHING AND DISCIPLINE

Desist strategies, reality therapy, and behavior modification have been presented as separate techniques for successful classroom management. The purist may refrain from mixing these techniques and may remain successful as a classroom manager. However, one technique should not be isolated from another. The classroom teacher should be able to use any and all strategies that personally suit his or her teaching style and learning goals. Teachers must decide very early in their professional careers what classroom management strategies they will feel comfortable with—emotionally and educationally—in the implementation and enforcement of classroom management strategies.

There are common elements in any management approach that suggest a systematic way of dealing with instructional and behavioral problems in the classroom. The following discussion may prove helpful in deciding on procedures for resolving real and simulated classroom management problems such as those listed in Table 10–3.

Preventing Discipline Problems

If the teacher is not faced with discipline problems, much more time is left for teaching and learning. The first step in preventing discipline problems is preparation. The teacher should think of possible problem areas and situations and devise a systematic procedure for removing the problem or dealing with the situation when it arises. As previously stated, teachers, either because of their lack of preparation or their incorrect reaction to a possible problem, can create discipline situations. In many cases, an alternative approach or sometimes no reaction at all on the part of the teacher will diffuse a problem. Organization and thoughtful preparation are the keys.

Sharing Responsibility with Students

It has been said that today's young people will not accept responsibility. We believe, however, that this age-old criticism of our younger generation is not completely justified. The easiest solution to a lack of student acceptance of responsibility and classroom discipline is for the teacher to give students

TABLE 10–3 Selected Problems Associated with Classroom Management

Problems of Motivation

1. Lack of activity for students
2. Apathetic student attitudes
3. Getting all students involved in activities
4. Uninvolved students
5. Daydreaming
6. Lack of success

Instructional problems

1. A need for variety of instructional techniques
2. Goals or objectives not clearly communicated to students
3. Pace too fast or too slow
4. Students who missed the orientation or prerequisite skills
5. Necessary prerequisite entry skills not developed; thus, students fail to achieve stated objectives
6. Students who are upset over their evaluation
7. Students not following directions
8. Failure to complete all assignments

Procedural Problems

1. Unclear assignments given by teacher
2. Moving the class to a different room
3. Establishing a systematic routine for procedural activities
4. Teacher did not reserve a special room or space for the activity
5. Projector or A-V equipment not previously checked out
6. Films not previewed by teacher; thus, inappropriate material presented
7. Necessary materials not available in the room

Disruptive Problems

1. Excessive talking at beginning of class
2. Note passing
3. Cheating
4. Stealing
5. Vandalism
6. Students seeking attention
7. Students arriving late for class
8. Teacher making unenforceable threats
9. Racial tensions
10. Teacher making value judgments about student's dress, home life, or parents
11. Obscene verbal or nonverbal gestures

more responsibility, the logic being that the student is more likely to learn about the obligations of responsibility by exercising it. Children will never learn how to handle money with only a penny in their pocket; there just is not much they can do with it. Thus, the teacher should make his or her students active participants in the dialogue of discipline.

This dialogue on discipline can take many forms: the establishment of

classroom rules and regulations; decisions concerning appropriate consequences for inappropriate behaviors; or the establishment of mutually acceptable behavior contracts. This principle is based on the individual's or
group's right to due process. There are many other rights guaranteed by our
form of government that this principle also seeks to protect (for example,
free speech and the right to assembly).

Solving the Problem

Ninety percent of the problems that occur in the typical classroom will not
be in the behavior problem category. They will be short in duration and will
not interrupt the instructional process. Such strategies as giving verbal and
nonverbal cues to the students will discourage these undesirable behaviors.
However, 10 percent or less of the problems that teachers face will fall into
the discipline problem category. These problems may be rectified by the
teacher's immediate attention (thus interrupting instruction) or may require long-term efforts on the teacher's part. In the latter case, the teacher
should seek the help of other school professionals who are familiar with the
student involved. The counselor is often the first to be consulted and can
inform the teacher of the student's past and present school history. In addition, both current and past teachers of the student—especially those who
have had success with the student—can usually offer insights into successful ways of coping with the student's problem. Gym coaches, teacher aides,
student teachers, and reading, art, media, and special-ed specialists should
not be overlooked.

It is important to remember that teachers should use all available strategies at their disposal prior to turning over a discipline or behavior problem
to a counselor, vice-principal, or principal. The teacher who uses the principal or vice-principal as a threat to make students behave or who sends a
student out of the classroom immediately following a behavior problem is
establishing a routine that suggests that (1) the teacher cannot control his
or her students; (2) the teacher believes a principal has nothing else to do
than to handle behavior problems; and (3) the teacher has little understanding of the principles of classroom management.

ON BEING ECLECTIC

When behavior problems arise, the teacher may wonder which classroom
management strategy is the most effective or whether or not several strategies can be combined successfully. Generally, the strategy that most often
produces the desired results with the lowest expenditure of the teacher's
time and effort is the most effective. *Effective* is a relative term and implies
a continuum of qualities that approximate effectiveness. The term also must
be understood as being "situational": In specific situations with a specific
student, reality therapy may be completely successful, while with other

individuals, desist strategies may be more effective. The teacher must make these observations and must decide on the most suitable course of action.

Classroom management strategies often can be mixed successfully. Although all three techniques are based on different theoretical premises, they are all oriented toward improving behavior in a positive, productive manner. To review, desist strategies systematically communicate the teacher's desire to stop or alter the behavior of a student and are heavily related to the teacher's power and authority. In contrast, reality therapy helps the individual to take responsibility for solving his/her own problems and requires positive, genuine, human involvement on the part of teacher and student. In somewhat of a different vein, behavior modification is an experimental approach to managing both individual and classroom behaviors that uses modern learning principles in the design and improvement of educational practice. In any one classroom, the teacher may find that there are individuals who have experiences that require many diverse management responses. In no case do we imply that the teacher should resort to negative behaviors such as sarcasm or ridicule, which, in our professional opinion, are never appropriate strategies for classroom management.

One last caution should be given on the eclectic approach. The effectiveness of any strategy often depends on the teacher's investment of time and energy and on his or her confidence in the technique. A possible pitfall is the teacher's moving quickly from one technique to another without expending the necessary time and energy. Such efforts are likely to be counterproductive, thus confusing the student and making management problems more severe.

Every teacher must use some type of classroom management system or systems. We have introduced three such systems, all of which tend to be humane. The final selection and implementation of any one strategy or combination of strategies rest solely with the teacher.

OTHER MANAGEMENT CONSIDERATIONS

Behavior problems and the appropriate classroom management strategies are some of the most important considerations in teacher decision-making. However, there are still other requirements that also demand the teacher's attention.

More than two-fifths of this book is devoted to interactive teaching strategies—discussions, inquiry, simulation, and classroom management. As you incorporate the various interactive techniques, you must be aware that they tend to be complex methods and as such the classroom routine changes quite drastically. For example, when using any inquiry strategy, you will find students working on tasks. Some students will be working in pairs, others in small groups, and yet others individually. This format requires far more teacher energy to manage than the class with every student in his or her place. As you use more materials, integrate microcomputers into the program, and establish a complex learning environment, you must also adapt your management styles.

Complex instructional environments require some student autonomy and self-direction. Without these traits the classroom would be chaotic. The complex instructional condition was examined by Elizabeth G. Cohen, Jo-Ann K. Intili, and Susan Hurevitz Robbins (1979). In their analysis, the role of the teacher as classroom manager changes as one evolves from large groups to complex designs. For example, in large groups or with teacher-directed instruction, student supervision tends to be routine with an authority figure (teacher) using rules or desist strategies. However, with complex designs (e.g., inquiry, discussions, or laboratories), the teacher must delegate authority and establish constructive behavior norms. Students are managed through extensive feedback, student-teacher communications, and systematic record keeping. Student cooperation and commitment are essential. Teachers work much harder, plan more thoroughly, and demonstrate greater numbers of interactions when using complex classroom designs.

In addition, we have observed that teachers can establish a positive classroom climate by (1) enriching the room with books, magazines, and wall charts; (2) ordering materials that are durable; (3) allowing some time for student-initiated learning; (4) making efficient transitions between activities; and (5) establishing procedures for classroom routines.

Punishment

Sometimes the school climate is not positive and some form of punishment must be administered. *Loss of privilege* is the most common form, for example, loss of recess, sports pass, or an assembly. *Corporal punishment* is lawful in nearly all states, but it must be administered cautiously. All school districts have a policy on this matter. Generally, *suspensions* are handled by the school principal. *In-school suspensions* are currently very common. This technique removes disruptive students or chronic mischief makers from a class and places them in a special isolated area when they must do their school work.

Expulsions are so serious that they are reserved to the local school board. Expulsion is the "court of last resort" and is administered most prudently.

Referral Agencies

A new teacher must know the school's policy on referral agencies. These include welfare organizations, youth advocacy groups, mental health clinics, juvenile court counselors, and ministers. It is common for teachers to use school-supported services such as counselors, social workers, coaches, special service personnel, and administrators.

All schools have policies relating to the role of the police in the schools and court referral systems. Teachers are not usually associated with these agencies.

Alcohol and Drug Management

The teacher in today's classroom will almost certainly come in contact with drug and alcohol abuse among his or her students. This is an especially difficult issue for the new teacher because of the widespread use of alcohol and drugs on college campuses. For many new teachers, alcohol and drug use is considered to be a question of personal choice and parental responsibility and not community-based law.

However, as a teacher you are responsible for developing and encouraging student understanding and value for our system of government and laws. Your role as teacher demands a high set of ethical standards because the community has given you charge of its youth. Further, professional ethics preclude your support of *student use* of alcohol or illegal drugs.

As a teacher you should watch for the early warning signs of alcohol and drug abuse.

- Sudden behavioral changes—classwork is lost, is not turned in, is copied, or declines in quality
- Attitudinal changes—comments are made to hurt others' feelings, or an "I don't care" demeanor emerges
- School problems—grades decline, difficulties with other teachers and school personnel appear, fights and arguments occur
- Changes in social relationships—new friends are involved in a different social scene
- Self-destructive behavior—student has injuries from falls or fights that he or she has difficulty recounting
- Avoidance—student withdraws or refuses to communicate, spends an inappropriate amount of time in isolated behavior

All teachers must be cautious in handling students suspected of drug or alcohol abuse. An accusation may lead to a lawsuit by the student or the parents of the student. Our advice is to check with school administrators on the accepted protocol for dealing with such problems. The alcohol and drug problem is not simply critical—it is pandemic!

Records Management

Every teacher faces the task of recording grades, attendance, absences, tardies, homework assignments, class participation, disciplinary actions, and other acts of classroom life. Issues of legality, fairness, consistency, and documentation suggest the need for a comprehensive and systematic approach to keeping records.

A major facet of records management is the establishment of a fair and equitable grading policy. You must establish guidelines for standards, quality, late work, missed assignments, bonus work, make-up tests, and class participation. Consistency and reasonableness are two criteria that help one to construct an appropriate grading policy.

Lastly, anecdotal records should be objectively recorded to document classroom incidents such as fights, inappropriate behavior, and cheating. Of course, you should also record student acts of courage, ingenuity, or creativity. These acts should be recorded when they happen. This record provides you with a chronicle of highlights that may provide evidence to support or oppose a student.

The teacher's understanding of these issues and his or her prompt decision when a problem arises help to develop teacher-student rapport and cooperation and to provide a role model for students. Collectively, classroom management considerations, although discussed only briefly, are often critical to the lives and safety of youngsters. The teacher's ability to fulfill these conditions is acquired by on the job training. Perhaps this is the only way the concepts of classroom management truly can be mastered—in a classroom with real students and a teacher who understands the theories and knows how to apply them.

FORMATIVE EVALUATION

Circle the letter in front of the best response to each question or the answer that best completes each statement.

1. Ms. Anderson has been teaching a difficult concept in chemistry, and one student has disrupted the class. What type of meeting would Glasser recommend?
   (a) Social problem-solving
   (b) Educational diagnostic
   (c) Open-ended
   (d) Task-oriented
2. Behavior modification will be effective if the following guideline is followed:
   (a) Work on one behavior at a time.
   (b) Use the same reinforcer for each class member.
   (c) Do not use group pressure.
   (d) Never use negative reinforcement.
3. Regarding discipline or classroom management, the text supports the position that:
   (a) There is one good, acceptable method of maintaining classroom discipline, and teachers should use it.
   (b) Most teachers tend to contribute to the problem.
   (c) There are several techniques that can be appropriately applied.
   (d) Most techniques are not based on any theory; you find out what works for you in practice.
4. Democratic discipline implies that:
   (a) No rules are permissible, for they imply authority and authority has no place in a democratic classroom.

(b) Rule-making should be limited to items that hinge on the state laws.

(c) Rule-making should reflect rational explanations of behavior.

(d) Because the teacher realizes that the students are mere juveniles, he or she makes the rules, which the students must endorse.

5. Teachers are most resistant to what phase of the behavior modification design?
   (a) Intervention phase
   (b) Reinstatement phase
   (c) Baseline phase
   (d) Reversal phase

6. Reality therapy is based on which one of the following assumptions or principles?
   (a) Punishment is an effective reinforcing technique.
   (b) Excuses are never accepted for not reaching goals.
   (c) Children from disadvantaged homes are not responsible for their behavior.
   (d) Remaining distant and objective is important in applying the principles.

7. The concept behind desist strategies is
   (a) Characterized by the teacher's power to reward and punish.
   (b) That a teacher's authority is never challenged.
   (c) One of student self-responsibility.
   (d) Essential to the collection of baseline data for a teacher intervention.

8. According to Wallen's level of force dimension, a "threat" is catagorized as
   (a) Low level of force
   (b) High level of force
   (c) Moderate level of force
   (d) None of the above

9. Which of the following is not an important element in establishing classroom regulations?
   (a) Enlist student aid in formulating classroom regulations.
   (b) Clearly and repeatedly state classroom regulations.
   (c) Provide variety in the classroom by frequent changes in expectations.
   (d) Maintain regulations with justice.

RESPONSES

1. (a)	6. (c)
2. (a)	7. (a)
3. (c)	8. (c)
4. (c)	9. (c)
5. (d)	

REFERENCES

Addison, Roger, and Donald T. Tosti. "Taxonomy of Educational Reinforcement." *Educational Technology* 19:1979, 24–25.

Berne, Eric. *Principles of Group Treatment.* New York: Oxford, 1964.

Birnbrauer, J. S., et al. "Programmed Instruction in the Classroom." In *Case Studies in Behavior Modification,* L. P. Ullmann and L. Kraemer (eds.). New York: Holt, Rinehart and Winston, 1965.

"Bottoms Up in Big D." *Newsweek* 77:1971, 99.

Canter, Lee, and Marlene Canter. *Assertive Discipline: A Take-Charge Approach for Today's Educator.* Los Angeles: Lee Canter and Associates, 1976.

Cohen, Elizabeth G., Jo-Ann K. Intilli, and

Susan Hurvetz Robbins. "Task and Authority: A Sociological View of Classroom Management." In Daniel L. Duke, ed., *Classroom Management*. The Seventy-Eighth Yearbook of the National Society for the Study of Education. Chicago: University of Chicago Press, 1979.

Cooper, Margaret L., Carolyn L. Thomson, and Donald M. Baer. "The Experimental Modification of Teacher Attending Behavior." *Journal of Applied Behavior Analysis* 3:1970, 153–157.

Curwin, Richard L. *The Discipline Book*. Reston, Va.: Reston, Inc., 1980.

Dreeben, Robert. "The School as a Workplace." In *The Second Handbook of Research on Teaching*, R. M. W. Travers (ed.). Chicago: Rand McNally, 1973, pp. 450–473.

Dreikurs, Rudolph. *Psychology in the Classroom*. New York: Harper & Row, 1957.

Dreikurs, Rudolph, and Loren Grey. *A New Approach to Discipline: Logical Consequences*. New York: Hawthorn, 1968.

Gallup, George H. "The 16th Annual Gallup Poll of the Public's Attitude Toward the Public Schools." *Phi Delta Kappan* 66(1):1984, 23–38.

Ginott, Haim G. *Teacher and Child*. New York: Avon, 1972.

Glasser, William. *The Identity Society*. New York: Harper & Row, 1972.

———. *Reality Therapy*. New York: Harper & Row, 1965, p: 6.

———. "Reality Therapy: An Anti-Failure Approach." *Impact* 2:1972, 6–9.

———. *Schools Without Failure*. New York: Harper & Row, 1969.

Gnagey, W. J. *Motivating Classroom Discipline*. New York: Macmillan, 1981.

Gordon, Thomas. *Teacher Effectiveness Training*. New York: Peter H. Wyden, 1974.

Grantham, Marvin L., and Clifton S. Harris, Jr. "A Faculty Trains Itself to Improve Student Discipline." *Phi Delta Kappan* 57:1976, 661–664.

Herman, S. H., and J. Tramontana. "Instructions and Group Versus Individual Reinforcement in Modifying Disruptive Group Behavior." *Journal of Applied Behavior Analysis* 4:1971, 113–120.

Homans, George C. *The Human Group*. New York: Harcourt, Brace, 1950, p. 123.

Johnson, David W. *The Social Psychology of Education*. New York: Holt, Rinehart and Winston, 1970.

Johnson, Lois V., and Mary A. Bany. *Classroom Management*. New York: Macmillan, 1970.

Koenig, Peter. "Glasser the Logician." *Psychology Today* 7:1974, 66–67.

Kohlberg, Lawrence. "The Cognitive-Developmental Approach to Moral Education." *Phi Delta Kappan* 56:1975, 670–677.

———. *Essays on Moral Development (Vol. 1: The Philosophy of Moral Development)*. New York: Harper & Row, 1981.

Kounin, Jacob S. *Discipline and Group Management in Classrooms*. New York: Holt, Rinehart and Winston, 1970, pp. 22–25.

Kounin, Jacob S., and Paul V. Gump, "The Ripple Effect in Discipline." *Educational Digest* 24:1959, 43–45.

Maslow, Abraham H. *Motivation and Personality*. New York: D. Van Nostrand, 1968.

McIntire, Roger W. "Spare the Rod, Use Behavior Mod." *Psychology Today* 4:1970, 42–44.

Premack, David. "Toward Empirical Behavior Laws: 1. Positive Reinforcement." *Psychology Review* 66:1959, 219–233.

Rosenfeld, Albert. "The 'Behavior Mod' Squad." *Saturday Review of the World* 2:1974, 49.

Sanford, Julie P., Edmund T. Emmer, and Barbara S. Clements. "Improving Classroom Management." *Educational Leadership* 40:1983, 56–60.

Schultz, Charles B., and Roger H. Sherman. "Social Class, Development, and Differences in Reinforcer Effectiveness." *Review of Educational Research* 46:1976, 25–59.

Silberman, Charles E. *Crisis in the Classroom*. New York: Random House, 1970.

Skinner, B. F. *Science and Human Behavior*. New York: Macmillan, 1953.

Sulzbacher, S. I., and J. E. Houser. "A Tactic to Eliminate Disruptive Behaviors in the Classroom: Group Contingent Consequences." In *Control of Human Behavior*, R. Ulrich, T. Stachnik, and T. Mabry (eds.) Glenview, Il.: Scott, Foresman, 1970.

Wallen, Carl J. "Establishing Teaching Principles in the Area of Classroom Management." In *Low Cost Instruction Simulation Materials for Teacher Education.* Monmouth, Oregon: Teaching Research, 1968. (U.S. Department of Health, Education and Welfare, Office of Education, Bureau of Research.)

INDEX